D1475854

Registration of Company Charges

REGISTRATION OF COMPANY CHARGES

Second edition

Gerard McCormack BCL, LLM, PhD
Barrister (Ireland)
Professor of Law at the University of Manchester

JORDANS
2005

Published by
Jordan Publishing Limited
21 St Thomas Street
Bristol BS1 6JS

Whilst the publishers and the author have taken every care in preparing the material included in this work, any statements made as to the legal or other implications of particular transactions are made in good faith purely for general guidance and cannot be regarded as a substitute for professional advice. Consequently, no liability can be accepted for loss or expense incurred as a result of relying in particular circumstances on statements made in this work.

British Library Cataloguing-in-Publication Data

A catalogue record for this book is available from the British Library.

ISBN 0 85308 981 7

Typeset by Columns Design Ltd, Reading, Berkshire
Printed and bound in Great Britain by Antony Rowe Ltd, Chippenham, Wilts

PREFACE

It is 11 years since the last edition of this book was published and in those years a lot has happened in this area. There have been major decisions of the House of Lords and Privy Council in *Re BCCI (No 8)* [1998] AC 214; *Re Brumark Ltd: Agnew v CIR* [2001] 2 AC 710; and *Re Leyland Daf Ltd: Buchler v Talbot* [2004] 2 AC 298. There have also been significant Court of Appeal decisions like *Re Spectrum Plus Ltd* [2004] Ch 307 which is covered extensively in Chapter 3. The House of Lords decision on the appeal in this case is eagerly awaited at the time of going to press.

The basic framework of the law has, however, remained unchanged since 1994. The fundamental reforms envisaged by the Company Law Review Steering Group and the Law Commission that would bring English law into line with Article 9 of the US Uniform Commercial Code have not yet come to pass. It remains to be seen whether these reforms will form part of the proposed new companies legislation or regulations made under such legislation. There is full discussion of the Law Commission proposals in Chapter 2.

In the writing of this book I have incurred many debts. Although we do not always agree, Richard Calnan of Norton Rose has been the source of wise counsel throughout, not least through his own writings on the subject. I would also like to thank my colleagues at the University of Manchester, particularly David Milman, Andrew Griffiths, John De Lacy and Michael Lower. Finally, much is due to Presy and Amelia and Anthony, who came along just as the ideas for the second edition were beginning to form.

Gerard McCormack
May 2005

CONTENTS

TABLE OF CASES

References are to paragraph numbers.

TABLE OF STATUTES

References are to paragraph numbers.
Paragraph references printed in **bold** type indicate where the Act is set out in part or in full.

TABLE OF STATUTORY INSTRUMENTS

References are to paragraph numbers.

Chapter 1

THE NATURE OF SECURITY INTERESTS

INTRODUCTION

1.1   The nature of security rights in property is an issue that has engendered countless debates and declarations over the years and contributed to the creation of countless paper mountains. In this chapter it is not proposed to augment this array of materials unduly but rather to essay some tentative observations. A leading commentator has suggested that a security interest is a right given to one party in the asset of another party to secure payment or performance by that other party or by a third party.[1] Lord Browne-Wilkinson in *Re Paramount Airways Ltd*[2] took on board the following definition of security that had been suggested by counsel: 'security is created where a person (the creditor) obtains rights exercisable against some property in which the debtor has an interest in order to enforce the discharge of the debtor's obligation to the creditor.' More recently, Lord Scott remarked in *Smith v Bridgend County Borough Council*[3] that 'a contractual right enabling a creditor to sell his debtor's goods and apply the proceeds in or towards satisfaction of the debt is a right of a security character.'

1.2   So in broad terms a security right is a right over property which is intended to ensure the performance of some obligation. A continental European legal observer might refer to this as 'real' security, as it is security over a 'res' or a thing. 'Real' security in this sense includes security over chattels and intangibles (personal property) as well as over land. 'Real' security may be contrasted with 'personal' security, which is understood as referring to the two main institutions of suretyship and independent or 'demand' guarantees as well as to obligations of lesser import so-called 'letters of comfort'. The expression 'quasi-security' has also recently come into vogue – by this is meant rights and transactions that serve as the functional equivalent of security but are not so in the strict legal sense.

1.3   The focus of this book is on the security rights that require registration under Part XII of the Companies Act 1985. These are 'real' security rights

---

1   See generally on this area R Goode *Legal Problems of Credit and Security* (Sweet & Maxwell, 3rd edn, 2003); P Ali *The Law of Secured Finance* (Oxford University Press, 2002); G McCormack *Secured Credit under English and American Law* (Cambridge University Press, 2004). See generally for a definitional exposition of security Fidelis Oditah *Legal Aspects of Receivables Financing* (Sweet & Maxwell, 1990) chapter one.

2   [1990] BCC 130 at 149.

3   [2002] 1 AC 336 at 355.

created by agreement between parties, ie mortgages and charges. But to make sense of Part XII it is necessary to look at the whole universe of security rights, including 'personal' security and 'quasi-security'. First I will look at 'real' security based on agreement, then at 'quasi-security' rights as these in a sense are also based on agreement or consent; then at security rights arising by operation of law and, finally, at 'personal' security.

'REAL' SECURITY – BASIC DISTINCTIONS

1.4 There are three basic distinctions: first, between legal and equitable security interests, secondly between possessory and non-possessory security interests, and thirdly between consensual and non-consensual security interests. These various distinctions cut across one another. The main types of security interest are mortgages, charges, pledges and liens. The distinction between legal and equitable security interests is perhaps most confusing to a non-common lawyer, but it is easy to exaggerate the importance of the distinction in practice. The distinction stems from the historical separation between law and equity and the fact that certain kinds of security right were only recognised in courts of equity, as distinct from courts of common law, prior to the unification of the court structure in the 1870s. For example, a mortgage of future property was void at common law and, consequently, any security interest in future personalty must necessarily be equitable in nature.[4] The distinction retains some importance in the context of priorities. Legal interests are said to bind the whole world, whereas equitable interests are said to bind all save for a bona fide purchaser of a legal interest in the same property for value without notice of the prior equitable interest. The priority issue is, however, affected by the question of registration because, generally speaking, a charge created by a corporate debtor is invalid in the event of the debtor going into liquidation.[5] Moreover, if an equitable security interest on property requires registration then the fact of registration should infect the holders of subsequent legal security interests in the same property with notice.[6]

1.5 The distinction between possessory and non-possessory security interests is highly significant in practical terms. Mortgages, charges and equitable liens are non-possessory security interests; in other words, the lender does not have possession of the items used as security, whereas the pledge and the common law lien are possessory in nature, ie the lender is entrusted with possession of

---

4   See eg *Lunn v Thornton* (1845) I CB 379; *Tailby v Official Receiver* (1888) 13 App Cas 523.
5   Companies Act 1985, s 395. See also the comments of Lord Hoffmann in *Smith v Bridgend County Borough Council* [2002] 1 AC 336, at 347–348:
> 'Section 395 ... was intended for the protection of the creditors of an insolvent company. It was intended to give persons dealing with a company the opportunity to discover, by consulting the register, whether its assets were burdened by floating and certain fixed charges which would reduce the amount available for unsecured creditors in a liquidation. Whether this was a realistic form of protection and whether the choice of registrable charges was entirely logical is not presently relevant.'
6   But see J De Lacy 'Reflections on the Ambit and Reform of Part XII of the Companies Act 1985 and the Doctrine of Constructive Notice' in J De Lacy (ed) *The Reform of United Kingdom Company Law* (Cavendish, 2002) 333 at 369–376.

the items used as security. Finally, mortgages, charges, pledges and contractual liens are consensual security interests, ie they are created by agreement between the parties. Common law and equitable liens, on the other hand, are non-consensual, ie they arise by operation of law, irrespective of the agreement of the parties, in certain defined circumstances. In *Re Cosslett (Contractors) Ltd*[7] Millett LJ provided a neat summary of the law in this area, stating:

> 'There are only four kinds of consensual security known to English law: (i) pledge; (ii) contractual lien; (iii) equitable charge and (iv) mortgage. A pledge and a contractual lien both depend on the delivery of possession to the creditor. The difference between them is that in the case of a pledge the owner delivers possession to the creditor as security, whereas in the case of a lien the creditor retains possession of goods previously delivered to him for some other purpose. Neither a mortgage nor [an equitable] charge depends on the delivery of possession. The difference between them is that a mortgage involves a transfer of legal or equitable ownership to the creditor, whereas an equitable charge does not.'

CONSENSUAL SECURITY RIGHTS – MORTGAGES AND CHARGES

1.6   This book is concerned with Part XII of the Companies Act 1985 dealing with the company charge registration system. Under Part XII the expression 'charge' is defined to include a mortgage.[8] Thus the word 'charge' is being used as a general umbrella expression to encompass also mortgages,[9] but on other occasions the two expressions are used interchangeably.[10] Indeed, both Lords Millett and Hoffmann appeared to use the expressions interchangeably in the House of Lords in *Re Leyland Daf Ltd: Buchler v Talbot*.[11] This usage has attracted criticism, for there is a technical distinction between a mortgage, strictly so-called, and a charge; this distinction has been expounded by judges like Slade J in *Re Bond Worth Ltd*.[12] A mortgage involves the transfer of ownership of the property used as security to the lender, with the borrower having a right to get the property back free from the mortgage once the loan secured has been repaid. A charge, on the other hand, does not involve any transfer of ownership.[13] The lender has 'ownership' rights, ie a right of recourse to the property once the loan secured has been repaid. To repeat, a

---

7   [1998] Ch 495 at 508.

8   Section 396(4) of the Companies Act 1985 as originally drafted.

9   Companies Act 1985, s 396(4) provides that 'charge' includes 'mortgage'.

10   Law of Property Act 1925, s 205(1)(xvi) states that 'mortgage' includes any charge or lien on any property for securing money or money's worth; and see also Insolvency Act 1986, s 248.

11   [2004] 2 AC 298 where Lord Millett suggested at [51] that where property is charged, irrespective of whether the charge is a fixed or floating charge, it belongs to the charge holder to the extent of the amount secured. Only the equity of redemption remains the property of the charger and falls within the scope of the chargor's liquidation. Lord Hoffmann at [30] also suggested that assets subject to a floating charge belong beneficially to the debenture-holder.

12   [1980] Ch 228 at 248.

13   Indeed, Millett LJ spelled out this very point in *Re Cosslett (Contractors) Ltd* [1998] Ch 495 at 508.

mortgage involves a conveyance of property subject to a right of redemption, whereas a charge conveys nothing and merely gives the chargee certain rights over the property as security for the loan.[14]

1.7   A charge is a very flexible instrument. In this connection it should be noted that Lord Hoffmann in *Re BCCI (No 8)*[15] said that legal concepts like 'proprietary interest' and 'charge' were no more than labels given to clusters of related and self-consistent rules of law. Such concepts did not have a life of their own from which the rules were inexorably derived. In Lord Hoffmann's view, the law should be slow to declare a practice of the commercial community to be commercially impossible given the fact that the law was fashioned to suit the practicalities of life. In fact, English law has long taken a non-doctrinaire view towards the recognition and enforcement of security interests in property.

1.8   In *Re BCCI (No 8)* Lord Hoffmann described an equitable charge as:[16]

'a species of charge, which is a proprietary interest granted by way of security. Proprietary interests confer rights in rem which, subject to questions of registration and the equitable doctrine of purchaser for value without notice, will be binding upon third parties and unaffected by the insolvency of the owner of the property charged. A proprietary interest provided by way of security entitles the holder to resort to the property only for the purpose of satisfying some liability due to him (whether from the person providing the security or a third party) and, whatever the form of the transaction, the owner of the property retains an equity of redemption.'

Lord Hoffmann pointed out that a charge is a security interest created without any transfer of title or possession to the beneficiary. An equitable charge could be created by an informal transaction for value and over any kind of property. The workhorse of the secured credit industry in England has traditionally been the charge, particularly the floating charge. The equitable charge is a creature of great flexibility and can venture into territory that is forbidden to the common law mortgage. For example, a mortgage of future property was void at common law and, consequently, any security interest in future personalty must necessarily be equitable in nature.[17]

1.9   This pragmatic nature of the charge is illustrated by *Re BCCI (No 8)* where a unanimous House of Lords categorically rejected the doctrine that it was conceptually impossible for a security interest to be taken by a creditor

---

14   *Re Bond Worth Ltd* [1980] Ch 228 at 250. See also the comments of Buckley LJ in *Swiss Bank Corporation v Lloyds Bank* [1982] AC 584 at 595:

'An equitable charge which is not an equitable mortgage is said to be created when property is expressly or constructively made liable or specifically appropriated, to the discharge of a debt or some other obligation, and confers on the chargee a right of realisation by judicial process, that is to say, by the appointment of a receiver or an order for sale.'

15   [1998] AC 214.
16   [1998] AC 214 at 226.
17   See e g *Lunn v Thornton* (1845) I CB 379; *Tailby v Official Receiver* (1888) 13 App Cas 523.

over his own obligations to the debtor, e g for a bank to be granted a charge over its own indebtedness to a customer.

1.10   In *Re TXU Europe Group plc*[18] Blackburne J suggested that to create an equitable charge what must be shown is:

'(1) that a particular asset (or class of asset) has been appropriated to the satisfaction of a debt or other obligation of the charger or a third party and (2) that the chargee has a specifically enforceable right to look to the asset (or class of asset) or its proceeds for the discharge of the liability. Whether a particular transaction gives rise to an equitable charge depends upon the intentions of the parties, ascertained from what they have done. Their intention may be express or inferred. An expression of intention will not be determinative of the legal effect of the transaction if, upon a proper understanding of the admissible evidence (including any material documents), the transaction in question has a different legal effect. Equally, it is irrelevant that the parties may not have realised that the legal effect of the transaction into which they have entered gives rise to an equitable charge if, upon a proper understanding of the admissible evidence, that is its legal effect.'

1.11   The relevant principles on the nature of an equitable charge were also considered by the House of Lords in *Swiss Bank Corporation v Lloyds Bank Ltd*.[19] The facts of the case are complicated, but the nub of the issue was whether a lender of money, the Swiss Bank Corporation, had obtained any kind of security interest in securities that the borrower wished to use the loan to invest in. The lender knew the purpose of the loan and, while the loan agreement did not actually confer a security interest, in it the borrower promised that it would observe all the conditions attached by the Bank of England to its consent for the loan. These conditions included the requirements that the loan was to be used exclusively for the purchase of certain foreign securities (FIBI securities) and that the interest on and capital of the loan were to be repaid to Swiss Bank out of the FIBI securities or the proceeds of their sale. The borrower subsequently charged the FIBI securities to Lloyds Bank as security for a guarantee given in respect of a further loan from that bank. When Swiss Bank sought repayment of the loan, it claimed to have a better interest in the securities than Lloyds Bank. Although the judge at first instance, Browne-Wilkinson J, held in the plaintiffs' favour, both the Court of Appeal and the House of Lords held against them.

1.12   None of the appellate judges in the *Swiss Bank* case could see anything in the loan which specifically said that the borrowers would repay the loan out of the FIBI securities, nor would they imply any such promise. Both the Court of Appeal and the House of Lords were content to apply the law as stated by Lord Wrenbury in *Palmer v Carey*:[20]

---

18   [2004] 1 P & CR D 20 at [35].
19   [1982] AC 584.
20   [1926] AC 703 at 706–707.

'an agreement between a debtor and a creditor that the debt owing shall be paid out of specific fund coming to the debtor, or an order given by a debtor to his creditor upon a person owing money or holding funds belonging to the giver of the order, directing such person to pay such funds to the creditor, will create a valid equitable charge upon such fund, in other words, will operate as an equitable assignment of the debts or fund to which the order refers. An agreement for valuable consideration that a fund shall be applied in a particular way may found an injunction to restrain its application in another way. But if there be nothing more, such a stipulation will not amount to an equitable assignment. It is necessary to find further, that an obligation has been imposed in favour of the creditor to pay the debt out of the fund.'

1.13 Finally, on a pragmatic note, there are some who might suggest that possibly it is a pointless jurisprudential exercise to attempt to define 'security interest' in the abstract,[21] or at least pointless in terms of practical results. The whole issue is context specific and that what matters is the definition in the sphere of a particular statute or *corpus* of law. Part XII of the Companies Act 1985, in one sense, is in this pragmatic tradition, for it does not define security rights in general but rather adopts the practical approach of setting out specifically the categories of charge that necessitate registration for effectiveness in the event of the chargor's liquidation.

Why consensual security rights are taken

1.14 Before proceeding further, a preliminary issue merits attention. One might inquire why a lender would wish to take security?[22] At first blush the answer appears obvious. As Lord MacNaghten put it as long ago as *Salomon v Salomon & Co*:[23] 'Everybody knows that when there is a winding-up debenture-holders generally step in and sweep off everything ...' The taking of security maximises a creditor's possibilities of recovery, whereas placement in the ranks of the ordinary unsecured creditor may leave a person with little hope of recovering anything. Moreover, judicial utterances to this effect are well borne out by the empirical evidence.[24] When a company or other debtor declines into

---

21 See e g Mr Justice Millett (1991) 107 LQR 679 reviewing Dr Fidelis Oditah's *Legal Aspects of Receivables Financing* (Sweet & Maxwell, 1990). See the statement in P Ali *The Law of Secured Finance* (OUP, 2002) at p 15: 'Despite the obvious importance of the concept of "security interest" to the law of secured transactions, the concept continues to evade precise definition.'

22 See generally M Bridge (1992) 12 OJLS 333, particularly at 333–342.

23 [1897] AC 22 at 53. See also Templeman LJ in *Borden v Scottish Timber Products Ltd* [1981] Ch 25 at 42: 'Unsecured creditors rank after preferential creditors, mortgagees and holders of floating charges and they receive a raw deal ...'

24 According to data from the Society of Practitioners of Insolvency, on average 75% of cases return nothing to unsecured creditors and in only 2% of cases can they expect to receive 100% returns: Eighth Survey of Company Insolvency by the Society of Practitioners of Insolvency (1997–1998) at p 20. The survey is referred to in their Preface by D Milman and D Mond *Security and Corporate Rescue* (Hodgsons, 1999). More recent findings suggest recovery rates for banks in the order of 77% and this compares with 27% for preference creditors and negligible returns for unsecured trade creditors. See the Department of Trade and Industry

insolvency there is, by definition, insufficient money in the corporate kitty to satisfy everybody. The basic principle of insolvency law is one of 'equality of misery' or equality of treatment of creditors, ie pari passu distribution of available assets amongst creditors.[25] This hallowed principle of insolvency law is, however, in fact somewhat hollow.[26] The law of insolvency privileges certain categories of claims by according them preferential status.

1.15   The categories of preferential debt are set out in Sch 6 to the Insolvency Act 1986 and until the reforms introduced by the Enterprise Act 2002 have basically comprised certain tax and employee claims.[27] A variety of arguments have been advanced for recognising claims by particular categories of creditors to preferential status.[28] As far as claims by governmental entities are concerned, such creditors are said to be involuntary and not consciously to have assumed the risk of the debtor's insolvency.[29] It is also arguable that they are not in a position effectively to monitor the debtor's behaviour and to assess the risk of default or insolvency. The main justification for according employees preferential status centres on inequality of bargaining power and rests on the fact that employees lack the economic strength to bargain for security rights and, consequently, may lose out in their employer's insolvency. The Enterprise Act 2002[30] abolishes Crown Preference (but not employee preference)[31] as part of an 'integrated package of measures' whereby, in return, secured creditors lose some of their existing entitlements.[32] Preferential creditors are paid ahead

---

report *A Review of Company Rescue and Business Reconstruction Mechanisms* (2000) at para 57. The information is drawn from research carried out by Professor Julian Franks and Dr Oren Sussman 'The Cycle of Corporate Distress, Rescue and Dissolution: A Study of Small and Medium Sized UK Companies', April 2000.

25   Insolvency Act 1986, s 107 which applies to voluntary liquidations and Insolvency Rules 1986, r 4.181(1) applicable to compulsory liquidations.

26   See generally R Mokal 'Priority as Pathology: The Pari Passu Myth' [2001] CLJ 581 who argues that the pari passu principle is rather less important than it is sometimes made out to be, and does not fulfil any of the functions often attributed to it.

27   Enterprise Act 2002, s 251 removes paras 1 and 2 (debts due to Inland Revenue), paras 3–5C (debts due to Customs and Excise), and paras 6 and 7 (social security contributions) from Sch 6 to the Insolvency Act 1986 and thereby puts into effect the abolition of Crown Preference.

28   See generally A Keay and P Walton 'The Preferential Debts Regime in Liquidation Law: In the Public Interest?' (1999) Company, Financial and Insolvency Law Review 84 and see also for a Canadian perspective S Cantlie 'Preferred Priority in Bankruptcy' in J Ziegel (ed) *Current Developments in International and Comparative Corporate Insolvency Law* (Oxford, Clarendon Press, 1994).

29   See generally the report by the Department of Trade and Industry and HM Treasury Review Group *A Review of Company Rescue and Business Reconstruction Mechanisms* (London, 2000).

30   The philosophy underlying the Enterprise Act is explained in the White Paper *Insolvency: A Second Chance* (2001) Cm 5234 (London, TSO, 2001) though as the legislation was in the process of gestation the banks won some significant concessions from the government.

31   For a succinct statement of the position see the White Paper *Insolvency: A Second Chance* at para 2.20: 'The preferential status of certain claims by employees in insolvency proceedings, such as wages and holiday pay within certain limits, will remain, as will the rights of those subrogated to them.'

32   Holders of existing floating charges, however, enjoy significant short-term benefits from the Enterprise Act, for they benefit from the immediate abolition of Crown Preference but are not

of general creditors and also of one type of secured creditor – namely the floating charge holder – but not other secured creditors. Failure on the part of a bank to take security will not only reduce the bank to the category of unsecured creditor but also means that its claim will rank after preferential creditors.

1.16 Security serves a raft of other functions as well as maximising the prospect of recovery in a debtor's insolvency.[33] The second reason for taking security focuses on control. If a lender takes security over a specific asset of the borrower then the borrower relinquishes exclusive control over that asset. The borrower may be more likely to pay the lender than general creditors because failure to pay may result in the loss of an asset that is essential to the conduct of the borrower's business. In certain circumstances, this factor may be the primary reason behind the taking of security by the lender. While priority over other creditors in the debtor's insolvency is often identified as the single driving force behind the taking of security, the focus on liquidation outcomes may be to present too simplistic a picture. An important empirical study suggests a more complex pattern of lender behaviour,[34] with the security devices available to a bank lender placing it in a powerful position to exert control over a company in financial distress, both within formal insolvency procedures and also in informal rescue contexts. This study demonstrates the existence, even in the case of small and medium sized companies, of an elaborate rescue process outside formal procedures. Banks, it appears, use their control rights to encourage or force financially distressed firms to undergo restructuring that would include downsizing and management replacement. As far as larger quoted companies in the UK are concerned, a well established but informal rescue procedure exists, namely the so-called 'London Approach',[35] and again a lender's security rights will enable it to exert an element of control over the terms of any corporate workout.

1.17 Thirdly, security over specific assets may enable the lender to sell off or take possession of the assets without having to seek judicial or other official intervention. This basically remains the position under the Enterprise Act 2002. Under previous law a floating charge holder over the whole or substantially the whole of a company's assets may appoint an administrative receiver to carry on

---

subject to any requirement to set aside a proportion of floating charge recoveries for the benefit of unsecured creditors. The latter requirement applies only with respect to floating charges created after the coming into force of the legislation on 15 September 2003.

33   See generally R Scott 'A Relational Theory of Secured Financing' (1986) 86 Columbia Law Review 901; A Schwartz 'A Theory of Loan Priorities' (1989) 18 Journal of Legal Studies 209.

34   See J Franks and O Sussman 'The Cycle of Corporate Distress, Rescue and Dissolution: A Study of Small and Medium Size UK Companies' (2000). This study was sponsored by the DTI/Treasury Working Group on Company Rescue and Business Reconstruction Mechanisms. See also G Cook, N Pandit and D Milman 'Formal Rehabilitation Procedures and Insolvent Firms: Empirical Evidence on the British Company Voluntary Arrangement Procedure' (2001) 17 Small Business Economics.

35   On the 'London Approach' see generally P Brierley and G Vlieghe 'Corporate workouts, the London Approach and financial stability' (1999) Financial Stability Review 168; P Kent 'Corporate Workouts – A UK Perspective' (1997) 6 International Insolvency Review 165; J Armour and S Deakin 'Norms in Private Bankruptcy: the "London Approach" to the Resolution of Financial Distress' [2001] Journal of Corporate Law Studies 21.

the business of the company with a view to optimal realisation of assets.[36] Although designated by statute as an agent of the company,[37] the basic function of the receiver is to realise the assets of the company for the benefit of the secured lender who made the appointment. The Enterprise Act abolishes administrative receivership in the generality of cases[38] but still allows a floating charge holder to make an out-of-court appointment of an administrator.[39] An administrator has somewhat wider duties than an old-style administrative receiver, including a duty to rescue the business of the company if at all viable.[40] Nevertheless, the essential point remains that even under the new regime a secured lender will retain a substantial measure of control over realising the assets of financially distressed firms. Timing the sale of secured assets is important from the point of view of increasing recoveries and it also avoids giving the appearance of a 'forced sale'. If the lender can control the time and manner of realisation of secured assets, then this strengthens his hand greatly both from a negotiating position vis-à-vis the borrower and in terms of optimising value from the security.

1.18   Fourthly, there is an argument that the taking of security obviates the need to conduct a possibly detailed and expensive investigation into the financial circumstances of the borrower. In theory, all that the lender need do is to check the value of the secured property so as to ensure that it serves as adequate security for the loan. Of course, the prudent lender will allow for a certain excess in the value of the security over the amount of the loan to cover for legal and practical obstacles to enforcement as well as unfavourable enforcement timing and conditions. In the words of one commentator, secured

---

36   Insolvency Act 1986, s 29(2). For a defence of receivership as traditionally understood see J Armour and S Frisby 'Rethinking Receivership' (2001) 21 OJLS 73. They examine two proposals for the reform of insolvency law: first, the idea of a debtor-in-possession reorganisation regime and, secondly, the imposition of more expansive duties of care and/or loyalty on administrative receivers and suggest that the case for reform is not made out. The legislature thought differently with the enactment of the Enterprise Act 2002.

37   Insolvency Act 1986, s 44.

38   Section 250 and Sch 16 of the Enterprise Act 2002; but, nevertheless, there are a substantial number of cases where the holder of a qualifying floating charge may still appoint an administrative receiver. Moreover, holders of existing floating charges continue to enjoy the right to appoint administrative receivers. The legislative restriction on the appointment of administrative receivers only applies with respect to floating charges created after the coming into force of the relevant provisions of the Enterprise Act on 15 September 2003.

39   Section 248 and Sch 16 of the Enterprise Act 2002.

40   See Sch 16, para 3(1) of the Enterprise Act 2002:
        'The administrator of a company must perform his functions – (a) with the objective of rescuing the company, or (b) where it is not reasonably practicable to rescue the company, with the objective of achieving a better result for the company's creditors as a whole than would be likely if the company were wound up (without first being in administration), or (c) where it is not reasonably practicable to rescue the company or achieve the result mentioned in paragraph (b), with the objective of realising property in order to make a distribution to one or more secured or preferential creditors. Furthermore, even in cases where rescue is not reasonably practicable, an administrator must not unnecessarily harm the interests of the creditors of the company as a whole.'

lending substitutes information about the secured property offered by the borrower for information about the borrower himself:[41]

'At its extreme, secured lending makes a nearly total substitution: a pawnshop, for example, asks no more information about the lender than is necessary to identify the borrower in the event that the borrower has stolen the pawned good. Rather, the pawnshop operator must know the value of the collateral and the price that can be realised from selling that collateral. The history of the borrower and the purpose of the loan are immaterial.'

1.19 The law facilitates secured financing for a variety of reasons. Security might be said to represent a fair exchange for the creditor; it might in certain circumstances lower the cost of a loan and, perhaps most importantly, it may encourage lenders to make loans they would not otherwise make and in this way it may help to stimulate economic activity.[42]

---

41   See generally Heywood Fleisig 'Economic Functions of Security in a Market Economy' in J Norton and M Andenas (eds) *Emerging Financial Markets and Secured Transactions* (Kluwer, 1998) p 15 at 19. Fleisig examines legal deficiencies in the framework governing secured transactions over movable property in Argentina. Theoretical and empirical perspectives are presented and the author concludes that 'three-quarters of the problem of high interest rates facing borrowers who do not use real estate as collateral is a problem that arises from the laws and legal procedures that govern lending against immovable property.' According to the author (at p 34): 'in most transitional and developing economies, instituting a modern system of secured transactions would probably reduce the cost of financing movable equipment to a few hundred basis points over the government dollar borrowing rate.'

42   The 'efficiency of secured credit' debate has become something of a veritable cottage industry in the United States. The literature is truly enormous and a lot of contributions seem to consist of assertions or attempts to demonstrate that most previous contributions to the debate have been flawed – see J White 'Work and Play in Revising Article 9' (1994) 80 Va L Rev 2089: 'a game with no purpose other than to satisfy and stimulate one's intellect.' For just a flavour of the available literature see T Jackson and A Kronman 'Secured Financing and Priorities Among Creditors' (1979) 88 Yale LJ 1143; S Levmore 'Monitors and Freeriders in Commercial and Corporate Settings' (1982) 92 Yale LJ 49; A Schwartz 'A theory of Loan Priorities' (1989) J Legal Stud 209; A Schwartz 'Security Interests and Bankruptcy Priorities: A Review of Current Theories' (1981) 10 J Legal Stud 1; A Schwartz 'The Continuing Puzzle of Secured Debt' (1984) 37 Vand L Rev 1051; R Scott 'A Relational Theory of Secured Financing' (1986) 86 Colum L Rev 901; P Shupack 'Solving the Puzzle of Secured Transactions' (1989) 41 Rutgers L Rev 1067; J White 'Efficiency Justifications for Personal Property Security' (1984) 37 Vand L Rev 473; B Adler 'An Equity-Agency Solution to the Bankruptcy-Priority Puzzle' (1993) 22 J Legal Stud 73; J Bowers 'Whither What Hits the Fan?: Murphy's Law, Bankruptcy Theory, and the Elementary Economics of Loss Distribution' (1991) 26 Ga L Rev 27; SL Harris and CW Mooney 'A Property-Based Theory of Security Interests: Taking Debtors' Choices Seriously' (1994) 80 Va L Rev 2021; H Kanda & S Levmore 'Explaining Creditor Priorities' (1994) 80 Va L Rev 2103; L LoPucki 'The Unsecured Creditor's Bargain' (1994) 80 Va L Rev 1887; R Picker 'Security Interests, Misbehavior, and Common Pools' (1992) 59 U Ch L Rev 645; G Triantis 'Secured Debt Under Conditions of Imperfect Information' (1992) 21 J Legal Stud 225. There are also symposia on the issue of the efficiency of secured credit in the 1994 Virginia Law Review and the 1997 Cornell Law Review. For slightly more general but specifically English contributions see R Mokal 'The Authentic Consent Model: Contractarianism, Creditors' Bargain and Corporate Liquidation' (2001) 21 Legal Studies 400; R Mokal 'Priority as Pathology: The Pari Passu Myth' [2001] CLJ 581; R Mokal 'The Seach for Someone to Save: A Defensive Case for the Priority of Secured Credit' (2002) 22 OJLS 687; V Finch 'Security, Insolvency and Risk: Who Pays the Price'

1.20   The Law Commission in its Consultative Report on *Company Security Interests*[43] agreed that it was 'possible to exaggerate the importance of secured credit'[44] but, nevertheless, managed to wax lyrical on its significance. The Law Commission said:[45]

> 'Any creditor faces the risk that the debtor will be unable to repay. A lender will often insist that the loan be secured by a mortgage or charge over the company's assets, so that if the company becomes insolvent the creditor may take the assets charged and sell them to pay off the debt. Secured lending is of great importance to small and medium-size enterprises, which may not have a sufficient credit-rating to be able to borrow on an unsecured basis at reasonable rates. It is of enormous importance in the financial sector, and it is frequently used by large companies to protect themselves when they are involved in projects through "single purpose vehicles" that they set up for the project.'

QUASI-SECURITY

1.21   There are various ways, outside the creation of a charge, in which a creditor may improve its position in the event of the debtor's insolvency, thereby removing itself from the general mass of creditors who have little hope of recovering anything. In *Chow Yoong Hong v Choong Fah Rubber Manufactory*[46] Lord Devlin made essentially the same point, observing that there are many ways of raising cash besides borrowing.[47] This was also a concern dear to the heart of the Law Commission in its recent Consultative Report on *Company Security Interests*. The Law Commission stated that the current law was open to fundamental criticism because it determined whether a transaction amounted to security on the basis of legal form, rather than looking at function. In its view:[48]

> 'There are many transactions which fulfil the same purpose as a charge, namely of securing an obligation, but which are not treated by the law as creating security. For example, when a company obtains goods on credit, the supplier may "retain" ownership of the goods ... so that, if the company defaults, it may repossess the goods to satisfy the debt due to it. Equally a financier may advance money to the company as against its future income, but rather than take a charge over the company's "receivables" it may simply "buy" them.'

(1999) 62 MLR 633; V Finch 'Is Pari Passu Passe' [2000] Insolvency Lawyer 194; V Finch *Corporate Insolvency Law: Perspectives and Principles* (CUP, 2002) at pp 75–105.

43   Law Commission Consultation Paper No 176 (September 2004).
44   Law Commission Consultation Paper No 176, p 3.
45   Law Commission Consultation Paper No 176, p xiv.
46   [1962] AC 209.
47   [1962] AC 209 at 216. See also the comments of Robert Walker LJ in *Lavin v Johnson* [2002] EWCA 1138 at [82]: 'But to say that the identification of a mortgage is a matter of substance, not form, is not to say that any transaction which is expected to produce the same economic consequences as a mortgage must be a mortgage in the eyes of the law.'
48   Law Commission Consultation Paper No 176, p xvi.

1.22   Quasi-security takes many forms. In other words, there are many ways in which a person loosely termed a creditor might enhance its prospects of recovery in the event of the debtor's insolvency besides being party to the creation of a charge. There is no simple comprehensive definition of quasi-security, but it is suggested that it includes the following:

(1)   sale and leaseback/hire purchase;
(2)   title retention/conditional sale;
(3)   agency sales financing;
(4)   factoring/assignment of receivables;
(5)   Quistclose trusts.

These are all 'quasi-security' devices and all of them will now be considered briefly, with the exception of title retention/conditional sales which will be addressed in detail in Chapter 5.[49]

Quasi-security – sale and leaseback/hire purchase

1.23   A not uncommon financing technique involves the sale of goods or land followed by a lease back. In all probability, the vendor will never have parted with possession and, in practice, it may be difficult to distinguish a genuine sale and lease-back from the creation of a charge over the property in question. In a leading case, *Re George Inglefield Ltd*,[50] Romer LJ attempted to explain the essential differences. He said:[51]

> 'In a transaction of sale the vendor is not entitled to get back the subject-matter of the sale by returning to the purchaser the money that has passed between them. In the case of a mortgage or charge the mortgagor is entitled, until he has been foreclosed, to get back the subject-matter of the mortgage or charge by returning to the mortgagee the money that has passed between them. The second essential difference is that if the mortgagee realises the subject-matter of the mortgage for a sum more than sufficient to repay him, with interest and the costs, the money that has passed between him and the mortgagor he has to account to the mortgagor for the surplus. If the purchaser sells the subject-matter of the purchase, and realises a profit, of course he has not got to account to the vendor for the profit. Thirdly, if the mortgagee realises the mortgage property for a sum that is insufficient to repay him the money that he has paid to the mortgagor, together with interest and costs, then the mortgagee is entitled to recover from the mortgagor the balance of the money ... If the purchaser were to resell the purchased property at a price which was insufficient to recoup him the money that he has paid to the vendor, of course he would not be entitled to recover the balance from the vendor.'

---

49   See generally S Worthington Proprietary Interests in Commercial Transactions (OUP, 1996).
50   [1933] Ch 1.
51   [1933] Ch 1 at 26–27. It was made clear in *Durham Bros v Robertson* [1898] 1 QB 765, however, that once the security nature of a transaction is established, equity will imply a right of redemption; see at 772 per Chitty LJ. Having regard to this fact Fidelis Oditah [1992] JBL 541 at 546 argues that the speech of Romer LJ gives very little, if any, useful guidance.

1.24 These distinctions, while easy to state on paper, may become blurred in practice. For example, sale agreements may include options to repurchase and also profit sharing clauses under which the original vendor shares in profits from resales as well as provisions whereby the vendor agrees to indemnify the buyer in respect of any losses incurred on a resale.

1.25 The modern form of hire purchase agreement in relation to goods builds on the clear theoretical distinction between a sale and a lease or hire of goods. Hire purchase entails a hiring coupled with an option to purchase. In legal terms, however, there is a lot to be said for the view that this description is a legal fiction that bears little or no relation to reality.[52] In legal terms there is a contract for the hiring of goods coupled with an option on the part of the hirer to purchase the goods.[53] While the agreement subsists, the property in the goods remains in the owner, and the hirer has no power to dispose of them. Moreover, although the hirer has an option to purchase the goods, it is not under a binding obligation to do so.[54]

1.26 Normally a hire purchase transaction involves three parties, namely a dealer, a finance house and a hirer. Goods are sold by the dealer to the finance house, who then lets them on hire-purchase terms to a hirer who had no prior interest in the goods. The tripartite nature of the transaction makes it difficult to argue that in reality it constitutes a loan. But the essential principle remains the same, irrespective of the fact that there are only two parties, as when the owner of goods sells them to a finance house and takes a lease-back under a hire purchase agreement.

1.27 It may be that, for one reason or another, the owner of goods finds a collusive dealer who represents to a finance house that it, in reality, is the owner of the goods. The dealer then purports to sell the goods to the finance house which then leases them on hire purchase terms to the original owner. All this occurred in *Eastern Distributors Ltd v Goldring*.[55] The finance house was not party to the fraud and it was held that there was a genuine sale and lease-back.

1.28 The fact situation was much the same in *Snook v London and West Riding Investments Ltd*.[56] Here it was contended that a supposed sale and re-letting was a sham, but the Court of Appeal by a 2:1 majority, Lord Denning dissenting, rejected the proposition.[57] Diplock LJ found it necessary to consider what, if any, legal concept was involved in the use of the popular and

---

52 See generally Crowther Committee Report on *Consumer Credit* Cmnd 4596 (1971), pp 175–176.

53 For a modern analysis see *Forthright Finance Ltd v Carlyle Finance Ltd* [1997] 4 All ER 90.

54 On hire purchase see generally R Goode *Consumer Credit Law and Practice* (Butterworths, looseleaf publication); A Guest *The Law of Hire-Purchase* (Sweet & Maxwell, 1966); R Goode *Hire-Purchase Law and Practice* (Butterworths, 2nd edn, 1970); R Goode *Commercial Law* (Penguin, 3rd edn, 2004) chapter 27.

55 [1957] 2 QB 600.

56 [1967] 2 QB 786.

57 In Lord Denning's view the transaction, though taking the form of a sale and reletting, was nothing more than a loan of money on the security of the goods and therefore illegal under the Bills of Sale Acts: see [1967] 2 QB 786 at 799.

pejorative word 'sham'.[58] He said that it meant acts done or documents executed by the parties to the 'sham' which were intended by them to give to third parties or to the court the appearance of creating between the parties legal rights and obligations different from the actual legal rights and obligations (if any) which the parties intend to create. For acts or documents to be a 'sham', however, all the parties thereto must have had a common intention that the acts or documents were not to create the legal rights and obligations which they gave the appearance of creating. No unexpressed intentions of a 'shammer' affected the rights of a party whom he had deceived.

1.29   Russell LJ was of a similar opinion. He said that to enable the court to hold that a transaction was intended to make a loan, it must find that both parties to a transaction so intended.[59] *Yorkshire Railway Wagon Co v Maclure*[60] and *Stoneleigh Finance Ltd v Phillips*[61] were quoted in support of this notion. Russell LJ was also a party to the decision in *Stoneleigh Finance Ltd v Phillips*. In that case he said that for some purposes the dealer may be regarded as agent for the finance company. There was no authority, however, for the proposition that in a case such as the present the dealer may be regarded as the agent of the finance company able to fix the latter with the intention which it never had, to enter into a transaction of secured loan under the cloak of a purchase and hire.[62]

1.30   A rare three party case where the genuineness of a sale and lease-back as between original owner and finance house was disputed is *North Central Wagon Finance Co Ltd v Brailsford*.[63] Here Cairns J observed that in considering whether the real transaction was one of loan, it was necessary to look behind the documents to discover its true nature. If the facts were not truly stated in the documents, that was a circumstance tending to show that the documents were a mere cloak.[64] In this particular case an agent of the finance company was party to various misstatements and this served to show that the documents obscured the true reality of the transaction.

1.31   *Polsky v S&A Services Ltd*[65] is a simple bipartite case where a purported sale and lease-back arrangement was struck down as being in reality a charge on the security of the goods. Lord Goddard CJ said that one of the most satisfactory ways of deciding what the true nature of the transaction was is to see whether the documents themselves accurately set out the deal between the parties as it took place and at the time when it took place.[66] Here there was no significant convergence between appearance and reality. A case to the same

---

58   [1967] 2 QB 786 at 802. See also *Ramsay v IRC* [1982] AC 300 at 323 per Lord Wilberforce.
59   [1967] 2 QB 786 at 804.
60   (1882) 21 Ch D 309.
61   [1965] 2 QB 537.
62   [1965] 2 QB 537 at 578–580. See also Davies LJ at 571.
63   [1962] 1 All ER 502.
64   [1962] 1 All ER 502 at 506–507. See also *Staffs Motor Guarantee Ltd v British Wagon Co Ltd* [1934] 2 KB 305.
65   [1951] 1 All ER 185. The judgment of Lord Goddard CJ was affirmed by the Court of Appeal [1951] 1 All ER 1062n.
66   [1952] 1 All ER 185 at 189.

effect is *Re Watson*[67] where there was an express finding of fact that no sale or hiring of the chattels was really intended. The object in truth was merely to create a security for a loan of money from the supposed vendor to the supposed purchaser.

Quasi-security – agency sales financing

1.32 Agency sales financing is a fairly complicated form of financing technique that was employed in *Welsh Development Agency v Export Finance Co Ltd*.[68] The case illustrates the complexity of modern financing techniques as well as the importance of the distinction between form and substance. It involved an intricate financing arrangement for a company, Parrot, that was in the business of exporting computer disks. Basically Parrot received funding from another company, Exfinco, in relation to its overseas sales. Whenever Parrot entered into a transaction for the sale of its goods to overseas buyers, Exfinco made a standing offer to buy all such goods that complied with certain warranties, from Parrot. Parrot in turn sold those goods as Exfinco's agent to the overseas buyers, with Exfinco acting as an undisclosed principal. Title did not pass to the overseas buyers until the purchase price of the goods had been paid. Payment by the overseas buyers was into a bank account in the name of Parrot but which was under the exclusive control of Exfinco. The price payable by Exfinco to Parrot for the goods was not fixed at the outset, but rather was subject to variation from time to time. As one might expect, the price related to the amount that was payable ultimately by the overseas buyers. Ninety per cent of this amount was covered by a guarantee from the Export Credit Guarantee Department (ECGD). In the account between Exfinco and Parrot, Exfinco were entitled: (i) to retain the amount not covered by the ECGD guarantee; (ii) to deduct a discount that mirrored the speed with which the overseas buyers paid their debts, such discount varying with the promptness of payments; and (iii) to debit a number of items such as bank charges against the account.

1.33 The outcome of these arrangements was that at all times Exfinco had a fund of 10% of the price of the goods sold, to meet further obligations of Parrot. It could discharge out of this fund liabilities that related to the whole of its dealing with Parrot. There was also a termination clause under which on cessation of the agreement Parrot would satisfy all claims owing to Exfinco by the overseas buyers and, when this payment had been made, Exfinco would transfer all interests that it had in the goods to Parrot.

1.34 Why adopt a complex funding scheme along these lines? Were not factoring and block discounting well tried and tested alternatives? Dillon LJ explained that these financing mechanisms were so well known that the debentures drawn up by banks sought to counter them. A standard clause in a debenture entailed a covenant by the company with the bank not to factor, discount or assign book debts. A breach of such a covenant might trigger the

---

67 (1890) 25 QBD 27.
68 [1992] BCLC 148. The case is analysed by F Oditah [1992] JBL 541. Contrast *Re Curtain Dream plc* [1990] BCLC 925.

appointment of a receiver over the company's undertaking. Hence Exfinco sought to structure its financing facilities in such a way that did not involve any assignment of book debts. But did they involve the creation of a charge over goods rather than an outright sale of such goods?

1.35 The Court of Appeal answered unanimously and negatively.[69] Staughton LJ pointed out that the sum payable by Exfinco to Parrot was related to the price payable by the overseas buyer, less a discount that was fixed at the time of the transaction but was subject to adjustment later by reference to the time that it took all overseas buyers to pay what was owed.[70] The judge took the view that this scheme was not inconsistent with a sale of goods, since parties may fix the price of goods in whatever way they wish. Moreover, the so-called discount was not incompatible with a contract of sale, as parties were free to agree that the buyer may deduct from the price a sum equal to interest on a debt that is paid late by some other person. Likewise with the termination clause and 'right of redemption' therein contained. Options to repurchase property were not unusual.[71]

1.36 The Exfinco-Parrot agreement applied to itself the label of outright sale. There were two escape routes from this characterisation.[72] One was to say that the documents drawn up were in essence a sham not intended to reflect the reality of the situation. The Court of Appeal rejected this proposition. The transaction was not a sham because there was no evidence that the parties intended rights and obligations to apply inter se other than those set out in the agreement. Moreover, looking at the internal workings of the transaction, there was nothing therein that was necessarily incompatible with the transaction being one of sale. The termination clause was like a repurchase agreement, and options to repurchase were not uncommon in sales transactions. Furthermore, price variation clauses were often found in sales contracts.[73]

---

69   The Court of Appeal overturned the first-instance decision of Browne-Wilkinson V-C who held that the financing arrangement, although it was drawn up in the form of a sale was in reality a disguised charge, as it was the transfer of goods to secure payment of a debt. For a defence of the first instance decision reported at [1990] BCC 933; [1991] BCLC 936 see WJ Gough *Company Charges* (Butterworths, 2nd edn, 1996) at pp 587–588.

70   [1992] BCLC 148 at 188.

71   [1992] BCLC 148 at 189. In *Alderson v White* (1858) 2 De G & J 97 Lord Cransworth said: 'an absolute conveyance, containing nothing to show that the relation of debtor and creditor is to exist between the parties, does not cease to be an absolute conveyance and become a mortgage merely because the vendor stipulates that he shall have the right to repurchase.' See also *Burlinson v Hall* (1884) 12 QBD 347; *Re Lovegrove* [1935] Ch 464; *Palette Shoes Pty Ltd v Krohn* (1937) 58 CLR 1.

72   See Staughton LJ [1992] BCLC 148 at 186.

73   See too the observations of Lord Hanworth MR in *Re Lovegrove* [1935] Ch 464 at 485:
      'What is the objection to that method of doing business? This is not a case in which some document is put forward to mask a device or stratagem for deceiving persons; it really is an agreement entered into for the purpose of enabling Mr Lovegrove to have money more quickly and more certainly on the sale of his goods, and one ought not to look at such a document with a sinister eye.'

1.37   The Court of Appeal was not impressed by the argument that the transaction should be regarded as creating a registrable charge merely because it involved a form of off-balance sheet financing. Ralph Gibson LJ said:[74]

> 'I do not think that there is any force in the fact that the transactions contemplated by the master agreement were, and were intended to be, "off balance sheet" … Other long-established forms of financing may also be "off balance sheet", namely factoring and block discounting.'

He added:[75]

> 'Those who were concerned with the financial stability of [the seller], over the short or longer term, could discover what charges were registered and could ask whether there are any off balance sheet lines of credit. Auditors could insist upon such a reference in the accounts to such lines of credit as would, in their judgment, give a true and fair picture. Those who provided credit on security could, if they judged it necessary, insert provisions which would prohibit the use of the sort of arrangement set out in the master agreement. If any mischief arising from off balance sheet financing is judged to be serious it could be prohibited by legislation. Under the law as it now stands, I could see no reason for giving, as it were, bad marks to the master agreement, in that it provides for off balance sheet financing, in the court's approach to the issue of construction.'

1.38   Certain commentators, however, are not so sanguine about off balance sheet financing, Gough, for example, suggests that it is unfortunate that 'the court did not take the opportunity … to strike down as an unregistered disguised charge the goods discounting arrangement which stretched the legal fiction of title security as a separate and independent form of financing to its most extreme extension, when that course was clearly available within the confines of established precedent … Stimulation of finance and security techniques involving the transfer of a company's trading stock and its normal trading function to some off balance sheet method of operation must be prejudicial to a fair, open and efficient system of secured financing.'[76]

1.39   The *Welsh Development Agency* decision recognises formalistic distinctions and, in this respect, resides somewhat uneasily with the path signified by the first instance decision of Knox J in *Re Curtain Dream plc*.[77] That case concerned a financier, Churchill, and a company, Curtain Dream. A facility letter was executed under which Churchill extended a general line of credit to the company of £500,000 and this facility letter was coupled with a general contract of trading. The facility letter contained terms to the effect that the company would invoice Churchill for the merchandise provided for in the contract of trading and that Churchill would reinvoice the merchandise to the company. The contract of trading stated that the goods were to remain the property of Churchill until there had been payment of the agreed price by

---

74   [1992] BCLC 148 at 177–178.
75   [1992] BCLC 148 at 178–179.
76   WJ Gough *Company Charges* (Butterworths, 1996) at pp 587–588 and see also A Berg 'Recharacterisation after Enron' [2003] JBL 205.
77   [1990] BCLC 925; on which see J De Lacy [1991] LMCLQ 39.

the company. Curtain Dream was also required to keep the goods separate from other goods so as to make them easily identifiable. The court had to decide whether the transaction taken as a whole involved the relationship of creditor and debtor between the parties or whether there was a sale and resale with the latter entailing also a reservation of title clause.[78] It was decided that, in substance, the transaction consisted of a loan. Terminological usages were employed in aid of this conclusion. There was reference in the documents to the establishment of a supplier credit line of up to 90 days for the company and the agreement spoke of a credit line. Moreover, there was an allusion to interest payable. Finally, and for the court decisively, there was what was seen as a compulsory redemption provision.[79] Curtain Dream was bound to transfer the property to Churchill and Churchill was bound to reconvey it.

1.40 With respect, however, it is difficult to appreciate the decisiveness of this feature. The agreement involved a sale plus a compulsory reservation of title resale as distinct from a compulsory rehiring. How this can be viewed as being the equivalent of an equity of redemption is difficult to conceive. It should be noted that Staughton LJ specifically reserved his opinion on the correctness of *Re Curtain Dream plc* in *Welsh Development Agency v Export Finance Co Ltd*.[80] The words of Lawrence LJ in *Re George Inglefield Ltd*[81] should be borne in mind in this context. He said:[82]

'As the law stands at present, there is nothing to prevent a limited company from selling its assets without giving notice of that sale to the public or to anyone else, remaining in possession of the assets so sold, with the consent of the buyer, and obtaining credit on the faith of that possession. If such a state of things ought to be remedied it is for Parliament to supply the remedy. All that the Court has to do … is to ascertain whether there has, in fact, been a sale of the assets and to give effect to the transaction if that be the case.'

Quasi-security – assignment of receivables

1.41 Lord Devlin in *Chow Yoong Hong v Choong Fah Rubber Manufactory*, after referring to the existence of means of raising cash other than by borrowing, mentioned the sale of book debts and the sale of unmatured bills of exchange, in each case for less than their face value.[83] He had earlier said that the business of buying bills at a discount (ie for their value at the date of purchase) was well known and quite distinct from moneylending. Usually the

---

78   [1990] BCLC 925 at 935.
79   [1990] BCLC 925 at 937.
80   [1992] BCLC 148.
81   [1933] Ch 1.
82   [1933] Ch 1 at 23. See generally F Oditah [1992] JBL 541 at 550–551.
83   For a general analysis of the various methods of unlocking wealth tied up in corporate debts see F Oditah *Legal Aspects of Receivables Financing* (Sweet & Maxwell, 1990) and see also F Oditah (1992) 108 LQR 459.

buyer was a bank or discount house, but the fact that it was neither did not transform the nature of the transaction, nor did the designation of the discount as interest.[84]

1.42 Receivables financing may take one of two forms – either the creation of charges, whether fixed or floating, on receivables (debts) or else the outright assignment of receivables, which is referred to as factoring.[85] A factoring transaction does not have to be registered, but where a company creates a charge over its debts, registration is a necessity.[86] Of course the factoring of debts equates to a loan of money on the security of debts to the extent that ready cash is released to the assignor. The latter receives money upfront rather than having to wait for the debts to mature, or to be collected. Factoring, however, can serve functions other than the immediate release of funds. For instance, if it is done on a notification basis, then the factor is relieved of the responsibility of collecting the debts. The factor may also take over the burden of accounts administration. Factoring may also take on some of the features of credit insurance if the factor assumes the responsibility for the debtor failing to pay as distinct from the assignor being under an obligation to accept a reassignment of bad debts.

1.43 Receivables financing is often carried out in a manner that blurs the distinction between the outright sale of receivables and their transfer by way of security.[87] It is possible to mortgage a debt by an assignment of the debt to the mortgagee coupled with a provision for reassignment of the debt once the obligation to which the mortgage relates has been discharged. The formalities for legal assignments of debts are laid down in s 136 of the Law of Property Act 1925. One of the requirements is that an assignment be 'absolute' and 'not purporting to be by way of charge only'.[88] Receivables financing is complicated by the fact that it is perfectly possible, nevertheless, that an assignment is 'absolute' for the purposes of s 136 and yet still operate by way of security. The test for the application of s 136 is whether, for the time being, the assignor has unconditionally transferred to the assignee the right to receive payment from the debtor. On the other hand, if the assignor is a corporate body, the transaction will require registration under Part XII of the Companies Act 1985 where the assignor retains an equity of redemption, ie if the transaction is by way of mortgage. With a mortgage the assignee has ownership of the debt transferred subject to the assignor's right of redemption. A charge of a debt, however, does not give the chargee ownership of the debt but instead

---

84 [1962] AC 209 at 215.

85 See generally F Salinger *Factoring Law and Practice* (Sweet & Maxwell, 3rd edn, 1999); F Oditah *Legal Aspects of Receivables Financing* (Sweet & Maxwell, 1990).

86 The distinction between factoring and the creation of a charge over debts was explored at length by the House of Lords in *Lloyds & Scottish Finance v Cyril Lord Carpet Sales Ltd* [1992] BCLC 609.

87 See M Bridge, R Macdonald, R Simmonds and C Walsh 'Formalism, Functionalism and Understanding the Law of Secured Transactions' (1999) 44 McGill LJ 567 at fn 46.

88 *Burlinson v Hall* (1884) 12 QBD 347. See also *Bovis International Inc v Circle Ltd Partnership* (1995) 49 Con LR 12 at 29 where Millett LJ said 'an assignment does not cease to be absolute merely because it is given by way of security and is subject to an express or implied obligation to reassign on redemption.'

preferential rights thereto.[89] It has been suggested that, to facilitate a transfer of the legal title to the debt in case the chargee wishes to dispose of it, the default provisions in the charge should confer a power of attorney on the chargee to collect or dispose of the debt and to convert the charge into a mortgage by executing an assignment in the name of the chargor.[90] These powers diminish to vanishing point any remaining distinctions between a mortgage and a charge.[91]

1.44   However, the distinction clearly remains between an outright transfer of debts on the one hand and the transfer subject to an equity of redemption, ie a mortgage or charge, on the other. In other words, there is still a fundamental distinction between factoring of debts and the creation of a security interest in the same.[92]

Quasi-security – Quistclose /conditional purpose trusts

1.45   Some trusts may be regarded as serving a security type function and, in particular, the conditional purpose or 'Quistclose' trust.[93] Under a 'Quistclose' trust money is advanced subject to the condition that it is applied for a particular purpose. If this purpose is not fulfilled or is no longer capable of accomplishment the money is said to be held on a secondary trust for the payer rather than being part of the debtor's assets available for payment to the debtor's general creditors.[94] The courts have held that debt and trust can coexist

---

89   Denman J stated in *Tancred v Delagoa Bay and East Africa Railway Co* (1889) 23 QBD 239 at 242 that '... a document given by way of charge is not one which absolutely transfers the property with a condition for reconveyance, but is a document which only gives a right to payment out of a particular fund or particular property, without transferring that fund or property'.

90   [1994] JBL 172 at 174.

91   See Fidelis Oditah *Legal Aspects of Receivables Financing* (Sweet & Maxwell, 1990) at p 96.

92   See also *Lloyds Bank plc v Clarke* [2002] 2 All ER (Comm) 992 where it was held by the Privy Council that a sub-participation agreement, entered into between two banks in respect of part of a Eurobond issue, did not confer upon the sub-participating bank any proprietary interest in the underlying bonds or their proceeds. The lead bank in this case had become insolvent and it was held that the sub-participating bank was merely an unsecured creditor of the lead bank. This was the generally accepted effect of a sub-participation agreement and also its effect in this particular case. Lord Hoffmann however, accepted (at [18]) that the 'legal rights and duties, as ascertained by construction, should be regarded as having a particular legal character was a question of law ... The label was not conclusive. Nor was it conclusive as to whether a transaction fell within a particular market category.'

93   See the leading case *Barclays Bank Ltd v Quistclose Investments Ltd* [1970] AC 567 and see now *Twinsectra Ltd v Yardley* [2002] 2 AC 164. See generally on the 'Quistclose' Trust L Priestley 'The Romalpa Trust and the Quistclose Trust' in Paul Finn (ed) *Equity in Commercial Relationships* (Law Book Company, 1987); W Goodhart and G Jones (1980) 43 MLR 489; M Bridge (1992) 13 OJLS 333; C Rickett (1991) 107 LQR 608; L Ho and P St J Smart (2001) 21 OJLS 267; JA Glister (2004) 63 CLJ 632.

94   This was the analysis adopted in the *Quistclose* case itself, but Lord Millett in *Twinsectra Ltd v Yardley* [2002] 2 AC 164 took a different approach. He said (at [100]) that the Quistclose trust was:

'an entirely orthodox example of the kind of default trust known as a resulting trust. The lender pays the money to the borrower by way of loan, but he does not part with the entire

– in other words, that the same transaction can give rise to the legal relationship of debt and also to a trust. It has been contended that a Quistclose trust constitutes a security interest in that the 'payer is to be protected from the claims of other creditors of the payee' on the latter's insolvency and thus 'clearly evinces an intention to seek and provide security'.[95] On this analysis, the Quistclose trust secures performance of the debtor's obligation to carry out the purpose of the advance.

1.46 On the other hand, it must be recognised that the Quistclose trust is not a conventional security interest. In the typical advance the secured assets and the monies advanced are quite clearly separate and the former secures the latter. With a Quistclose trust the payer is asserting a de facto security interest in the advance itself and it is not the failure to repay that is secured but rather the execution of the purpose. If the purpose is carried out, the payer is converted from a secured into an unsecured creditor.[96] Under a 'Quistclose' trust the payee (debtor) never acquires beneficial ownership but is rather a trustee – a conduit for the transmission of funds.

SECURITY RIGHTS ARISING BY OPERATION OF LAW

1.47 It is a fundamental condition of the application of the registration of company charges regime contained in Part XII of the Companies Act 1985 that there is in existence a charge created by a company that is registered in England and Wales. If there is no charge the registration obligation does not apply nor does it apply where the security right in question has been brought into being by operation of law. Security rights arising by operation of law will now be considered.

---

beneficial interest in the money, and in so far as he does not it is held on a resulting trust for the lender from the outset ... When the purpose fails, the money is returnable to the lender, not under some new trust in his favour which only comes into being on the failure of the purpose, but because the resulting trust in his favour is no longer subject to any power on the part of the borrower to make use of the money. Whether the borrower is obliged to apply the money for the stated purpose or merely at liberty to do so, and whether the lender can countermand the borrower's mandate while it is still capable of being carried out, must depend on the circumstances of the particular case.'

See also the article by P Millett QC (as he then was) 'The *Quistclose* Trust: Who Can enforce It?' (1985) 101 LQR 269 and see also William Swadling *The Quistclose Trust: Critical Essays* (Hart, 2004) ; JA Glister 'The Nature of Quistclose Trusts: Classification and Reconciliation' (2004) 63 CLJ 632.

95   See M Bridge (1992) OJLS 333 at 345–346 and 360–361.

96   See M Bridge, R Macdonald, R Simmonds and C Walsh 'Formalism, Functionalism and Understanding the Law of Secured Transactions' (1999) 44 McGill LJ 567 at fn 156. See the comments of Lord Millett in *Twinsectra Ltd v Yardley* [2002] 2 AC 164 at [72]: 'Arrangements of this kind are not intended to provide security for repayment of the loan, but to prevent the money from being applied otherwise than in accordance with the lender's wishes. If the money is properly applied the loan is unsecured.'

Liens – common law liens

1.48 A common law lien is a right to retain possession of an asset until discharge of an outstanding debt and is to be distinguished from an equitable lien which is essentially a form of non-possessory security interest arising by operation of law. The distinction between the two concepts has been expounded in the following terms:[97]

'An equitable lien differs from a common law lien in that a common law lien is founded on possession and, except as modified by statute, merely confers a right to detain until payment, whereas an equitable lien, which exists quite irrespective of possession, confers on the holder the right to a judicial sale.'

1.49 In *Tappenden v Artus*[98] Diplock LJ compared the common law remedy of a possessory lien with other 'primitive remedies' such as abatement of nuisance, self-defence or ejection of trespassers to land. The remedy was a self-help one. Diplock LJ said the possessory lien was a remedy in rem exercisable on the goods and its exercise required no intervention by the courts, for it was exercisable only by a person who had actual possession of the goods subject to the lien. A common law lien afforded a defence to an action for recovery of the goods by a person who, but for the lien, would be entitled to immediate possession.

1.50 Common law liens are non-consensual in nature and are confined to historically determined situations. As one commentator has noted, the modern law is content to leave the existence of a common law lien to legal history without making any real attempt to rationalise its existence in contemporary conditions.[99] Statute, however, has sometimes recognised or created lien-type rights. Section 88 of the Civil Aviation Act 1982 which was considered in *Bristol Airport plc v Powdrill*[100] serves as a case in point. The section conferred on airport authorities the right to detain aircraft to force payment of unpaid airport charges. The Court of Appeal took the view that the statutory right of detention was a 'lien or security' over property within the meaning of s 248 of the Insolvency Act 1986. In general, a common law lien equals a passive power of detention. The lienee may, however, have a power of sale in the case of a statutorily-conferred lien as is the situation with s 88 of the Civil Aviation Act 1982. Moreover, statute sometimes invests a lienee with a power of sale in other circumstances.[101]

---

97 *Halsbury's Laws of England* (4th edn reissue 1997) vol 28, para 754. The relevant chapter is by Professor Norman Palmer and Sir Anthony Mason, former Chief Justice of Australia.

98 [1964] 2 QB 185.

99 See M Bridge *Personal Property Law* (OUP, 3rd edn, 2002) at pp 170–171. Professor Bridge points to general confluence between the conferment of a lien and the exercise of a common calling. See also A Bell *Modern Law of Personal Property in England and Ireland* (Butterworths, 1989) at pp 138–139.

100 [1990] Ch 744.

101 See, for example, Torts (Interference with Goods) Act 1977, ss 12 and 13. Moreover, under the Civil Procedure Rules 1998, r 25.1(1)(c)(v) the court has power on the application of any party to a cause or matter to order the sale of any property which is the subject of a claim or as to

Liens – equitable liens

1.51 Equitable liens are more expansive in nature than common law liens in that they are not dependent on possession.[102] It has even been suggested that 'the equitable lien is a dangerous and elusive enemy of the law of [pari passu distribution of a debtor's assets in an insolvency]' and that as 'applied to some bankruptcy cases, it seems as well named as the Holy Roman Empire, for it is neither equitable nor a lien'.[103] An equitable lien is a form of equitable charge arising by operation of law. In other words, it[104] is a right against property which arises automatically by implication of equity to secure the discharge of an actual or potential indebtedness.[105] An equitable lien may be enforced by obtaining an order of sale from the court.[106] The best known equitable liens are the vendor's lien for unpaid purchase money and the purchaser's lien, both arising in the case of contracts for the sale of land.[107] The former is founded on the principle that 'a person, having got the estate of another, shall not, as between them, keep it, and not pay the consideration'.[108] The purchaser's lien rests on the converse principle that he who has agreed to convey property in return for a purchase price will not be allowed to keep the price if he fails to convey the property as agreed.[109] It should be noted that an equitable lien differs from a traditional mortgage in that no title to the property is transferred to the lien-holder and so the lien cannot be enforced by foreclosure.

1.52 The question arises whether the categories of equitable liens are closed. Maybe this is a bit like asking whether the Pope is a Catholic, in that arguments for expanding the boundaries of equitable liens will always be made. On the other hand, one could adopt the statement of Bagnall J in *Cowcher v Cowcher*[110] and say that while equity is not beyond childbearing in this

---

which any question may arise on a claim and which is of a perishable nature or which for any other good reason it is desirable to sell quickly.

102 Adopting the words of Lord Mersey in *Kreglinger v New Patagonia Meat and Cold Storage Co Ltd* [1914] AC 25 at 46. See generally on equitable liens the decision of the High Court of Australia in *Hewett v Court* (1983) 57 ALJR 211 which case is extensively discussed by I Hardingham 'Equitable Liens for the Recovery of Purchase Money' (1985) 15 Melbourne University Law Review 65.

103 M McLaughlin (1927) 60 Harvard Law Review 341 at 389 referred to by J Phillips in chapter 39 of N Palmer and E McKendrick (ed) *Interests in Goods* (Lloyds of London Press, 2nd edn, 1998) at pp 992–993.

104 See *Hewett v Court* (1983) 57 ALJR 211; on which see I Hardingham 'Equitable Liens for the Recovery of Purchase Money' (1985) 15 Melbourne University Law Review 65.

105 (1983) 57 ALJR 211 at 220. Reference was made inter alia in this connection to *Re Bernstein* [1925] Ch 12 at 17–18 and *Re Bond Worth Ltd* [1980] Ch 228 at 251.

106 *Bowles v Rogers* (1800) 31 ER 957; *Re Stucley* [1906] 1 Ch 67.

107 Under ss 41–43 of the Sale of Goods Act 1979 an unpaid seller of goods has a possessory lien and also a right to stop goods in transit, but the courts have refused to recognise equitable liens that operate independently of the legislation in sale of goods transactions – *Re Wait* [1927] 1 Ch 606.

108 *Mackreth v Symmons* (1808) 15 Ves 329 at 340; 33 ER 778 at 782.

109 See *Rose v Watson* (1864) 10 HL Cas 672 at 684.

110 [1972] 1 WLR 425 at 430. Somewhat more controversially Bagnall J also said that in determining rights, particularly property rights, the only justice that can be attained by mortals, who are fallible and not omniscient, was justice according to law, namely the justice

particular area, its progeny must, however, be legitimate: by precedent out of principle. Any extension of the scope of equitable liens is likely to be by way of expansion of existing categories rather than by the development of wholly new categories. The procreational qualities of equitable liens will be discussed in the context of two leading cases on purchaser's liens, one Irish and the other Australian, namely *Re Barrett Apartments Ltd*[111] and *Hewett v Court*[112] though there is obvious linkage with the issue of the remedial constructive trust, which will be considered later.

1.53 In *Re Barrett Apartments Ltd* the company owned a site on which it proposed to build a block of flats. 'Booking deposits' were paid by prospective purchasers of the flats and a further sum was to be paid on the execution of a building agreement. Building agreements were signed in only a couple of cases. A receiver was appointed to the company and the question arose whether the depositors had secured claims against the company. A distinction was drawn between depositors who had, and those who had not, signed a legally enforceable contract for the purchase of premises. The liquidator paid off the two who had signed such agreements. He rejected, however, all other claims. The Irish Supreme Court said that he was right in so doing.

1.54 The depositors relied heavily on the words of Vaughan Williams LJ in *Whitbread and Co Ltd v Watt*[113] that the lien was a right invented for the purpose of doing justice. The Supreme Court, however, were unmoved by this argument. Henchy J stated that depositors as a class did not have an equity to be treated as secured creditors, while other creditors, whose debts could be more deserving of payment and no less closely connected with the property, were left to languish as unsecured creditors without hope of payment at the tail end of the queue of creditors.[114] In his view, the rationale behind allowing a purchaser a lien on the property in respect of a deposit paid to the vendor was that by paying the deposit in pursuance of the contract, the purchaser acquired an equitable estate or interest in the property.[115] Therefore the purchaser should be allowed to follow that estate or interest by being accorded a lien on it.[116]

---

which flowed from the application of sure and settled principles to proved or admitted facts. But one need not necessarily take on board this baggage.

111 [1985] IR 350 on which see G McCormack (1986) 7 Co Law 113; P Coughlan (1988) 10 Dublin University Law Journal 90.

112 (1983) 57 ALJR 211. See also *Lord Napier and Ettrick v Hunter* [1993] AC 713. Here the House of Lords held that the doctrine of subrogation conferred on an insurer an equitable proprietary lien or charge on the monies recovered by the insured person from a third party in respect of the insured loss. The court did not feel it necessary to decide whether the equitable lien or charge attached also to the rights of action vested in the insured person to recover from a third party.

113 [1902] 1 Ch 835 at 838. See also *Combe v Lord Swaythling* [1947] 1 Ch 625. McCarthy J argued ([1985] IR 350 at 360) that the judge merely meant to say that an express agreement for the grant of a lien was not necessary. He did not purport to remove the necessity for a contractual setting.

114 [1985] IR 350 at 358–359. For an argument supporting a more individuated claim to a lien see P Coughlan (1988) 10 Dublin University Law Journal 90 at 104–106.

115 [1985] IR 350 at 357–358. Reference was made to *Rose v Watson* (1864) 10 HLC 672 and *Tempany v Hynes* [1976] IR 101.

116 It has been argued that this view is at odds with the accepted learning that equitable charges

Where no contract of purchase was entered into by the depositor, the payment of the booking deposit did not give the payer any estate or interest in the property. McCarthy J was of the same opinion. He said that those who paid advances in respect of an anticipated contract should not be placed in a more advantageous position than that of trading creditors or professional creditors who put their goods or their services at the disposal of the self-same debtor without payment and whose claims could only rank as those of unsecured creditors.[117]

1.55 *Re Barrett Apartments Ltd* may be looked at from the point of view of a judicial reaction to the multiplicity of arguments for secured status in corporate insolvency. The Irish Supreme Court viewed ratable allocation of available resources as a principle of overriding weight and importance. Any suggested departure from this desideratum was treated with considerable caution. The court conceived the case almost entirely in terms of policy. What was fair or just for the judges to decide? Even-handed distribution of corporate assets appears to have been taken as a touchstone of justice. Some would say, however, that the decision gives moneyed might priority over social justice.[118] Certainly the majority of the High Court of Australia took a more expansive view of equitable liens in *Hewett v Court*.[119] First, they decided that the availability of specific performance to a purchaser was not essential in deciding upon an equitable lien.[120] Specific performance results in fulfilment of the contract, whereas an equitable lien came about in the event of the contract not being performed. Logically the two were quite distinct. A decree of specific performance might be withheld from an innocent purchaser on grounds which had nothing to do with the question whether the purchaser should be accorded security for the return of the purchase money.[121]

1.56 In *Hewett v Court* a company agreed with purchasers to construct a transportable house according to agreed plans and specifications and to

---

are not dependent on possession or ownership, either at law or equity. See P Coughlan (1988) 10 Dublin University Law Journal 90 at 96.

117 [1985] IR 350 at 361.

118 To use a turn of phrase associated with Lord Denning in *Williams & Glyn Bank v Boland* [1979] Ch 312 at 333. The decision was affirmed by the House of Lords [1981] AC 487 where Lord Scarman said (at 510) that the court should not be perturbed by supposed difficulties as a result of the decision in the banking or conveyancing sectors. Bankers and solicitors existed to provide the services which the public needed. They could adjust their practice if it was socially required. Some might say that at the end of the day the consumer loses because the banks will pass on the losses associated with judicial rejection of their claims in the form of increased charges.

119 (1983) 57 ALJR 211.

120 The issue is most fully considered by Deane J ((1983) 57 ALJR 211 at 221–223). Gibbs CJ opined (at 215) that specific enforceability was not relevant in adjudicating upon a purchaser's lien but did not conclusively rule out the proposition that specific enforcement was a prerequisite to an unpaid vendor's lien. Deane J took the view that specific enforceability was irrelevant to equitable liens generally and Murphy J appears to have been of a similar opinion.

121 In *Re Barrett Apartments Ltd* [1985] IR 350 Keane J in the Irish High Court took the view that the availability of the remedy of specific performance was not a precondition for the existence of an unpaid purchaser's lien. The Supreme Court, however, did not adopt a view on the matter.

transport it to the site of the purchasers and place it in position on blocks there. Property in the home, it was agreed, was to remain with the company until the contract price had been paid in full. The price was payable in stages, a deposit on entry into the contract followed by instalments at various stages of the operations. The company went into liquidation, however, before the stage of completion, but it was held that the purchasers had an equitable lien over the buildings in respect of their pre-payments. It was held unanimously that the relevant contract was one for the provision of work and materials and not one for the sale of goods, but the court differed on the availability, or otherwise, of an equitable lien. Gibbs CJ, Murphy and Deane JJ were in the majority. Gibbs CJ observed that the fact there was no authority precisely in point did not mean that a lien could arise. In his view, the rules of equity were not so rigid and inflexible that it was necessary to discover precise authority for the existence of a lien before one could be held to have been created. The present case was analogous to that of a purchaser's lien. Technically, the contract was not one of sale and purchase, but the doctrines of equity attached more importance to substance than to technicalities.[122]

1.57 In a succinct judgment, Murphy J confronted 'head-on' the questions of policy involved. He said an equitable lien such as this will often be necessary to protect consumers, who, unlike traders, cannot be expected to enquire into the solvency of the person with whom they are dealing. He noted, however, that, as so often happens in commercial and conveyancing cases, the court was not assisted by any 'commercial impact statement' of what would be the effect in commerce generally of equitable liens arising in such circumstances.[123]

1.58 Deane J adopted a more traditional case-based analysis. He outlined a number of factors that, in his view, were sufficient for the implication, independently of agreement, of an equitable lien between contracting parties with the criteria being satisfied in the present case. The factors are as follows:[124]

(a)   an actual or potential indebtedness by the owner of the property the subject of the contract to the other party arising from a payment or promise thereof of consideration in relation to the acquisition of the property or of an expense incurred in relation to it;

(b)   the property is specifically identified and appropriated to the performance of the contract; and

(c)   the relationship between the indebtedness and the property is such that it would be unconscientious or unfair for the owner to dispose of the property without the consent of the other party or discharge of the liability.

---

122   (1983) 57 ALJR 211 at 215.
123   (1983) 57 ALJR 211.
124   (1983) 57 ALJR 211 at 223. John Phillips in chapter 39 of NE Palmer and E McKendrick (eds) *Interests in Goods* (Lloyds of London Press, 2nd edn, 1998) has persuasively argued (at p 990) that the principles expounded by Deane J, based as they are on the concepts of appropriation and unconscientious dealing, make it difficult to determine in any given factual situation whether or not a lien will arise.

1.59 It has been argued that the concepts of unconscientiousness and appropriation are so opaque as to make it difficult to determine whether, in any particular case, an equitable lien will be held to have arisen. It may be that, given the difficulties that the tests engender, the appropriate approach is that of Gibbs CJ, ie of reasoning by reference to established categories of liens. If, however, the tests are applied to the facts of *Re Barrett Apartments* it seems clear that no lien would have arisen. An apartment could not be said to have been appropriated to the performance of a contract unless a contract for the purchase of the same had been signed.

1.60 It should be noted that an equitable lien may be qualified or negatived by agreement between the parties. The issue of express or implied ouster of the intervention of equity, as it were, has arisen particularly in the context of vendor's liens. A vendor's lien will now be considered.

Existing categories of equitable lien – the vendor's lien

1.61 An unpaid vendor has a lien on the property to secure payment of the balance of the purchase price. The lien is enforceable by the unpaid vendor seeking an order for the sale of the property from the court. Again, the unpaid vendor's lien, while obviously in the broadest sense a security interest of some species, arises by operation of law. Consequently, it is outside the scope of the company charge registration system.

1.62 The lien by operation of law cases are, however, to be distinguished from cases where there is an equitable mortgage by deposit of title deeds with an ancillary right to retain the title deeds until the loan has been repaid. An instance of this is *Re Molton Finance Ltd*[125] where a firm of stockbrokers lent money to a company and as security the company deposited deeds and documents with the stockbrokers 'to the intent that the same may be equitably charged with the repayment'. The charges created were not registered and the company later went into liquidation. The liquidator claimed that the deeds and documents deposited were void against him for want of registration and for their delivery up by the stockbrokers. The latter contended that they had a common law lien on the documents but this proposition was rejected.

1.63 According to the Court of Appeal, the deposit of the deeds and documents was simply an adjunct to the equitable charge. The contractual right to the retention of these materials was lost when the charge was avoided for non-registration. Lord Denning observed that when an equitable mortgage or charge is created by deposit of title deeds, there is an implied contract that the mortgagee or chargee may retain the deeds until he is paid. This implied contract was part and parcel of, and had no independent existence apart from, the equitable mortgage or charge. When the mortgage or charge was avoided

---

125 [1968] Ch 325, on which see J Sunnucks (1970) 33 MLR 131. See also *Re Farm Fresh Foods Ltd* (Irish High Court, unreported) 23 June 1980, referred to by G McCormack (1984) 2 Irish Law Times (New Series) 67 at 68.

for non-registration, then everything that was ancillary to it was avoided also. Thus the contractual right of retention went by the board too.[126]

1.64 The rationale for non-registrability of an unpaid vendor's lien was discussed by Brightman J in *London and Cheshire Insurance Co Ltd v Laplagrene Co*.[127] He said that if such a lien was registrable the time for registration would expire 21 days after the exchange of contracts for sale, because it was at that time that the lien was created. The lien was not created on completion because the purchase price was unpaid, but was discharged on completion to the extent that the purchase price was paid. In many cases, the 21-day period for registration would expire well before completion. It would be a great inconvenience, therefore, if every vendor to a company were compelled as a matter of course to register an unpaid vendor's lien on the exchange of contracts, on the off-chance that circumstances might arise in the future which would render it desirable for the vendor to be able to rely on an unpaid vendor's lien.[128]

1.65 The question arises as to the kinds of property over which an unpaid vendor's lien may exist.[129] Like the case of a purchaser's lien, an unpaid vendor's lien is capable of existing in relation to land and likewise with intangible personal property. Both the vendor's lien as well as the purchaser's lien may subsist in this sphere.[130] In *Langen & Wind Ltd v Bell*[131] Brightman J observed that an unpaid vendor's lien extends not only to land but to all property over which a court of equity will assume jurisdiction in the case of a contract of sale.[132] So an unpaid vendor's lien has been held to arise on the sale of shares,[133] debts,[134] patents[135] and interests under trusts.[136] The position is different in relation to a lien over goods. The shutters appear to come down on the recognition process no matter whether one is concerned with a vendor's lien or a purchaser's lien.[137]

1.66 Most often cited in this connection are the observations of Atkin LJ in *Re Wait*.[138] He said:[139]

---

126 [1968] Ch 325 at 333.
127 [1971] Ch 499.
128 [1971] Ch 499 at 514. See also Lawrence J in *Re Beirnstein* [1925] Ch 12 at 17.
129 See generally Andrew P Bell *Modern Law of Personal Property in England and Ireland* (Butterworths, 1989) at pp 180–181.
130 For the purchaser's lien see *Barker v Cox* (1876) 4 Ch D 464 and *Imperial Ottoman Bank v Trustees, Executors and Securities Insurance Corpn* (1895) 13 R 287.
131 [1972] Ch 685.
132 [1972] Ch 685 at 692.
133 *Langan and Wind Ltd v Bell* [1972] Ch 685.
134 *Collins v Collins (No 2)* (1862) 31 Beav 346.
135 *Dansk Rekylriffel Syndikat Aktieselskab v Snell* [1908] 2 Ch 127.
136 *Davies v Thomas* [1900] 2 Ch 462; *Re Stucley* [1906] 1 Ch 67.
137 The situation according to *Re Dyton, Appleton v Hole* (1952) 102 LJ 669 is different where the contract is for the sale of goods and other property and the goods element is not severable.
138 [1927] 1 Ch 606.
139 [1927] 1 Ch 606 at 639; Atkin LJ also said at 635–636:
        'The total sum of legal relations (meaning by the word "legal" existing in equity as well as in common law) arising out of the contract for the sale of goods may well be regarded as

'The unpaid vendor has a lien which is a possessory lien; and has a right of stoppage in transitu; but in my experience no one has ever claimed or been given in the countless cases that have arisen of vendors of goods remaining unpaid after delivery, a right to a lien over the goods in the possession of the purchaser. Similarly, the purchaser who in pursuance of the contract of sale has paid the purchase price or part of it before delivery has never claimed or received a lien over the property which is in the hands of the vendor. I am satisfied that such liens would be quite inconsistent with the provisions of the Code, and do not exist.'

1.67 To the same effect are the observations of Simonds J in *Transport and General Credit Corpn v Morgan*[140] who said it would be quite inconsistent with the exhaustive statement of the law in the Sale of Goods Act that there be any lien other than the possessory lien which the statute itself provides.[141] The High Court of Australia grappled with the same issue in *Hewett v Court*[142] but a less conclusive answer was provided and Gibbs CJ expressly left open the question whether there was any room for the existence of equitable liens by operation of law in the case of contracts for the sale of goods.[143] Deane J adopted a similar approach. He found it unnecessary to consider whether there was a comprehensive legislative code which precluded the implication of an equitable lien to secure payment or repayment of purchase price under a contract for the sale of goods.[144] As far as the Sale of Goods Act constituting a comprehensive legislative code there is much to be said for the view that it should not be regarded as exclusive on such a collateral matter as lien securities.[145] After all, the Act is not exhaustive on the general rules of contract law, e g principles of offer and acceptance insofar as a contract for the sale of goods is concerned.[146] On the other hand, it would seem much too late in the day to argue for the existence of an unpaid vendor's lien in a sale of goods contract. Commercial

---

defined by the Code. It would have been futile in a code intended for commercial men to have created an elaborate structure of rules dealing with rights at law, if at the same time it was intended to leave, subsisting with the legal rights, equitable rights inconsistent with, more extensive, and coming into existence earlier than the rights so carefully set out in the various sections of the Code.'

140 [1939] 1 Ch 531.
141 [1939] 1 Ch 531 at 546.
142 (1983) 57 ALJR 211.
143 (1983) 57 ALJR 211 at 213.
144 (1983) 57 ALJR 211 at 221. See also the non-committal views of Wilson and Dawson JJ at 217.
145 See Phillips at pp 983–984 of NE Palmer and E McKendrick (eds) *Interests in Goods* (Lloyds of London Press Ltd, 2nd edn, 1998) where reference is made to the observations of Kearney J in the Supreme Court of New South Wales in *Electrical Enterprises Retail Pty Ltd v Rodgers* (1989) 15 NSWLR 473. In this case Kearney J of the Supreme Court of New South Wales said at 492–493 that having regard to the particular provisions of the Sale of Goods Act in New South Wales, in appropriate cases equitable principles could apply to a contract for the sale of goods.
146 Section 61(2) of the Sale of Goods Act 1979 provides:
'The rules of the common law including the law merchant except insofar as they are inconsistent with the provisions of this Act, and in particular the rules relating to the law of principal and agent and the effect of fraud, misrepresentation, duress or coercion, mistake or other invalidating cause, apply to contracts for the sale of goods.'

common sense would militate against acceptance of the existence of a lien. Certainly, in *Re Bond Worth Ltd*[147] Slade J took the view that no equitable lien could arise in such circumstances.

Subrogation to an unpaid vendor's lien

1.68　A variant on the theme of vendor's lien is for a person who has advanced money to finance the acquisition of property to claim that it is subrogated to an unpaid vendor's lien. The possibility of such a claim was recognised by the House of Lords in *Orakpo v Manson Investments Ltd* where Lord Diplock considered the nature of subrogation and suggested that the mere fact that money lent has been expended upon discharging a secured liability of the borrower did not give rise to any implication of subrogation unless the loan contract provided that the money was to be applied for this purpose.[148] He suggested that the origin of the right of subrogation was the contract of loan between borrower and lender. If there was no contractual obligation upon the borrower to apply the monies in discharging a security on the property of the borrower in favour of a third party, the expectation of the parties that the money would in fact be used for this purpose did not give rise to any right of subrogation in the lender even if the money was so applied. On the other hand, Lord Diplock said 'where a contract of loan provides that monies lent by L to B are to be applied in discharging a liability of B to C secured on property, it is an implied term of that contract that L is to be subrogated to C's security'. This view has been criticised on the basis that it must be open to question whether such evidence should be regarded as conclusive of the parties' intentions, in the absence of any express agreement between the lender and the borrower that the loan should be secured.[149]

1.69　Lord Keith, however, was of a broadly similar opinion to Lord Diplock. He said that if a person had simply borrowed money without any strings attached and then voluntarily used it to complete contracts for the purchase of land or to pay off the holders of existing charges, no question of subrogation would have arisen.[150] Lord Keith went on to say:[151]

> 'If it had been a term of the contract of loan that the money was to be used for such purposes, and there had been no agreement for fresh security to be given to the lenders, then upon the money being so applied the lenders would by operation of law have been subrogated to the security rights of the vendor and of the existing charge holders. It is not inconceivable that a money lender should be prepared to proceed on that basis, intending and expecting that he would be so subrogated by operation of law. He might indeed expressly stipulate for such subrogation but that would not be necessary. Subrogation would be the legal result of carrying out the contract entered into.'

147　[1980] Ch 228 at 251.
148　[1978] AC 95 at 105.
149　See Charles Mitchell *The Law of Subrogation* (Clarendon Press Oxford, 1994) at p 146.
150　[1978] AC 95 at 119.
151　[1978] AC 95.

1.70   The old authority of *Wylie v Carlyon* appears to illustrate a stricter approach towards subrogation to security rights than the views articulated in *Orakpo*.[152] In *Wylie v Carlyon* it was contended that persons were entitled, under the doctrine of subrogation, to be placed in a mortgagee's shoes by reason of the fact that their monies were used to pay off the mortgagee. Eve J rejected the proposition, stating that an individual who advances money to another for the purpose of enabling that other to pay specific debts does not, in the absence of 'a special bargain', acquire the rights against the property of those whose debts are thereby discharged.[153]

1.71   More recently the juridical basis of the doctrine of subrogation was considered by the House of Lords in *Banque Financière De La Cité v Parc (Battersea) Ltd*.[154] In this case a Swiss bank (Banque Financière) partly refinanced an existing secured bank loan made available by Royal Trust Bank to Parc for the purpose of buying development land in Battersea. Parc was part of the Omni Group of companies of which the ultimate holding company was Omni Holding AG. The comparatively simple refinancing transaction was structured in a somewhat complicated way so as to avoid reporting requirements. The essential point, however, was that Banque Financière was granted a letter of postponement by the general manager of Omni Holding AG. that purported to subordinate loans made by Holding, and other intra-group lending, to the loan made to Parc by Banque Financière. It was held, however, that while the letter of postponement was intended to be directly binding on all companies in the Omni Group, the general manager had no authority to bind such companies, in particular a company called OOL that had a charge on the property of Parc that ranked after the secured loan that had been partly repaid. Parc became insolvent with insufficient assets to repay both Banque Financière and OOL. It was crucial therefore to determine whose claim had priority.

1.72   Since the principles of the law of agency were of little avail to the Swiss bank, they had recourse to the law of unjust enrichment arguing that the existence of the letter of postponement meant that they should have priority over OOL, whether by way of subrogation to the secured loan which had been partly discharged or otherwise. The House of Lords unanimously accepted this contention. The fullest discussion of legal principle occurs in the judgment of Lord Hoffmann who suggested that subrogation could be a contractual arrangement for the transfer of rights against third parties or an equitable remedy to reverse or prevent unjust enrichment.[155] Lord Hoffmann said that it was a mistake to regard the availability of subrogation as a remedy to prevent unjust enrichment as turning entirely upon the question of intention, whether common or unilateral. He added that one is here concerned with a restitution-ary remedy and the appropriate questions were therefore, first, whether the defendant would be enriched at the plaintiff's expense; secondly, whether such

---

152   [1922] 1 Ch 51. Lord Diplock does, however, refer to *Wylie v Carlyon* with approval in *Orakpo* [1978] AC 95 at 105.
153   [1922] 1 Ch 51 at 63.
154   [1999] 1 AC 221.
155   [1999] 1 AC 221 at 230–231.

enrichment would be unjust; and thirdly, whether there were nevertheless reasons of policy for denying a remedy. Lord Hoffmann continued:[156]

> 'subrogation is not a right or a cause of action but an equitable remedy against a party who would otherwise be unjustly enriched ... When judges say that the charge is "kept alive" for the benefit of the plaintiff, what they mean is that his legal relations with a defendant who would otherwise be unjustly enriched are regulated *as if* the benefit of the charge had been assigned to him. It does not by any means follow that the plaintiff must for all purposes be treated as an actual assignee of the benefit of the charge and, in particular, that he would be so treated in relation to someone who would not be unjustly enriched.'

1.73 *Banque Financière* has attracted some criticism from commentators. There was a concern that the introduction of free-wheeling restitutionary principles might destabilise the well-established law of subrogation and maybe indeed have a knock-on effect on the company charge registration system.[157] The decision also appears to allow a creditor who has made a loan on an unsecured basis to claim subrogation to the rights of a secured creditor.

1.74 In later decisions, however, the Court of Appeal has been minded to explain and distinguish *Banque Financière* on the basis that the Swiss bank, only against OOL and not more generally, was entitled to the benefit of the security that had been partly discharged by the new loan. A case in point is *Halifax plc v Omar*[158] where again a lender advanced money for the purchase of a property. The lender meant to take a charge over the property but, due to a fraud, no charge was ever executed. The property subsequently came into the hands of a purchaser who, on the assumed facts, was both innocent of the fraud and unaware of the bank's interest. The bank had an equitable security in the property by virtue of subrogation to the vendor's lien, whereas the purchaser also had an equitable interest. Applying the normal 'first in time has priority' principle to resolve conflicts between competing equitable interests, the bank would have priority. The purchaser, however, argued that the bank's claim to subrogation was based on the reversal of unjust enrichment and the unjust enrichment claim was subject to the defence of bona fide purchase which the purchaser could legitimately advance.

1.75 The Court of Appeal, however, rejected this contention stating that the lender's subrogation claim was based not on unjust enrichment but rather on well established principles of property law. Jonathan Parker LJ distinguished between subrogation to a security and subrogation merely to the indebtedness

---

156 [1999] 1 AC 221 at 236. Reference was made to the observations of Millett LJ to this effect in *Boscawen v Bajwa* [1996] 1 WLR 328 at 335.

157 S Midwinter [2003] LMCLQ 6. In his view unjust enrichment doctrine is an unnecessary complication that does not advance the intellectual or moral basis of the law at all. Midwinter points out that the House of Lords in *Banque Financière* state repeatedly that subrogation is based either on contract or unjust enrichment and it is simply implausible that, amongst the generalised statements of the law to be found in that case, the 'ordinary' case could have slipped through, unmentioned. Midwinter suggests that is difficult to avoid the conclusion that the *Omar* reasoning is not consistent with that in *Banque Financière*.

158 [2002] 2 P & CR 26.

itself. In the former case the remedy of subrogation gives effect to a property right which already exists in equity, ie the right to be regarded as chargee of the property in question. A claimant who is subrogated to a security right is treated in equity as if he had that security, and where the security takes the form of an unpaid vendor's lien he is an equitable chargee to the extent his money was used to pay the purchase price for the property.

1.76 The stance adopted in *Omar* was endorsed by a differently constituted Court of Appeal in *Eagle Star v Karasiewicz*.[159] In this case an existing secured loan over property to which an equitable owner had consented was replaced by a new loan to which the consent of the equitable owner had, mistakenly, not been obtained. The equitable owner contended that she was not bound by the new security as she had not given her consent to it, whereas the new lender contended that it was subrogated to the rights of the lender whose security had been discharged by the proceeds of the fresh loan. The subrogation claim succeeded. Arden LJ suggested that *Halifax plc v Omar* explained the more usual case of subrogation where money was lent to pay off a secured claim. She continued:[160]

> 'The effect of the ... decision is that ... the creditor who seeks to be subrogated is given the remedy by way of satisfaction of a pre-existing equitable proprietary right which is vindicated by the order for subrogation ... [T]here may be factors which would lead the court to the conclusion that subrogation was not the appropriate relief ... where there was waiver of the security; or where it is clear that the party advancing money intended to do so on an unsecured basis. But apart from those exceptional situations ... it must be right that where a creditor has advanced money intending to take security, and the money has been used to pay off a secured debt and he does not receive the security he expected to receive, he should in general be subrogated to the rights of a secured creditor whom he has paid off.'

1.77 *Omar* is a case where a charge over the property was never executed, but alternative possibilities exist under which the charge is avoided for want of compliance with the company charge registration requirements. In this scenario, the lender might wish to fall back on its claim by subrogation to an unpaid vendor's lien. Such a claim succeeded in the Irish case *Bank of Ireland Finance Ltd v DJ Daly Ltd*.[161] The facts were that the Bank had agreed to make an advance to the company to enable it to purchase certain lands and they received an undertaking from the company's solicitors to lodge the title deeds

---

159 [2002] EWCA 940.
160 [2002] EWCA 940 at [19].
161 [1978] IR 79. See also *Highland Finance Ireland Ltd v Sacred Heart College* [1992] 1 IR 472 where it was held that the bargain between the plaintiff and first defendant, which entitled the plaintiff to loan repayments through complex and unique arrangements, was inconsistent with the retention of the entitlement to be subrogated to the right of an unpaid vendor to immediate payment of the purchase price. Murphy J, however, reluctantly rejected the argument that the right of subrogation should be confined to those cases like *Thurstan v Nottingham Permanent Building Society* [1903] AC 6 where the lender had no right of action in personam against the borrower, so that, in the absence of a right of subrogation, the borrower would be unjustly enriched.

of the property on completion of the transaction, and pending completion to hold them in trust for the bank, and further to lodge the proceeds of resale of the property with the bank. The bank made the advance and the defendant, having already paid a deposit, used some of the monies so advanced to pay the vendor the balance. Subsequently, the title deeds came into the possession of the bank, but not by way of security for an advance. It was held, however, that the solicitors' undertaking created an equitable charge in itself[162] but this charge was never registered.

1.78 It was contended on behalf of the company that the bank, having so obtained an equitable charge, was precluded from claiming to be subrogated to an unpaid vendor's lien. The court, however, took the view that the plaintiff's lien was not defeated by merger in, or inconsistency with, the equitable charge created by the defendant's letter. Any question of possible inconsistency was resolved in favour of the lender. McMahon J put the matter thus:[163]

> 'The security by subrogation is not inconsistent with the security by deposit of title deeds. Each is an equitable security of the same rank, but the deposit of title deeds, if implemented, would enable the bank to impede or prevent any dealing in the legal estate in the property without the bank's consent. I think that the security by deposit of title deeds can be regarded as a security which is additional to the security by subrogation rather than as a substitute for it.'

1.79 In the *Daly* case, the plaintiff bank was able to escape, somewhat fortuitously, the general obligation of registration through making use of the law relating to subrogation and unpaid vendor's liens. The decision seems questionable, since it seems to undermine the foundations of the registration system. Fortunately, a different view was taken in England in *Burston Finance Ltd v Speirway Ltd* on the issue of abandonment of an unpaid vendor's lien.[164]

1.80 It was in *Burston Finance* held that simply taking security in addition to the unpaid vendor's lien would not necessarily, without more, involve an abandonment of the unpaid vendor's lien. Where, however, a lender took a security which satisfied certain conditions then, according to the court, it would be straining credulity to suggest that the lender did not intend to abandon the ordinary lien and to rely upon the security so selected. These conditions entailed a security which (a) was for the full amount of the outstanding purchase price; (b) extended over the whole of the property conveyed;

---

162 *Simmons v Montague* [1909] 1 IR 87 was referred to as authority for that proposition. In that case, the debtor deposited title deeds of his hotel along with a map of the property but he had a possessory title only to part of the property. The deposit was, nevertheless, held to be sufficient evidence of an agreement to charge all his interest in the hotel, including that part held under a possessory title and as regards which no deeds were deposited.

163 [1978] IR 79 at 84.

164 [1974] 1 WLR 1648. For an endorsement of the decision see C Mitchell *The Law of Subrogation* (Clarendon Press Oxford, 1994) at p 142.

(c) reserved a much higher rate of interest than would be covered by the ordinary unpaid vendor's lien; and (d) comprised all the remedies afforded by that lien.[165]

1.81   In *Burston Finance* the legal charge taken by the vendor satisfied all of these conditions, but the vendor relied heavily on the principle that an unpaid vendor's lien could co-exist with a security that was, from its inception, either wholly void or otherwise unenforceable. In other words, a vendor did not get what she bargained for when all she got was a charge that was void *ab initio*.[166] Walton J, however, decided that it was quite impossible to equate a legal charge that only became void subsequent to its creation, and then only to a strictly limited extent, with charges that were wholly ineffective from their inception. The lenders got what they bargained for and were merely lax in not taking steps to ensure that what they bargained for remained good against the world by embarking upon the process of registration.[167]

1.82   In *Orakpo v Manson Investments*[168] the House of Lords added a gloss to the line of cases relied upon by the lender in *Burston Finance Ltd v Spierway Ltd*. In particular, the House of Lords refused to equate situations where the lender's charge had been rendered void with cases where it was merely unenforceable.[169] In the former case, the lender obtained nothing in return for her loan, whereas in the latter the lender obtained a valid legal charge. So co-existence of an unpaid vendor lien with a charge that was wholly void was possible, but not co-existence with a charge that was merely unenforceable.

The remedial constructive trust

1.83   At a very general level, one might say that the function of equity is to mitigate the rigour of the law. The question therefore arises whether a person, who would otherwise be within the category of general creditors, may invoke the assistance of equity to leapfrog the queue of creditors? In particular, may such a person assert a proprietary right in an asset of the insolvent that allows him to take priority over other creditors, including secured creditors? The courts generally are loath to entertain such claims. Judicial reticence is reflected in the remarks of Judge Paul Baker in *Re Stapylton Fletcher Ltd*.[170] He said:

---

165   [1974] 1 WLR 1648 at 1653.
166   [1974] 1 WLR 1648 at 1652–1653. Reference was made in this connection to *Thurstan v Nottingham Permanent Benefit Building Society* [1902] 1 Ch 1; *Congresbury Motors Ltd v Anglo-Belge Finance Co Ltd* [1971] Ch 81; and *Ghana Commercial Bank v Chandiram* [1960] AC 732.
167   *Capital Finance Co Ltd v Stokes* [1969] 1 Ch 261 and *Coptic Ltd v Bailey* [1972] Ch 446 not followed.
168   [1978] AC 95. On *Orakpo* generally, see P Birks *An Introduction to the Law of Restitution* (paperback edition, 1989) at pp 391–392.
169   [1978] AC 95 at 106 per Lord Diplock; at 114 per Lord Edmund-Davies; and at 118 per Lord Salmon. *Congresbury Motors Ltd v Anglo-Belge Finance Co Ltd* [1971] Ch 81 was overruled.
170   [1994] 1 WLR 1181 at 1203.

'The court must be very cautious in devising equitable interests and remedies which erode the statutory scheme for distribution on insolvency. It cannot do it because of some perceived injustice arising as a consequence of the insolvency.'

1.84 A leading authority is the Privy Council decision in *Re Goldcorp Exchange Ltd.*[171] In this case a bank holding a charge had appointed receivers over the assets of a company. Some of the customers of the company had purchased gold bullion for future delivery but, at the date when the receivers were appointed, there had not been any appropriation of specific and segregated parcels of bullion to the individual purchase contracts. These facts suggested that the bullion was swallowed up, as it were, by the bank's charge, but the claimants invoked a number of arguments including that of the constructive trust. The Privy Council, however, rejected the proposition that the court should create in favour of the non-allocated claimants a remedial restitutionary right superior to the security created by the charge. Lord Mustill pointed out that the bank relied on the floating charge to protect its assets, whereas the customers relied on the company to deliver the bullion. The fact that the claimants were private citizens whereas their opponent was a commercial bank could not justify the court in simply disapplying the bank's valid security. That, in the court's view, would be to stretch a nascent doctrine beyond breaking point.[172]

1.85 Not all judges sing from the same hymn sheet, however. In this connection one might cite the observations of Lord Browne-Wilkinson in *Westdeutsche Landesbank v Islington London Borough Council.*[173] He said that the introduction into English law of the remedial constructive trust may provide a more satisfactory road forward and added:

'The court by way of remedy might impose a constructive trust on a defendant who knowingly retains property of which the plaintiff has been unjustly deprived. Since the remedy can be tailored to the circumstances of the particular case, innocent third parties would not be prejudiced and restitutionary defences, such as change of position, are capable of being given effect. However, whether English law should follow the United States and Canada by adopting the remedial constructive trust will have to be decided in some future case when the point is directly in issue.'

1.86 As a general proposition it is submitted that the doctrine of the remedial constructive trust should be kept within very narrow bounds. There is a

---

171 [1995] 1 AC 74; on which see E McKendrick (1994) 110 LQR 509.

172 There was a group of claimants – the Walker & Hall claimants who were able to demonstrate sufficient appropriation to establish a shared interest in the pooled bullion. On a conventional tracing analysis, however, their claim was limited to the lowest balance of metal held by Goldcorp between the accrual of their rights and the commencement of receivership. They attempted to circumvent this limitation by arguing for the existence of a general equitable lien on the basis of *Space Investments Ltd v Canadian Imperial Bank of Commerce Trust Co (Bahamas) Ltd* [1986] 1 WLR 1072 but Lord Mustill refused to declare such a lien on the grounds that it would be inequitable in the particular circumstances of the case: [1995] 1 AC 74 at 108–110.

173 [1996] AC 669 at 716.

dichotomy which must be observed between family and commercial cases. The remedial constructive trust, if recognised at all, should be confined to the family sphere. Application of a more discretionary approach in the sphere would be in line with the expectation of the parties and might be productive of no greater uncertainty than the lengthy and detailed search for an elusive, if not wholly fictitious common intention, that the present law seems to require. In commercial cases, however, the very rationale of a constructive trust claim in most situations is to obtain priority over other creditors. The reason that a constructive trust is invoked is to achieve this preference. A discretionary approach towards the recognition of equitable proprietary remedies would work to the detriment of third parties and, moreover, is potentially disruptive of commercial life.

1.87 The later case of *Re Polly Peck International (No 5)*[174] supports the proposition that the remedial constructive trust should not be allowed to disrupt the process of insolvency distribution. The backdrop to this case is the Turkish occupation of Northern Cyprus in the 1970s and the confiscation and illegal use of Greek-owned property in Northern Cyprus. The applicants contended that their property had been, with knowledge of the wrongs committed against them and their property, illegally occupied and exploited by subsidiaries of Polly Peck International (PPI), a Turkish Cypriot controlled business that was now in administration. The applicants claimed that a substantial sum received by the administrators represented the profits and proceeds of wrongdoing that had been received by PPI who were thereby unjustly enriched at the applicants' expense. They claimed that this sum was subject to a remedial constructive trust for their benefit, but the argument failed to pass judicial muster. Mummery LJ said that the effect of the statutory scheme applicable on insolvency was to shut out a remedy that would, if available, have the effect of conferring a priority not accorded by the provisions of the statutory insolvency scheme. In his opinion, the law could not be moved legitimately by judicial decision down a road signed 'No Entry' by Parliament. In a colourful turn of phrase he suggested that the insolvency road was blocked off to remedial constructive trusts, at least when judge driven in a vehicle of discretion.[175]

PERSONAL SECURITY

1.88 The expression 'personal security' refers to two major legal institutions, ie suretyship and independent or demand guarantees.[176] Contracts of surety-ship have been recognised for centuries, but the judicial recognition of 'demand

---

174 [1998] 3 All ER 812 at 831; Nourse LJ defined a remedial constructive trust (at 831) as: 'an order of the court, granting, by way of remedy, a proprietary right to someone who, beforehand, had no proprietary right.'
175 See also the comments of Millett LJ in *Paragon Finance v Thakerar* [1999] 1 All ER 400.
176 See generally on this area J O'Donovan and J Phillips *The Modern Contract of Guarantee* (Sweet & Maxwell, 3rd edn, 2003); G Andrews and R Millett *Law of Guarantees* (Thomson, Sweet & Maxwell, 4th edn, 2005); K McGuinness *Law of Guarantee* (Carswell, 2nd edn, 1996).

guarantees' or 'performance bonds' is a relatively recent phenomenon, although it was remarked in *Gold Coast Ltd v Caja de Ahorros* that they have now been a feature of commercial life for many years. In 1978 in the *Edward Owen* case[177] Lord Denning said that the 'performance bond is a new creature as far as we are concerned.'

1.89 Generally speaking, confusion in terminology abounds, for the expression 'guarantee' or 'contract of guarantee' is often, and traditionally, used to refer:

> 'exclusively to contracts of suretyship whereas independent or demand guarantees are often called performance bonds. Moreover, the term "performance bond" or "performance guarantee" is sometimes used to denote a genuine contract of guarantee or indemnity. To make matters even more confusing, a guarantee or indemnity may be given in circumstances in which one might expect to find a true performance bond. The nature of the particular contract, whether it happens to be a guarantee or an indemnity, or a performance bond, and whether the normal incidents of a contract of that class have been modified, is ultimately a question of construction in each case, and is often very difficult to resolve ...'[178]

Surety guarantees

1.90 There is no modern statutory definition of suretyship, but the expression is described in s 4 of the Statute of Frauds 1677 as 'any special promise to answer for the debt, default, or miscarriage of another person'. The description has been turned into modern legal terminology as a promise to accept liability for the failure of another party to perform legal obligations, existing and future, and arising from any source.[179] A suretyship contract is a secondary or accessory contract. In other words, the liability of a surety is conditional on the liability of a principal debtor and is co-terminous with that liability. If certain circumstances arise which happen to reduce the liability of the principal debtor or even to extinguish it altogether, then the liability of the surety is proportionately reduced or eliminated. A surety guarantor is relieved from liability, either absolutely or to the extent by which its position has been prejudiced, where there has been some alteration of the creditor/principal debtor relationship that is potentially to the detriment of the surety. If, for example, a creditor binds itself contractually to give a principal debtor more time to pay the debt, without reserving its rights against the surety, the surety may be detrimentally affected.[180] A surety is entitled to be indemnified by the principal debtor in respect of any sums that it is required to pay to the creditor and, by giving a

---

177 *Edward Owen Engineering Ltd v Barclays Bank International Ltd* [1978] 1 QB 159 at 169.
178 *American Home Assurance Co v Hong Lam Marine Pte Ltd* [1999] 3 SLR 682, a decision of the Singapore Court of Appeal that is referred to by R Jack, A Malek and D Quest *Documentary Credits* (Butterworths, 3rd edn, 2001) at p 357.
179 *Hampton v Minns* [2002] 1 WLR 1 at 24.
180 See generally on discharge of a surety from liability *Moschi v Lep Air Services* [1973] AC 331; *Natwest Bank v Riley* [1986] BCLC 268; *Ankar Proprietary Ltd v Natwest Finance* (1987) 162 CLR 549; *Standard Chartered Bank v Walker* [1982] 1 WLR 1410; *China and South Sea Bank v Tan* [1990] 1 AC 536.

principal debtor more time to pay, a creditor may conceivably increase the likelihood that a surety's indemnity vis-à-vis the principal debtor could become worthless. The creditor has changed the risk position of the surety, without its consent, and for this reason the surety is relieved of responsibility. The liability of the surety is tied strictly to the underlying base contract, and legally binding modifications of that base contract which are not obviously to the surety's advantage will discharge the surety.

Demand guarantees

1.91 The courts in England have treated the demand guarantee as an autonomous performance undertaking analogous to the commercial letter of credit.[181] Demand guarantees are sometimes used to secure the performance of the seller under a sales contract and are commonly used to secure the performance of a contractor's obligations to the employer in the case of a construction contract. In the latter situation, a bank will provide the guarantee at the request of a contractor and the guarantee is issued for the benefit of the employer. The contractor stands in a similar position to the applicant for a commercial credit and the position of the bank equates with that of the issuing bank in the letter of credit context. Moreover, the position of the employer is analogous to that of the beneficiary under a letter of credit. The guarantee undertaking given by the bank to the employer is separate and distinct from the original base contract and the bank is not concerned with disputes between employer and contractor. One can stretch the letter of credit analogy too far, however.[182] The bank under a letter of credit is the first port of call for payment insofar as the seller of goods is concerned. If the underlying base contract is performed according to its terms, then the seller will receive payment from the bank and the bank, in turn, will be reimbursed by the buyer. On the other hand, a demand guarantee should only be called in practice if something has gone wrong in terms of the underlying base contract. Nevertheless, the courts have stressed the letter of credit analogy in cases such as *Edward Owen v Barclays Bank International*[183] where Lord Denning said:

'A performance bond ... has many similarities to a letter of credit ... It has long been established that when a letter of credit is issued and confirmed by a bank, the bank must pay it if the documents are in order and the terms of the credit are satisfied. Any dispute between buyer and seller must be settled between themselves ...

All this leads to the conclusion that the performance guarantee stands on a similar footing to a letter of credit. A bank which gives a performance guarantee must honour the guarantee according to its terms. It is not concerned in the least with the relations between the supplier and the customer; nor with the question whether the supplier is in default or not. The bank must pay according to its guarantee, on demand, if so stipulated

---

181 See generally R Jack, A Malek and D Quest *Documentary Credits* (3rd edn, 2001), chapter 12.
182 See the comments of Eveleigh LJ in *Potton Homes Ltd v Coleman Contractors Ltd* (1984) 28 BLR 19 at 29.
183 [1978] 1 QB 159 at 171. See also *Esal (Commodities) Ltd v Oriental Credit Ltd* [1985] 2 Lloyds Rep 546.

without proof or conditions. The only exception is where there is a clear case of fraud of which the bank has notice.'

1.92 Under English law demand guarantees and standby letters of credit are treated alike. The difference between the two is more a matter of business practice than strict legal rights.[184] A standby credit is payable against documents which evidence or at least suggest that the applicant is in breach of an obligation owed to the beneficiary. The underlying obligation may be the performance of a supply or construction contract or the repayment of a loan. In the international oil trade standbys are used as a fallback payment mechanism. Because of the difficulty of obtaining a set of documents which conform to letter of credit stipulations, standbys are used which can be satisfied by the submission of less rigorous documentation if, following an agreed period after the oil has been delivered, the supplier has not been able to obtain payment by other means. The demand guarantee follows the substance of the standby credit in that the bank gives its irrevocable undertaking to pay against specified documents but, in its purest form, the bank simply undertakes to pay against the beneficiary's first written demand for payment without any further documentation. Unlike the case of standbys, the conventional letter of credit structure of advice and confirmation of the credit by a foreign bank is not appropriate. Instead, the beneficiary will normally require that a local bank actually issue the demand guarantee and the applicant's bank will authorise or mandate the issue. The applicant's bank issues its own undertaking to the local bank to reimburse that bank for any payment it makes under the prime instrument.

The demand guarantee/surety guarantee distinction

1.93 Demand guarantees should be distinguished from guarantees by way of surety. The essence of a surety-type guarantee is that, unless otherwise agreed between the parties, the guarantor's liability is co-extensive with that of the party for whose obligation the guarantee is given. Consequently, the guarantor is liable only when that party is liable and only to the extent of that party's liability. By way of contrast, a demand guarantor or issuer of a standby credit is liable when the conditions stipulated in the undertaking are fulfilled, without regard to the underlying contractual position. The issuer of a demand guarantee or standby credit may, therefore, be liable to pay the beneficiary even where

---

184 The similarity between the two undertakings was explored in *Kvaerner John Brown Ltd v Midland Bank plc* [1998] CLC 446 at 449 where Creswell J said:
　　'Standby credits issued by banks at the request of a seller or contractor in favour of a buyer or employer are sometimes used in lieu of first demand bonds in respect of major long-term sales or construction contracts ... Similar principles for present purposes apply both in relation to standby credits and first demand bonds. In the case of a first demand bond or a standby credit, banks assume irrevocable obligations. It is only in exceptional cases that the courts will interfere with the machinery of irrevocable obligations assumed by banks. Such obligations are regarded as collateral to the underlying rights and obligations between the businessmen at either end of the banking chain.'

the applicant is not actually in default and may be liable to pay sums in excess of those for which the applicant would be personally liable.[185]

1.94 This difference in legal result has spawned considerable litigation exploring the parameters of the distinction between demand guarantees and surety guarantees. For example, in the construction industry, advance payment guarantees are often issued to employers who make stage payments to contractors and, similarly, refund guarantees are a common feature of the shipbuilding industry. It appears, however, that there is no standard practice in relation to such guarantees: they can either be in the form of demand guarantees or surety guarantees. In *Gold Coast Ltd v Caja de Ahorros del Mediterraneo*[186] Tuckey LJ explained that, in deciding upon the nature of the undertaking in a particular case, the court had to construe the instrument in its factual and contractual context having regard to its commercial purpose. In the *Caja de Ahorros* the Court of Appeal referred approvingly to the following illumination of the distinction offered in a leading practitioner textbook:[187]

> 'Where an instrument i) relates to an underlying transaction between parties in different jurisdictions, ii) is issued by a bank, iii) contains an undertaking to pay on demand (with or without the words first and/or written) and iv) does not contain clauses excluding or limiting the defences available to a guarantor, it will almost always be construed as a demand guarantee.'

1.95 Often the courts will face a difficult task of construction in correctly classifying the nature of the legal relationships assumed by the parties. For example, as in *Trafalgar House Construction Ltd v General Surety and Guarantee Co Ltd*,[188] the contract may contain somewhat contradictory language, describing itself as a performance bond but also using language redolent of suretyship. In *Trafalgar House* the House of Lords decided that the instrument in question was a surety guarantee for a number of reasons. It used suretyship expressions and, moreover, bonds in similar form had existed for more than 150 years and had been treated by the parties thereto and by the courts as guarantees.[189]

1.96 Because of the fact that a demand guarantee is independent of the underlying base contract, a demand guarantor cannot avail itself of traditional defences available to a surety guarantor. The independence principle means that there is no room for traditional surety defences to operate. In actual fact, the wording of the contract between creditor and surety guarantor will often

---

185 See R Jack, A Malek and D Quest *Documentary Credits* (3rd edn, 2001) at p 357: 'under [a demand] guarantee, payment must be made against documents, under a [surety] guarantee, proof of primary liability is required which means that there will have to be an extensive investigation of the facts and possibly a lengthy trial before payment will be ordered.' See also on this area *Howe-Richardson v Polimex-Cekop* [1978] 1 Lloyd's Rep 161; *Esal (Commodities) Ltd v Oriental Credit Ltd* [1985] 2 Lloyd's Rep 546.

186 [2002] 1 Lloyds Rep 617.

187 Mark Hapgood (ed) *Paget's Law of Banking* (11th edn, Butterworths, 1996).

188 [1996] 1 AC 199. See also *Marubeni Hong Kong and South China Ltd v The Mongolian Government* [2004] 2 Lloyd's Rep 198.

189 [1996] 1 AC 199 at 205 per Lord Jauncey.

exclude or restrict the operation of surety defences. This has led some commentators and courts to the view that there is not so much a stark dichotomy
between surety guarantees on the one hand and demand guarantees on the
other, but rather a spectrum of guarantees. In *Moschi v Lep Air Services Ltd*,[190]
for example, Lord Reid said that there was not a general rule applicable to all
guarantees. Parties were free to make any agreement they liked and the court
had to determine the meaning of the particular agreement. Lord Diplock said
in the same case that, where a contractual promise could correctly be classified
as a guarantee, it was open to the parties expressly to exclude or vary any of
their mutual rights or obligations which would otherwise result from its being
classifiable as a guarantee.[191] Every case, he added, depended upon the true
construction of the actual words in which the promise was expressed.

1.97   The spectrum of guarantees would range from traditional surety guarantees, with all the implied trappings and trimmings at one end, to completely
autonomous demand guarantees at the other. The mere fact, however, that a
document uses words excluding traditional surety defences will not transform
what is otherwise a demand guarantee into a surety guarantee. Such a
clause was one of the features which persuaded the House of Lords in
Trafalgar House that the relevant instrument was a true guarantee, but it did
not prove decisive in tipping the balance in favour of a suretyship construction
in the *Caja de Ahorros* case.

Letters of comfort

1.98   Insofar as surety guarantees are at the bottom end of the spectrum to
the extent that liability is concerned, then so-called 'letters of comfort' are off
the spectrum. In more cases than not under English law a 'letter of comfort'
will provide only moral comfort to a creditor. The leading case is *Kleinwort
Benson v Malaysia Mining Corpn*[192] where the Court of Appeal held that a
letter of comfort to a lender stating that it was the policy of the parent
company to ensure that its subsidiary was 'at all times in a position to meet its
liabilities' in respect of a loan made by the lender to the subsidiary did not have
contractual effect as a promise regarding the parent company's future intentions towards its subsidiary. On the facts, the letter of comfort was expressed to
be only a statement of present fact and not a promise as to future conduct.
Bearing in mind the context in which the letters were written they were not
intended to be anything other than a representation of fact giving rise to a
moral responsibility. It should be noted, and was noted by the Court of
Appeal, that during the course of the negotiations the parent company was
asked by the lender to provide a legal guarantee of the subsidiary's debts.[193] It

---

190 [1973] AC 331 at 344.
191 [1973] AC 331 at 349.
192 [1989] 1 WLR 379.
193 Templeman LJ put the point well in *Re Southard & Co Ltd* [1979] 1 WLR 1198 at 1208 when
he said:
> 'English company law possesses some curious features, which may generate curious results.
> A parent company may spawn a number of subsidiary companies, all controlled directly
> or directly by the shareholders of the parent company. If one of the subsidiary companies,

had refused and, in consequence of so doing, the subsidiary was charged a higher rate of interest on the loan to reflect the increased risk that the lender was assuming.

1.99   The *Kleinwort Benson* decision has been criticised as excessively technical[194] but, nevertheless, the case does not foreclose the possibility that 'letters of comfort' will be held to have legal consequences where the facts are stronger and different. This point was reiterated in *Re Atlantic Computers plc*[195] by Chadwick J who said that the question for the court in each case is whether, as a matter of construction, in the light of whatever surrounding circumstances may be relevant and admissible, the parties intended to make a contractual promise for the future or to give only a warranty as to present intention.

CONCLUSION

1.100   In this chapter the variety of security interests that are known to English law have been considered. It has also been demonstrated that there are various mechanisms by which a person might improve its prospects of recovery in the event of a company's liquidation. These methods do not necessarily involve the creation of a charge. Indeed, the chapter has focused upon those facilities which do not involve resort to the process of charge creation such as the use of absolute title of security and equitable liens. In subsequent chapters detailed attention will shift to the specific mechanics of the company charge registration system.

---

to change the metaphor, turns out to be the runt of the litter and declines into insolvency to the dismay of its creditors, the parent company and the other subsidiary companies may prosper to the joy of the shareholders without any liability for the debts of the insolvent subsidiary.'

194 See the Australian case *Banque Brussels Lambert SA v Australian National Industries* (1989) 21 NSWLR 502. Some commentators have distinguished between 'hard' and 'soft' letters of comfort. Basically a letter of comfort is considered 'soft' if all it includes is the issuer's statement of his awareness of his transaction and a description of his connection with the affiliate. A mere indication that the issuer does not have the intention of decreasing his stake in the affiliate in the foreseeable future does not necessarily change the nature of the facility. It becomes a 'hard' letter of comfort only if the issuer assumes a commitment of one type or another, such as his undertaking to see to it that the affiliate remains in a position to perform its financial duties or a promise to retain the existing shareholding. The letter of comfort in the *Kleinwort Benson* case, on this analysis, would be of the 'hard' variety and thus legally binding.

195 [1995] BCC 696. See also *Chemco Leasing SpA v Rediffusion plc* [1987] 1 FTLR 201.

Chapter 2

THE OBJECTIVES OF THE COMPANY CHARGE REGISTRATION SYSTEM

INTRODUCTION

2.1   The requirement to register with the Registrar of Companies details of certain charges created by a company was first introduced by s 14 of the Companies Act 1900. In this chapter it is proposed to examine the purposes underlying the requirement of registration. The legislative history of the registration provisions will also be traced in broad detail. The chapter will conclude with a study of the ideas advanced by the Law Commission for the replacement of the present system of company charge registration with a new system of 'notice filing' modelled along the lines of Article 9 of the United States Uniform Commercial Code. This Code was first promulgated in 1951 by the National Conference of Commissioners on Uniform State Laws and the American Law Institute. Article 9 applies to any transaction (regardless of form) which is intended to create a security interest in personal property. The policy is to treat like transactions treated alike, notwithstanding differences of a formal nature. Article 9 also deems certain transactions to constitute security interests.[1] The US Article 9 approach has been followed in the Personal Property Security Acts in the common law provinces of Canada and in 1999 in New Zealand.[2]

THE DAVEY COMMITTEE

2.2   Section 14 of the 1900 Act followed the recommendations of the Davey Committee on Company Law Amendment.[3] The Committee reported in 1895. The principal motive behind the concept of a register open to public inspection appeared to be the consideration that the provisions relating to a company's internal register of charges had become a dead letter. The obligation on a company to keep a register of mortgages and charges at its own registered

---

1   See generally M Bridge [1992] JBL 1 and G McCormack *Secured Credit under English and United States Law* (CUP, 2004).
2   Information on the New Zealand legislation can be found on the website – www.ppsr.govt.nz.
3   C 7779, paras 46–50 on which see p 98 of *A Review of Security Interests in Property* (HMSO, February 1989) – a report prepared by Professor Aubrey Diamond for the Department of Trade and Industry. See also WJ Gough *Company Charges* (Butterworths, 2nd edn, 1996) at pp 450–458.

office dated from 1862 and still survives, in an amended form, in s 407 of the Companies Act 1985. In a number of cases, however, it was held that failure to comply with the provisions in respect of an internal register did not invalidate the charge.[4]

2.3   First, one might refer to *Re General South American Co*.[5] Here there was a failure to keep the required particulars in the company's internal register as required by s 43 of the Companies Act 1862. Malins V-C held that, although the law had not been complied with, the innocent holders of the debentures were not affected on account of the non-performance of the duty by the officers of the company in not keeping the register in a proper form.[6] A second case that merits attention is *Wright v Horton*.[7] This is a case where debentures were issued to a director of a company. They were not registered in accordance with the requirements of s 43 of the Companies Act 1862. The company went into liquidation and the validity of those debentures was contested by unsecured creditors. The House of Lords took the view that the mere omission to register did not invalidate the debentures. Lord Halsbury LC made a couple of observations. First, the validity of a mortgage or charge was not made to depend in express terms, at all events by s 43, upon its registration. Secondly, it was only persons who were already members or already creditors who had a right to see the register at all. In conclusion, the legislature had simply enacted a pecuniary penalty for the non-performance of the statutory duty when that statutory duty was knowingly and wilfully omitted.[8]

2.4   The Davey committee was mindful of these decisions and took the view that there should be a public register of charges for companies. On the other hand, the committee took the view that there were liens, mortgages and charges of daily occurrence in the usual transactions of business which it would be inconvenient to register, and the validity of which should not be dependent on their registration. In the Committee's opinion, invalidation as against liquidators and creditors was appropriate because this ensured that it was in the interest of the mortgage holder to attend to registration.

2.5   Following the Davey Committee recommendations the Companies Act 1900 was enacted. The requirement to register was laid down in respect of four categories of charges. These were a charge for the purpose of securing any issue of debentures, a charge on uncalled capital of the company, a charge created or evidenced by an instrument which, if executed by an individual, would require registration as a bill of sale, and a floating charge on the undertaking or property of the company. The Companies Bill 1900 was

---

4   See generally WJ Gough *Company Charges* (Butterworths, 2nd edn, 1996) at pp 450–452.

5   (1876) 2 Ch D 337.

6   (1876) 2 Ch D 337 at 344.

7   (1887) 12 App Cas 371. See also *Re Wynn Hall Coal Company* (1870) LR 10 Eq 515 and *Re General Provident Assurance Company* (1874) LR 14 Eq 50, though certain aspects of the judgment in *Re Wynn Hall Co* were criticised in *Wright v Horton* (1887) 12 App Cas 371.

8   (1887) 12 App Cas 371 at 376–377. See also Lord Watson at 380–381 and Lord FitzGerald at 384.

introduced in the House of Commons by the President of the Board of Trade, Mr Ritchie. He said[9] apropos the registration provisions:

'Another evil which at present exists is that when it comes to the winding up of some companies it is found that the whole of the available assets of the company are mortgaged, and there is nothing at all to divide amongst the unhappy creditors. The only remedy which can be applied to this particular evil is to take care that publicity is given to any mortgages which exist. It is therefore provided that any mortgages shall be registered with the Registrar of Joint Stock Companies and be open to public inspection, and that any mortgages not so registered shall be invalid.'

JUDICIAL RATIONALISATION OF THE REGISTRATION REGIME

2.6   There are many cases in which judges have expounded the rationale behind the idea of registration. One might, for instance, mention *Re Yolland, Husson and Birkett Ltd.*[10] Here Cozens-Hardy MR said:[11]

'I approach section 14 of the Companies Act 1900 as one is bound to do, by considering what was the mischief which had to be remedied. It was that companies were allowed to issue debentures charging very frequently all their present and future assets, and there might be no means of ascertaining, at all events for a considerable time, whether any debentures were issued, and therefore for the protection of the general creditors of the company or of persons desiring to trade with the company, it was thought fit to require that there should be a register of mortgages of that particular kind not merely in the company's own books, but by the Registrar.'

2.7   It is relatively easy to multiply examples. In *Re Jackson and Bassford Ltd*[12] Buckley J noted that under s 14 of the Companies Act 1900 provision is made for the registration of mortgages or charges which are given by limited companies. He went on to say that the object of that legislation is that those who are minded to deal with limited companies shall be able by searching a certain register, to find whether the company has encumbered its property or not.[13] The same judge spoke in a similar vein in *Re Cardiff Workmen's Cottage Co Ltd.*[14] In that case he said that the purpose of the Act of Parliament in requiring, within 21 days, registration of securities on the company's property is to ensure the means of notice to those who contemplate giving credit to the company.[15] The observations of Sargant J in *Esberger & Son Ltd v Capital and Counties Bank*[16] are along the same lines. He stated that

---

9   *Hansard*, HC Deb, vol 84, ser 4, col 1143.
10   [1908] 1 Ch 152.
11   [1908] 1 Ch at 156.
12   [1906] 2 Ch 467.
13   [1906] 2 Ch at 476.
14   [1906] 2 Ch 627.
15   [1906] 2 Ch at 629.
16   [1913] 2 Ch 366.

the statute, in providing for the keeping of a register, aims to show what monies are owing by the company on certain securities, so that creditors may have some notion of how far the property of the company is unencumbered.[17] In *Dublin City Distillery v Doherty*[18] Lord Parker talked about the object of the section as being to give notice to all who deal with a company of certain matters which vitally affect the company's credit. More recently, however, a somewhat more sceptical note was sounded by Lord Hoffmann in *Smith v Bridgend County Borough Council*[19] who said of the section:

> 'It was intended to give persons dealing with a company the opportunity to discover, by consulting the register, whether its assets were burdened by floating and certain fixed charges which would reduce the amount available for unsecured creditors in a liquidation. Whether this was a realistic form of protection and whether the choice of registrable charges was entirely logical is not presently relevant.'

EXTRA-JUDICIAL ASSESSMENT OF THE BENEFITS AFFORDED BY COMPANY CHARGE REGISTRATION

2.8   The Diamond Report identified a number of factors as underlining the requirement of registration.[20] The main consideration was the provision of information for persons who wished to assess the creditworthiness of the company, such as credit reference agencies and the like. Financial analysts and prospective investors might also find the information of assistance. A prospective chargee could ascertain whether or not the assets of the company were encumbered. Moreover, the absence of reference to charges on the register enabled a company to provide some sort of assurance that its assets were unencumbered. Finally, the registration requirement was a litmus test for a receiver or liquidator in considering whether to acknowledge the validity of a charge. The combined weight of these considerations was so strong that, in submissions to Diamond, the general requirement for the registration of charges under the Companies legislation commanded almost universal support and there was no demand for its abolition.[21]

2.9   In Australia, a fundamentally similar system for the registration of company charges exists. The Eggleston committee which examined the Australian system in 1972 identified the raison d'être of the registration obligation in succinct terms.[22] Briefly they said it was to protect creditors who extend credit to a company believing that it has unencumbered assets, when in fact those assets have been charged in favour of another creditor. The issue was gone into

---

17   [1913] 2 Ch at 374.
18   [1914] AC 823 at 854.
19   [2002] 1 AC 336 at [19].
20   HMSO, February 1989 at p 98. See also p 54.
21   See the clear statement to that effect at p 54 of the report.
22   Seventh Interim Report of the Company Law Advisory Committee 'Registration of Charges' (Parliament of the Commonwealth of Australia, July 1972, Parliamentary Paper No 230, para 4).

in more detail by the Australian Law Reform Commission in 1991 when looking at Personal Property Securities law reform.[23] The Commission pointed out that an intending investor in a company, for example, would want to be able to gauge the company's gearing, ie ratio of debt to equity.[24] Part of that information might be gleaned by seeing how much of its property was secured. In addition, an intending purchaser would want to know whether any money was owing on the property he or she intended to buy. Furthermore, regulatory agencies such as the Australian Securities Commission (ASC) wished to monitor a company's exposure to debts as a concomitant to their task of ensuring a healthy corporate sector. Information on secured lending practices filled in part of the picture but did not tell the whole story, as information on unsecured borrowings was also very important.

2.10 The Australian Law Reform Commission spoke of laws affecting personal property securities as having the key goal of information maximisation. The Commission said:[25]

'An efficiently functioning commercial system depends on those who make decisions within it being able to assess accurately the risks involved. The availability of information about whether assets are being used as security, who holds the security and the rights the lender has will determine how accurate their assessments are ... Having more relevant information will tend to increase the potential for accurate risk assessments, and thus the efficiency of lending and borrowing decisions ... It will also tend to

–   increase the efficiency of the decisions of those who are deciding whether to invest in, or keep investments in, companies and business

–   help corporate and business regulators (such as the ASC) to fulfil effectively their function of prudential oversight of the corporate and business sectors.'

DEVELOPMENT OF THE REGISTRATION PROVISIONS

2.11 The provisions relating to the registration of company charges have grown and developed since the introduction of the registration requirement in 1900. This is true in the sense that the list of charges requiring registration has been added to over the years. Charges on any land, wherever situated or any interest therein, and charges on book debts of the company became registrable in 1907.[26] 1928 saw another extension of the ambit of the registrable charge, with charges on calls made but not paid, on a ship or any share in a ship, and a charge on goodwill, patents, trade marks and copyright becoming subject to the

---

23   Personal Property Securities – Draft Proposals (30 May 1991). See also *Personal Property Securities* Discussion Paper No 52 produced by the Australian Law Reform Commission in August 1992 in association with the NSW Law Reform Commission (Discussion Paper No 28).

24   See para 2.1 of the report containing the draft proposals.

25   Paragraph 3.15 of the report.

26   Companies Act 1907, s 10.

registration obligation.[27] Charges on aircraft were brought within the scope of the obligation by the Mortgaging of Aircraft Order 1972.[28]

2.12 Despite these modifications, it is possible to discern essential features of the scheme introduced in 1900 which have remained unchanged. Registration was a requirement imposed in respect of only a limited category of enumerated charges. An unregistered but registrable charge became void against a certain stated class of persons. Registration was not a reference point for determining priorities. There was provision for a certificate of due registration issued by the Registrar. Also, registration out of time necessitated an application to the court.

2.13 Some, but not all, of these features remained in the registration regime that was contained in the Companies Act 1989. The Act might be viewed as essentially an exercise in legislative fine-tuning but, of course, the scheme therein contained with respect to registration of charges has not been implemented. The legislative changes were heralded by two Department of Trade and Industry discussion documents of 2 September 1987 and 7 July 1988. In formulating proposals for change, the Department had also the benefit of draft recommendations by Professor Diamond, propounded as part of his DTI-commissioned study of security interests in property other than land. The Diamond report was eventually published in February 1989 after a long gestation period. There are two aspects to Diamond. Firstly, the report in Part II details a blueprint for a comprehensive register of security interests along the lines of Article 9 of the United States Uniform Commercial Code. Secondly, Part III of the report embodied suggestions for immediate changes in the company charge sphere.[29]

2.14 The Companies Act 1989 went for interim reform, but what eventually emerged onto the statute book was introduced only at a very late stage of the parliamentary process. We had the situation where legislative clauses already widely consulted upon were dropped wholesale in favour of clauses that had not been the subject of any consultation. The end result was highly technical legislation that may not have been practically workable. A major difficulty arose over the interaction between company charge registration and the land registration process. Where a company grants a charge over land, in respect of which it is the registered proprietor, the charge is registrable both at the Land Registry and with the registrar of companies. The practice is first to register with the registrar of companies and then with the Land Registry. Currently, the registrar of companies issues a certificate which is conclusive evidence that all the requirements as to company charge registration have been complied with. Part IV of the Companies Act 1989 proposed to take away the evidentiary conclusiveness attached to the registrar's certificate and, with it, came a practical problem. How could the Land Registry be sure that a charge created

---

27 Companies Act 1928, s 43.
28 SI 1972/1268.
29 Diamond Report (HMSO 1989) at p 14. According to the report, given the fact that the present system was widely acknowledged to be seriously defective and that over 350,000 companies had charges registers at that time, big improvements were possible and worthwhile to make even as a short-term operation.

by a company is validly created without a certificate by the registrar of companies to prove this? If there is no such assurance about the validity of the charge, then the chargee cannot be registered, in the charges register of a particular title folio at the Land Registry, as the proprietor of a charge affecting the property.

2.15 Under the present system, there is a requirement to submit the original instrument of charge along with relevant particulars of the charge to the registrar of companies.[30] The registrar compares the instrument with the particulars submitted and, if there is a correspondence, issues a certificate of due registration which is stated to be conclusive evidence that all the specifications of the Act with respect to registration have been complied with. This work entails a considerable administrative burden and the idea behind Part IV of the Companies Act 1989 appears to have been to alleviate this burden. Henceforth, there was to be no obligation to submit the original instrument of charge, hence no checking of particulars and no conclusive certificate of due registration. To offset the possibility of a loss of accuracy in the register a chargee was precluded from asserting rights conferred by the charging instrument in excess of those referred to in the particulars delivered for registration.

2.16 There seems to be no enthusiasm in the commercial world for implementation of Part IV and it is unlikely ever to be brought into force in its present form. The practical difficulty already alluded to, as well as other imperfections, appear to have doomed it. Something may be salvaged from the wreckage, however. It is certainly conceivable that some of the provisions in Part IV may find a place in future legislation on the subject of company charges.

2.17 Part II of the Diamond report contained proposals for a Comprehensive Register of Security Interests along United States Article 9 lines.[31] Diamond thought that the present law relating to security interests should be replaced by new legislation, containing a simpler and unified system. Similar rules should apply to all types of security interest, except where the security agreement provided otherwise or where there were good policy reasons for the differences. The legislation would apply to security interests created by agreement.[32] The definition of 'security interest' would be such as to include mortgages, charges and 'security' in a strict sense, as well as any other transfer or retention of any interest in or rights over property or land which secures the payment of money or the performance of any other obligation. Excluded from the definition

---

30 For more details on the mechanics of registration see Chapter 6.
31 For a discussion of the report see M Lawson 'The Reform of the Law Relating to Security Interests in Property' [1989] JBL 287; A Diamond 'The Reform of the Law of Security Interests' (1989) 42 CLP 231. See also IR Davies (1988) 37 ICLQ 465 and (1990) 32 Mal LR 88; R Goode (1984) 100 LQR 324.
32 Diamond Report (HMSO 1989) at p 35. He suggested that the legislation should be based closely on Article 9 of the American Uniform Commercial Code and the Personal Property Security Acts introduced into several Canadian provinces, though it need not slavishly follow any of the precedents, since the needs in the UK were not necessarily the same as those in North America.

would be guarantees, indemnity policies and performance, although in a broad sense these 'secured' payment or performance, for they did not involve an interest in or right over property.[33]

2.18   A written security agreement was required, or a note or memorandum of the agreement, signed by or on behalf of the debtor, identifying the property subject to the security interest and indicating that the creditor is to have an interest in the property.[34] Informal non-possessory security interests would not be effective as against third parties, nor even between creditor and debtor themselves. In relation to possessory security interests, however, no mandatory requirement of writing was specified. It was suggested that the same situation should obtain for the deposit of contractual documents with the intention of creating a security interest over the debtor's rights under the contract.[35]

2.19   Under the new regime, priorities would depend on a system of notice filing.[36] The proposal was for a register of security interests with the register consisting of a collection of forms submitted by the applicant. The form submitted was not to be the security agreement but rather a 'financing statement'. The function of the financing statement was to put on record that a named debtor may have created a security interest in favour of a named creditor. It was sufficient if the types of property affected were described in the document. The financing statement was not tied to any specific time span, although, in general, priority in the queue of creditors was dependent upon the date of registration of the financing statement, save for possessory security interests where filing was not necessary for priority purposes, so long as the goods remained with the secured party.[37] No mandatory requirement to file a financing statement was proposed. A financing statement, in Diamond's view, should not, however, operate to protect a security interest created more than 21 days before the filing if insolvency occurs within 12 months of the date of filing.

2.20   Purchase money security interests received favourable treatment under the Diamond proposals.[38] Such interests were afforded a priority over pre-existing security interests that included after-acquired property. The justification for this favouritism is that, whereas a security interest granted over property already owned may remove that property from the debtor's estate, a security interest over newly-acquired property to secure the price paid for that property is neutral in its effect. The debt in respect of the price is offset by the addition of the property. Moreover, if the new property helped the debtor's

---

33   Diamond Report (HMSO, 1989).

34   Diamond Report at p 47.

35   Diamond Report at p 50. Diamond was not reporting for the Department of Trade and Industry in a vacuum. The Crowther Committee on Consumer Credit had traversed part of the same terrain in its 1971 Report (Cmnd 4596), as had a Working Party established by the Scottish Law Commission and chaired by Professor JM Halliday which looked at security over movable property. The report of the Working Party was published by the Scottish Law Commission in March 1986.

36   See chapter 11 of the Report.

37   Diamond Report at p 58.

38   See generally pp 64–65 and 88 of the Report.

business to earn extra profits it would strengthen the position of existing creditors by swelling their security interest. In addition, if an earlier creditor could rely on an after-acquired property clause to the prejudice of a purchase money security interest holder, he would obtain a wholly unjustified windfall at the expense of the later creditor whose money enabled the additional property to be acquired. Diamond also suggested that the special treatment should extend to a claim in respect of the proceeds generated by resales of the property. In general, Diamond recommended that if goods (or other property) subject to a security interest were sold, the money received in exchange for them should, so long as it was in the hands of the debtor and identifiable, be the subject of a security interest in favour of the creditor.[39]

2.21   Diamond also talked about the enforcement of security. In essence, a secured party would have the remedies available to a creditor under a mortgage or charge, including the right to appoint a receiver where the security agreement so provided. If property subject to a security agreement was sold by the creditor, any surplus would belong to the debtor.[40]

2.22   Part II of the Diamond Report was never implemented. In response to a parliamentary question[41] the official position was stated as follows:

> 'A clear majority of those representing interests governed by English law argued against major reform. Reform would be complex and in view of the proposed registration requirements, potentially costly to the Government and business. It could be contemplated only if there was a strong commercial justification. That did not emerge from the consultation and I have therefore decided not to accept the recommendations in Part II of the [Diamond] report for England and Wales.'

2.23   As well as the so-called inertia factor, there was also the European Community dimension that inhibited independent national legislative activity. For instance, the Law Society's Company Law Committee together with the Joint Working Party of the Law Society on Banking Law, recommended caution towards the fundamental reforms proposed by Diamond because of the possibility of European Community harmonisation measures in this sphere.[42]

THE COMPANY LAW REVIEW AND THE LAW COMMISSION PROPOSALS

2.24   As we have seen, proposals for the introduction of an Article 9 type system in the Diamond Report in 1989[43] and also by the Crowther Committee

39   Diamond Report at p 80.
40   See chapter 14 of the Report.
41   *Hansard*, HC Deb, vol 189, col 482 (24 April 1991).
42   A memorandum by these bodies was issued in November 1989. It is commented upon by Ferran and Glass [1991] JBL 152.
43   *A Review of Security Interests in Property* (1989); on which see generally D Prentice 'The

on Consumer Credit in 1971[44] floundered on a sea of legal and business objections. The issue of company charge registration was revisited, however, in 2000 as part of the fundamental reform of company law being undertaken by the Company Law Review Steering Group. In October 2000 the Steering Group produced a consultation document 'Registration of Company Charges' that recommended incremental changes to the present system. The final report of the Company Law Steering Group in July 2001 *Modern Company Law for a Competitive Economy*,[45] however, put the idea of Article 9 style reforms back on the agenda and led to a reference of the matter to the Law Commission. The final Steering Group report came as something of a surprise and was inspired, it seems, by some determined arm-twisting behind the scenes by some convinced advocates of the North American approach.[46] Professor Sir Roy Goode, a consultant to the Law Commission on this project and a member of the Company Law Review Advisory Group on company charges is one such advocate. Professor Goode has criticised the present English position in trenchant terms stating that:[47]

> 'this state of affairs continues to be tolerated in the 21st century, when the United States and Canada have for many years had highly developed, market-responsive legislation which has worked and when successive government reports have recommended the adoption of similar legislation in this country, is a shocking indictment of the indifference of successive governments to the modernisation of our commercial law.'

Professor Goode concludes that now 'the groundwork is being laid for a modern personal property security law which responds to the needs of the market rather than being rooted in outdated concepts and doctrine.'[48]

2.25 Following the reference, in July 2002 the Law Commission produced a consultation paper on 'Registration of Security Interests'[49] and this was followed up by a 'consultative report'[50] in September 2004 with the promise of

---

Registration of Company Charges: Ripe for Reform' (1985) 101 LQR 330; I Davies 'The Reform of English Personal Property Security Law' (1990) 32 Malaya Law Review 88; M Lawson 'The Reform of the Law Relating to Security Interests in Property' [1989] JBL 287; A Diamond 'The Reform of the Law of Security Interests' (1989) 42 CLP 231.

44 (1971) Cmnd 4596, Parts IV and V.

45 July 2001. The final report of the Company Law Review Steering Group led to the reference to the Law Commission.

46 See generally R Goode 'Insularity or Leadership? The Role of the United Kingdom in the Harmonisation of Commercial Law' (2001) 50 ICLQ 751 at 759–760.

47 *Legal Problems of Credit and Security* (Sweet & Maxwell, 3rd edn, 2003) at p 156.

48 Ibid.

49 Consultation Paper No 164 (henceforth referred to as CP 164). See generally on the consultation paper L Gullifer 'Will the Law Commission sink the floating charge?' (2003) LMCLQ 125; G McCormack 'Quasi-securities and the Law Commission Consultation Paper on security interests – a brave new world' (2003) LMCLQ 80 and see more generally I Davies 'The Reform of English personal property security law: functionalism and Article 9 of the Uniform Commercial Code' (2004) 24 LS 295.

50 *Company Security Interests* (September 2004). This will be referred to as 'CR'. For a discussion of the consultative report see R Calnan 'The Reform of Company Security Interests' [2005] Butterworths Journal of International Banking and Financial Law 25 which contains an edited version of the first chapter of a report on the recommendations by the

a Final Report some time in 2005. Basically, the Law Commission suggest replacing the present transaction based system of company charge registration under Part XII of the Companies Act 1985 with a notice-filing system. The Law Commission pointed out that Part XII provides information as to the state of a company's secured borrowings – information that is of assistance to later secured parties, prospective investors, credit reference and rating agencies, financial analysts and the like. Part XII also assists in determining priorities between competing security interests in that a registrable but unregistered security interest is void in the event of the creator's liquidation. The Law Commission suggested that company charge registration was intended to prevent the implication of false wealth, whereas its role in governing priorities had developed almost by accident. Its proposals involved a shift in emphasis. Registration would be made easier and there would be clearer and more rational priority rules but at the expense of some loss of information.[51]

2.26 The new notice-filing system envisaged by the Law Commission would be keeping with the North American and New Zealand models. The decision to use overseas legislation as a guide was taken partly because of constraints of time but also because the Law Commission saw 'no need to re-invent the wheel.'[52] According to the Law Commission there was not necessarily an assumption that what has worked well in North America will work well in England. Nevertheless, 'the fact that Article 9 and the PPSAs have been so successful means that they deserve very careful consideration.'[53] The notice filing/transaction filing distinction is central to the Law Commission proposals and has been explained in the following terms:[54]

'The most characteristic difference between notice filing and traditional systems of registration is that notice filing is parties-specific rather than transaction-specific. What is filed are not the details of a particular security but notice that certain parties have entered into, or may in future enter into, a secured transaction in relation to specified property. This approach has certain implications. A notice may be filed in advance of the transaction and the proposed transaction may never take place. The same notice may serve a series of connected transactions. And the information given on the register is necessarily rather general in character, being an invitation to further inquiry rather than a full account of the right in security.'

2.27 Currently, the list of registrable security interests is set out in s 396(1) of the Companies Act 1985. To be registrable a security interest must constitute a 'charge', be created by a company and also come within the list set out in the

---

Financial Law Committee of the City of London Law Society. The full report can be accessed from www.citysolicitors.org/. See also G McCormack (2005) 68 MLR 286. This section of the chapter is based on this article.

51 CR, para 2.46 and see also J De Lacy 'Reflections on the ambit and reform of Part XII of the Companies Act 1985 and the doctrine of constructive notice' in J De Lacy (ed) *The Reform of United Kingdom Company Law* (Cavendish, 2002) at p 76.

52 CR, para 1.20.

53 CR, para 1.5.

54 Scottish Law Commission discussion paper *Registration of Rights in Security by Companies* (October 2002) at p 8.

section.[55] If the security interest falls down on any of these criteria then it is outside the scope of the registration obligation.[56] The Law Commission suggested that the notice filing system could be applied to a broader range of security interests and also include functionally equivalent legal devices – 'quasi-security' – such as the assignment of receivables (factoring) and retention of title clauses in sale of goods contracts. There might also be a comprehensive restatement of the law of security interests and, in time, the scheme could be extended to non-corporate legal actors. In the first instance, however, it was suggested that the reform would involve the introduction of notice filing for an amended list of company charges and possibly also for 'quasi-interests'. The instrument of reform was likely to be provisions in, and regulations made under, a general comprehensive Companies Bill.

2.28   In the period since the original Law Commission consultation paper, however, there has been no sign of a general Companies Bill. Consequently, the reform effort by the Law Commission appears to have stalled somewhat. There also appears to be an increasing amount of practitioner resistance,[57] with leading lawyers warning about the dangers of throwing out the baby with the bathwater and suggesting that there was nothing fundamentally wrong with the present system that a bit of incremental amendment could not mend.[58] One commentator remarks:[59]

> 'The Law Commission's imperative seems to be to introduce a US-style functional system as a wholesale replacement for our current system. On a cost-benefit analysis, this seems difficult to justify. The implementation costs will be very large, and it is difficult to see what material benefits will result from it.'

He adds that one of the advantages of English law for domestic and international investors is the ease of creation of security and quasi-security and it would be most unfortunate if the effect of the Law Commission proposals were to make such facility more complicated and expensive.

2.29   On the other hand, the Law Commission believe that their recommendations provide:

---

55   See generally H Bennett 'Registration of Company Charges' in J Armour and H Bennett (eds) *Vulnerable Transactions in Corporate Insolvency* (Hart, 2003) 217 at 243.

56   'Charge' is said by CA 1985, s 396(4) to include a mortgage, but there is no other amplification of the term in the statute. Basically, however, a charge equals a right of recourse against property to ensure the payment of money due or the performance of some other obligation. It is a consensual security right created by agreement between the parties under which the debtor retains possession of the asset used as security; see generally *Swiss Bank Corpn v Lloyds Bank* [1982] AC 584 at 595.

57   CR, para 2.7, fn 21: 'We understand that at least one respondent representing legal practitioners may now have moved to a position where it considers only minor reform of the law relating to registration of company charges is desirable.'

58   See R Calnan 'The Reform of the Law of Security' [2004] Butterworths Journal of International Banking and Financial Law 88.

59   Ibid at 92. For a response by the Law Commissioner responsible for the Commercial and Common Law team, Professor Hugh Beale, see 'Reform of the Law of Security – Another View' [2004] Butterworths Journal of International Banking and Financial Law 117.

'significant improvements and cost-savings in secured finance for com-panies.[60] The use of technology can made the registration of company charges much easier, cheaper and quicker. The low cost of registration makes it feasible to provide lenders with a wide range of useful information about a company's property. The law on the priority of competing interests and the remedies available in the case of default can be made simpler, clearer and better suited to the needs of modern business finance.'[61]

The Law Commission however, may have been guilty of over-egging the pudding on occasion when expounding upon the worldwide acceptance of notice-filing. The Report states:[62]

'Notice filing also forms the basis of a Model Law promulgated by the European Bank for Reconstruction and Development. Legislation based on this model has been adopted in ten jurisdictions of Central and Eastern Europe.'

2.30 The European Bank for Reconstruction and Development (EBRD) Model Law is, however, based not on notice filing but on transaction filing and involves the submission of a registration statement to the relevant registry within 30 days of the execution of an instrument of charge.[63] Moreover, American style notice filing has singularly failed to flower in the transitional economies of Central and Eastern Europe with their civil law systems and this replicates the experience through out the world.[64] Indeed, the Scottish Law Commission in a paper published after their English counterparts produced 'Registration of Security Interests' said, with reference to notice-filing, 'Not for us'. Its Discussion Paper states:[65]

---

60 For a discussion of the importance of secured credit see CP, paras 1.7 and 1.8 and also see R Mokal 'The Authentic Consent Model: Contractarianism, Creditors' Bargain and Corpo-rate Liquidation' (2001) 21 Legal Studies 400; R Mokal 'Priority as Pathology: The Pari Passu Myth' [2001] CLJ 581; R Mokal 'The Search for Someone to Save: A Defensive Case for the Priority of Secured Credit' (2002) 22 OJLS 687; G McCormack 'The Priority of Secured Credit' [2003] JBL 389; V Finch 'Security, Insolvency and Risk: Who Pays the Price' (1999) 62 MLR 633; V Finch 'Is Pari Passu Passe' (2000) Insolvency Lawyer 194; V Finch *Corporate Insolvency Law: Perspectives and Principles* (CUP, 2002) at pp 75–105.

61 Press release 'Law Commission consults on Provisional Recommendations on Company Security Interests', 16 August 2004.

62 CR, para 1.5.

63 Articles 8 and 33 of the Model Law. The Model Law does not provide for advance registration. Registration must therefore relate to a specific transaction, though there is provision for an 'enterprise charge' – more or less the equivalent of an English floating charge. See generally on the Model Law L Mistelis (1998) 5 Parker School Journal of East European Law 455; G McCormack and F Dahan [1999] Company, Financial and Insolvency Law Review 65.

64 According to the Scottish Law Commission the only civil law jurisdictions to have introduced notice filing are Quebec and Louisiana; see Discussion paper *Registration of Rights in Security by Companies* (October 2002) at para 1.28 and see further T Harrell 'A Guide to the Provisions of Article 9 of Louisiana's Commercial Code' (1990) Loyola Law Review 711; MG Bridge, RA Macdonald, R Simmonds and C Walsh 'Formalism, Functionalism and Understanding the Law of Secured Transactions' (1999) 44 McGill LJ 567.

65 Scottish Law Commission Discussion Paper No 121 *Registration of Rights in Security by Companies* (October 2002) at para 1.28.

'Existing models of notice filing presuppose Anglo-American property law and turn on distinctions between creation, attachment and perfection which are unknown in Scots law or in other systems drawn from the Germanic stream of the civil law tradition. A system of notice filing suited to English property law could not readily be modified or adapted to accommodate the very different structures and concepts of Scots property law.'

2.31   One selling point used by the Law Commission to advance the cause of notice-filing is that of internet registration. Filing could be done online and by a secured party at the press of a computer button. Undoubtedly this idea seems infinitely more attractive than an old paper-based registration system that has been around for over 100 years. Its attractions in an era of e-government are axiomatic. However, there is no necessary connection between notice filing and internet registration. Indeed the Article 9 notice filing system dates from the 1950s and a time when computers were certainly not de rigueur. The original notice filing systems were paper-based. Moreover, the present transaction based registration under Part XII of the Companies Act 1985 could be shifted online. There is no necessary incompatibility between transaction registration and online filing. After all, one can search the register online at the moment. It does not require a fundamental change to switch the registration part of the process online.[66]

2.32   The Law Commission suggested that a notice filing scheme would have the following principal advantages:[67]

(1)   Electronic online filing would be fast, simple and cheap in the long run.
(2)   In a companies-only scheme the risk of an error that might invalidate a filing would be very small since companies have a unique registration number.
(3)   A simple description of the secured property (collateral) would suffice. This would reduce the risk of inaccurate descriptions and also protect third parties because a security interest would not be effective as regards collateral that falls within the description in the financing statement.
(4)   Advance filing is permissible so that a lender's priority position could be protected while negotiations over security are continuing.
(5)   Dual registration of charges over land, ships, aircraft and intellectual property rights in the companies register as well as in specialist property registers 'will generally no longer be necessary.'
(6)   The time of filing would generally determine priorities between competing security interests in the same collateral with an exception for purchase money security interests (PMSIs) which would enjoy priority over pre-existing security interests, subject to certain conditions. 'The rules of

---

66   See the Companies House Strategy document (April 2003) *Strategic Direction 2003/2006: The Future for Companies House* at pp 6–7:
   '[W]e will investigate the potential to develop an on-line service for the registration of mortgages and charges. However, as both company and land registration law is changing over the life of this plan we need to make a careful assessment of when it would be appropriate to invest in the delivery of this new service.'
67   CR, para 2.43.

priority will be more rational and better suited to modern conditions, for example in relation to assignments of receivables. They will still be complicated but they will be significantly clearer than under current law.'[68] A PMSI is basically the provision of funds tied to the acquisition of particular collateral with the provider of funds obtaining an interest in the property thereby acquired.

(7)   The distinction between fixed and floating charges and the associated uncertainty over the boundary between them will in practice disappear. The floating charge would be superseded by a single type of security interest that has all the advantages of a floating charge but fewer disadvantages to the lender.

2.33   In response to the Law Commission one might say that these are not necessarily advantages of notice filing per se. These outcomes or advantages – call them what you will – could all be realised in a revamped version of the present transaction based registration system. 'Dual registration', for example, and the presence or absence thereof has nothing to do with notice filing. One could have notice filing with dual registration of particular types of collateral still being required and transaction filing with cases of dual registration eliminated from the system. The same is the case with respect to the methods for determining priorities between competing security interests in the same secured property. Under the present regime, time of registration is not a priority reference point and if one had two fixed equitable charges over the same property then priority between them is determined by the time of their respective creation and not by reference to the time of registration.[69] One could easily, however, devise a transaction based registration system where priorities turn on the time of registration rather than the time of creation of the security interests. Indeed, the Irish Company Law Review Group has recently produced a draft Companies Bill which includes such a provision.[70]

2.34   Moreover, recognition of the purchase money security interest (PMSI) is not a complete novelty as far English law is concerned.[71] One has the decision of the House of Lords in *Abbey National v Cann*[72] giving effect to the PMSI in the context of domestic conveyancing. This recognition was carried a stage further by the Court of Appeal in *Whale v Viasystems Ltd*,[73] where the court endorsed the sentiments expressed by Professor Goode about 'the inequity that would result in allowing the prior chargee a windfall increase in his security

---

68   CR, para 2.43.

69   See eg *Re Ehrmann Bros Ltd* [1906] 2 Ch 697; *Watson v Duff, Morgan and Vermont (Holdings) Ltd* [1974] 1 WLR 450; and see generally RM Goode *Legal Problems of Credit and Security* (3rd edn, 2003) at p 168 et seq.

70   The draft Bill is available on the Review Group website – www.clrg.org/.

71   See also *United Malayan Banking Corpn v Aluminex* [1993] 3 MLJ 587 which recognises the purchase money security interest in Malaysia on the basis of old English authorities like *Re Connolly Bros Ltd (No 2)* [1912] 2 Ch 25 and *Wilson v Kelland* [1910] 2 Ch 306.

72   [1991] 1 AC 56; on which see generally J De Lacy 'The Purchase Money Security Interest: A Company Charge Conundrum?' [1991] LMCLQ 531; H Bennett and C Davis 'Fixtures, Purchase Money Security Interests and Dispositions of Interests in Land' (1994) 110 LQR 448.

73   [2002] EWCA Civ 480.

brought about not with the debtor's money or new funds injected by the prior chargee but with financing provided by a later incumbrancer.'[74] Jonathan Parker LJ said:[75]

> 'It must now be taken as settled law that, in the context of an issue as to priorities between equitable interests, the court will have regard to the substance, rather than the form of the transaction or transactions which give rise to the competing interests; and in particular that conveyancing technicalities must give way to considerations of commercial and practical reality ... [T]his approach is not limited to cases involving the purchase of a property coupled with the grant of a mortgage or charge to secure repayment of the funds which were required to enable completion of the purchase to take place ... [I]t falls to be adopted generally, in every case where an issue arises as to priority as between equitable interests.'

2.35 Legislation may be needed to bed down the purchase money security interest more firmly in the fabric of the law and to fix its precise parameters, but such legislation is not dependent on the introduction of a notice filing system for company securities more generally. The legislation in question could be completely independent.

2.36 The theoretical justification for recognising PMSIs rests on the fact that the release of funds by the creditor increases the debtor's total pool of assets.[76] The debtor is enabled in consequence to acquire new assets as distinct from merely rolling over existing debt. Whereas a security interest granted by the debtor over property that it already owns is potentially harmful to existing creditors, a security interest granted over newly acquired property to secure the price paid for that property is neutral in its effect on existing creditors. The debt incurred to pay for the property is offset by the addition of the property. Moreover, if an earlier creditor could rely on a provision in the instrument of charge that catches after-acquired property to the prejudice of a PMSI holder, the earlier creditor would gain an undeserved windfall, for it was the advance of funds by the later creditor that enabled the property to be acquired.[77] Some US commentators suggest that the purchase money super priority is best thought

---

74   *Legal Problems of Credit and Security* (2nd edn, 1988) at pp 99–100; and see now the third edition at pp 190–193.
75   [2002] EWCA Civ 480 at [72].
76   See also A Schwartz 'The Continuing Puzzle of Secured Debt' (1984) 37 Vanderbilt Law Review 1051 who argues that whereas a general financier takes account of average risk, the PMSI lender may have particular skills and is able to lend on particularly advantageous terms because of its special knowledge of the collateral.
77   See the discussion at para 17.7 of the Diamond report, *A Review of Security Interests in Property* (HMSO 1989) and for a law and economics perspective see H Kanda and S Levmore 'Explaining Creditor Priorities' (1994) 80 Virginia Law Review 2103 at 2138–2141.

of as a device for alleviating the situational monopoly created by an after-acquired property clause.[78] The debtor is not restricted to the earlier lender in its borrowing opportunities and is in a better position to tap alternative sources of finance. On the other hand, privileging the PMSI in this way seems to assume that the release of funds so as to acquire new assets is more valuable to a debtor's business than, say, advances to pay the salaries of existing employees. One might legitimately ask whether one of these advances is of greater social benefit than the other?[79]

2.37 A lender who advances funds so as to enable employees to be paid may claim to be subrogated to the preferential rights of these employees. For a couple of reasons, however, these subrogation rights are less valuable than PMSI status. First, preferential claims are subject to strict monetary limits under Sch 6 of the Insolvency Act 1986. Secondly, the enactment of the reform scheme envisaged by the Law Commission will necessitate consequential changes to the Insolvency Act and it is still unclear how preferential claims will fare under the new dispensation.[80]

2.38 A lender might also claim protection under a conditional payment or 'Quistclose trust'[81] by suggesting that, if the funds are not expended for the stated purpose, they should then be returned to the lender as the beneficiary under a trust.[82] Another area of uncertainty under the Law Commission scheme, however, concerns the treatment of 'Quistclose' trusts. It is not clear whether they would be deemed to create a security interest and hence become

---

78   T Jackson and A Kronman 'Secured Financing and Priorities among Creditors' (1979) 88 Yale LJ 1143 at 1171–1178.
79   See WJ Gough *Company Charges* (Butterworths, 2nd edn, 1996) at p 436, who argues that credit, as a matter of business need, is 'indivisible in the sense that all business inputs, including wages, overheads, equipment and supplies are all vital to an ongoing business.'
80   See CR, para 3.411: 'One obvious amendment that will be needed is in relation to references to the floating charge (and the knock-on effects for preferential creditors, for example).'
81   Called after the leading case *Barclays Bank Ltd v Quistclose Investments Ltd* [1970] AC 567.
82   See also *Twinsectra Ltd v Yardley* [2002] 2 AC 164 at [100] where Lord Millett described the 'Quistclose' trust as:
     'an entirely orthodox example of the kind of default trust known as a resulting trust. The lender pays the money to the borrower by way of loan, but he does not part with the entire beneficial interest in the money, and in so far as he does not it is held on a resulting trust for the lender from the outset ... When the purpose fails, the money is returnable to the lender, not under some new trust in his favour which only comes into being on the failure of the purpose, but because the resulting trust in his favour is no longer subject to any power on the part of the borrower to make use of the money. Whether the borrower is obliged to apply the money for the stated purpose or merely at liberty to do so, and whether the lender can countermand the borrower's mandate while it is still capable of being carried out, must depend on the circumstances of the particular case.'
     In effect, he adopted the interpretation of a Quistclose trust that he suggested extra-judicially while still a QC in 'The Quistclose Trust: Who can Enforce it?' (1985) 101 LQR 269 and see also L Ho and P St J Smart 'Reinterpreting the Quistclose Trust: A critique of Chambers' (2001) 21 OJLS 267. See generally W Swadling (ed) *The Quistclose Trust: Critical Essays* (Hart Publishing, 2004). The question of the proper jurisprudential basis of the Quistclose trust has generated considerable controversy. Lord Millett remarked, perhaps slightly ruefully, in the Preface to the latter book that 'It was too much to hope that a single decision of the House of Lords would put an end to controversy.'

subject to registration requirements. Since the object of the trust is to give the provider of funds priority over other creditors, in the event that the recipient of the funds becomes insolvent, it seems to fall within the functional definition of security.[83] Nevertheless, in its initial consultation paper, the Law Commission provisionally concluded that special purpose trusts should be outside the requirement to register (either because no security arises, or alternatively because any security arises through operation of law).[84] In the Consultative Report, the Law Commission suggest a different view stating that 'on further reflection we do not think our draft regulations should seek to determine the issue one way or the other. It should be left to the courts to determine the issue if and when it should arise in litigation.'[85]

NOTICE FILING AND THE FLOATING CHARGE

2.39   One could, in theory at least, have a notice filing system which preserves the traditional floating charge and all its trappings such as crystallisation and automatic crystallisation.[86] Accommodation of the floating charge/fixed charge distinction in a new regime is difficult, however, since the new regime is based on a 'first to file has priority' principle, whereas the floating charge has a lower ranking status than a fixed charge on specific assets. The Canadian and New Zealand PPSAs assimilate fixed and floating charges under the new dispensation.[87] The Canadian Supreme Court in *Royal Bank of Canada v Sparrow Electric Corpn*[88] declared that the effect of the legislation is to sweep away the distinction between fixed and floating charges as well as between legal and equitable security interests notwithstanding the fact that the security agreement used by the parties may have employed the old floating charge terminology.[89]

---

83   For discussion see M Bridge 'The Quistclose Trust in a World of Secured Transactions' (1992) 12 OJLS 333 at 345–346.

84   Paragraph 7.54.

85   CR, para 3.61. The Law Commission add that its position should not cause significant problems in practice since the secured party will in any event be able to preserve its position by filing a financing statement 'just in case' the Quistclose trust is held to be a consensual security interest.

86   See the leading cases *Re Brightlife Ltd* [1987] Ch 200; *Re Woodroffes (Musical Instruments) Ltd* [1986] Ch 366.

87   See generally G McCormack 'The Floating Charge in England and Canada' in J De Lacy (ed) *The Reform of United Kingdom Company Law* (Cavendish, 2002).

88   (1997) 143 DLR (4th) 385; on which see generally K Davis 'Priority of Crown Claims in Insolvency' (1997) 29 Canadian Business Law Journal 145.

89   See the comment by Catherine Walsh in 'The Floating Charge is Dead: Long Live the Floating Charge' in Agasha Mugasha (ed) *Perspectives on Commercial Law* (Prospect, 1999) 129 at 146:

'Although the Court ultimately divided, the majority and minority opinions were ad idem on the proprietary character of the bank's PPSA security interest in the debtor's inventory: it was fixed and legal in nature ... In a PPSA statutory regime, all security interests attach on the debtor's acquisition of rights in the collateral, regardless of whether the collateral is specific or circulating, and regardless of the scope of the debtor's licence to deal. In thus establishing a unitary attachment regime independent of the concept of crystallisation, the PPSA legislators had effectively signalled to the courts that all security interests were henceforth to be characterised as fixed and legal in their proprietary effect.'

This is also the position in New Zealand. As Lord Millett presciently remarked in *Re Brumark Ltd: Agnew v Commissioner of Inland Revenue*:[90] 'A curiosity of the case is that the distinction between fixed and floating charges, which is of great commercial importance in the United Kingdom, seems likely to disappear from the law of New Zealand when the Personal Property Security Act 1999 comes into force.'

2.40 The Law Commission, however, in its initial consultation paper proposed the retention of the floating charge stating that 'a charge that permits the debtor to dispose of the assets in the ordinary course of business free of the charge may still be described accurately as a floating charge ...'[91] The initial consultation paper attracted criticism on this score with commentators suggesting that it generated unnecessary complexities.[92] Not only would practitioners have to learn a whole new notice filing system, they would have to bear in mind too the old fuzzy fixed/floating charge distinction and its continued importance.[93] The change of tack by the Law Commission is welcome but, nevertheless, the basic point remains that the fixed/floating charge distinction might be regarded as independent from the notice filing/transaction filing debate.

2.41 The consultative report does not highlight to any great extent the change of approach by the Law Commission on the floating charge. Reasons for this reticence are not hard to find. The floating charge is very much the workhorse of the secured credit industry in England and has been the mainstay of bank lending for over a century.[94] One of the precursors to the Law Commission Consultation Paper, the Crowther Report, observed that the floating charge was so fundamental a part of commercial lending practice that its abolition could not seriously be contemplated.[95] The centrality of the floating charge in lending practice was also acknowledged by the Privy Council in *Re Brumark Ltd: Agnew v Commissioner of Inland Revenue*.[96] Lord Millett said:

'The floating charge is capable of affording the creditor, by a single instrument, an effective and comprehensive security upon the entire undertaking of the debtor company and its assets from time to time, while at the same time leaving the company free to deal with its assets and pay its trade creditors in the ordinary course of business without reference to the holder. Such a form of security is particularly attractive to banks, and it rapidly acquired an importance in English commercial life which ... should not be underestimated.'

---

90 [2001] 2 AC 710 at 716.
91 CP, para 4.133.
92 See, for example, L Gullifer 'Will the Law Commission sink the floating charge?' (2003) LMCLQ 125 at 144.
93 Leading cases on the distinction include *Re Brumark Ltd: Agnew v Commissioner for Inland Revenue* [2001] 2 AC 710 and *Re Spectrum Plus Ltd* [2004] Ch 307.
94 See J Ziegel 'The New Provincial Chattel Security Regimes' (1991) 70 Canadian Bar Review 681 at 712.
95 *Consumer Credit* Report of the Committee on Consumer Credit (1971 Cmnd 4596) at para 5.7.77.
96 [2001] 2 AC 710.

Banks and bank lending documentation are very rooted in the language and concepts of the floating charge and might be most reluctant to see its disappearance unless this vanishing act is very carefully managed and 'spun' as a transformation.

2.42   Pre-Article 9 United States law did not have any equivalent of the floating charge[97] and essentially there were two grounds for this lack of recognition. First, there was the conceptual point that a debtor could not create a security interest over future property, ie property that he did not yet own and, secondly, there was the more instrumental argument that a debtor should have a cushion of free assets to which general creditors were entitled to look to for payment.[98] Over time, however, a sophisticated avoidance industry developed and the effect of this was to permit large scale receivables and other financing.[99] As a result, most types of personal property, whether tangible or intangible, became available as collateral to secure loans.[100] On the other hand, each separate security device might be the subject of a distinct filing system.[101]

2.43   Article 9 rationalised this complicated state of affairs by a straightforward provision that permitted the creation of a 'floating' security interest in a shifting subject-matter.[102] The floating charge has been likened to a charge over a fund of assets[103] and the Article 9 security interest has been analogised in similar terms. What Article 9, in essence, did was to say that there was no necessary incompatibility between a fixed security interest and the debtor's freedom to dispose of the charged assets in the ordinary course of business.

---

97   The progenitor of Article 9, Professor Grant Gilmore, has argued that if floating charges had been accepted in the US, then some of the pressure for change which brought about Article 9 would have been absent – *Security Interests in Personal Property* (Little Brown, 1965) at pp 359–361.

98   See *Zartman v First National Bank of Waterloo* (1907) 189 NY 267; *Benedict v Ratner* (1925) 268 US 353; and see generally JO Honnold, SL Harris, CW Mooney *Security Interests in Personal Property* (Foundation Press, 3rd edn, 2001) at pp 452–456.

99   See generally Grant Gilmore *Security Interests in Personal Property* (Little Brown, 1965) vol 1, chapters 1–8.

100   Article 9 has been described as 'an anthological collection of the most celebrated security law controversies of the preceding forty years' in Grant Gilmore 'Security Law, Formalism and Article 9' (1968) 47 Nebraska LR 659 at 671.

101   See the official comment attached to the 1972 version of Article 9–101. Grant Gilmore notes in *Security Interests in Personal Property* (Little Brown, 1965) at p 463:
      'The typical pre-Code pattern included separate filing systems for chattel mortgages, for conditional sales, for trust receipts, for factor's liens and for assignments of accounts receivable. In such a situation the expense and difficulty of making a thorough credit check are obvious. Since the filing requirements were themselves frequently obscure and tricky, the chances were good that a lender who, through his counsel, was familiar with one device would inadvertently go wrong in attempting to comply with another and fail to perfect his security interest.'

102   Grant Gilmore has said in 'Security Law, Formalism and Article 9' (1968) 47 Nebraska LR 659 at 672:
      'Article 9 draftsmen argued from the premise that, under existing security law, a lender could take an enforceable interest in all of a debtor's present and future personal property to the conclusion that the new statute should provide for the accomplishment of this result in the simplest possible fashion.'

103   See e g RC Nolan 'Property in a Fund' (2004) 120 LQR 108.

Article 9–205 provides that a security interest is not invalid or fraudulent against creditors solely because the debtor has the right or ability to '(a) use, commingle, or dispose of all or part of the collateral, including returned or repossessed goods; (b) collect, compromise, enforce or otherwise deal with collateral; (c) accept the return of collateral or make repossessions; or (d) use, commingle, or dispose of proceeds;' or because the secured party fails to require the debtor to account for proceeds or replace collateral.

2.44   Translated into English law terms, an Article 9 security interest is a fixed charge coupled with a licence to deal. In England, however, if a security giver purported to dispose of assets that were the subject of a fixed charge in the ordinary course of business then this would breach the covenants in the loan agreement, whether these covenants are express or implied.[104] While the language has not been entirely consistent, in the main the English courts have insisted on the proposition that a floating charge is not a fixed charge with a superadded licence to deal.[105] As Buckley LJ explained in *Evans v Rival Granite Quarries Ltd*:[106]

> 'A floating security is not a future security, it is a present security, which presently affects all the assets of the company expressed to be included in it. On the other hand, it is not a specific security: the holder cannot affirm that the assets are specifically mortgaged to him. The assets are mortgaged in such a way that the mortgagor can deal with them without the concurrence of the mortgagee. A floating security is not a specific mortgage of the assets, plus a licence to the mortgagor to dispose of them in the course of his business but is a floating mortgage applying to every item until some event occurs or some act of the mortgagee is done which causes it to crystallise into a fixed security.'

2.45   The new super security interest contemplated by the Law Commission would change this conceptual structure fundamentally, but this is being done without much fanfare and the rolling of drums. It is almost if the changes are being smuggled in silently. Observers have written elegies to the floating charge. Does it not deserve a decent burial? One might accept the proposition that the benefits of the floating charge in terms of comprehensiveness, lack of formalities and ease of use could be retained if English law moved over to an Article 9 type system.[107] Indeed, the disappearance of the floating charge might be

---

104   One commentator has talked about the 'mental block experienced by the courts in the early floating charge cases when they were quite unable to fathom the idea of a fixed mortgage or charge over trading assets coupled with a licence to dispose of those assets in the ordinary course of business' – see D McLauchlan (1999) 115 LQR 365 at 367.

105   See, however, R Calnan 'Floating charges: A Proposal for Reform' [2004] Butterworths Journal of International Banking and Financial Law 341, who refers to the observations of Buckley LJ in *Cretanor Maritime v Irish Marine* [1978] 1 WLR 966 at 978:
> 'The debenture created an immediate equitable charge on the assets of the [company], wherever situated, subject to a power in the [company], so long as the charge continued to float, to deal with their assets in the ordinary course of their business, notwithstanding such a charge, as though it did not exist.'

106   [1910] 2 KB 979 at 999. See also *Re Gregory Love & Co* [1916] 1 Ch 203.

107   Professor Sir Roy Goode has long propounded this view arguing that:
> 'a unified concept of security interests in which rules of attachment, perfection and

proclaimed more widely as one virtue of the adoption of a radically new system of secured credit law. While the floating charge is an instrument of great power it is also the source of perhaps of even greater mystery.[108] The existence of the floating charge may in fact puzzle foreign observers from civilian jurisdictions and cloud understanding of this branch of law by non-specialists. On the other hand, the floating charge was undoubtedly a great invention by Victorian lawyers and entrepreneurs and its death would be mourned by many.

RADICAL CRITICISMS OF A PROPOSED NOTICE FILING SYSTEM

2.46 There are more radical critics of the kind of notice filing system advocated by the Law Commission. One New Zealand commentator suggests that:[109]

> 'the expensive PPSA registration system embraces information which is, for the large part, already available in financial statements, in company records and at credit reporting agencies. On the other hand, secured financing is flourishing in jurisdictions which have rejected the art 9 model in favour of registrationless regimes for personal property security.'

2.47 Another distinguished American commentator contends that the filing system hardly looks like a significant variable in the search for a successful mercantile economy and adds, perhaps slightly tongue-in-cheek:[110]

> 'The filing system is an integral part of the most sophisticated secured lending system known to mankind. Only by an effective filing system can a secured lender know of other lenders and only by it can later secured lenders and unsecured lenders be encouraged to lend. Without such a system, lenders would grow wary, commerce would be hobbled, and the manifold commercial ends that are met by commercial lenders would be stunted, rendered more costly, or stymied altogether ... I can see generations of law students writing this down and repeating this incantation in negotiations, in court, and elsewhere. This view even extends to Americans abroad who approach the English, Dutch and Germans with an air of

---

>   priority are clearly laid out and are designed to produce results that are fair in the typical
>   case is greatly preferable to the uncodified and unsystematised collocation of rules we have
>   painfully developed in this country over the past century.'
>   See 'The Exodus of the Floating Charge' in D Feldman and F Meisel (eds) *Corporate and
>   Commercial Law: Modern Developments* (Lloyds of London Press, 1996) chapter 10 at
>   pp 202–203.

108 For accounts of the juridical nature of the floating charge see E Ferran 'Floating Charges –
     The Nature of the Security' [1988] CLJ 213; S Worthington 'Floating Charges – An
     Alternative Theory' [1994] CLJ 81; K Naser 'The Juridical Basis of the Floating Charge'
     (1994) 15 Company Lawyer; R Gregory and P Walton 'Fixed Charges over Changing Assets –
     the Possession and Control Heresy' [1998] CFILR 68.

109 B Dugan 'PPSA – The Price of Certainty' [2000] NZLJ 241 at 242.

110 J White 'Reforming Article 9 Priorities in Light of Old Ignorance and New Filing Rules'
     (1995) 79 Minnesota Law Review 529 at 530.

superiority, asserting the superiority of our filing system and belittling the European efforts to put together a filing system worthy of the name.'

2.48 While these are dissenting, even maverick voices, in the Anglo-Saxon world, in the Continental European legal community, such views are more mainstream and even commonplace. Indeed, the doyen of comparative law studies in the personal property security field, Professor Ulrich Drobnig, has recently remarked apropos whether a notice filing system is really necessary:[111]

'if all the information it offers is a notice that there may exist a security interest, so that intending creditors are put on notice but have to turn to the debtor in order to verify the true state of affairs. Is not nearly the same effect achieved in countries without a registration system where the courts proceed from a general presumption that business people must know that any major piece of equipment is bought on credit? Does not this presumption also put intending creditors on notice so that they also have to verify the true state of affairs? I remain to be convinced of the true necessity of a filing system.'

2.49 Closer to home, Mr Richard Calnan, a partner in Norton Rose solicitors, has suggested that the notice filing system may lead to the underproduction of valuable information in that a searcher of the register does not know whether a particular registration relates to an actual transaction or to an intended transaction that never in fact materialised. In addition, fewer details of the transaction are available than under transaction-filing.[112] Rather paradoxically, computerisation and the information age produces less, rather than more, information on the public register about the state of a debtor's secured borrowings. The Law Commission in the Consultative Report dealt firmly with the 'less information' and 'clutter' points, stating that the reduction of information on the financing statement was not significant as compared to what is currently required:[113]

'In fact the current scheme requires only two additional items: the amount secured by the charge and the date it was created ... The statement of the amount secured is not a useful piece of information since, unless the charge is for a fixed amount, it is most unlikely to be accurate by the time anyone searches the register. To provide the date on which the charge was created is not possible in a system that has the advantage of allowing filing before the charge has been agreed or has attached.'

---

111 'Present and Future of Real and Personal Security' (2003) European Review of Private Law 623 at 660. A common lawyer might respond to this by saying that Article 9 in a sense facilitated a movement from status to contract. As Professor Alison Dunham said with reference to the pre-Article 9 US position in 'Inventory and Accounts Receivable Financing' (1949) 62 Harvard Law Review 588 at 611: 'One banker thought the question [about sources of debtor information] "silly" because his bank did not make a loan unless the borrower "was properly introduced" and therefore a fraudulent borrower was an impossibility.'

112 'The Reform of the Law of Security' [2004] Butterworths Journal of International Banking and Financial Law 88 at 89–90: 'the effect of the proposals would be to make the system less informative and reliable.'

113 CR, para 2.47.

Moreover, the Law Commission considered that the risk of clutter was small
for two reasons:[114]

> 'First, filing will only be effective if done with the debtor's consent and it
> can be expected that debtors will be circumspect in giving their consent to a
> filing. Secondly, if further finance is sought from another secured party, it
> will insist before anything else that any filings that are not concerned with
> existing security agreements are removed.'

2.50   Another way of avoiding 'clutter' would be to have in effect a system of
provisional registration of the kind suggested in the draft Irish Companies Bill.
Under this scheme a filing can be submitted prior to completion of a
transaction provided a further filing evidencing the actual creation of a security
interest is filed with the registrar within 21 days of the first filing of the
intention to create a security interest. In these circumstances the security would
take effect as to priority from the date of the first preliminary filing. On the
other hand, in the absence of the second filing within 21 days of the
preliminary filing, the preliminary filing would lapse.[115]

QUASI-SECURITIES

2.51   A radical change envisaged by the Law Commission is the extension of
the filing system to cover functionally equivalent legal device – quasi-securities
like the assignment of receivables and title-retention devices such as hire-
purchase agreements, finance leases and conditional sales. These proposals
were made in the consultation paper and the Consultative Report is to the same
effect despite some objections and reservations from consultees.[116] The opposition was less manifest in the case of outright assignment of receivables for two
reasons. First, it is often very difficult to distinguish between an outright
assignment of receivables and a security assignment. The latter is presently
within the scope of the company charge registration system but the former is
not. The second reason lies in the present unsatisfactory priority principles.
Under present law, where there is more than one assignment of the same
receivable, priority goes to the first assignee who gives notice to the debtor,
provided that that assignee did not have actual or constructive notice of an
earlier assignment at the time of the second assignment.[117] As the Law
Commission point out, it is not practicable to check 'with each account debtor
to find out whether a notice of assignment of the debt has been given, nor will
the assignee always wish to give notice simply in order to preserve its priority as
against a competing assignment.'[118] A 'first to file has priority' rule appeared to
be much more suitable to modern conditions than the existing rule. It was
therefore recommended that all sales of receivables should be within the new

---

114 CR, para 2.54.
115 See the provisions of the draft Bill and explanatory notes from the Irish Company Law
     Review Group on the website – www.clrg.org/.
116 CR, para 2.87.
117 This is the rule in *Dearle v Hall* (1828) 3 Russ 1; for criticism of the rule see F Oditah
     'Priorities: Equitable versus Legal Assignments of Book Debts' (1989) 9 OJLS 521.
118 CR, para 2.87.

regime for purposes of perfection and priority but not for purposes of enforcement.[119] The Law Commission did not try to separate sales of receivables with recourse against the assignor from those without recourse because 'it is so hard to distinguish between those that resemble a secured transaction and those that do not ...'[120]

2.52 There was a greater division of opinion about the proposals to bring title-retention devices within the new regime. The fact is that with these transactions the parties do not consider that they are creating a security interest at all.[121] The parties have deliberately chosen a different structure and it would require a major exercise of legislative fiat to re-characterise their efforts as a 'deemed' security interest. As one commentator has remarked in a broader context:[122]

> 'There are two features of the UCC, Article 9 approach that appear to be troublesome even to those who are attracted to it. The first is the total reconceptualisation that it requires in the context of types of transactions that traditionally are not viewed as secured financing devices ... The second feature ... is the extent to which it requires a bifurcated approach to the characterisation of certain types of transactions. Since a title retention sales contract or a lease falls within a secured financing regime because it functions as a security device, it follows that the seller or lessor is not the owner of the goods sold or leased ... What is troublesome is that outside this regime, the recharacterisation might not be acceptable with the result that same transaction is viewed differently depending on the legal issues being addressed.'

2.53 Although accepting the cogency of some of the points made by objectors, the Law Commission was basically unmoved. It concluded that, on balance, the new scheme should cover quasi-securities and these provisions should also be included at the 'companies-only' stage. The proposals involve a

---

119 CR, para 2.88. This is because a buyer of receivables would not expect to owe any duties to the assignor in relation to enforcing the debt vis-à-vis the account debtor. The Law Commission recommendations mirror the approach adopted in Article 9 of the US Uniform Commercial Code; on which see generally G McCormack *Secured Credit under English and American Law* (CUP, 2004) at pp 237–239: 'The basic distinction between the sale and securing of accounts is seen in the fact that any surplus from collections goes to the buyer in the case of a sale and to the seller in the case of a security assignment.'

120 CR, para 2.87.

121 See the comment by I Davies 'The reform of English personal property security law' [2004] LS 295 at 321:
> 'The difficulty with the functionalism as applied in Article 9-type regimes is that it can be both over-inclusive and also under-inclusive at the same time. A more appropriate approach in any reform of English personal property security law is to operate within the existing legal landscape rather than to seek to transform it.'

122 See the comments by Professor Ronald Cuming 'The Internationalisation of Secured Financing Law' in Ross Cranston (ed) *Making Commercial Law: Essays in Honour of Roy Goode* (OUP, 1997) at pp 522–523. The same point has later been made by the Financial Law Committee of the City of London Law Society – see R Calnan 'The Reform of Company Security Interests' [2005] Butterworths Journal of International Banking and Financial Law 25 at 31.

major expansion in the scope of the filing system and failure to file means loss of the deemed security interest in the debtor's insolvency. If, say, a finance lessor fails to file notice of his interest against the lessee and the latter goes into liquidation, the lessor loses his 'ownership' interest. Effectively the lessor's title disappears. The same is true of a supplier who delivers goods to a company but retains title to the goods until the goods have been paid for by the corporate buyer. If the company goes into liquidation, then the supplier can no longer rely on the retention of title clause in the conditions of sale and his claim for the unpaid purchase price of the goods is that of an unsecured creditor.

2.54 The New Zealand Personal Property Securities Act provides protection for the finance lessor or unpaid seller in this situation by allowing an unregistered security interest to remain valid in the lessee's or buyer's liquidation. Failure to file means loss of priority to competing parties claiming an 'ownership' or security interest in the goods.[123] An unregistered security interest, including a deemed security interest, however, will still give priority over unsecured creditors.[124] The thinking behind the New Zealand legislation is that the new registration obligations brought many previously unregistrable transactions within the scope of the registration net. It would be unfair to penalise parties to such transactions, who might never have thought to register, with being reduced to the ranks of unsecured creditors. Unsecured creditors, it is argued, do not rely on the register and consequently are not prejudiced by the non-appearance of a registrable interest on the register.[125] The Law Commission rejected this proposition and suggested that unsecured creditors, or at least credit rating agencies, do in fact rely on the register.[126]

2.55 More generally, the Law Commission accepted that its proposed scheme would mean some re-characterisation of the transaction, but suggested that the degree of change on this point may easily be overstated. A consequence of re-characterisation is that legal title may be lost if the security interest is not filed but, under current law, a buyer in possession could pass title that it does

---

123 See e g New Zealand Personal Property Securities Act 1999, s 52.

124 See the New Zealand Law Commission Report No 8 *A Personal Property Securities Act for New Zealand* (1989) at p 115:

'In practice, only two parties are possibly misled by the absence of a registration statement. The first is the prospective creditor who would normally advance credit only against a first ranking security in a debtor's goods. Under the proposed statute, if such a creditor files a registration statement, it is protected against any unperfected security interests ... Creditors, who supply goods or funds on an unsecured basis are generally either not concerned about the presence of outstanding interests or assume that such interests exist. Prospective buyers and lessees, like prospective secured creditors, also rely heavily on the ostensible ownership of their transferor. Accordingly, they are protected from unperfected security interests ... unless they have knowledge of the security interest.'

125 This view is not one, however, that appeals to all New Zealand commentators. See, for instance, D McLauchlan 'Unperfected Securities under the PPSA' [1999] NZLJ 55, who argues that if the policy objective of adherence to the perfection requirement is to be achieved, then failure to perfect should have the meaningful penalty of defeating the security interest on the insolvency of the debtor. In McLauchlan's view this is a bare minimum step that the law should take in redressing the balance somewhat in favour of unsecured creditors.

126 CR, para 2.49.

not have. The scheme involved widening the exceptions to the basic principle that a person cannot pass a title that it does not have. The Law Commission state:

> 'The hirer or lessee is not an owner, but if the financier has not filed, a sale or other disposition by the hirer or lessee should give the innocent purchaser rights in priority to those of the financier. What to lawyers may be a painful change to familiar conceptual structures may be precisely the practical relief that industry needs.'[127]

2.56   Commentators on the consultation paper contended that there was 'little in it' for retention of title claimants – some disadvantages without commensurate benefits.[128] A supplier of inventory to multiple buyers who relied on retention of title clauses in the conditions of sale would, under the new scheme, have to file against each buyer. Moreover, under current law, if the retention of title clause is valid, the supplier has in effect super-priority status by being able to repossess the goods in the event of the buyer's insolvency. Under the new regime, however, achieving an equivalent status would depend on fulfilling potentially onerous conditions that might include notification of the buyer's other creditors. The Law Commission recognised that the questions whether or not the ultimate scheme of registration and priority should include title-retention devices and whether such inclusion should occur at the companies-only stage 'are difficult and controversial'[129] but nevertheless favoured inclusion. The Law Commission admitted that there was no obvious advantage for the retention of title supplier. It endeavoured, however, to accentuate the positive by saying that filing on-line would be easy and cheap and, for high volume users like suppliers who normally used retention of title clauses in their conditions of sale, special arrangements were envisaged under which information entered into a secured party's own system could be forwarded to the registry without further data input.[130]

2.57   There was a strong argument that it would be inappropriate to include title-retention devices in a 'companies only' scheme. The law on title-retention devices would become very messy and complicated if different rules applied depending on whether the lessee/hirer/buyer, as the case may be, was a company or was unincorporated. Here the Law Commission fell back on the principle that the best was the enemy of the good, stating:[131]

> 'The anticipated Companies Bill gives us an opportunity to establish the notice-filing scheme for companies. If we do not seize that opportunity, we reduce the chance that any of the scheme will ever reach the statute book. A Bill introducing this scheme from scratch would require much more Parliamentary time and Departmental effort than to take powers, and have regulations made, under a Companies Bill. It is true that primary legislation would then be needed in order to extend the scheme to unincorporated

---

127   CR, para 2.108.
128   See, for example, G McCormack 'Quasi-securities and the Law Commission Consultation Paper on security interests – a brave new world' [2003] LMCLQ 80 at 86–91.
129   CR, para 2.132.
130   CR, para 2.103.
131   CR, para 2.122.

debtors; but it would in substance be merely a re-enactment of the companies scheme with a wider scope of application. That should require much less Parliamentary time and Departmental effort. It would be ideal to insist on enactment of the entire scheme all at one but those with close knowledge of the legislative process have advised us not to recommend an all-or-nothing approach.'

FINANCIAL COLLATERAL AND RESPONSIVENESS TO CONSULTEES

2.58 In the Consultative Report, the Law Commission was particularly responsive to issues raised by consultees with respect to financial collateral. Under the original Law Commission proposals the only way of establishing a security interest over shares or other financial collateral was by the secured party asserting 'control' over the collateral. Where the shares were entered in the books of a financial intermediary, one method of asserting control was by drawing up a control agreement under which the securities intermediary agreed to respond to instructions from the secured party rather than from the debtor. 'Control' was the sole possible perfection method, however, with perfection by registration not being a permissible alternative.[132] Under existing law it is possible to create a floating charge over shares and, if the charge is registered, then it is good in the debtor's liquidation.[133] The security taker does not have 'control', but instead its security interest is 'perfected' by registration. Under the original Law Commission scheme this would not have been possible, and the proposals were criticised for being unnecessarily restrictive and excluding a not uncommon method of taking security. The taking of security was forced into a relatively tight straightjacket and this seemed to contradict the goals of the new system, which is supposed to be facilitative and enabling. The Law Commission has now had a welcome change of heart and considers that filing should be an alternative perfection method with respect to financial collateral.[134]

2.59 The position is the same with respect to security over bank accounts. In the initial consultation paper the Law Commission recommended the enactment of provisions in relation to bank accounts that closely paralleled the US Article 9. Article 9 does not permit a security interest over a bank account to be perfected otherwise than by control, and the depositary bank could effectively

---

132 The consultation paper viewed the latter as an unnecessary refinement: para 5.24.
133 On the other hand, a fixed charge over shares does not require registration: *Arthur D Little v Ableco Finance* [2003] Ch 217, but a charge over the dividend income from shares may be registrable as a charge over book debts – see CR, para 2.141.
134 CR, para 2.139. In fairness to the Law Commission it did ask in the consultation paper whether 'control' should be the only perfection method for shares and bank accounts and left it up to consultees to come up with alternatives.

veto the grant of a security interest over the account in favour of a third party lender.[135] The limitation has now been described by the Law Commission as seemingly illogical.[136]

THE CHANCES OF IMPLEMENTING THE LAW COMMISSION REFORM PROPOSALS

2.60   The Law Commission has undoubtedly produced an impressive con-sultative report, but serious question marks remain about the overall political acceptability of its proposals. For a start, the recently enacted and implemented Enterprise Act 2002 will have to be rewritten. The Enterprise Act, for example, gives the holders of general floating charges over the assets of a company power to appoint an administrator to the company without having to go to court.[137] It also sets aside a proportion of floating charge realisations for the benefit of unsecured creditors.[138] More generally, the insolvency legislation gives preferential creditors first bite out of floating charge realisations.[139] Were the floating charge to disappear or be assimilated with the fixed charge, as the Law Commission now recommend, these provisions would have to be reframed. Finding measures to offer an equivalent level of protection to unsecured and preferential creditors may not be easy, as the Law Commission itself recognises. More generally, the Law Commission also recognises that insolvency is a potential political hot potato stating:[140]

> 'Policy issues relating to insolvency are issues for the Government rather than the Law Commission: our brief does not include insolvency. However, it is clear that if the scheme we provisionally propose were to be imple-mented, a good deal of consequential amendment would be needed to the current insolvency legislation. We have discussed our scheme with the Insolvency Service, and although we have identified some areas that will need amendment, we are continuing to work on this area. It is our intention that our reforms should effectively be insolvency-neutral.'

2.61   The second political issue concerns the vehicle and timing of reform. According to the Law Commission,[141] work on the project has always been based on an understanding from the DTI that the most likely way of imple-menting any recommendations would be by secondary legislation under a forthcoming Companies Bill. But this is a second best solution in that other

---

135   For Canadian criticism of the Article 9 position in this regard see J Ziegel (1999) 14 Banking and Finance Law Review 131.

136   CR, para 2.157. The limitation was not supported by any consultees.

137   What is now Sch B1, paras 14–21 of the Insolvency Act 1986.

138   Section 176A of the Insolvency Act 1986 as inserted by Enterprise Act 2002, s 252. Under the Insolvency Act 1986 (Prescribed Part) Order 2003 the proportion is based on a sliding scale and calculated as 50% of the first £10,000 of net property, then 20% of the remainder but subject to a ceiling so that the fund for unsecured creditors shall not exceed £600,000.

139   Sections 40 and 175 of the Insolvency Act 1986; for the interpretation of these provisions see *Re Leyland Daf Ltd: Buchler v Talbot* [2004] 2 AC 298.

140   CR, para 2.60.

141   CR, para 1.18.

jurisdictions would have Personal Property Security statutes, whereas England would have secondary legislation.[142] Of course, one could utter the usual clichés about half a loaf being better than no bread at all and the best being the enemy of the good. Parliamentary time is short and to insist upon a separate Bill for the introduction of a notice filing system might be to give up on the project as a matter of practical political reality. On the other hand, regulations made under a Companies Bill could not be extended to security interests created by non-incorporated business debtors, and still less to security interests created by consumers. Consequently, we are likely to have a truncated personal property security regime for many years to come. On the other hand, proceeding by way of secondary legislation provides flexibility, as regulations can be amended with much less fuss and inconvenience than primary legislation. In this way the fate of Part IV of the Companies Act 1989 may be avoided.

2.62 A third political point relates to the European dimension and the possibility of EC harmonisation measures in this sphere. As we have seen, this possibility was mentioned by the then government in deciding not to proceed with the Diamond recommendations in 1991. While there have been no comprehensive EC initiatives, neither has the EC gone away, and the Brussels bureaucrats have dipped their toes into the security law waters with not insignificant measures on Financial Collateral[143] and simple retention of title clauses.[144] Despite the Law Commission seeming to will the contrary, civilian jurisdictions, including Scotland, have not embraced the idea of notice filing. It is unlikely that any future EC initiatives would have notice-filing as their centrepiece; nor, indeed, would they necessarily be compatible with a general notice filing system. Finally, banks generally have what they want under the present regime, including the ability to take security in almost any asset with the minimum of formalities, with priority over most other creditors, and with the ability to enforce their security interest without undue hindrance.[145] In

---

142 See CR, para 1.19, fn 22:
   'As a result, instead of the approach generally taken by the PPSAs, of having the main provisions in primary legislation with detailed additional requirements introduced by secondary legislation, we are proposing that any Companies Bill which implements our draft regulations give the Registrar rule-making powers in certain areas (such as determining the exact detail of a financing statement) ...'
143 Directive 2002/47/EC implemented in England by the Financial Collateral Arrangement (No 2) Regulations 2003.
144 Article 4(1) of Directive 2000/35/EC on combating late payment in commercial transactions (OJ L 2000/35) provides:
   'Member States shall provide in conformity with the applicable national provisions designated by private international law that the seller retains title to goods until they are fully paid for if a retention of title clause has been expressly agreed between the buyer and the seller before the delivery of the goods.'
   On this see generally G McCormack 'Retention of Title and the EC Late Payment Directive' (2001) I Journal of Corporate Law Studies 501; G Monti, G Nejman and W Reuter 'The Future of Reservation of Title Clauses in the European Community' (1997) 47 ICLQ 866; I Davies 'Retention of Title Clauses and Non-Possessory Security Interests: A Secured Credit Regime within the European Union?' in I Davies (ed) *Security Interests in Mobile Equipment* (Dartmouth, 2002).
145 See generally M Bridge 'How Far is Article 9 Exportable? The English Experience' (1996) 27 Canadian Business Law Journal 196 at 221.

addition, the practising legal profession have their precedent banks and are comfortable and familiar with the status quo. Whatever the theoretical benefits of notice filing, the Law Commission has a very difficult job in persuading old dogs to learn new tricks, especially when the old tricks seem to work most of the time. Moreover, financial markets lawyers have expressed concerns 'that many of the proposals will make the law less flexible and more complex than it is at present, will create greater uncertainty, will provide less information to those dealing with companies, and will place unnecessary restraints on freedom of contract in business transactions.'[146]

---

146 See 'Commentary by the Financial Law Committee of the City of London Law Society on Law Commission Consultation Paper No 176', Executive summary at para 4.

Chapter 3

CHARGES REQUIRING REGISTRATION

INTRODUCTION

3.1 Part XII of the Companies Act 1985 adopts the approach of itemising specifically the charges that require registration.[1] This in line with the view that it is fairer to leave the unknown non-registrable and to bring it into the list, if and when desired, rather than to make the unknown registrable to the possible prejudice of a creditor or at the risk of inhibiting a commercial activity.[2] The Secretary of State was, however, empowered under the unimplemented s 93 of the Companies Act 1989 to add any description of charge to, or remove any description of charge from, the list of registrable charges. Perhaps the best course is to set out the list of charges that require registration and then to go through the list while dwelling on the heads of charge that have proved particularly contentious or controversial. The following charges need to be registered under Companies Act 1985, s 396(1):

(a)   a charge for the purpose of securing any issue of debentures;

(b)   a charge on uncalled share capital of the company;

(c)   a charge created or evidenced by an instrument which, if executed by an individual, would require registration as a bill of sale;

(d)   a charge on land (wherever situated) or any interest in it, but not including a charge for any rent or other periodical sum issuing out of the land;

(e)   a charge on book debts of the company;

(f)   a floating charge on the company's undertaking or property;

(g)   a charge on calls made but not paid;

(h)   a charge on a ship or aircraft, or any share in a ship;

(i)   a charge on goodwill, or on any intellectual property.

It is also fundamental to the application of the section that the charge in question be created by a company to which Part XII applies, ie a company registered in England and Wales. This requirement has posed particular problems when it comes to charges created by trustee companies.

---

1   On the other hand, as far as practitioners are concerned and given the serious consequences of non-registration, clearly the safest approach is to register if there is any risk that the transaction might be deemed to create a registrable security interest.

2   A Review of Security Interests in Property (HMSO, February 1989) at p 107.

CHARGES CREATED BY TRUSTEE COMPANIES

3.2   As the Company Law Review Steering Group point out, the current practice of Companies House is to register a charge submitted by a trustee company where the trustee makes its status as trustee known to Companies House but to record on the register that the charger is acting as the trustee.[3] Such a note assists the trustee because certain trustees, particularly banks, are sensitive to any adverse implications that the registration of a charge might have upon their financial standing. On the other hand, there is the question whether such a charge is properly registrable. The beneficiary, even if it is a registered company, has not created the charge and the trustee company is not the beneficial owner of the assets in question and, consequently, the assets might not be regarded as the company's property for the purpose of s 395 etc. The Company Law Review Steering Group pointed out that 'the sanction of invalidity would be irrelevant in such a case because the liquidator of the trustee would obtain no benefit if the unregistered charge were void against him, because the trustee would not be the beneficial owner of the charged property, which would not be available to the trustee company's creditors in any event'.[4] Section 283(a) of the Insolvency Act 1986 states that any property which is held by the bankrupt's estate on trust for any other person does not constitute part of the bankrupt's estate for the purpose of the legislation. Somewhat surprisingly, there is no equivalent provision as regards corporate insolvency, though it is clear that a similar principle should apply. A liquidator can have no better claim to the assets than the company as trustee had. While not directly in point, the decision of the House of Lords in the Scottish appeal *Heritable Reversionary Company Ltd v Millar*[5] does have some bearing on the matter. In that case Lord Watson said:[6]

> 'An apparent title to land or personal estate, carrying no real right of property with it, does not, in the ordinary or in any true legal sense, make such land or personal estate the property of the person who holds the title. That which, in legal as well as conventional language, is described as a man's property is estate, whether heritable or moveable, in which he has a beneficial interest which the law allows him to dispose of. It does not include estate in which he has no beneficial interest, and which he cannot dispose of without committing a fraud.'

3.3   The Steering Group, however, also pointed to a contrary view that:

> 'the sanction of invalidity is not the only sanction for non-registration and is not the only rationale for the requirement to register. There are two other sanctions: the making of the money secured by the non- registrable charge

---

3   See the consultation document from the Company Law Review Steering Group 'Registration of Company Charges' (October 2000) at para 3.61.
4   'Registration of Company Charges' at para 3.59. See also R Goode *Legal Problems of Credit and Security* (3rd edn, 2003) at p 78.
5   [1892] AC 598. See generally Hamish Anderson 'The Treatment of Trust Assets in English Insolvency Law' in Ewan McKendrick (ed) *Commercial Aspects of Trusts and Fiduciary Obligations* (OUP, 1992) 167 at 171–172.
6   [1892] AC 598 at 614.

immediately payable; and the fine for the contravention of the requirement to register the charge. As trustee, the charging company is the legal owner of the trust property and, in that sense, the property is the company's property for the purposes of registering any charge upon it.'[7]

It could also be added that the trustee might be more than the bare holder of the legal title.

3.4   The Steering Group recommended that the law should be clarified to the effect that company trustees charging trust property should register such charges and disclose in the particulars that they do so as trustee of the charged property. Broadly speaking, the Law Commission endorsed this recommendation in the proposed new notice filing context. It also suggested that the filed information should state not only that the charger was acting as trustee but for which corporate beneficiary.[8]

A CHARGE FOR THE PURPOSE OF SECURING ANY ISSUE OF DEBENTURES

3.5   Of course, most issues of debentures are supported by a floating charge, so even if CA 1985, s 396(1)(a) were absent from the legislation, charges securing an issue of debentures would still be registrable in the generality of cases. Moreover, even if there is no floating charge underlying an issue of debentures, there might well be a fixed charge registrable by virtue of some other paragraph.

3.6   So far as the discussion has preceded on elephantine assumptions as to a debenture – ie an elephant is difficult to define but you know it when you see it; so too with a debenture. The phrase is in fact defined in s 744 of the Companies Act 1985: ' "debenture" includes debenture stock, bonds and any other securities of a company, whether constituting a charge on the assets of the company or not.' But that definition is not much good in the present context. The expression is generally understood to refer to a document evidencing indebtedness.[9] An English case often cited is *Levy v Abercorris Slate and Slab Co.*[10] In that case Chitty J opined that a debenture means a document which either creates a debt or acknowledges it, and any document which fulfils either of these conditions is a 'debenture'. He went on:[11]

'I cannot find any precise legal definition of the term, it is not either in law or commerce a strictly technical term, or what is called a term of art. It

---

7   'Registration of Company Charges' at para 3.59.
8   Consultation Paper No 164 *Registration of Security Interests* (2002) at para 5.65.
9   See generally on this area WJ Gough *Company Charges* (Butterworths, 2nd edn, 1996) at pp 645–657. Gough at p 646 cites the High Court of Australia in *Handeval Pty Ltd v Comptroller of Stamps (Victoria)* (1985) 157 CLR 177 at 195: 'it has been generally agreed that two characteristics of a debenture are, first, that it is issued by a company and, secondly, that it acknowledges or creates a debt.'
10   (1888) 37 Ch D 260.
11   (1888) 37 Ch D 260 at 264.

must be "issued", but "issued" is not a technical term, it is a mercantile term well understood; "issue" here means the delivery over by the company to the person who has the charge ...'

Chitty J expressly rejected the argument that a debenture must be one of a series of debentures or issued pari passu with the others. He also referred back to his earlier judgment in *Edmonds v Blaina Furnaces*[12] where he said on the subject of debentures:[13]

> 'But although it is not a term with any legal definition, it is a term which has been used by lawyers frequently with reference to instruments under Acts of Parliament, which when you turn to the Acts of Parliament themselves are not so described. The "debentures" of a railway company are frequently spoken of; but the Companies Clauses Act of 1845 speaks of "bonds and mortgages and not 'debentures'", in argument, however, they are frequently so called. In the same way the instruments of a company incorporated under the Act of 1862, of which a register must be kept, are commonly called debentures, but the term in the Act is "mortgages" and "charges". It is an expression used frequently in the Law Courts both by counsel and Judges, and it is a very convenient term, but it has no legal definition ... The term itself imports a debt – an acknowledgment of a debt.'

3.7   Section 6(2) of the Interpretation Act 1978 provides that unless the contrary intention appears, words in the plural include the singular. It is submitted that a contrary intention clearly appears in the case of CA 1985, s 396(1)(a) and that debentures means debentures in the plural. This interpretation accords with the generally accepted view. Professor Aubrey Diamond in his report for the DTI states that what para (a) ought to apply to, and probably does apply to, is a charge for the purpose of securing an issue of a series of debentures and those circumstances alone. In *Automobile Association (Canterbury) Incorporated v Australasian Secured Deposits Ltd*[14] the New Zealand Court of Appeal, construing identical legislation, rejected the proposition that the wording caught the issue of a single debenture. Richmond J suggested that the Legislature had in mind primarily a large scale issue of debentures.[15] He added, however, that the words used may well be capable of application even to an issue of two debentures secured by one charge. Redrafting of the legislative language has been recommended in the Diamond Report. It was suggested, though, that the phrase used in s 396 to describe an issue of debentures should follow the wording employed in s 397.[16] That section deals with the formalities of registration where a company creates 'a series of debentures containing, or giving by reference to another instrument, any charge to the benefit of which the debenture holders of that series are entitled pari passu.'

---

12   (1887) 36 Ch D 215.
13   (1887) 36 Ch D 215 at 218–219.
14   [1973] 1 NZLR 417.
15   [1973] 1 NZLR 417 at 426.
16   A Review of Security Interests in Property (HMSO, February 1989) at p 119.

3.8 Diamond considered that if a series of debentures were created, secured only on assets not caught by any of the other heads of registrable charge, it was right and necessary that it should be registered:[17]

> 'It is right that it should be registered because the issue of such a series is likely to be a relatively significant event for the company, notice of which should be made available to persons sufficiently interested to search the charges register, and it is necessary to do so because it enables the debenture holders, or their trustee, to be confident that notice of the charge has been given, and it affords a useful assurance to them.'

A CHARGE ON UNCALLED SHARE CAPITAL OF THE COMPANY OR CALLS MADE BUT NOT PAID

3.9 Companies Act 1985, s 396(1)(a) refers to a charge on uncalled share capital of the company and section 396(1)(g) refers to charges on call made but not paid. Section 396(1)(g) presumably covers a charge on instalments due as part of the issue price of shares. These instalments are not calls in the strict sense. Otherwise, as certain commentators have pointed out, a notable lacuna in the registration system would be revealed.[18] Section 262(1)(b) of the Australian Corporations Law goes even further by making registrable a charge on uncalled share premiums. The further reference was added in Australia to take account of the distinction drawn in *Re South Australian Barytes Ltd (No 2)*[19] between uncalled share capital and uncalled share premiums.[20]

3.10 It should be noted that this head of registrable charge does not extend to a legal or equitable mortgage of shares held by a company in another company, even where that other company is a wholly owned subsidiary.[21] This form of security is much more likely to occur today than a charge on uncalled capital. It should also be noted that s 150 of the Companies Act 1985 restricts the right of public companies to security rights over their own shares.

---

17 At p 119 of the Report.
18 See e g I Snaith *The Law of Corporate Insolvency* (1989) at p 163.
19 (1977) 3 ACLR 52.
20 The change was in fact accomplished by s 200 of the Companies Code 1981: see generally WJ Gough *Australian Supplement to Company Charges* (1983), p 15, fn 6.
21 *Arthur D Little Ltd (in Administration) v Ableco Finance LLC* [2003] Ch 217. The non-registrability of charges over shares is discussed in Chapter 4. It should be noted, however, that a charge on share dividends may be registrable as a charge on book debts.

A CHARGE CREATED OR EVIDENCED BY AN INSTRUMENT WHICH, IF EXECUTED BY AN INDIVIDUAL, WOULD REQUIRE REGISTRATION AS A BILL OF SALE

3.11   As numerous commentators and official bodies have pointed out, including the Diamond report, the Bills of Sale Acts are verbose and unclear.[22] The legislation governing bills of sale is contained in the Bills of Sale Act 1878 and the Bills of Sale Act (1878) Amendment Act 1882.[23] Bills of sale which fall within the legislation are of two kinds. First, there are those which constitute absolute assurances of chattels and, secondly, there are bills of sale given by way of security. The former are regulated by the 1878 Act, whereas the latter are affected both by the 1878 and 1882 Acts. The statutory definition of a bill of sale is contained in s 3 of the Bills of Sale Act 1878 which lays down that the Act shall apply to 'every bill of sale ... whereby the holder or grantee has power ... to seize or take possession of any personal chattels'. Section 4 of the same Act sets out three categories of bill of sale:

(1)   assignments, transfers, declarations of trust without transfer, inventories of goods with receipt thereto attached or receipts for purchase monies of goods, and other assurances of personal chattels;

(2)   powers of attorney, authorities or licences to take possession of personal chattels as security for any debt;

(3)   agreements by which a right in equity to any personal chattels or to any charge or security thereon shall be conferred.

Section 4 goes on to set out a list of documents that are specifically exempted from the definition of a 'bill of sale'. The exceptions include a transfer of goods in the ordinary course of business of any trade or calling. The expression 'bill of sale' is given the same meaning in the Act of 1882.[24]

3.12   The raison d'être of the 1878 and 1882 Acts was explained by Lord Herschell in *Manchester, Sheffield and Lincolnshire Railway Co v North Wagon Railway Co*.[25] He said the former enactment was designed for the protection of creditors, and to prevent their rights being affected by secret assurances of chattels which were permitted to remain the ostensible possession of a person who had parted with the property in them. The statutory scheme of protection is for a bill of sale to be attested and to be registered in a public register within seven days. Failure to comply with the registration requirements renders the bill void, but only as against creditors or their representatives.[26] As between the parties thereto, an unregistered bill of sale remains perfectly valid. On the other

---

22   Diamond A Review of Security Interests in Property (HMSO, February 1989) at p 14.

23   See also the Bills of Sale Acts 1890 and 1891 which exempt certain letters of hypothecation from the operation of the Bills of Sale Acts. For accounts of the bills of sale legislation see AG Guest *The Law of Hire Purchase* (London, 1966), chapter 4; RM Goode *Hire Purchase Law and Practice* (2nd edn, London, 1970), chapter 4; and see also WJ Gough *Company Charges* (Butterworths, 2nd edn, 1996), chapter 25.

24   Bills of Sale Act (1878) Amendment Act 1882, s 3.

25   (1888) 13 App Cas 554.

26   Bills of Sale Act 1878, s 8.

hand, the second statute was intended to prevent needy persons being entrapped into signing complicated documents which they might often be unable to comprehend and so being subjected by their creditors to the enforcement of harsh and unreasonable provisions. Lord Herschell added:[27]

> 'A form was accordingly provided to which bills of sale were to conform, and the result of non-compliance with the statute was to render the bill of sale void even as between the parties to it. But this being the object, the enactment is … limited to bills of sale given "by way of security for the payment of money by the grantor thereof".'

3.13   In the unimplemented Part IV of the Companies Act 1989 the legislature avoided reference to the Bills of Sale Acts and opted for more direct wording that made reference to a charge on goods as being registrable. The change in wording, however, signified an extension of the categories of registrable charge because oral charges are not caught by the current dispensation. The Bills of Sale Acts have a restricted scope and apply only to charges on goods that are created or evidenced by an instrument of some sort.[28] *Newlove v Shrewsbury*[29] illustrates the limited operation of the Bills of Sale legislation. In that case an oral agreement was made under which title to a personal chattel was given by way of security for an advance. The grantor of the chattel signed a 'receipt' and it was held by the Court of Appeal that this document, not being an assurance of personal chattels, was not a bill of sale within s 4 of the 1878 Act. Lindley LJ suggested that the agreement to give security was by way of an oral agreement that was antecedent to the receipt. The defendant, upon obtaining possession of the chattel, could defend possession by proof of the oral agreement and without having to make reference to the receipt.[30]

3.14   The exception in the Bills of Sale legislation for the transfer of goods in the ordinary course of any trade or calling means that there is scope for the argument that what might appear to be a charge created by a company is in reality a transfer of goods in the ordinary course of a business and hence not registrable. The Bills of Sale Acts exception has provoked a fair degree of litigation. In *King v Greig*[31] it was held that the words 'transfer of goods in the ordinary course of business of any trade or calling' refer to transfers in the ordinary course of the business, trade or calling of the transferor. Cusson ACJ denied, however, that the business, trade or calling (if any) of the transferee or supposed transferee was never of any importance.[32] In *Tennant v Howatson*[33] the Privy Council took into account, in determining the applicability of the exception, the frequency of transactions like the transaction under examination which occurred in the particular trade.

---

27   (1888) 13 App Cas 554 at 560–561.
28   Diamond Report at p 121.
29   (1888) 21 QBD 41.
30   (1888) 21 QBD 41 at 44–45. Lindley LJ said that the right to possession conferred by such an oral agreement could not be upset by reference to the receipt.
31   [1931] VR 413.
32   [1931] VR 413 at 423.
33   (1888) 13 App Cas 489.

3.15   If a particular kind of transaction is commonplace by the standards of a trading community it is likely to come within the exception. For instance, in *Re Young Hamilton & Co*[34] Bigham J, deciding that a particular transaction was not registrable as a bill of sale, observed:[35] 'This document evidences a transaction of a most ordinary kind as between bankers and merchants. Such transactions happen by the score every day of the week in places of business like Manchester.'

3.16   It is for a person relying on the 'ordinary course of business' exception to establish the existence of the exception in the particular case before the court. There must be evidence adduced as to the particular trade or calling, for the court was most unlikely to infer that the exception applied merely by reference to the volume of reported cases on a particular topic.[36]

3.17   In the Australian case *Wangaratto Brewery Co v Betts*[37] a sale by a trader of goods as part of the sale of the whole business was held not to be within the exclusion. It should be noted that in Australia the requirement to register company charges still does not apply to a transfer of goods in the ordinary course of the practice of any profession or the carrying on of any trade or business: see s 262(2)(d) of the Corporations Law.[38]

3.18   Other exceptions from the category of registrable bills of sale include:

(a)   bills of sale of goods in foreign parts or at sea. The Bills of Sale Acts 1890 and 1891 widened this exception to encompass an instrument charging or creating any security on or declaring trusts of imported goods given or executed at any time prior to their deposit in a warehouse, factory, or store, or to their being re-shipped for export, or delivered to a purchaser not being the person giving or executing such instrument;

(b)   bills of lading, warehouse-keeper's certificates, warrants or orders for the delivery of goods;

(c)   other documents used in the ordinary course of business as proof of the possession or control of goods, or authorising or purporting to authorise, either by indorsement or by delivery, the possessor of such document to transfer or receive goods thereby represented. In *Dublin City Distillery Co Ltd v Doherty*[39] the House of Lords rejected the proposition that the kind of delivery orders considered in that case fell within the exception, as no proof had been offered of their usage in the ordinary course of the distillery business.

3.19   At different times, various formulations have been suggested to update the Bills of Sale Acts exemption relating to the category of registrable charges over goods. According to the Diamond Report a charge should not be

---

34   [1905] 2 KB 381.
35   [1905] 2 KB 381 at 389.
36   *Ian Chisholm Textiles Ltd v Griffiths* [1994] BCC 96.
37   (1870) 1 AJR 79.
38   Also excluded is a dealing, in the ordinary course of the practice of any profession or the carrying on of any trade or business, in respect of goods outside Australia: Corporations Law, s 262(2)(e).
39   [1914] AC 823.

registrable where it related to pledges or possessory liens on goods or arose by way of pledge, deposit, letter of hypothecation or trust receipt of bills of lading, dock warrants or other documents of title to goods.[40] The unimplemented Part IV of the Companies Act 1989 adopted more straightforward drafting and excepted from the registration requirement a charge under which the security taker was entitled to possession either of the goods or of a document of title to the goods.[41]

CHARGES ON LAND

3.20 Companies Act 1985, s 396(1)(d) makes registrable with Companies House a charge on land (wherever situated) or any interest in it, but not including a charge for any rent or other periodical sum issuing out of the land. Section 396((3) declares that the holding of debentures entitling the holder to a charge on land is not for the purposes of this section deemed to an interest in land.

3.21 It should be noted that, under s 3(7) and (8) of the Land Charges Act 1972, charges affecting unregistered land must be registered under the Land Charges Act 1972 as well as under the Companies Act 1985.[42] This requirement of dual registration, however, affects only fixed charges.[43] Floating charges are still exempted from registration in the Land Charges Registry, though a floating charge over land is a somewhat rare occurrence.[44]

3.22 In the case of registered land, the Land Registration Act 1925 (now the Land Registration Act 2002) has always required registration at both the Land Registry and the Companies Registry. The procedure for registration with the Land Registry differs depending on whether the charge is fixed or floating. Where the charge is fixed, the charge itself is capable of substantive registration and the chargee is given a charge certificate. With a floating charge, however, the interest is protected by a notice in the register and there is no charge certificate. Unless protection for the chargee's interest is achieved in the requisite manner, a purchaser under a registered disposition will take free of the chargee's interest whether or not he has notice thereof: express, implied or constructive.

---

40 (HMSO 1989) at p 120. This position mirrors relevant provisions of the Ghana Companies Code on charges on goods that were drafted by Professor LCB Gower.

41 Companies Act 1989, s 93.

42 Section 97 of the Law of Property Act 1925 states that every 'mortgage affecting a legal estate in land ... whether legal or equitable ... shall rank according to its date of registration as a land charge pursuant to the Land Charges Act.'

43 Section 4(5) of the Land Charges Act 1972 provides that if the land is unregistered, a puisne mortgage or a general equitable charge will be void as against a purchaser of the land charged with it, or of any interest in such land, unless the land charge is registered in the appropriate register before the completion of the purchase.

44 Section 3(7) of the Land Charges Act 1972 provides that registration of floating charges under the Companies Act 1985 is sufficient in place of the Land Charges Act, and that once registered under the 1985 Act, the charge has effect as though it had been registered under the Land Charges Act 1972.

CHARGES ON BOOK DEBTS

3.23   According to s 396(1)(e) of the Companies Act 1985 a charge on book debts of a company is registrable. It should be noted that s 396(1)(f) makes registrable all types of floating charge including floating charges over book debts and other receivables. The application of the company charge registration provisions to fixed charges over book debts has, however, provoked some controversy. Essentially the debate has been over the precise definition of a 'book debt' and also over the fine dividing line between the creation of a charge over debts and the outright assignment of such debts in a factoring transaction. These controversies will be explored fully in this chapter. On the other hand, the appropriateness of the registration obligation per se has gone largely unquestioned. Many of the reasons underlying the registration obligation were articulated in the Diamond report, which made the point that it is common for trade debtors to be given a period of credit. Thus, many companies had substantial sums due to them for services rendered or goods supplied by the company. In Diamond's view, a charge over book debts was a major weapon in the hands of the charge holder and the existence of such a charge could cause considerable disadvantage to other creditors.[45]

Use of the expression 'book debts' rather than 'receivables'

3.24   Section 396 of the Companies Act 1985 uses the phrase 'book debts' rather than the more modern and somewhat wider expression 'receivables'. In the Diamond report it was suggested that the relevant legislation should substitute the phrase 'receivables' for 'book debts' since 'book debts' is a rather antiquated phrase, although it is the expression used in s 344 of the Insolvency Act 1986.[46] It was also suggested that the concept of 'book debts' should be defined as 'debts due or to become due to the company in respect of goods supplied or to be supplied or services rendered or to be rendered by the company in the course of the company's business, whether entered in a book or not.'[47] This definition differs somewhat from that found in s 262(4) of the Australian Corporations Law which reads as follows:

> 'The reference in paragraph (1)(f) to a charge on a book debt is a reference to a charge on a debt due or to become due to the company at some future time on account of or in connection with a profession, trade or business carried on by the company whether entered in book or not, and includes a reference to a charge on a future debt of the same nature although not incurred or owing at the time of the creation of the charge but does not

---

45   See Diamond Report *A Review of Security Interests in Property* (1989) at pp 109–110. See also the somewhat blunt statement at para 7.35 of the Law Commission Consultation Paper *Registration of Security Interests* (2002): 'A security over receivables should be registrable under a notice-filing system as a charge.'

46   Diamond Report (HMSO 1989) at pp 121–122.

47   See Diamond Report *A Review of Security Interests in Property* (HMSO, 1989) at p 121.

include a reference to a charge on a marketable security, on a negotiable instrument or on a debt owing in respect of a mortgage, charge or lease of land.'[48]

3.25   Part IV of the Companies Act 1989 did not propose the use of the phrase 'receivables' rather than 'book debts' and, in fact, did not favour any changes in this area save for a minor amendment making it explicit that charges on book debts assigned to the company are registrable.[49] The legislature even resisted an amendment suggested by the Opposition that would have incorporated into the section the definition of book debts suggested in the Diamond Report.[50] A government minister, however, suggested that a definition of 'book debts' might be included in regulations to be made under the Act. The Act, of course, has never come into force and these regulations have never been made.

Definition of book debts

3.26   The definition of book debts has provoked much controversy over the years. In the leading case of *Shipley v Marshall*[51] book debts were taken as meaning debts that could or would in the ordinary course of a business be entered in well-kept books relating to that business. Buckley J in *Independent Automatic Sales Ltd v Knowles and Foster*[52] amplified this definition of 'book debts', stating that a debt arising in the course of business and due or growing due to the proprietor of that business could properly be called a book debt. This was so whether in fact the debt was entered in the books of the business or not. In *Robertson v Grigg*[53] Gavan Duffy CJ and Starke J in the High Court of Australia construed the expression 'book debts' as pointing to debts owing to a business of a kind usually entered in books of account of the business and in fact so entered. In the New Zealand case *Stanley Stamp Co v Brodie*[54] Stout CJ described book debts as including all such as are entered, or even usually entered in the account books of the vendor. It is clear that actual entry in books of account of a company is not required in England.[55]

---

48   The key feature in this exhaustive definition is the debt charged has to be one due or to become due to the company by reason of or in connection with a profession, trade or business carried on by a company. The debt is not required to be entered in a book and the concept encompasses a future debt not incurred or owing at the creation of the charge.

49   Section 396(1)(c)(iii).

50   House of Commons Standing Committee D, 20 June 1989, col 405.

51   (1863) 14 CB NS 566.

52   [1962] 1 WLR 974, on which see WJ Gough *Company Charges* (Butterworths, 2nd edn, 1996) at p 688.

53   (1932) 47 CLR 257 at 262. For a more recent Australian interpretation see *Waters v Widdows* [1984] VR 503 where a loan made by a company to an associated company was held to be a book debt.

54   (1914) 34 NZLR 129 at 148.

55   In *M O'Donnell & Sons (Huddersfield) Ltd v Midland Bank plc* [2001] EWCA Civ 2108 it was decided by the Court of Appeal that a sum arising from the sale of the entirety of a company's business operations was not a 'book debt' but came within the expression 'other debts' in a bank debenture. Another relevant authority is *Hart v Barnes* [1983] 2 VR 517 where it was held that amounts realised on a sale of the company's stock in trade and plant were not book debts, as they were not realised in the ordinary course of the business of the company.

Application to future debts and to contingency contracts

3.27 It is submitted that the registration requirements embrace both existing and future debts, but not contingency contracts. On this analysis, the law can be summed up in three propositions:[56]

'(i)   Registrability is tested at the date of creation of the charge.

(ii)   If, at the date of creation of the charge, what is charged is a contract which does not of itself constitute a book debt, the charge will not be registrable even if a book debt may arise out of the contract at some future date.

(iii)   If, however, on its true construction the charge is over book debts arising in the future, the fact that the debts are not in existence when the charge is created does not preclude the charge from registration.'

3.28 The leading case is *Independent Automatic Sales Ltd v Knowles and Foster*.[57] Here a company that manufactured and dealt in automatic washing machines from time to time entered into hire-purchase agreements for the disposal of its machines. Subsequently, the company obtained borrowing facilities from a lender and, as part of the 'lending package', created a security interest in favour of the lender over the benefits flowing to the company from the hire purchase agreements.[58] The court held that the lending agreement constituted a charge on book debts and, consequently, was void against the liquidator of the company for non-registration. There was an argument that the registration of charge provisions did not, on their true construction, require a charge on future book debts to be registered; in other words, 'book debts' in the statute meant only existing book debts. Buckley J had two answers. His first point was that the hirer became liable immediately upon the agreement coming into operation to the extent of his minimum liability under it notwithstanding that some part of that liability was to be discharged by future payments and that the debts so constituted were existing book debts at the date of the deposit. Secondly, he held that a charge exclusively on future book debts of a company was registrable, stating:[59]

'That is competent for anyone to whom book-debts may accrue in the future to create an equitable charge upon those book-debts which will attach to them as soon as they come into existence is not disputed (see *Tailby v Official Receiver*).[60] That such a charge can accurately be described as a charge on book-debts does not appear to me to be open to question ... A charge of book-debts, present and future, is not an unusual form of security in the commercial world, and it would seem to me strange if such a charge were registrable (as it undoubtedly is) and a charge confined to future book-debts were not.'

---

56   See M Lawson [1988] LMCLQ 141 at 145.
57   [1962] 1 WLR 974.
58   In American Article 9 parlance the lender is a chattel paper financier.
59   [1962] 1 WLR 974 at 985.
60   (1888) 13 App Cas 523.

3.29 There is a school of thought[61] that relies on *Paul and Frank Ltd v Discount Bank (Overseas) Ltd*[62] and which argues that a charge on future book debts is non-registrable. The *Paul and Frank* case, however, appears distinguishable from *Independent Automatic Sales Ltd v Knowles and Foster*. In *Paul and Frank* it was held by Pennycuick J that a letter of authority authorising the payment of the proceeds of an insurance policy to the defendant did not create a registrable charge. The court held that where the item of property charged was the benefit of a contract and, at the date of the charge, the benefit of the contract did not comprehend any book debt, the contract was not registrable merely by reason of the fact that it might ultimately result in a book debt.[63]

3.30 The views propounded in *Paul and Frank Ltd* on the non-registrability of contingency contracts were approved of by Lynch J in the Irish High Court in *Farrell v Equity Bank Ltd*.[64] That was a case where the liquidator of a company asserted an entitlement to the receipt of part premiums refunded by various insurers. The refunds were made when policies of insurance were cancelled before the expiration of the periods of insurance for which the premiums were paid. The monies required to pay such premiums had earlier been advanced by Equity Bank Ltd, the defendants. The terms of the advance gave Equity Bank the prior right to receive such refunds until the whole of the advance had been repaid. The judge took the view that a charge had been created in favour of Equity Bank over the refunds if and when they might become payable. The bare possibility, however, that future refunds of premiums might become payable in amounts that were wholly unascertained, and might never arise, from the perspective of the date of creation of the charge, did not have the effect of constituting the transaction a book debt.

3.31 Somewhat more controversially, in *Re Brush Aggregates Ltd*[65] it was suggested that the purchase price of property sold by a company may not be a

---

61 See J Parris *Effective Retention of Title Clauses* (Basil Blackwell, 1986) at p 114. See generally on this area G McCormack [1989] LMCLQ 198 at 206–209.

62 [1967] Ch 348.

63 The court distinguished *Independent Automatic Sales Ltd v Knowles and Foster* [1962] 1 WLR 974 on the basis that if a charge upon its proper construction covers future debts, in the sense of debts under a future contract which, when that contract comes to be made, will constitute book-debts (eg an ordinary contract for the sale of goods on credit), there was no reason why the registration requirement should not be fairly applicable to the charge. In *Contemporary Cottages (NZ) Ltd v Margin Traders Ltd* [1981] 2 NZLR 114 at 126 Thorp said:

'There seems to me to be a basic conflict between the proposition that registration may be required in respect of a debt not existing at the time of the charge, and the concept that the test is to be the character of the property assigned and charged at the date of creation of the charge. I prefer the proposition which lies behind the judgment of Buckley J, ie that the charge over future book debts is created at the time of execution of an appropriate assignment pursuant to *Tailby*'s case, to distinguishing between book debts which arise from existing contracts and book debts which arise from non-existent contracts on any basis which makes charges over the latter registrable but charges over the former not registrable. That consequence, which is necessarily involved in the proposals by Pennycuick J, is one which seems to me, with respect, to indicate the illogicality of the distinction.'

64 [1990] 2 IR 549. This case is discussed by H Linnane (1990) 11 Co Law 230–232.

65 [1983] BCLC 320.

book debt if the precise sum payable has to be ascertained in the future by reference to the quantity supplied, although otherwise it would be a book debt. It should be noted, however, that a determination on the point was not necessary to a decision in the case. The case concerned a company which agreed to sell a gravel pit and there was a facility for adjustment of the payments between the parties according to the reserves of sand and gravel in the pit. The company assigned to various creditors portions of the money it was owed under the agreements. None of the assignments were registered. The judge reached the conclusion, after a close analysis of the transactions, that the assignments were present charges on future book debts, as and when they arose, rather than assignments of a contingent contractual right. Accordingly they were unenforceable as against the liquidator. The assignments were looking to the money when it became due as the subject of the charge rather than to the contingent contractual right.

3.32   The suggestion made in *Re Brush Aggregates Ltd*[66] that the purchase price of property may not be a book debt if the precise sum payable has to be calculated in the future with reference to the quantity supplied was not welcomed by in the Diamond report. It was commented that a charge on such a future debt should be registrable as a charge on a book debt. Part IV of the Companies Act 1989, however, did not contain any specific provision to deal with this situation.

A shipowner's lien on subfreights

3.33   In certain first instance cases, a shipowner's lien on subfreights has been held void as an unregistered charge.[67] The first case is *Re Welsh Irish Ferries Ltd (The Ugland Trailer*[68] where a receiver was appointed to a company that chartered a ship. The vessel was chartered in accordance with conditions which provided 'that the owners shall have a lien upon ... all sub-freights for amounts due under the charter'. Nourse J held that this contractual provision operated as an equitable assignment to the shipowners, by way of security for the money that the company owed them, of the company's right to require payment from the shipper. In his view, it was established law that an equitable assignment of a chose in action by way of security created an equitable charge on the chose. Consequently, the shipowner's contractual lien was a charge on the book debts of the company and registrable as such. The analysis was carried a stage further in *The Annangel Glory*.[69] In this case Saville J decided

---

66   [1983] BCLC 320.
67   Companies Act 1989, s 93 declared that a shipowner's lien on subfreights shall not be treated as a charge on book debts or as a floating charge, but this provision has not been implemented. For criticism of this provision see M Lawson [1989] JBL 287 at 289 who argued that the special treatment given to a vessel owner could have resulted in an anomaly. Typically, a bank financing the purchase of a ship would take as part of its security an assignment of the vessel's earnings. The bank would have to register its security in circumstances in which a ship owner claiming a lien over sub-freights would not.
68   [1986] Ch 471; see M Wilford [1986] LMCLQ 1.
69   [1988] 1 Lloyd's Rep 45; on which see M Wilford [1988] LMCLQ 148 and see also *The Attika Hope* [1988] Lloyd's Rep 439.

that the same provision created a floating charge on a specified part of the charterer's property (namely subfreights to become due to the charterers in respect of the vessel). The floating charge was registrable under s 396(1)(f) of the Companies Act 1985. In his view, an instrument creating a floating security on specified future book debts could properly be described as a floating charge on the company's property or undertaking whether or not such debts exist at the date of the instrument.[70] The judge also cast doubt on the assumption that a floating charge on book debts could not be a charge on book debts, or, in other words, that the latter type of charge was confined to fixed or specific charges.

3.34 The charge thesis has not gone unchallenged[71] and it is a pity, perhaps, that these first instance decisions were not taken to a higher court. For instance, a contractual lien for subfreight does not give a right to follow, wherever the fund may be found, a sum of money merely because it is the proceeds of a debt due for freight.[72] This limitation on the right is difficult to reconcile with the charge conception. It has been persuasively argued that the lien is a personal contractual right of interception analogous to an unpaid seller's right of stoppage in transit and should be treated as such.[73] Lord Millett has now endorsed this academic viewpoint, albeit in an obiter pronouncement, in *Re Brumark Ltd: Agnew v Commissioner of Inland Revenue*.[74] He suggested that a lien on subfreights was not a charge at all, but merely a personal right to intercept freight before it is paid to the owner. These comments are obviously of great persuasive value, coming from a judge of the authority of Lord Millett, but they have the effect of destabilising first instance decisions that have now stood for a considerable period of time. Moreover, the opportunity has not been taken of bringing the statutory reversal of *Welsh Ferries* into force.

3.35 The decision in *Re Welsh Irish Ferries Ltd* did cause some concern in the commercial community, however, and indeed some of the adverse consequences were acknowledged by Nourse J himself in that case. He adverted to the fact that charterparties are negotiated by shipbrokers and others, and not by lawyers. In addition, while they were sometimes of relatively short duration, the 21 day period would normally expire before the charter came to an end, so that registration would have to be effected in almost all cases. This would be enormously inconvenient to shipowners. Furthermore, the raison d'être of the system of registration was to warn unsuspecting creditors, whereas anyone dealing with a corporate charterer must know that it has created liens on subfreight.[75]

---

70 At p 50.
71 See F Oditah [1989] LMCLQ 191.
72 See *Tagart, Beaton & Co v James Fisher & Sons* [1903] 1 KB 391 at 395 per Lord Alverstone. See also *The Nanfri* [1979] AC 757 at 784.
73 F Oditah [1989] LMCLQ 191 at 197.
74 [2001] 2 AC 710 at [41].
75 [1986] Ch 471 at 480. See also the Diamond Report *A Review of Security Interests in Property* (1989) at p 111.

Debt subordination trusts

3.36 In essence the concept of debt subordination is a straightforward one.[76] One creditor (the senior creditor) agrees not to be paid until a particular other creditor (the junior creditor), or perhaps all other creditors are paid in full. Debt subordination agreements often take the form of a mere contractual arrangement between senior and junior creditor but, sometimes, the creation of a trust is involved.[77] With contractual debt subordination the junior creditor agrees that it will not be paid unless and until the senior creditor is paid in full. With a subordination trust, on the other hand, the senior creditor receives a double dividend. The junior creditor agrees to claim the junior debt when it matures or on liquidation and to hold the receipts on trust for the senior creditor.[78] It is possible to envisage more intricate forms of arrangement. An example would be where the basic provision is that of contractual subordination and this is coupled with a covenant by the debtor or junior creditor not to amend the subordination provisions. The debtor or junior creditor then declares a trust over the benefit of that covenant in favour of the senior creditor.[79] In economic terms, there is much to be said for the view that a subordination trust represents a charge over the junior debt, or the proceeds of

---

76 See generally P Wood *The Law of Subordinated Debt* (Sweet & Maxwell, 1990); WJ Gough *Company Charges* (Butterworths 2nd edn, 1996) chapter 40; B Johnston [1991] JBL 225; J Powell [1993] LMCLQ 357; and R Nolan [1994] JBL 485. See also B Johnston [1987] Australian Business Law Review 80 and P Wood [1985] International Financial Law Review 11.

77 Geoffrey Fuller in *Corporate Borrowings: Law and Practice* (Jordans, 1995) at pp 73–75 refers to three main reasons why debt subordination is employed. First, in the case of banks it is done to increase their capital base for regulatory purposes. He refers in this connection to the July 1988 Report on International Convergence of Capital Measurement and Capital Standards by the Basle Committee on Banking Regulations and Supervisory Practices. Secondly, the technique is used so that lenders on a senior basis will be more likely to lend greater amounts and, finally, so that external lenders can be sure that the proceeds of their loans are not used to repay debts to 'insiders', such as a parent company or a major shareholder.

78 In *Re SSSL Realisations (2002) Ltd* [2004] EWHC 1760 Lloyd J distinguished between two different types of subordinated debt agreement:
    'There are those by which the debts owed to one creditor or group of creditors are subordinated to those of others, leaving all others to compete equally between themselves, pari passu. The alternative approach, sometimes called "turnover subordination", is one whereby one creditor agrees with another to hold on trust for the other all dividends or other payments received in respect of his own debt (or at any rate the amount required to pay the other creditor in full), unless and until the other is paid in full. The latter approach would only arise in the context of an agreement between creditors, whereas the former could apply either in an agreement between creditors or in the terms of the issue of subordinated debt as between debtor and creditor. As regards the interest of the creditor seeking to be preferred over another, depending on the likely competition from other creditors not party to the agreement, the latter may well be a more beneficial arrangement than the former, because the former limits the competition, but gives the advantage of that to all the creditors who are not subordinated.'

79 See generally on trusts of covenants *Fletcher v Fletcher* (1844) 4 Hare 67; 67 ER 564. See also *Re Cook's Settlement Trusts* [1965] Ch 902. For commentary see D Elliott (1960) 76 LQR 100; J Barton (1975) 91 LQR 236; R Meagher and J Lehane (1976) 92 LQR 427; C Rickett (1979) 32 CLP 1 and (1981) 34 CLP 189; D Goddard [1988] Conveyancer 19.

that debt, in favour of the senior creditor[80] but, of course, 'economic effect' is not the current legal test. If, in law, a subordination trust does entail the bringing into existence of a security interest the consequences are profound where the junior debtor is a company that has gone into liquidation. The view has been expressed that a subordination trust represents the creation by a junior debtor of a registrable charge over its book debts. One leading commentator, Phillip Wood, puts forward the following opinion:[81]

'The better view is that a properly drafted subordination trust of proceeds should not create a security interest under English law but the matter is undecided and, in light of the potentially disastrous consequences if this view is wrong, a doubt must be recorded.'

3.37 Professor Sir Roy Goode is more dogmatic on the point but also approaches the matter from a slightly different perspective.[82] He suggests that it is necessary to distinguish between an undertaking to hand over recoveries prior to the debtor's liquidation and an undertaking as to proof and application of dividends in the winding-up of the debtor. Outside the context of the liquidation of the debtor, where the undertaking to account creates a trust in favour of the senior creditor, it will create a charge on the junior creditor's book debts and will be void if not registered and where the junior creditor is in liquidation. This invalidity in the event of liquidation does not, however, affect the senior creditor's right to retain sums paid over by the junior creditor prior to the commencement of its liquidation. Goode also argues that the liquidation of the junior creditor does not have any effect on sums received from the debtor by the junior creditor before winding-up and not yet paid over to the senior creditor. The argument proceeds on the basis that upon payment a book debt ceases to exist. Therefore the provision invalidating unregistered charges over book debts has no cutting edge in this instance.

3.38 Insofar as an obligation undertaken by the junior creditor to hand over to the senior creditor dividends received in the debtor's winding-up is concerned, Professor Goode contends that there is no question of a registrable charge being created. An entitlement to a dividend in a liquidation cannot be classified as a debt.[83] While a liquidator in a winding-up has statutory duties to perform he is not a debtor in respect of dividends declared by him.[84]

3.39 Other commentators have argued that a subordination trust of debt proceeds does not create a charge on the basis that there is no equity of

---

80 See the observations by P Wood *The Law of Subordinated Debt* (1990) at 38:
   'A subordination trust is in economic substance a collateral charge by the junior creditor over the junior creditor's debt or the proceeds of that debt to secure the senior debt, but without imposing any personal liability on the junior creditor to pay the senior debt himself. The question is whether the transfer of proceeds is in law a security interest.'
81 The Law of Subordinated Debt (1990) at 39.
82 Commercial Law (3rd edn, Penguin, 2004) at pp 614–616.
83 See the definition of book debts offered by Lord Esher MR in *Official Receiver v Tailby* (1886) 18 QBD 25 at 29: 'debts arising in a business ... which ought to be entered in the company's books.'
84 See also on this point P Wood *The Law of Subordinated Debt* (1990) at 38.

redemption involved in the transaction.[85] The existence of an equity of redemption in the chargor is an essential feature of the creation of a charge. If there is no equity of redemption, there is no charge.[86]

> 'A trust and a charge are two mutually exclusive institutions ... [I]t is simply incorrect to say that a trust can at the same time be a charge. One litmus test that distinguishes a trust from a charge is who has the ability to benefit from the rise in value of the property in question. Only the beneficial owner has such ability which is the inherent corollary of beneficial ownership. Thus any rise in value of the trust property naturally inures to the beneficiary. In contrast, a chargee due to his lack of beneficial ownership, does not benefit from the rise in value of the charged property. A chargee's interest is confined to the satisfaction of the obligation secured by the charge.'[87]

3.40   The use of absolute title as security is well established in certain commercial spheres. One might highlight in this connection finance leasing and the factoring of book debts. Philip Wood suggests that a trust of receipts, by the junior creditor in favour of the senior creditor, up to an amount equal to the senior debt, leaves no equity of redemption since the junior creditor never transfers more than is required to pay the senior debt. In his view, there is no surplus to swing back with the beneficial ownership in the proceeds split.[88] Wood draws an analogy with the tracing aspects of reservation of title clauses in sale of goods contracts. With such a provision the seller of goods retains title to the goods until the goods have been paid for, notwithstanding delivery of the goods to the buyer. The buyer is permitted to resell the goods in the ordinary course of business, but the original seller lays claim to the resale proceeds up to the amount of the original contract debt. Is such a claim a legally viable one? The answer would appear to be in the negative on the basis of the more recent case law[89] and this is where the analogy breaks down.[90]

---

85   For a development of this argument see B Johnston [1987] Australian Business Law Review 80 at 133–135.

86   See also JR Lingard *Bank Security Documents* (3rd edn, 1993) at p 335, who argues that the primary reason why an agreement for postponement of a debt is not a charge is that it confers no right on the bank to sell or otherwise realise the subordinated debt, nor is there any intention to create a charge. He cites the observations of Peter Gibson J in *Carreras Rothmans Ltd v Freeman Mathews Ltd* [1985] Ch 207 that the rights to enforce a trust are wholly different from the rights of a chargee. A beneficiary under a trust did not have a power of sale, nor was there any equity of redemption in the trust beneficiary.

87   See Look Chan Ho 'A Matter of Contractual and Trust Subordination' (2004) 19 JIBLR 494 at 496.

88   Wood The Law of Subordinated Debt (1990) at pp 39–40.

89   *Compaq Computer Ltd v Abercorn Group Ltd* [1991] BCC 484 and *Modelboard Ltd v Outer Box Ltd* [1992] BCC 945; and see also *Pfeiffer Weinkellerei-Weineinkauf GmbH & Co v Arbuthnot Factors Ltd* [1988] 1 WLR 150; *Tatung (UK) Ltd v Galex Telesure Ltd* (1989) 5 BCC 325. See generally Chapter 5.

90   Advancing an argument similar to that of Wood, Look Chan Ho in 'A matter of Contractual and Trust Subordination' (2004) 19 JIBLR 494 at 497 relies on the Australian case *Associated Alloys v ACN 001 452 106* (2000) 202 CLR 588, but it is submitted that this case is almost impossible to reconcile with the English cases.

3.41 A possible way around the registration difficulties has also, however, been outlined by Wood.[91] He states that a subordination trust may be constituted by a trust deed under which the junior debt is payable to a trustee who holds the recoveries for the benefit first of the senior creditor and then the junior creditor. The debtor may be authorised to pay the creditors direct until an event of default occurs, in which event the debtor must pay the trustee. The proposition is that the trustee is not creating a charge because the trustee has no property of its own to charge. The junior creditor is not conveying any proprietary interest to the senior creditor but is merely taking a limited interest under the trust. As Wood himself recognises, the matter has not been decided and the same strictures levelled against debt subordination trusts per se might seem to apply. There is also an analogy that may be drawn with direct payment clauses in building contracts.[92] The debtor is authorised to pay creditors direct until some default happens at which time payment must thereafter be made to the trustee. In the construction context such clauses were upheld in *Re Tout and Finch Ltd*[93] but the correctness of this decision has been questioned in the light of the House of Lords decision in *British Eagle International Airlines Ltd v Compagnie Nationale Air France*[94] and the principle articulated in *Ex parte Mackay*[95] that a person is not allowed, by stipulation with a creditor, to provide for a different distribution of his effects in the event of bankruptcy from that which the law provides.[96]

3.42 The decision of Lloyd J in *Re SSSL Realisations (2002) Ltd*[97] suggests, however, that even if a debt subordination trust creates a charge, such a charge is not registrable. He referred to a trust arrangement whereby one creditor, A, agrees to hold on trust monies received from a common debtor for the purpose of paying or securing payment of another creditor, B. In the *SSSL Realisations* case, however, the subordination arrangement was of the contractual variety, with the trust element ancillary to the former. Its effect was to prevent a parent company, unless and until certain conditions were satisfied, from taking steps to collect in a debt owed to it by a subsidiary. This had the effect of putting certain creditors in a better position in the liquidation of the insolvent subsidiary. Nevertheless, Lloyd J commented:[98]

---

91 *The Law of Subordinated Debt* (Sweet & Maxwell, 1990) at 39–40. See also B Johnston [1987] Australian Business Law Review 80 at 135.

92 See generally on this area D Capper 'Direct Payment Clauses and the Pari Passu Principle' [1998] LMCLQ 54; R Davis *Construction Insolvency* (Palladian Law Publishing, 2nd edn, 1999) chapter 6.

93 [1954] 1 All ER 127; and see also *Re Wilkinson ex parte Fowler* [1905] 2 KB 713.

94 [1975] 1 WLR 758.

95 (1873) 8 Ch App 643 at 647.

96 For a trenchant criticism see Look Chan Ho 'A Matter of Contractual and Trust Subordination' (2004) 19 JIBLR 494 at 499:
    'A proper reading of the decision in *Re SSSL* confirms yet again that that *British Eagle* is wholly unconcerned with the principle of pari passu distribution. Hence the standard de rigueur caution against the enforceability of subordination agreements on *British Eagle*/pari passu grounds is simply misconceived. Decades of concern over the *British Eagle*/pari passu violation is in fact a schism over an ism that is now an anachronism.'

97 [2004] EWHC 1760.

98 [2004] EWHC 1760 at [50].

'it does not do so by way of security over an asset belonging to [the parent]. The fact that it achieves a result which is, in some respects, similar to that which would be achieved by a charge is of course relevant, but it cannot be characterised as a charge merely because the effects are in some ways similar. The document must be examined and analysed and its true legal nature ascertained ...'

More controversially, Lloyd J suggested that even if the subordination agreement was of the true 'trust' variety, it would not create a registrable charge over book debts. It had been argued that there was nothing inherently wrong with such a transaction, which did confer proprietary rights, but that if the junior creditor later became insolvent, the arrangement was likely to be a charge over its book debts, and accordingly void against other creditors unless registered. Lloyd J, however, accepted a definition of 'book debt' as being a debt owing to a company connected and arising out of the company's trade and business, which is entered or commonly would be entered, in the ordinary course of business, in well kept books of a trade or business.[99] He took the view that a sum of cash in the hands of the junior creditor could not in any sense be regarded as a book debt. It was possible to create a charge over a sum of money held by a person once it has been paid to him, without necessarily also creating a charge over the debt or other right in respect of which it may come to be paid. The charge over the sum of money would not be registrable as a charge over book debts.

Negotiable instruments exception

3.43 In *Dawson v Isle*[100] it was held that a book debt arises where a bill of exchange has been received and entered in the books of the company. However, CA 1985, s 396(2) provides that where a negotiable instrument has been given in payment of any book debts the deposit of the negotiable instrument for the purpose of securing an advance shall not be regarded as a charge on those book debts.

3.44 The Hong Kong equivalent of this provision was considered by the Privy Council in *Chase Manhattan Asia Ltd v First Bangkok City Finance Ltd.*[101] The facts are quite complicated, but basically the transaction consisted of an assignment to Chase of part of a loan made by FBCF (to a third party). This was secured by the assignment to Chase of a promissory note issued to FBCF by the third party borrowers, and an undertaking by FBCF to buy back the assigned loan from Chase, whereupon Chase would re-endorse and re-deliver the note. The Privy Council took the view that there was a charge over a book debt of FBCF, ie the original loan which was void against the liquidator of FBCF for non-registration under the Hong Kong Companies Ordinance. Lord Templeman observed that, although the promissory note was a negotiable instrument given by the borrower to secure payment of the lenders' book debt,

---

99 Reference was made to *Shipley v Marshall* (1863) 14 CB (NS) 566; *Official Receiver v Tailby* (1886) 18 QBD 25.
100 [1906] 1 Ch 633.
101 [1990] 1 WLR 1181.

the assignee was unable to rely on the Hong Kong equivalent of s 396(2) of the Companies Act 1985 because of its failure to receive the note.[102] It was said that the provision exempts from registration only the holders of a negotiable instrument and that exemption must have been granted in order that the benefits of, and consequences of, negotiability should not be prejudiced by the insolvency of the company which deposits that instrument.

Factoring or the outright assignment of debts

3.45 It is vitally important to distinguish between the outright assignment ('factoring') of book debts and the creation of a charge over such debts.[103] Section 136 of the Law of Property Act 1925 specifies the following conditions which must be met before an assignment of debts or other choses in action can operate as a legal assignment:

(1)   the assignment must be absolute and not by way of charge;
(2)   the assignment must relate to the whole of the debt;
(3)   the assignment must be in writing under the hand of the assignor;
(4)   notice in writing of the assignment must be given to the debtor.

Even if these conditions are not met, an assignment may still be effective in equity provided that consideration has been provided and the intention to assign is clear. As Lord Macnaghten remarked in *Tailby v Official Receiver*,[104] it has long been settled that future property, possibilities and expectancies are assignable in equity for value. In his view, the mode or form of assignment was absolutely immaterial provided that the intention of the parties was clear. The judge added that to effectuate the intention:

> 'an assignment for value, in terms present and immediate, has always been regarded in equity as a contract binding on the conscience of the assignor and so binding the subject-matter of the contract when it comes into existence, if it is of such a nature and so described as to be capable of being ascertained and identified ...'

3.46 Notice to the debtor is not required to perfect the title of an equitable assignee. It should be noted too that assignments of part of a debt are possible only in equity. In *Ashby Warner & Co v Simmons*[105] it was explained that the common law failed to recognise that any common law rights could be created by an order for payment of a sum out of a larger sum. It was not regarded at common law either as a security or as an assignment. Equity, however, prevailed now in all courts and equity did justice to the party who obtained an

---

102   [1990] 1 WLR 1181 at 1184.

103   See also *Lloyds TSB Bank plc v Clarke (Liquidator of Socimer International Bank Ltd)* [2002] UKPC 27, [2002] 2 All ER (Comm) 992, PC where it was held by the Privy Council that a sub-participation agreement that was entered between two banks as part of a Eurobond issue did not invest the sub-participating bank with any proprietary interest in the underlying bonds or their proceeds. The lead bank had become insolvent but, since the agreement did not amount to the assignment of a proprietary interest in the proceeds, the money formed part of the insolvent estate and the sub-participating bank was merely an unsecured creditor.

104   (1888) 12 App Cas 523.

105   [1936] 2 All ER 697; (1932) 52 TLR 613.

assignment of part of a larger sum by holding that that assignment gave him an equitable right on the fund when the fund came into existence.

3.47 In commercial practice, factoring of debts is often done on a non-notification basis and this necessarily involves equitable assignment. The distinction between notification factoring and non-notification factoring is quite crucial in practical terms. With the former, notice of the assignment is given to the debtor and the factor invariably collects the debts. In the second situation, the assignor maintains direct relations with its customers by continuing to collect the debts. The factor remains in the background with the proceeds of the debts being remitted to it. The distinction between legal and equitable assignment has some practical consequences in terms of actions against the debtor. Basically a legal assignee can sue a debtor in his name without involving the assignor in the proceedings, whereas in the case of an equitable assignment the assignor should be joined as a co-plaintiff if he is willing and as a co-defendant if he is not.[106] In certain circumstances, however, this rule may be waived.[107]

3.48 While the legal/equitable distinction may have some practical import, the difference between outright assignments on the one hand, whether legal or equitable, and charges, on the other, is of far more profound consequence. Factoring, or the outright sale of book debts, is a business that is outside the ambit of the company charge registration system.[108] As the Privy Council noted in *Chow Yoong Hong v Choong Fah Rubber Manufactory*:[109] 'There are many ways of raising cash besides borrowing. One is by selling book debts ...'

3.49 In *Welsh Development Agency v Export Finance Co Ltd*[110] Browne-Wilkinson V-C explained that it has been firmly established for many years that

---

106   *Weddell v JA Pearce & Major* [1988] Ch 26 at 40–41.

107   See *William Brandt's Sons & Co v Dunlop Rubber Co Ltd* [1905] AC 454; *Hendry v Chartsearch Ltd* [1998] CLC 1382; and see also *Raffeisen Zentralbank Österreich AG v Five Star* [2001] 3 All ER 257.

108   See generally on factoring F Salinger *Factoring Law and Practice* (Sweet & Maxwell, 3rd edn, 1999).

109   [1962] AC 209 at 216. See also the comments of Lord Scarman in *Lloyds & Scottish Finance Ltd v Cyril Lord Carpet Sales Ltd* [1992] BCLC 609 at 618–619:
       'Block discounting is a well known service offered by certain finance houses to traders who do a substantial business by way of hire-purchase or credit-sale agreements with their customers. Though there are variations in detail, the essential feature of the service is that in return for an immediate advance the trader sells to the finance house at a discount his interest in the agreements he has with his customers. The trader gives the house his guarantee of due performance by his customers of their obligations. He includes a number, often a very large number, of hire-purchase or credit-sale agreements in each discounting transaction: hence the City's name "block discounting" for this type of transaction. The service is similar to many other financial services offered in the City of London and elsewhere – an immediate advance of money against documents, which are purchased at a discount. It is an adaptation of the historic business of discounting bills and notes to the particular circumstances of the hire-purchase and credit-sale trade. The finance house looks only to the discount for his profit. Once the trader has met his commitment for the advance and the discount charge (out of the moneys received or receivable from his customers whose debts he has sold), the finance house is content that the trader should keep for himself whatever else is collected from the customers.'

110   [1990] BCC 393.

debt factoring agreements and agreements for the block sale of hire purchase agreements at a discount are not secured loans but sales. The respective rights of a finance and other creditors of the 'seller' depended entirely on the legal garb in which the finance house clothed the transaction. The judge went on to say:[111]

> 'The transaction is essentially the same in commercial terms whatever legal structure is adopted: the finance house has advanced money to a company in need of money on terms that the finance house is to recoup itself (either from a third party or from the borrower/seller) the sum advanced plus its "turn" on the deal. If the advance is by way of secured loan, it will be registrable: others dealing with the company will know of the secured position of the finance house and can adjust their dealings accordingly. If, on the other hand, the advance is by way of sale, the finance house is, in commercial terms, fully secured but others dealing with the company are ignorant of the fact.'

In the Court of Appeal in the same case Dillon LJ observed:[112]

> 'The essence of the transaction when a trader raises finance by factoring book debts or block discounting hire-purchase agreements is that the trader sells the book debts to a finance company for a price which is necessarily discounted from the full aggregate face value of the debts. It is discounted, primarily, because the trader will be getting an immediate payment, while the finance company will have to wait for the debts to come in from the debtors and they may well not be presently payable. Indeed with hire-purchase agreements the debt will be payable by the hirer by instalments over what may be a considerable period. The rate of discount will also no doubt take into account the risk the finance company is assuming that the debtor will fail to pay the debts; ... It is normal, therefore, that the rate of discount for the finance company will be calculated by reference to the appropriate rate of interest for the period for which the finance company is out of its money.'

Exploring the outright assignment/security interest distinction

3.50 While the distinction is of profound practical significance, often the difference between, for example, an equitable assignment of debts and a security interest in debts may seem like an exercise in splitting hairs. Nevertheless, the distinction was confirmed by the House of Lords in *Lloyds & Scottish Finance v Cyril Lord Carpet Sales*.[113] This is a case where Lloyd & Scottish (the factor) agreed to buy credit sale agreements from Cyril Lord (the assignor). The parties entered into a master trading agreement which was stated to govern all subsequent transactions. The trading agreement provided that every assignment of debts should be an absolute assignment and sale, and that it should be

---

111 [1990] BCC 393 at 405; and see also the view expressed by Staughton LJ when the case went on appeal: [1992] BCLC 148 at 185–186.
112 [1992] BCLC 148 at 165–166.
113 [1992] BCLC 609. The case was originally decided in 1979 and is reported at (1979) 129 NLJ 366. On the case see A Giddins 'Block Discounting – Sale or Charge' (1980) 130 NLJ 207.

in the form specified in a schedule to the master agreement. The purchase price was calculated as 80% of the balances due under the credit sale agreements purchased less a discount to be agreed from time to time. This discount was the factor's 'turn' or profit on the deal. The factor was entitled to give notice of assignment to the debtors but, at its discretion, however, it could choose not to do so, and, in that situation, the factor would continue to collect the debts as agent for the assignor. The assignor gave bills of exchange or banker's orders to the assignor in respect of an agreed percentage of the debts. This percentage was in practice always 80%, payable by 24 or 30 monthly instalments. 100% of the debts remained, of course, due to the factor, and the assignor guaranteed payment of this. A provision in the master trading agreement stated that upon fulfilment of the assignor's obligations in respect of all assignments, the factor would pay a further purchase price of what was, in effect, the further 20% of the value of the debts assigned. After entry into the trading agreement, 200 assignments of batches of credit sale agreements were carried out by the parties in the agreed form.

3.51   The House of Lords held that the transaction constituted a genuine sale and purchase of debts. In its view, the trading agreement formed the basis of the contract and all subsequent assignments took place subject to it. The circumstances indicated that when the original negotiations took place a lot of importance was placed on the trading agreement being executed before any assignment had been effected. The trading agreement was a central feature in the parties' contractual intentions and there was no evidence that they intended to execute an agreement for a loan secured by a charge. Lord Wilberforce stated quite clearly that the court should not scrutinise minutely documents so as to produce a contractual intention that was manifestly negated by the trading agreement and by other evidence.[114] He remarked that:[115]

'parties to discounting arrangements often confuse the terminology appropriate to such arrangements with that which describes loan transactions: in the present case there are frequent references to "advances", "repayments", or "credit lines" and one witness went so far as to say that in talking to ordinary men and women this language had to be used or they would not understand. It is regrettable that the artificial character of the substantive law should lead to these inaccuracies, but the courts have to look at the nature of the transaction which they profess to describe ... loose descriptions have become commercial vernacular.

3.52   The factor did not seek to recover the surplus of debts due above the 80% figure. Their sole objective was to collect the amount that they had paid to

---

114   The precedent value of three old cases was stressed by the House of Lords – *Re George Inglefield Ltd* [1933] 1 Ch 1; *Olds Discount Co Ltd v John Playfair Ltd* [1938] 3 All ER 275; and *Olds Discount Co Ltd v Cohen* [1938] 3 All ER 281n. Lord Wilberforce stated ([1992] BCLC 609 at 618):

'It cannot be denied that in some respects there were rough edges in the way that business was done; commercial practicality may have taken precedence over legal exactitude. But over the whole field, given the flexibility of the [master] trading agreement and the great number of transactions handled, I cannot find that the parties were not, in substance, carrying out the trading agreement.'

115   [1992] BCLC 609 at 616.

the assignor and, in addition, the service fee. The account in respect of an individual assignment was closed as soon as this amount was received, with the assignor collecting and keeping the balance. The House of Lords, however, likened this situation to one of set-off and said that the fact did not demonstrate the existence of a loan. The assignor was liable to account to the factor in respect of the 20% balance; yet under another clause in the trading agreement the factor was under an eventual obligation to pay to the assignor a further purchase price equivalent to that balance. It simplified matters if the assignor was allowed to retain the 20% balance rather than handing it over, and receiving an equivalent sum back, by way of payment of the additional purchase price. The fact that only 80% of the face value of the debts had to be paid by the buyer at the outset created in effect a form of reserve or protection for the buyer. Lord Wilberforce commented:[116]

> 'In block discounting "transactions", the purchaser is acquiring an asset (viz a book debt) which he did not create, as to the validity of which he has no knowledge, which he is not going to collect, and of any default in whose realisation he may be ignorant. He naturally requires a certain margin, or reserve, as is sometimes said, security to ensure, so far as possible, that he will get what he has bargained for. But it is a fallacy (into which the [dealer's] argument falls) to argue from this towards a conclusion that the transaction as a whole is one of security or charge. There are many contracts, of sale, or for building work, or otherwise, where some security is required by one party that the other will fulfil his promise. But this does not alter the nature of the contract itself or turn it into a contract by way of charge. In the present case, the fact the purchasers wanted guarantees, or security, or reserves, to ensure that they received the whole of what they had bought, cannot convert a transaction of purchase into one of charge.'

3.53   The *Lloyds & Scottish* case involved an example of non-notification factoring. Often this form of factoring seems suspiciously like the creation of a charge, and the same is true where factoring of debts is done on a recourse basis. This circumstance alone, however, will not lead to recharacterisation of the transaction by the courts.[117] In other words, the fact that the 'purchaser' of book debts has a right of recourse against the 'seller' of the debts in the event of the debtor's non-payment is not necessarily incompatible with the transaction being one of sale. An option to repurchase is viewed as being essentially different from an equity of redemption.[118]

3.54   The outright assignment/security assignment distinction also arises in the context of one-off transactions as well as under medium to long-term

---

116 [1992] BCLC 609 at 616.
117 For further exploration of the distinction between charges and factoring of debts see the judgment of Browne-Wilkinson V-C in *Welsh Development Agency v Export Finance Co Ltd* [1990] BCC 393.
118 See *Welsh Development Agency v Export Finance Co Ltd* [1992] BCLC 148 at 154 where Dillon LJ commented that factoring or block discounting amounts to a sale of book debts, rather than a charge on book debts, even though the purchaser of the debts under the relevant agreement is given recourse against the vendor in the event of default in payment by the debtors.

factoring arrangements. A leading authority is *Re Kent and Sussex Saw-mills Ltd*[119] where the transaction was held to fall on the 'security assignment' side of the line. This is a case where a company contracted with the Ministry of Fuel and Power for the supply of logs. Thereafter it was extended considerable overdraft facilities by its bank with the overdraft conditional on the company sending a letter to the Ministry directing them to pay all monies payable to the company under the contract, into the bank, to the company's account, such directions not to be revoked without the consent in writing of the bank. A subsequent contract with the Minister was financed by a letter in the same terms. It was held that the letters were assignments of book debts to the bank by way of security for the overdraft and not having been registered were void against the liquidator in the winding up. Wynn Parry J propounded a general rule. He said that prima facie, at any rate when one has to look at a document brought into existence between a borrower and a lender in connection with a transaction of borrowing and lending, one must approach the consideration of that document with the expectation of discovering that the document is intended to be given by the borrower to the lender in order to secure repayment of a proposed indebtedness of the borrower to the lender.[120] The important factor here was that the directions in the letters to the Ministry were revocable. Wynn-Parry J opined that the Ministry was in no way concerned with the position as between the bank and the company, and as between those two parties there was no ground, either at law or in equity, on which the bank could have resisted a request or a requirement by the company to cancel the instructions.

3.55 More recently, there appears to be a greater propensity on the part of the courts for inferring the existence of an absolute assignment of debts rather than a security assignment. *Re Kent and Sussex Sawmills*, for example, was distinguished in *Siebe Gorman & Co Ltd v Barclays Bank Ltd*.[121] In this case Siebe Gorman had supplied goods to a company and was owed for the same. The company, however, had bills of exchange payable over a period of six months for just less than the amount of the debt. The bills of exchange had been handed to Barclays Bank for collection. The company executed a deed assigning the bills to Siebe Gorman as 'security' for the debt owed to Siebe Gorman. It also sent a letter to Barclays Bank directing it to pay the proceeds of the bills direct to Siebe Gorman. This letter was expressed to be an irrevocable instruction. Was there an absolute assignment of the debts or an assignment by way of charge only? Slade J observed that the ultimate test of whether the document amounted to a charge was whether there could be discovered from the deed, either in express words or by necessary implication, an equity of redemption in the company. For this purpose the court should have regard to the substance of the transaction as reflected in the document, when properly construed, rather than the minutiae of particular phrases appearing in it.[122] In this particular case the irrevocable letter of mandate to

---

119 [1947] Ch 177.
120 [1947] Ch 177 at 181.
121 [1979] 2 Lloyd's Law Reports 142. The last is perhaps best known for the holding that it is possible to create a fixed charge over future book debts of a company. See also on this point *Re Keenan Bros Ltd* [1986] BCLC 242 and *Re Brightlife Ltd* [1987] Ch 200.
122 [1979] 2 Lloyd's Law Reports 142 at 161.

Barclays Bank, which could properly be regarded as forming part of the same transaction as the deed of assignment, was scarcely consistent with the existence of an equity of redemption.[123]

3.56 *Re Kent and Sussex Sawmills Ltd* was also distinguished in *Re Marwalt Ltd*.[124] This is a case where an exporter, BSC, had agreed to supply a Chilean company with tinplate. It sold the tinplate to Marwalt (which had export credit guarantee insurance) for on-sale at the same price. Marwalt was indemnified by the exporter and received a commission and expenses. The proceeds of sale were paid into a separate account at a bank which was under instructions to pay the sums credited to the account immediately to BSC. BSC contended that the proceeds belonged to it beneficially, whereas the bank argued that it was entitled to the monies either to set off against another account or under a debenture. The judge held that the arrangements between Marwalt and BSC involved an out and out assignment of future receipts and not an assignment by way of charge only and, furthermore, the bank had notice of the assignment. Moreover, the proceeds, having been assigned to BSC, were not in the beneficial ownership of Marwalt and were not available for set-off, nor were they caught by the debenture. The judge said there was one essential difference between *Re Kent and Sussex Sawmills Ltd*[125] and the present case. In *Re Kent and Sussex Sawmills Ltd* there was no correlation between the amount to be paid by the debtor to the creditor, and the amount due to the bank, which took the form of a fluctuating overdraft. Thus, the court was driven to the conclusion that it was a charge only, and accordingly void. But in the present case there was an exact correlation between the monies which were to come in from the Chilean company and the monies which were to go out to BSC.[126]

3.57 Nevertheless, the courts may still hold that what purports to be an absolute assignment of debts is, in reality, a security assignment. A case in point is *Orion Finance Ltd v Crown Financial Management Ltd*[127] where there was a full analysis of the relevant legal principles by Millett LJ. In this case it was held that what purported to be an absolute assignment of sub-rental income from an intermediate lessor to a head lessor was in reality a security assignment. It was intended to secure performance of the obligations due under the head lease and was properly characterised as a charge. Millett LJ said more generally:[128]

> 'The first task is to determine whether the documents are a sham intended to mask the true agreement between the parties. If so, the court must disregard the deceptive language by which the parties have attempted to conceal the true nature of the transaction into which they have entered and must attempt by extrinsic evidence to discover what the real transaction

---

123 *Re Kent and Sussex Sawmills Ltd* [1947] Ch 177 was distinguished.
124 [1992] BCC 32.
125 [1947] Ch 177.
126 [1992] BCC 32 at 41. The judge placed particular reliance on *Ashby, Warner & Co Ltd v Simmons* [1926] 2 All ER 697.
127 [1996] BCC 621; [1996] 2 BCLC 78.
128 [1996] 2 BCLC 78 at 84.

was ... Once the documents are accepted as genuinely representing the transaction into which the parties have entered, its proper legal categorisation is a matter of construction of the documents. This does not mean that the terms which the parties have adopted are necessarily determinative. The substance of the parties' agreement must be found in the language they have used; but the categorisation of a document is determined by the legal effect which it is intended to have, and if when properly construed the effect of the document as a whole is inconsistent with the terminology which the parties have used, then their ill-chosen language must yield to the substance.'

According to Millett LJ there is a presumption of conformity between form and substance, but this presumption was liable to be defeated. He said:[129]

'The question is not what the transaction is but whether it is in truth what it purports to be. Unless the documents taken as a whole compel a different conclusion, the transaction which they embody should be categorised in conformity with the intention which the parties have expressed in them.'

A FLOATING CHARGE ON THE WHOLE OR PART OF THE COMPANY'S PROPERTY

3.58   Section 396(1)(f) of the Companies Act 1985 renders registrable a floating charge on the company's undertaking or property. The unimplemented Part IV of the Companies Act 1989 revised this wording to make it clear that a floating charge over part only of the company's property was registrable. In fact, the redrafting process merely confirms the outcome of case law. In *Re Yorkshire Woolcombers Association Ltd*[130] Romer LJ said that for a charge to be a 'floating charge on the undertaking or property of the company' it could not be contended that it was essential that the charge must be on the whole undertaking, or on the whole property of the company. To the same effect is *Hoare v British Columbia Development Association*[131] where a company was negotiating an arrangement with various railway companies. The company charged all its rights and interests both present and future, under or by virtue of any such arrangement, and all profits therefrom. The business was run as if no such deed of covenant had been entered into, subject to the right of the charge holders to intervene. Thus, one had a floating charge over part only of the company's undertaking or property and it was held by Neville J to be registrable.[132]

3.59   There is no statutory definition of floating charge in s 396(1)(f) of CA 1985 and it is generally accepted that one must fall back on the common law definition. In *Smith v Bridgend County Borough Council*[133] Lord Scott seemed

---

129   [1996] 2 BCLC 78 at 85.
130   [1903] 2 Ch 284 at 294.
131   (1912) 107 LT 602.
132   See also *Mercantile Bank of India v Chartered Bank of India, Australia and China and Strauss & Co* [1937] 1 All ER 231 at 241.
133   [2002] 1 AC 336 at 357.

to suggest, however, that in the statutory context the definition of 'floating charge' may be broader than the traditional conception. He accepted that, at common law, the floating charge was a present security but said that this did not preclude the grant of future security rights from constituting a floating charge for s 395 registration purposes:

> 'In my opinion, a charge expressed to come into existence on the occurrence of an uncertain future event and then to apply to a class of assets that cannot be identified until the event has happened would, if otherwise valid, qualify for registration as a floating charge. The future charge would have the essential characteristic of floating, remaining dormant, until the occurrence of the specified event. It would, I think, come within the mischief sought to be dealt with by the section 395 requirement of registration of floating charges.'

The other judges, however, did not offer any support for this analysis and appeared to apply the common law definition of floating charge in the statutory setting. It is submitted that Lord Scott's reasoning, if followed, would introduce an undesirable degree of uncertainty. It is submitted also that the mischief he sought to address is adequately catered for by the fact that a floating charge, although a present security, can catch property rights that spring into existence at some future date.

Nature of a floating charge[134]

3.60 The seminal account of a floating charge is contained in the judgment of Romer LJ in *Re Yorkshire Woolcombers Association Ltd*[135] which refers to the nature of the assets over which the security is taken.[136] Romer LJ said:[137]

> '[If] a charge has the three characteristics that I am about to mention it is a floating charge. (1) If it is a charge on a class of assets of a company present and future; (2) if that class is one which, in the ordinary course of the business of the company, would be changing from time to time; and (3) if you find that, by the charge, it is contemplated that, until some future step is taken by or on behalf of those interested in the charge, the company may carry on business in the ordinary way as far as concerns the particular class of assets I am dealing with.'[138]

---

134 See generally on this area R Pennington 'The Genesis of the Floating Charge' (1960) 23 MLR 630; E Ferran 'Floating Charges – The Nature of the Security' [1988] CLJ 213; S Worthington 'Floating Charges: An Alternative Theory' [1994] CLJ 81 and R Nolan 'Property in a Fund' (2004) 120 LQR 108.

135 [1903] 2 Ch 284.

136 A floating charge was first mapped out by the Court of Appeal in Chancery in *Re Panama, New Zealand and Australian Royal Mail Co* (1870) 5 Ch App 318.

137 [1903] 2 Ch 284 at 295.

138 It should be stressed that it is the members of the class rather than the class itself which is changing.

3.61 *Re Yorkshire Woolcombers Association Ltd* was appealed to the House of Lords, where it is reported under the name of *Illingsworth v Houldsworth*.[139] There Lord MacNaghten drew a distinction between the fixed charge and the floating charge in the following terms:[140]

'A specific charge, I think, is one that without more fastens on ascertained and definite property or property capable of being ascertained and defined; a floating charge, on the other hand, is ambulatory and shifting in its nature, hovering over and so to speak floating with the property which it is intended to affect until some event occurs or some act is done which causes it to settle and fasten on the subject of the charge within its reach and grasp.'

3.62 There are difficulties, however, with this attempt at definition, principally on grounds of vagueness. Use of the words 'ambulatory' and 'shifting' mystify rather than enlighten. In fact Lord MacNaghten provided a more focused definition of the floating charge in the earlier case of *Governments Stock and other Securities Investment Co v Manila Railway Co*:[141]

'A floating security is an equitable charge on the assets for the time being of a going concern. It attaches to the subject charged in the varying condition in which it happens to be from time to time. It is of the essence of such a charge that it remains dormant until the undertaking charged ceases to be a going concern, or until the person in whose favour the charge is created intervenes.'

3.63 The essence of the floating charge is that it does not inhibit a company from disposing of assets within the category covered by the charge in the ordinary course of its business without reference to, or the consent of the person entitled to the benefit of the charge. A specific charge, on the other hand, prevents a company from disposing of an unencumbered title to the assets, the subject-matter of the charge. If a security giver purported to dispose of assets that were the subject of a fixed charge in the ordinary course of business, then this would constitute a breach of a covenant in the loan agreement, whether express or implied.[142] The security taker could appoint a receiver, whether under a provision contained in the debenture or via a court application, since the security is clearly in jeopardy. The English courts have been adamant that a floating charge is not a fixed charge coupled with

---

139 [1904] AC 355.
140 [1904] AC 355 at 358.
141 [1897] AC 81 at 86.
142 One commentator has talked about the 'mental block experienced by the courts in the early floating charge cases when they were quite unable to fathom the idea of a fixed mortgage or charge over trading assets coupled with a licence to dispose of those assets in the ordinary course of business' – see D McLauchlan (1999) 115 LQR 365 at 367.

a licence to deal.[143] As Buckley LJ explained in *Evans v Rival Granite Quarries Ltd*:[144]

'A floating security is not a future security, it is a present security, which presently affects all the assets of the company expressed to be included in it. On the other hand, it is not a specific security: the holder cannot affirm that the assets are specifically mortgaged to him. The assets are mortgaged in such a way that the mortgagor can deal with them without the concurrence of the mortgagee. A floating security is not a specific mortgage of the assets, plus a licence to the mortgagor to dispose of them in the course of his business but is a floating mortgage applying to every item until some event occurs or some act of the mortgagee is done which causes it to crystallise into a fixed security.'

3.64   This statement has been criticised on the basis that it asserts distinctions without a difference.[145] A floating charge is stated to be 'present' but not 'specific' and to 'apply' to the assets concerned from the date of creation, but not 'specifically affecting' them until crystallisation. Nevertheless, it is easy to be over-critical, for the element of mystery about the floating charge cannot be denied.[146] Once an instrument of charge has been executed, the floating charge is a presently existing security interest even though it does not attach to any specific property until crystallisation.[147] This seems a subtle distinction – presently existing but not attaching.[148] In one sense it seems to exist, yet on the other hand, it does not. The 'present existence' of the floating charge is demonstrated by three factors. First, if the floating charge extends over land the security instrument must comply with the formality requirements laid down in the Law of Property (Miscellaneous Provisions) Act 1989 and the predecessor provisions in the Law of Property Act 1925 on the basis that the agreement

---

143   According to P Ali *The Law of Secured Finance* (OUP, 2002) at p 121 the 'licence' theory of floating charges is 'now widely regarded as without any legitimate basis'; but cf R Calnan 'Priorities Between Execution Creditors and Floating Charges' (1982) 10 NZULR 111. For a slightly different perspective see R Nolan 'Property in a Fund' (2004) 120 LQR 108 at 117:

'The floating charge is a charge over a fund of assets, in the sense that the chargee has an immediate security interest in identified assets owned by the chargor, which is nevertheless subject to, and restricted by, the superior but limited power of the chargor (as owner) to manage and alienate those assets free of the chargee's interest. In addition, the chargee will almost invariably have security in identifiable future assets if, as and when acquired by the chargor.'

This perspective, however, may be somewhat difficult to reconcile with *Re Leyland Daf Ltd: Buchler v Talbot* [2004] 2 AC 298.

144   [1910] 2 KB 979 at 999. See also *Re Gregory Love & Co* [1916] 1 Ch 203.

145   See R Calnan 'Floating Charges: A Proposal for Reform' [2004] Butterworths Journal of International Banking and Financial Law 341.

146   See generally R Goode 'The Exodus of the Floating Charge' in D Feldman and F Meisel (eds) *Corporate and Commercial Law: Modern Developments* (Lloyds of London Press, 1996) 193 at 203.

147   See also the observations of Kekewich J in *Brunton v Electrical Engineering Corpn* [1892] 1 Ch 434 at 440.

148   Note the statement of Dixon J in *Barcelo v Electrolytic Zinc Co of Australasia Ltd* (1932) 48 CLR 391 at 420 that 'some degree of abstraction is involved in this description of the operation of a floating charge as a present security over assets.'

creates an immediately subsisting 'interest in land'.[149] Secondly, the floating charge holder can apply for an injunction to restraint the debtor from disposing of assets otherwise than in the ordinary course of business.[150] Thirdly, and this covers largely the same territory as the second point, the floating charge holder has an inherent right to apply to the court for the appointment of a receiver if his security is in jeopardy.[151] Finally, the overall message is further reinforced by an analysis of the priority picture that arises when two floating charges containing after-acquired property clauses, are in competition. Assuming that both have been duly registered, the first in point of time prevails,[152] whereas if there was no security agreement in existence until the property came into existence, one would assume that the two agreements would rank equally. The answer lies in the fact that from the very moment that the first security instrument is executed there is a presently existing security. As one commentator puts the matter:

> 'In other words, it creates an inchoate security interest which is waiting for the asset to be acquired so that it can fasten on to the asset but which, upon acquisition of the asset, takes effect as from the date of the security agreement.'[153]

The fixed/floating charge distinction

3.65   The fact that all floating charges require registration but fixed charges require registration only if they are specifically set out in s 396 of the Companies Act 1985 provides merely one reason for distinguishing between fixed and floating charges over property.[154] There are many other reasons for making the distinction. Firstly, under Insolvency Act 1986, ss 239 and 245 the floating charge is more vulnerable to challenge in a liquidation than a fixed charge. Both fixed and floating charges as well as other forms of transaction are subject to attack under s 239, which renders voidable acts or things done by an insolvent company in the period immediately prior to liquidation or administration which have the effect of putting a creditor in a better position than it would occupy in the event of the company's insolvent liquidation and where the company was influenced by a desire to prefer the creditor or a guarantor for the debt. The relevant period is six months generally but two

---

149 *Driver v Broad* [1893] 1 QB 744; *Wallace v Evershed* [1899] 1 Ch 891.

150 *Re Woodroffes (Musical Instruments) Ltd* [1986] Ch 366 at 377–378 per Nourse J; *Tricontinental Corpn Ltd v Commissioner of Taxation* [1988] 1 Qd R 474 at 484.

151 *McMahon v North Kent Ironworks Co* [1891] 2 Ch 148; *Edwards v Standard Rolling Stock Syndicate* [1893] 1 Ch 574; *Re Victoria Steamboats Ltd* [1897] I Ch 158; *Re London Pressed Hinge Co Ltd* [1905] 1 Ch 576; *Norton v Yates* [1906] 1 KB 112; and see generally WJ Gough Company Charges (London, Butterworths, 2nd edn, 1996) at pp 132–134.

152 *Re Benjamin Cope & Sons Ltd* [1914] 1 Ch 800; but cf *Re Automatic Bottle Makers Ltd* [1926] Ch 412.

153 RM Goode *Legal Problems of Credit and Security* (London, Sweet & Maxwell, 3rd edn, 2003) at p 70.

154 See generally R Calnan 'Floating Charges: A Proposal for Reform' [2004] Butterworths Journal of International Banking and Financial Law 341 at 345–346.

years where the transaction is in favour of a person connected with the company. Such a person has also the onus of establishing that the company was not influenced by a desire to prefer.

3.66 The 'influenced by a desire' criterion has been interpreted as requiring a subjective wish to improve the creditor's position.[155] Objective intention is not enough. Moreover, if the preference has been produced by pressure on the part of the creditor it seems that the element of pressure negates the requisite desire.[156] The 'influenced by a desire' requirement means that in practice there is very little chance of setting aside transactions unless the benefit has gone to a connected person. On the other hand, floating charges alone are caught by the more draconian and far-reaching Insolvency Act 1986, s 245. This provision invalidates floating charges granted by insolvent companies to secure past indebtedness in the 12-month period prior to liquidation or administration. Once again, where the beneficiary of the security is a connected person, challenges become easier, but the major limitation on the operation of s 245 is its restriction to floating charges.[157]

3.67 Secondly, the fixed charge outranks the floating charge for priority purposes. Where there are two charges over the same property; one fixed and one floating, the fixed charge holder will generally prevail over the floating charge holder in any priority battle. This has given rise to the expression 'The fixed charge for priority; the floating charge for control'.

3.68 Thirdly, under what is now s 176A of the Insolvency Act 1986, introduced by the Enterprise Act 2002, s 252, a proportion of set floating charge recoveries are set aside for the benefit of unsecured creditors.[158] The percentage is calculated on a sliding scale basis and constitutes 50% of the first £10,000, then 20% of the remainder but subject to an overall ceiling of £600,000 so that the fund for unsecured creditors will not in any case exceed £600,000.[159] The set aside provisions, however, only operate in respect of floating charges. If a security taker has the benefit of a fixed charge, its security will not be subject to the carve-out for unsecured creditors. Fourthly, preferential claims are payable out of floating charge assets in priority to the floating charge holder, though

---

155 *Re MC Bacon Ltd* [1990] BCC 78.

156 The Cork Committee (1982, Cmnd 8558) at para 1256 suggested that pressure for payment by the creditor should continue, as under the former law, to afford a defence to a claim for the avoidance of a preference.

157 The Cork Committee (para 1553) suggested that this was a desirable limitation as the floating charge could potentially extend to future assets not yet paid for by the company, whereas the fixed charge is restricted to existing assets of the company. The position could be criticised on the basis that the dichotomy postulated by the Cork Committee does not exist. See generally on this Howard Bennett 'Late Floating Charges' in J Armour and H Bennett (eds) *Vulnerable Transactions in Corporate Insolvency* (Hart Publishing, 2003) 183 at 184–186.

158 The Enterprise Act abolished Crown Preference and the fund for unsecured creditors was established as a balancing measure to ensure that the benefits of the abolition did not enure exclusively for the benefit of unsecured creditors. The fund has its origins in a recommendation of the Cork Committee on Insolvency Law and Practice (Cmnd 8558 at para 1538) that 10% of net realisations of property subject to a floating charge should be set aside for unsecured creditors.

159 Insolvency (Prescribed Part) Order 2003 (SI 2003/2097).

the latter can recoup itself out of the free assets of the company to the extent that these assets are sufficient to satisfy the claims secured by the floating charge.[160] In *Re Leyland Daf Ltd: Buchler v Talbot*[161] the House of Lords, however, made it clear that the general costs and expenses of liquidation could not be paid out of floating charge realisations in the same way that they cannot be paid out of fixed charge realisations. Lord Millett said:[162]

> 'In considering the incidence of the costs and expenses of the winding up it must be borne in mind that there are two distinct funds: (i) the proceeds of the free assets which belong to the company and are administered by the liquidator in a winding up and (ii) the proceeds of the assets comprised in a floating charge which belong to the charge holder to the extent of the security and are administered by the receiver. In principle ... the costs of administering each fund are borne by the fund in question.'

Leyland Daf was decided on the basis that floating charge assets constitute a separate fund distinct from the company's own assets and that the charge holder 'owns' these assets.

3.69   Fifthly, in an administration it appears that under Sch B1, para 99(3) of the Insolvency Act 1986 the administrator's remuneration and expenses are payable out of floating charge assets in priority to the floating charge holder, but these items cannot be paid in the same way out of fixed charge assets.[163]

3.70   Finally, under the Insolvency Act 1986 the holder of a floating charge over the whole or substantially the whole of a company's assets was given the power to appoint an administrative receiver out-of-court over the assets of a company, and also the power to block the appointment of an administrator.[164] These powers, it seems, were conferred on the holder of an all-assets floating charge because of the possibility that an administrator might continue trading, deplete the assets of the company and run up large expenses that would be payable ahead of the floating charge holder. The Enterprise Act 2002 has changed the position somewhat by removing the right to appoint an administrative receiver in the generality of cases but also substituting a new right to

---

160 Insolvency Act 1986, ss 40 and 175.
161 [2004] 2 AC 298. For criticism of the decision see See Riz Mokal 'Liquidation expenses and floating charges – the separate funds fallacy' [2004] LMCLQ 387 and V Selvam 'Questioning Fundamentals: *Leyland Daf* and the "Ownership" of Charged Property' (2004) 67 MLR 832. The decision has been criticised on the basis that it ignores the fundamental nature of a 'charge'. As traditionally understood, a charge does not involve the transfer of ownership as such to the charge holder but merely gives the latter a right of recourse to the property for payment of the debt or performance of the obligation secured. Nevertheless, in defence of the doctrinal merits of the decision, one might say that a charge holder possesses 'property' or 'ownership' rights. While the charge holder may not own the property of the company, the charge holder clearly owns 'something', whatever that 'something' is. The charge holder is not confined to merely personal rights against the company. Without stretching metaphysics too far, it hardly seems farfetched to say that the charge holder has 'ownership' rights in something that constitutes a separate fund.
162 [2004] 2 AC 298 at [62].
163 See also Insolvency Act 1986, s 19.
164 Insolvency Act 1986, ss 8, 9 and 29.

appoint an administrator out-of-court.[165] The company itself also has such a right to make an out-of-court appointment but, in this instance, prior notice must be given to a qualifying floating charge holder and the latter can then choose to make its own appointment.[166] In court proceedings for the appointment of an administrator, a qualifying charge holder can also intervene and apply for the appointment of a particular person. The court is obliged to accede to this application unless it 'thinks it right to refuse the application because of the particular circumstances of the case.'[167]

Freedom to deal with charged assets

3.71   Although the nature of the property charged provides a reasonably safe guide for characterising the type of security as fixed or floating, it is not a completely reliable guide. The trend of the case law focuses more on the management autonomy that a floating charge confers on the security giver. With a floating charge, the security giver has management autonomy with respect to the assets within the security umbrella until that autonomy is brought to an end by a process known as crystallisation, whereupon the floating charge becomes fixed.[168]

3.72   The freedom on the part of the debtor to deal with assets in the ordinary course of business in the case of a floating charge was considered in *Re Cosslett Contractors*.[169] In *Cosslett* the Court of Appeal were faced with provisions in a construction contract which provided that the contractor's plant, goods and materials when on site should 'be deemed to be the property of the employer'. Plant etc could not be removed from the site. It was also provided that if the contractor should become bankrupt or abandon the site, the employer upon giving seven days' notice in writing could enter upon the site and expel the contractor therefrom and himself complete the works, or employ another contractor to complete the works and use the plant etc for this purpose. The employer was also empowered to sell the plant etc and apply the proceeds of sale towards satisfaction of the sums due to him from the contractor.

3.73   The Court of Appeal decided that the council's right to retain possession of the plant and use it to complete the works did not constitute an equitable charge because it did not give the council a proprietary interest in the plant but only rights of possession and use. Neither was it by way of security. Millett LJ said:[170]

---

165   Insolvency Act 1986, ss 72A–H (which were added by Enterprise Act 2002, s 250) and Sch B1 which contains the substantive law on new-style administrations.
166   Insolvency Act 1986, Sch B1, paras 22–26.
167   Insolvency Act 1986, Sch B1, para 36.
168   [1904] AC 355 at 358. The floating charge has been described as an instrument of power and mystery, and part of the mysterious aura derives from the concepts of crystallisation and automatic crystallisation – see generally R Goode 'The Exodus of the Floating Charge' in D Feldman and F Meisel (eds) *Corporate and Commercial Law: Modern Developments* (Lloyds of London Press, 1996) 193 at 203.
169   [1998] Ch 495.
170   [1998] Ch 495 at 508.

'It is of the essence of a charge that a particular asset or class of assets is appropriated to the satisfaction of a debt or other obligation of the charger or a third party, so that the chargee is entitled to look to the asset and its proceeds for the discharge of the liability. This right creates a transmissible interest in the asset. A mere right to retain possession of an asset and to make use of it for a particular purpose does not create such an interest and does not constitute a charge.'

3.74 Millett LJ added more fundamentally that the right at issue in this particular case did not constitute a charge or other kind of security interest because it did not secure the performance of the contract by the company but merely enabled the council to perform the contract in its place. On the other hand, the right to sell the plant and to apply the proceeds in discharge of any indebtedness due from the council to the company did constitute a charge. The court decided that this charge was floating rather than fixed in nature. Millett LJ observed:[171]

'The essence of a floating charge is that it is a charge, not on any particular asset, but on a fluctuating body of assets which remain under the management and control of the chargor, and which the chargor has the right to withdraw from the security despite the existence of the charge. The essence of a fixed charge is that the charge is on a particular asset or class of assets which the chargor cannot deal with free from the charge without the consent of the chargee. The question is not whether the chargor has complete freedom to carry out his business as he chooses, but whether the chargee is in complete control of the charged assets.'

3.75 In this particular case the company's business was to carry out civil engineering works, and in prohibiting the company from removing from the site plant or materials that was required for the completion of the works, the council was restricting the way in which the company could carry on business. This restriction, however, bore no relation to the council's security in that the council's purpose was to ensure that the company would give proper priority to the completion of the works and a similar restriction would have been appropriate where the company had not taken any security interest. The relevant provisions of the contract constituted a floating charge which was void for want of registration in the company's liquidation.

3.76 In *Re Cimex Tissues Ltd*[172] a 'badly-drafted' debenture[173] expressly created a fixed charge over plant and machinery used in the company's manufacturing business. There was a further provision that the company should not 'sell, mortgage or otherwise deal with the charged property' otherwise than for the purpose of getting in and realising such property in the ordinary course of, and for the purposes of, carrying on the trading business, except with the consent in writing of the lender. The court held that the licence giving the chargor limited power to deal with the charged assets was not inconsistent with the charge being fixed. The extent to which a licence to deal

---

171   [1998] Ch 495 at 510.

172   [1995] 1 BCLC 409.

173   See the comments of the judge, Stanley Burnton QC, at paras 6, 15 and 16.

was incompatible with a fixed charge depended on all the circumstances of the case and, in particular, on the scope of the licence and the nature of the charged property.

3.77 It has been held that the existence of a right on the part of a chargor unilaterally to require a chargee to release property from a charge does not transform what is otherwise a fixed charge into a floating charge.[174] In *Re Queen's Moat Houses plc* Lightman J suggested that there is a critical difference between the right of a corporate chargor to deal with and dispose of a property free from a charge without reference to the chargee and the right of a corporate chargor to require the chargee to release the charged property from the charge and to substitute alternative security of equal value.[175]

3.78 In *Ashborder BV v Green Gas Power Ltd*[176] Etherton J suggested that what must be ascertained, as a matter of standard interpretation of written documents, is whether, on the language used, the express power to dispose of assets in the ordinary course of business was limited to particular assets or applied to all assets of the company. In this context, while the nature of the assets in question forms part of the factual background against which the standard process of documentary interpretation takes place, the ordinary and natural meaning of the words used is the primary touchstone. Where there was no express provision permitting disposals in the ordinary course of business, the nature of the charged assets assumed a much greater significance in establishing whether the intention was to create a fixed charge or a floating charge over the assets in question.

3.79 Like the Privy Council in *Countrywide Banking Corpn Ltd v Dean*[177] Etherton J in *Ashborder* did not attempt any particular formulation of the test for determining whether a transaction falls within the ordinary course of a company's business for the purpose of a floating charge, or to make any comprehensive statement of the criteria for determining when a transaction is to be held to have taken place in the ordinary course of business for that purpose. On the other hand, he did suggest that the following were relevant considerations:[178]

> '(1) The question whether a particular transaction is within the ordinary course of a company's business in the context of a floating charge is a mixed question of fact and law; (2) it is convenient to approach the matter in a two stage process; (3) first, to ascertain, as a matter of fact, whether an objective observer, with knowledge of the company, its memorandum of association and its business, would view the transaction as having taken place in the ordinary course of its business, and, if so (4) second, to

---

174 *Re Queen's Moat Houses plc* [2004] NPC 67.
175 [2004] NPC 67 at [27].
176 [2004] EWHC 1517.
177 [1998] AC 338. The Privy Council emphasised the diversity of contexts in which courts had given consideration to 'the ordinary course of business'. Some were in relation to statutory provisions concerning fraudulent preference and personal and corporate insolvency, whereas others concerned the disposal of assets subject to a floating charge.
178 [2004] EWHC 1517 at [227].

consider whether, on the proper interpretation of the document creating the floating charge, applying standard techniques of interpretation, the parties nonetheless did not intend that the transaction should be regarded as being in the ordinary course of the company's business for the purpose of the charge; (5) subject to any such special considerations resulting from the proper interpretation of the charge document, there is no reason why an unprecedented or exceptional transaction cannot, in appropriate circumstances, be regarded as in the ordinary course of the company's business; (6) subject to any such special considerations, the mere fact that a transaction would, in a liquidation, be liable to be avoided as a fraudulent or otherwise wrongful preference of one creditor over others, does not, of itself, necessarily preclude the transaction from being in the ordinary course of the company's business; (7) nor does the mere fact that a transaction was made in breach of fiduciary duty by one or more directors of the company; (8) such matters in (6) and (7) may, however, where appropriate and in all the circumstances, be among the factors leading to the conclusion that the transaction was not in the ordinary course of the company's business; (9) transactions which are intended to bring to an end, or have the effect of bringing to an end, the company's business are not transactions in the ordinary course of its business.'

Fixed and floating charge over receivables

3.80   Notwithstanding the longevity of the floating charge, the precise parameters of the floating charge have provoked some controversy from the 1970s onwards. The reason appears to have been the increase in the extent and monetary limits of preferential claims. In a receivership or liquidation, statute declares that preferential creditors should be paid ahead of the floating charge holder,[179] but fixed charges enjoy priority over preferential creditors as a matter of general law. In this climate secured creditors tried to outflank preferential creditors by expanding the territory of the fixed charge so as to take up ground traditionally occupied by the floating charge.[180]

3.81   The scope for boundary dispute litigation was highlighted by Hoffmann J in *Re Brightlife Ltd*[181] who said that a floating charge, like many other legal concepts, was not susceptible of being defined by the enumeration of an exhaustive set of necessary and sufficient conditions. One could enumerate its standard characteristics but it did not follow that the absence of one or more features or the presence of others would prevent the charge from being categorised as 'floating'. In his view there are bound to be penumbral cases in which it may be difficult to say whether the degree of deviation from the

---

179   Sections 40 and 175 of the Insolvency Act 1986.
180   See the comments of Lord Millett in *Re Brumark Ltd: Agnew v Commissioner of Inland Revenue* [2001] 2 AC 710 at [17]:
> 'By the 1970s, however, the banks had become disillusioned with the floating charge. The growth in the extent and amount of the preferential debts, due in part to increases in taxation and in part to higher wages and greater financial obligations to employees, led banks to explore ways of extending the scope of their fixed charges.'
181   [1987] Ch 200.

standard case is enough to make it inappropriate to use such a term. He added that the rights and duties which the law may or may not categorise as a floating charge are wholly derived from the agreement of the parties, supplemented by the terms implied by law. It was fallacious to argue that once the parties have agreed on some terms which are thought sufficient to identify the transaction as a floating charge, they are then precluded from agreeing to any other terms that were not present in the standard case.

3.82 A floating charge is clearly compatible with some restrictions on the debtor's management autonomy.[182] For example, the existence of a negative pledge provision in the security documentation does not turn what would otherwise be a floating charge into a fixed charge. The real issue is about how extensive these restrictions must be before the charge becomes a fixed charge. It is clear, however, that characterisation of the nature of a security interest by the parties is not conclusive. To use an analogy, and to borrow language used in a different context, a four-pronged instrument for manual digging cannot be changed into a spade merely by the parties calling it a spade.[183] If a security agreement has the usual attributes of a floating charge in terms of debtor autonomy, the parties cannot transform the agreement into a fixed charge merely by labelling it as such. There is a whole line of cases, particularly in the context of receivables financing, where the courts have disregarded the characterisation applied to a security interest by the parties and instead construed the parties' agreement in the round and in the light of the surrounding circumstances.[184]

3.83 Regard must be had to the general commercial background and the intention of the parties as construed objectively. It is arguable, however, that the controversial decision of Slade J in *Siebe Gorman & Co Ltd v Barclays Bank Ltd*[185] minimised the significance of what the parties intended to happen in practice. In *Siebe Gorman* the relevant debenture purported to create a fixed charge on existing and future debts owing to the charger and also contained a negative pledge clause – the company was prohibited from charging or assigning the debts in favour of anybody else other than the bank. Slade J was more persuaded, however, by a third feature of the debenture which obliged the debtor, even before the bank had taken any steps to enforce its security, to pay into the debtor's account with the bank all monies which it might receive in respect of the debts. While there were no express prohibitions on withdrawals from this account, Slade J held that the debenture on its true construction gave the bank rights to prevent the company from spending in the ordinary course of business all or any of the proceeds of book debts paid into the account.

---

182 See the comments of Hoffmann J in *Re Brightlife Ltd* [1987] Ch 200 at 209:

> 'But a floating charge is consistent with some restriction upon the company's freedom to deal with its assets. [F]loating charges commonly contain a prohibition upon the creation of other charges ranking prior to or pari passu with the floating charge.'

Professor John Farrar has suggested that restrictive clauses may be inconsistent with the nature of a floating charge, but reaches the conclusion that 'it would now seem too late for the point to be raised': (1974) 38 Conv (NS) 315 at 318.

183 See the judgment of Lord Templeman in *Street v Mountford* [1985] AC 809.

184 Cases like *Re Brumark Ltd: Agnew v CIR* [2001] 2 AC 710.

185 [1979] 2 Lloyd's Rep 142.

Were this not so, he would have been inclined to regard the charge, for all the wording of the debenture, as doing no more than 'hovering over' and, so to speak, floating with the book debts.

3.84 In *Siebe Gorman* inferences were made about the spending of debt proceeds that ultimately proved decisive in the resolution of the fixed/floating charge debate. Hoffmann J was not prepared, however, to make similar inferences in *Re Brightlife Ltd*.[186] In this case the debenture described the charge as a first specific charge and the chargor was not allowed to sell, factor or discount the debts without the written consent of the chargee. There was no provision referring to collection of debts or disposal of the proceeds thereof other than a general clause that the chargor should not deal with the debts 'otherwise than in the ordinary course of getting in and realising the same'. Hoffmann J pointed out that a floating charge was consistent with some restriction on the company's freedom to deal with its assets. Such charges commonly contained a prohibition on the creation of other charges ranking prior to or pari passu with the floating charge. According to Hoffmann J the chargor was free to collect its debts and pay the proceeds into its bank account and, once in the account, they would be outside the charge over debts and at the free disposal of the company. He went on to say that a 'right to deal in this way with the charged assets for its own account is a badge of a floating charge and is inconsistent with a fixed charge.'[187]

3.85 The *Brightlife* decision allows proper leeway for the operation of party autonomy or contractual freedom – call it what you will – but the parties must set out clearly what they want. The courts cannot give effect to unexpressed intentions that run counter to what is likely to happen in commercial practice. This philosophy also seems to underlie *Re Brumark Ltd: Agnew v Commissioner of Inland Revenue*[188] where the Privy Council suggested that restrictions on debt proceeds withdrawals must be real and substantial in practice. In other words, a charge on book debts could be a fixed charge if the proceeds of the debts collected by the chargor were required to be paid into a blocked account with the charge holder. Lord Millett said:[189]

> 'Such an arrangement is inconsistent with the charge being a floating charge, since the debts are not available to the company as a source of its cash flow. But their Lordships would wish to make it clear that it is not enough to provide in the debenture that the account is a blocked account if it is not operated as one in fact.'

---

186 [1987] Ch 200. See also *Hart v Barnes* (1982) 7 ACLR 310; *Supercool Refrigeration and Air Conditioning v Hoverd Industries Ltd* [1994] 3 NZLR 300; *Re Cosslett (Contractors) Ltd* [1998] Ch 495.

187 [1987] Ch 200 at 209.

188 [2001] 2 AC 710; and see also the decision of the House of Lords in *Smith v Bridgend County Borough Council* [2002] 1 AC 336.

189 [2001] 2 AC 710 at [48].

3.86 Subsequently, in *Smith v Bridgend County Borough Council* the House of Lords endorsed *Brumark* in general terms about the degree of control that must be exercised by a charge holder before a charge can be characterised as a floating charge.[190]

3.87 Somewhat surprisingly, the Court of Appeal has now taken a different approach in *NatWest Bank plc v Spectrum Plus Ltd*.[191] The Court of Appeal said that Slade J could properly have held in *Siebe Gorman* that the charge on book debts created by the debenture was a fixed charge simply because of the requirements (i) that the book debts should not be disposed of prior to collection and (ii) that, on collection, the proceeds should be paid to the bank itself. A fortiori, Slade J was entitled to hold that the debenture, imposing (as he found) restrictions on the use of the proceeds of book debts, created a fixed charge over the book debts.[192]

3.88 More generally, Lord Phillips MR in *Spectrum* said:[193]

'I do not consider it satisfactory that the limited restraint that Slade J held arose under the debenture should be the critical factor in determining whether the charge should be categorised as a fixed or a floating charge. It seems to me that it is at least arguable that a debenture which prohibits a chargor from disposing of book debts before they are collected and requires him to pay them, beneficially to the chargee as and when they are collected properly falls within the definition of a fixed charge, regardless of the extent of his contractual right to draw out sums equivalent to the amounts paid in. Strictly speaking the chargor is neither entitled to dispose of the book debts before they fall due for payment, nor to dispose of the proceeds. What he does enjoy are contractual rights to payments, whether as a lender or as a borrower, from the bank. The extent to which, at any moment in time, a bank is contractually bound to permit a customer who has charged his book debts to make withdrawals which are back to back with the amounts of book debts collected will depend upon the terms of the contract between banker and customer and possibly on the financial

---

190 *Smith v Bridgend County Borough Council* [2002] 1 AC 336 involves further litigation arising out of the same set of facts as *Re Cosslett (Contractors) Ltd*: Lord Hoffmann said (at [41]):
'I do not see how a right to sell an asset belonging to a debtor and appropriate the proceeds to payment of the debt can be anything other than a charge. And because the property ... (constructional plant, temporary works, goods and materials on the site) was a fluctuating body of assets which could be consumed or (subject to the approval of the engineer) removed from the site in the ordinary course of the contractor's business, it was a floating charge: see *Agnew* ... [T]he intentions of the parties ... are relevant only to establish their mutual rights and obligations. Whether such rights and obligations are characterised as a floating charge is a question of law (see *Agnew*'s case ...). The answer to this question may come as a surprise to the parties but that is no reason for adopting a different characterisation.'
191 [2004] Ch 337. The case has already generated a very extensive literature and for a very small sample of relevant comment see A Berg [2004] JBL 581; F Oditah (2004) 120 LQR 533. It should be noted that the Court of Appeal overturned the decision of Morritt V-C who held at first instance that *Siebe Gorman* was wrongly decided.
192 [2004] Ch 337 at [96].
193 [2004] Ch 337 at [94].

consequences of mutual dealings. It is not satisfactory that the categorisation of a charge created by a debenture should turn upon the precise details of a bank's relationship with its customer.'

Lord Phillips added that for 25 years parties have used the form of debenture used in *Siebe Gorman* in reliance upon the understanding that its meaning and effect was that accorded to it by Slade J. In the circumstances he was inclined to hold that the debenture had, by customary usage, acquired the meaning and effect that had been attributed to it.[194] It is submitted that the *Spectrum* decision is difficult to defend in the light of *Brumark* and it is questionable whether the reasoning will withstand an appeal to the House of Lords.

3.89   Central to the fixed/floating charge characterisation debate is an unresolved tension in that the lender wishes to have a fixed charge but the borrower wants to be able to use the proceeds of charged debts in the ordinary course of its business. Legal doctrine, however, insists that some restrictions on this freedom are necessary before a fixed charge label can properly be attached to the security interest. One might attempt to square the circle by imposing formal restrictions on debt proceeds withdrawals but, simultaneously, establishing a 'consent to withdrawls' procedure whereby the borrower can, in practice, benefit from having collected the debts. Alternatively, a lender might suspend the operation of direct control over the bank account into which the proceeds of book debts are paid, thus permitting the company to carry on trading in a more normal fashion than strict compliance with the terms of a fixed charge would permit.

3.90   On the other hand, there is another general principle that a contract like a debenture should be interpreted against its general commercial context. If the parties never seriously intended that restrictions in a debenture should operate, then this is part of the general business backdrop and points to a floating charge construction. In *Investors Compensation Scheme v West Bromwich Building Society*[195] Lord Hoffmann formulated some general principles concerning the construction of contractual documents and if these are translated into the fixed/floating charge context they point unequivocally to the conclusion that a so-called blocked account must be operated as one in practice before a fixed charge designation can be upheld. Lord Hoffmann described interpretation as the ascertainment of the meaning which the document would convey to a reasonable person having all the background knowledge that would reasonably have been available to the parties in the situation in which they were at the time of the contract. He said:

'This background includes anything which would have affected the way in which the language of the document would have been understood by a reasonable man. The background may not merely enable the reasonable man to choose between the possible meaning of words which are ambiguous but even to conclude that the parties must, for whatever reason, have used the wrong words or syntax. The rule that words should be given their

---

194   [2004] Ch 337 at [97]. The Irish Supreme Court, however, took a different view on the interpretation of a similarly worded debenture in *Re Holidair Ltd* [1994] IR 416.
195   [1998] 1 WLR 896 at 912–913.

natural and ordinary meaning reflected the common sense proposition that we do not easily accept that people have made linguistic mistakes, particularly in formal documents. Nevertheless, if one could conclude from the background that something must have gone wrong with the language, the law does not require judges to attribute to the parties an intention which they plainly could not have had. The law however excludes from the admissible background the previous negotiations of the parties and their declarations of subjective intent.'

Combined fixed/floating charges

3.91 As far as the lender is concerned, the ideal state of affairs is that the borrower should have freedom to conduct normal business operations while solvent but combined with servitude to the lender while insolvent.[196] In *Re New Bullas Trading Ltd*[197] a debenture purported to create a fixed charge on book debts while uncollected and to combine this with a floating charge on the proceeds of the debts. *New Bullas* has been criticised on the basis that the distinction between the book debts before collection and after realisation is unrealistic and artificial and that the characterisation of a security over book debts cannot be divorced from contractual provisions relating to the application of the proceeds.[198] As one commentator suggests:[199]

'The distinctive feature of debts as an object of security is that they are realised by payment, upon which they cease to exist. If the chargor is authorised to collect them, then so long as his authority to do so continues, the only way in which the chargee can assert his security interest as a fixed interest is through the proceeds. It is by a contractual provision controlling the proceeds that the chargee establishes that the debts themselves are collected for his account, not for that of the chargor. Without such a contractual control, the chargee's supposed fixed security over the debts has no meaning, for the chargor is then collecting the debts for his own account.'

3.92 There is force in these criticisms of *New Bullas* but, on the other hand, a book debt is clearly worth something in money terms if it is sold as distinct from being collected. Moreover, in a number of different contexts, debts and debt proceeds have been treated as separate items of property. The courts, for

---

196 The debenture that was used and judicially approved in *Re New Bullas Trading Ltd* [1994] 1 BCLC 485 appeared to combine these ideals in an admirable fashion. As was stated (at 487): 'There being usually no need to deal with it before collection, [a company's book debt] is at that stage a natural subject of the fixed charge. But once collected, the proceeds being needed for the conduct of the business, it becomes a natural subject of the floating charge. While the company is a going concern, it is no less an advantage to the lender that the debt should be collected and the proceeds used in the business. But on insolvency, a crystallised floating charge on proceeds which, in the event supposed, are all the more likely to have been dissipated, may be worthless; whereas a fixed charge enabling the lender to intercept payment to the company may be of real value.'

197 [1994] 1 BCLC 485.

198 'Charges over Book Debts: A Missed Opportunity' (1994) 110 LQR 592.

199 Ibid at 602.

example, have held that a contractual prohibition on the assignment of debts does not prevent the assignee from having to account for the proceeds of the debts, once received, to the assignor.[200] This conclusion strongly suggests that debts and debt proceeds are being viewed as comprising distinct items of property.

3.93　On the other hand, the Privy Council in *Re Brumark Ltd* clearly held that it is not possible, practically speaking, to create a fixed charge over uncollected book debts and to couple this in the same debenture with a floating charge on the proceeds of realisation of these debts. In deciding whether a charge over receivables was fixed or floating one had to consider what was going to happen to the proceeds of the receivables.[201]

A CHARGE ON A SHIP OR AIRCRAFT, OR ANY SHARE IN A SHIP

3.94　This category of charge is made registrable by s 396(1)(h) of the Companies Act 1985 with the registrar of companies, but there are also parallel systems of specialist registers. The Civil Aviation Act 1982, s 86 requires the registration of mortgages of aircraft in a 'Register of Aircraft Mortgages' to be maintained by the Civil Aviation Authority and also makes provision for the priorities of registered mortgages. The details of the law on aircraft mortgages are laid down in the Mortgaging of Aircraft Order 1972 (MAO)[202] and have been succinctly summarised in the Law Commission Consultative Report on *Company Security Interests* as follows:[203]

> 'The MAO provides that an aircraft registered in the UK nationality register, or such an aircraft together with any store or spare parts for that aircraft, may be made security for a loan or other valuable consideration.[204] Registered mortgages have priority over unregistered mortgages and charges, and priority between registered mortgages is decided by reference to the date of registration, although nothing in the priority rules is to be construed as giving a registered mortgage any priority over any possessory lien for work done to the aircraft or statutory right of detention.[205] Priority notices may also be entered in the mortgage register.'[206]

200　*Linden Gardens Trust Ltd v Lenesta Sludge Disposals Ltd* [1994] 1 AC 85; *Re Turcan* (1888) 40 Ch D 5.

201　See, however, *Re Spectrum Plus Ltd* [2004] Ch 337 where the Court of Appeal felt themselves to be bound by the earlier decision of the Court of Appeal in *New Bullas* [1994] 1 BCLC 486 even though the Privy Council had refused to follow it in *Re Brumark Ltd* [2001] 2 AC 710.

202　SI 1972/1268; and for a more detailed treatment see Peter Thorne 'Aircraft mortgages' in N Palmer and E McKendrick (eds) *Interests in Goods* (Lloyds of London Press, 2nd edn, 1998); N Meeson *Ship and Aircraft Mortgages* (Lloyds of London Press, 1989); WJ Gough *Company Charges* (Butterworths, 2nd edn, 1996) chapter 36.

203　Law Commission Consultation Paper No 176 at para 3.314.

204　MAO, art 3.

205　MAO, art 14.

206　MAO, art 5(1).

3.95 The category of charge made registrable at Companies House by CA 1985, s 396(1(h) includes a legal or equitable mortgage on a ship or a share in a ship. The Merchant Shipping Act 1995 and the Merchant Shipping (Registration of Ships) Regulations 1993[207] lay down that legal mortgages of ships must be in a prescribed form[208] and also provide for a centralised single register for ships, which is divided into separate Parts for different kinds of ship. The prescribed form requirements, however, do not apply to equitable mortgages. There is a statutory scheme of priority for registered mortgages based on the order of registration.[209]

A CHARGE ON GOODWILL OR INTELLECTUAL PROPERTY

3.96 Section 396(1)(j) of the Companies Act 1985 makes a charge on goodwill or on any intellectual property registrable. The phrase 'intellectual property' is defined to mean

'(i) any patent, trade mark, service mark, registered design, copyright or design right, or
(ii) any licence under or in respect of any such right.'

Charges on registered designs or design rights did not require registration up until the enactment of the Copyright, Designs and Patents Act 1988 when the relevant provisions were amended to include them.[210] It should also be mentioned that charges on patents,[211] trade marks[212] and registered designs[213] must, in addition, be notified to the Patents Office.

---

207 SI 1993/3138.
208 Merchant Shipping Act 1995, Sch 1.
209 For more details see the Law Commission Consultation Paper No 176 *Company Security Interests*, para 3.324; and see also WJ Gough *Company Charges* (Butterworths, 2nd edn, 1996) chapter 35.
210 Copyright, Designs and Patents Act 1988, s 303(1) and Sch 7, para 31(1).
211 Patents Act 1977, s 33(2).
212 Trade Marks Act 1938, s 25(1).
213 Registered Designs Act 1949, s 19(1) as amended by Copyright, Designs and Patents Act 1988, Sch 3, para 18.

Chapter 4

CHARGES AND CONSENSUAL SECURITY RIGHTS NOT REQUIRING REGISTRATION

INTRODUCTION

4.1 Part XII of the Companies Act 1985, like corresponding registration provisions in other company statutes, takes the line of setting out specifically a list of charges that require registration.[1] This chapter will look at the kinds of charges that still fall outside the scope of the registration system. First of all, it is appropriate to note that according to the definition in s 395 a charge to be registrable must be created by a company. Therefore a charge arising by operation of law is not within the compass of the registration obligation. The impracticability of having to register an unpaid vendor's lien was discussed by Brightman J in *London & Cheshire Insurance Co Ltd v Laplagrene Property Co Ltd*.[2] He pointed out that an unpaid vendor's lien was a creature of the law, and that it did not depend on contract but on the fact that the vendor had the right to specific performance of its contract. The lien was created on the formation of the contract of sale and the time for registration would therefore expire after 21 days. The lien was not discharged until the purchase money was paid on completion. If registration were necessary, every vendor selling to a company would be considerably inconvenienced in having to register the unpaid vendor's lien on the off chance that circumstances might arise in which it would be necessary to rely on the lien.

CHARGES ON SHARES

4.2 Where a prospective lender wishes to take a security interest over shares held by the debtor, a number of security possibilities present themselves.[3] The first is the pledge, but this can only be used in relation to bearer shares, which

---

1 No change to this position was proposed by the Companies Act 1989. Section 93 of that Act referred to a charge as: 'any form of security interest (fixed or floating) over property, other than an interest arising by operation of law ...'

2 [1971] Ch 499.

3 See generally for a brief discussion of the process involved in the taking of security over shares Richard Calnan 'Taking Security in England' in Michael Bridge and Robert Stevens (eds) *Cross-Border Security and Insolvency* (OUP, 2001) 17 at pp 40–41; and for a discussion of the impact of 'dematerialisation' see Joanna Benjamin *Interests in Securities* (OUP, 2000) and Jacqueline Lipton *Security over Intangible Property* (LBC Information Services, 2000) at pp 69–84.

are most uncommon in England.[4] The second is the floating charge which may be, and is, employed with facility and ease. On the other hand, the floating charge holder is in a weaker priority position than other secured creditors with fixed security interests. For this reason, lenders may wish to take either a legal mortgage or an equitable charge over shares. A legal mortgage is possible only in relation to existing shares, whereas an equitable charge may extend over after-acquired shares. With a legal mortgage the lender becomes the legal owner of the shares, and is registered as such in the books of the relevant company and there is a covenant to reconvey the shares to the borrower once the loan is repaid. Lenders, however, may be reluctant to go on the register of members and this leaves the equitable charge as the alternative security option. The equitable charge, though, can be trumped by subsequent registered holders of the shares who acquire the shares bona fide, for value, and without notice of the earlier equitable interest. Because of the absence of any registration requirement pertaining to shares, the status of a bona fide purchaser may be relatively easy to establish. For this reason, equitable chargees may wish to obtain possession of the relevant share certificates but, of course, this is not possible where the shares exist in so-called 'dematerialised' or uncertificated form.[5] However, under the securities settlement system operating in London for dematerialised shares ('Crest'), where a Crest member wishes to grant a security interest over uncertificated securities to another Crest member it may do this by transferring the securities to a sub-account known as the escrow balance within its general securities account. As one commentator explains:[6]

> 'Here the securities are blocked from the control of collateral giver and subject to the control of the collateral taker. The collateral taker may instruct Crest to release the securities back into the general account of the collateral giver (which it will do on discharge of the secured obligation) or alternatively instruct Crest to transfer them to its own account (which it will do on the default of the collateral giver, in order to enforce its security interest). Crest does not monitor whether such enforcement action is authorised under the terms of the collateral agreement.'

4.3 A fixed charge (whether legal or equitable) over a corporate debtor's portfolio of shares does not have to be registered under Part XII of the Companies Act 1985, though a similar floating charge, like all floating charges, would have to be registered. The presence or absence of registration require-ments has occasionally provoked lively debate and a security taker runs the risk that what purports to be a fixed charge will be recharacterised as a floating charge and hence require registration.[7] The non-registrability of charges over

---

4   *Harrold v Plenty* [1901] 2 Ch 314.
5   The practical steps a lender might take to protect itself in this situation are discussed in J Lipton *Security over Intangible Property* (LBC Information Services, 2000) at pp 69–84.
6   Joanna Benjamin *Interests in Securities* (OUP, 2000) at p 209; and see also J Coiley 'New Protections for Cross-Border Collateral Arrangements' [2001] JIBL 119 at 121.
7   A Singaporean case in point is *Dresdner Bank v Ho Mun-Tuke Don* [1993] 1 SLR 114. Here, as security for financial facilities, a stockbroking company, City Securities, executed letters of hypothecation in favour of various banks charging shares listed in periodical certificates to be issued to the banks. There was, however, no actual physical delivery of the shares listed in the certificates to the banks, and City Securities dealt with the shares in question in their trading.

shares is perhaps the most significant gap in the existing registration regime in that a relatively easy way to circumvent the registration requirements is for a company to transfer its assets to a subsidiary and then to charge the shares in the subsidiary. The loophole was successfully availed of in *Arthur D Little v Ableco Finance*[8] where a company purported to create, inter alia, a 'first fixed charge' on shares in a subsidiary together with 'distribution rights'. The judge noted that the description of the security did not determine the issue of categorisation. In his view, the characterisation question was to be resolved by looking at the effect of the terms and provisions of the debenture in the light of the circumstances prevailing when the charge was created. The totality of the circumstances indicated that a fixed charge construction was appropriate. The chargor was not free to dispose of or deal with the shares and these could not to be replaced by other collateral. The judge added that the fact that certain clauses in the lending agreement also charged the 'distribution rights' did not alter the fixed charge character of the security over the shares:

> 'The use of the words "together with" shows that the intention of the parties was to include the shares as charged and everything that went with them. What was being charged was the entire bundle of rights making up the shares, including the right to receive dividends and to exploit the shares. True it is ... that the "distribution rights" are merely ancillary to and a composite part of the bundle of rights making up the shares so that it is not possible to sever these rights from the shares.'[9]

4.4 The court was unperturbed by the fact that, after the granting of the charge, the company continued to have the right to receive dividends. That mere fact did not render the charge over the shares and all the ancillary rights thereto a floating charge. An analogy was drawn with a charge over land and, as Nichols LJ remarked in *Re Atlantic Computer Systems plc*:[10] 'A mortgage of land does not become a floating charge by reason of a mortgagor being permitted to remain in possession and enjoy the fruits of the property charged from time to time.' Reference was also made to the observations of Lord Millett in the *Brumark* case that a fixed charge could allow the security taker to exploit the characteristics inherent in the nature of the asset itself.[11]

The Singapore Court of Appeal held that, despite the terms of the letters of hypothecation and the periodical certificates, the freedom which the banks allowed the stockbroking firm to deal with the shares resulted in the creation of floating charges and not fixed charges. LP Thean J said that the shares charged to the banks in the ordinary course of business of the stockbroking firm changed from time to time, and, until some steps were taken by the banks to enforce the charges, the stockbrokers were at liberty to carry on business in the ordinary way as far as concerned the shares charged. In essence, the security giver and not the security taker had control over the assets in question. See on this point the later comments of Millett LJ in *Re Cosslett (Contractors) Ltd* [1998] Ch 495 at 510.

8   [2003] Ch 217.
9   [2003] Ch 217 at [45].
10   [1992] Ch 505 at 534.
11   [2001] 2 AC 710 at 727.

REFORMING REGISTRATION REQUIREMENTS WITH RESPECT TO SHARES

4.5 There have been various suggestions over the years that charges over shares should become registrable, either in whole or in part.[12] For example, the Jenkins Committee on Company Law Reform, which reported in 1962, considered that charges on shares in a subsidiary should become registrable.[13] Jenkins adopted the analogy of a company carrying on business through branches. If the company raised a loan on the security of assets used by one of the branches, then the charge was registrable, whereas if a company conducted business through subsidiary companies, charges on shares in the subsidiaries were not registrable. This analogy was, however, not accepted by the Diamond Report[14] and also by Parliament when considering the provisions that became Part IV of the Companies Act 1989. At that time an amendment to the legislation was rejected that would have made registrable charges on shares in subsidiaries.[15] The main objection to registration raised in the Diamond Report rests on the fact that a company's portfolio of shares may be changing all the time. If each purchase or sale of shares were accompanied by an obligation to file details of a charge thereon, or to file a memorandum of satisfaction, as the case may be, a great deal of paperwork would be generated[16] and lenders might become reluctant to accept shares as security.[17] One commentator has concluded that, if expediency is to be preferred over general principles, then Diamond is probably correct in his assessment, but it does seem somewhat anomalous to exclude a common and often major asset from public disclosure.[18]

4.6 Moreover, in Australia s 262(1)(g) of the Corporations Act 2001 makes registrable a charge on a marketable security, not being (i) a charge created in whole or in part by the deposit of a document of title to the marketable security; or (ii) a mortgage under which the marketable security is registered in the name of the chargee or a person nominated by the chargee. In the Diamond Report it was commented, however, that the Australian exclusions would probably exclude the vast majority of charges on shares in England.[19] The first exclusion is the equivalent of a pledge or deposit of negotiable instruments or documents of title to goods. The second exclusion seems premised on the

---

12 For an example of such 'plugging of the gap' see s 131(3) of the Singapore Companies Act.
13 Cmnd 1749, para 301.
14 A Review of Security Interests in Property (HMSO, 1989) at pp 115–118.
15 *Hansard*, HL Deb, vol 504, cols 121–123 (14 February 1989).
16 Diamond Report at p 117.
17 Diamond also considered that it was inadvisable to make registrable charges on shares in subsidiaries but not on other shares, because of the risk that a searcher might be misled into thinking that there is no such charge, whereas the reality is that the charge is created before the relationship of holding and subsidiary company existed. Further, there were difficulties for a charge holder in determining whether a particular company was a subsidiary – see generally on these points pp 116–117 of the Report.
18 See M Lawson [1989] JBL 287 at 303.
19 See Diamond Report at p 116.

assumption that there is no fear of persons being misled as to the creditworthiness of the person creating the charge, since that person no longer appears as the registered owner of the shares.

4.7   Under a notice-filing system the reasons traditionally given for excluding shares from the category of registrable securities no longer seem to be valid. By virtue of a single filing, it would be possible to create a valid security interest fully enforceable against third parties over a changing portfolio of shares. Nevertheless, the Law Commission, more recently, did not recommend the extension of the notice-filing system to shares. In its view, there were good reasons of principle for making registration of charges over shares and investment securities unnecessary under a notice-filing regime. In arriving at this conclusion, the Law Commission referred back to the public notice function that the registration system was designed to serve. The rationale disappeared where relevant information was readily available elsewhere. Consequently, the register need not duplicate information from other sources or warn about securities that would be obvious to third parties. The Law Commission stated:[20]

> 'A mortgage or charge over shares may be created by a simple agreement, but in practice the mortgagee or chargee will wish to protect the security interest against third parties. There are two ways of what amounts to perfecting a charge over shares. One is to take custody of any share certificates, usually together with a transfer form signed in blank by the share owner. The other is to have the shares registered in the name of the mortgagee or chargee ... In either case, the position will be clear to third party enquirers; and Article 9 treats securities that are under the control of the secured party as perfected, just as it does possessory securities once the collateral is in the possession of the creditor.'

4.8   The US Uniform Commercial Code in Articles 8 and 9 permits the perfection of security interests over investment property (including shares) by filing as well as by 'control', though 'control' is recognised as a superior method of perfection.[21] In other words, a secured party who is perfected by control will have priority over an earlier secured party who is perfected by filing.[22] The approach originally envisaged by the Law Commission was more restrictive in that 'control' would become the sole permissible method of perfecting a

---

20   Consultation Paper No 164 at para 5.24.
21   For a definition of 'control' see Article 9–106. Control over a securities account is defined in terms of obtaining control over the security entitlement. As the official comment explains:
> 'an agreement that provides that (without further consent of the debtor) the securities intermediary or commodity intermediary will honor instructions from the secured party concerning a securities account ... described as such is sufficient. Such an agreement necessarily implies that the intermediary will honor instructions concerning all security entitlements ... carried in the account and thus affords the secured party control of all the security entitlements ...'
22   Article 9–328. The official comment explains the rationale of the control priority rule on the basis that parties who deal in securities never developed a practice of searching the UCC files before conducting securities transactions. The primary that is afforded control is designed to take account of the circumstances of the securities markets.

security interest in shares and investment securities.[23] Under the original proposals, the only way of establishing a security interest over shares or other financial collateral was by the secured party asserting 'control' over the collateral. Where the shares were entered in the books of a financial intermediary, one method of asserting control was by drawing up a control agreement under which the securities intermediary agreed to respond to instructions from the secured party rather than from the debtor. It was only possible to perfect such a security interest by 'control', however, with the alternative of perfection by registration denied.[24] Existing law, of course, permits the creation of a floating charge over shares and, assuming that the charge has been duly registered, then it will be valid in the event of the debtor's liquidation.[25] The security taker does not have 'control' but, instead, its security interest is 'perfected' by registration. Under the original Law Commission scheme this would not have been possible, and the proposals were criticised for being unnecessarily restrictive in excluding a not uncommon method of taking security. The goals of the new system were supposed to facilitate and enable the taking of security, but in this respect the goals appeared to be compromised by the specific proposals. In the Consultative Report the Law Commission has changed its mind, and this suggests that it should be possible to 'perfect' a security interest over financial collateral through filing.[26]

4.9   The Law Commission proposals are designed to be compatible with the EC Financial Collateral Directive.[27] The Financial Collateral Directive was implemented in England by the Financial Collateral Arrangements (No 2) Regulations 2003 and is part of the EC's Financial Services Action Plan.[28] It contains a number of provisions that impact on the English law of security interests.

THE EC FINANCIAL COLLATERAL DIRECTIVE

4.10   The Directive makes provision for the establishment of a community-wide regime under which financial instruments (securities) and cash may be

---

23   It should be noted too that under Article 9–309(10) security interests in investment property that have been created by a broker or securities intermediary are automatically perfected. The Official Comment explains that this provision is designed to facilitate current secured financing arrangements for securities firms as well as to provide sufficient flexibility to accommodate new arrangements that develop in the future.

24   The consultation paper viewed the latter as an unnecessary refinement: para 5.24.

25   On the other hand, a fixed charge over shares does not require registration (*Arthur D Little v Ableco Finance* [2003] Ch 217), but a charge over the dividend income from shares may be registrable as a charge over book debts – see CR, para 2.141.

26   CR, para 2.139. In fairness to the Law Commission it did ask in the Consultation Paper whether 'control' should be the only perfection method for shares and bank accounts and left it up to consultees to come up with alternatives.

27   Directive 2002/47/EC on financial collateral arrangements (OJ L168, 27.6.02). At para 5.31, fn 52 of the Consultation Paper the Law Commission recognise that the Collateral Directive does not seem to preclude registration as an alternative method of perfecting a charge.

28   COM (1999) 232. The Financial Services Action Plan is designed to contribute to the creation and maintenance of more efficient and competitive financial markets in Europe.

used as collateral under both security interest and title transfer structures.[29] According to the somewhat long-winded preamble, this will aid in the 'integration and cost-efficiency of the financial market as well as to the stability of the financial system in the Community, thereby supporting the freedom to provide services and the free movement of capital in the single market in financial services.'[30] The preamble also refers to the need to achieve a balance between market efficiency and the safety of the parties to the arrangement and of third parties. Consequently, the Directive is limited in its application to those financial collateral arrangements which provide for some form of dispossession, ie 'the provision of the financial collateral, and where the provision of the financial collateral can be evidenced in writing or in a durable medium, ensuring thereby the traceability of the collateral.'[31] Moreover, Member States may exclude the application of the Directive where either the collateral-giver or the collateral-taker is other than a public authority or financial institution, provided that the other party to the transaction is one of the aforementioned.[32] In fact the Financial Collateral Arrangements (No 2) Regulations 2003 in the UK adopt the approach of maximum compliance and apply the new regime to all cases where the collateral-provider and the collateral-taker are both non-natural persons.[33]

4.11   Essentially, the Financial Collateral Directive seeks to resolve the main problems affecting cross-border use of collateral in wholesale financial markets. The Directive attempts to create a clear framework that brings about legal certainty in the sphere of collateral. It does this by ensuring that an effective and simple community-wide regime exists for the creation of collateral under both security interest and title transfer collateral arrangements. Such title transfer arrangements are required to be recognised in all Member States and freed from the risk of being recharacterised as invalidly created security interests. 'Title transfer' is directive-speak for sale and repurchase agreements in respect of securities (or 'repos'). The Directive also seeks to restrict the

---

29   For a definition of cash and financial instruments see Article 2 of the Directive. See generally on this whole area of security over shares and investment property the website of the Financial Markets Law Committee – www.fmlc.org/.

30   Paragraph 3 of the preamble.

31   Paragraph 10 of the preamble.

32   Article 1(3) of the Directive. In other words, Member States may limit the application of the Directive to transactions amongst public authorities and financial institutions. It may be that if Member States exercise this option they will restrict significantly the usefulness of the Directive and the degree of harmonisation and simplification achieved by it.

33   SI 2003/3226, reg 3. The discussion paper 'Implementation of the Directive on Financial Collateral Arrangements' (July 2003) from HM Treasury (at para 2.4) canvassed the possibility of going further and applying the same principles to all financial collateral arrangements, including those involving individual natural persons: 'However, our view is that this is unlikely to be legally feasible using the implementing powers in the European Communities Act 1972.'

imposition of onerous formalities on either the creation or enforcement of collateral arrangements.[34] According to the European Commission:[35]

> 'collateral takers today must comply with impractical publicity require-ments, sometimes dating back many centuries, to ensure that third parties are aware that the assets being provided as collateral would not be generally available in an insolvency situation. In today's fast-moving securities mar-ket the application of these rules can be difficult and inconvenient, but failure to comply can result in the invalidity of the collateral.'

4.12 All this is explained in the preamble,[36] but unfortunately, however, like some other emanations from Brussels,[37] the length of the preamble does not necessarily mean greater clarity and there may be discordance between the substantive provisions of the Directive and the provisions of the preamble. It is stated in Article 3 that Member States shall not require that the creation, validity, perfection, enforceability or admissibility in evidence of a financial collateral arrangement or the provision of financial collateral under a financial collateral arrangement be dependent on the performance of any formal act. But does this provision preclude filing or registration as an alternative method of perfection?[38] If this were the case, perfection, in the words of para 10 of the preamble, would not be made dependent on the performance of any formal act such as the execution of any document in a specific form or in a particular manner, the making of any filing with an official or public body or registration in a public register. Perfection is not dependent on filing, but filing is, nevertheless, one of the ways in which perfection may be achieved: the other

---

34   Furthermore, the Directive permits the re-pledging of collateral, provides limited protection of collateral arrangements from some rules of insolvency law that might inhibit the use of top-up or substitute collateral, and endeavours to create legal certainty in respect of book-entry securities by extending the principles enshrined in the Settlement Finality Direc-tive (98/26/EC) so as to determine where such securities are located (place of the relevant intermediary account).

35   See p 2 of the document 'Proposed Directive on financial collateral arrangements – frequently asked questions' of 30 March 2001 available at www.europa.eu.int/.

36   Paragraphs 9 and 10.

37   See the European Insolvency Regulation (EC) 1346/2000, OJ 2000 L160/1 where the preamble has been criticised by H Rajak 'The Harmonisation of Insolvency Proceedings in the European Union' [2000] CFILR 180 at 187 in the following terms:

> 'This preamble ... is unstructured, overlong and unnecessarily complex. It goes well beyond the generally accepted role of a preamble – to provide a context for the substance of the Regulation and thereby to assist in its interpretation. It will be left to judges to decide which provisions in the preamble are of substantive effect and to be treated as within the body of the Regulation and which are simply prefatory and providing a context. With the likelihood that hundreds, possibly thousands of courts in the EC will be required to interpret and apply provisions of this Regulation, the present state of the preamble will be likely to be the cause of growing uncertainty and disharmony.'

Professor Rajak adds (at 189) that the provision comes close to contradicting provisions in the body of the Regulation.

38   Law Commission Consultation Paper *Registration of Security Interests* (2002) seemed to think not; see p 136, fn 52. It may be, however, that the Law Commission had a previous draft of the Directive in mind when framing this comment.

way being control. It is not clear, however, whether this is a correct interpretation of the Directive and the matter, ultimately, will only be solved by the intervention of the European Court of Justice on an interpretative question.

4.13 A second area of doubt concerns the status of the floating charge over securities which, like all floating charges created by companies, is registrable under Part XII of the Companies Act 1985. The argument for exempting floating charges over securities from registration requirements goes as follows – one of the objectives of the Directive is to permit the substitution of collateral without throwing into doubt the validity of the collateral arrangements or making it subject to 'onerous' formality requirements like registration.[39] Provision for collateral substitution may mean that the collateral arrangement would be categorised in England as a floating charge,[40] though the recharacterisation risk is reduced, if not entirely eliminated, by standard market documentation which provides that the ability of the collateral giver to substitute assets is subject to the consent of the collateral taker.[41] Certainty would only be achieved by disapplying registration requirements from all types of financial collateral. It would be a rather strained and strong reading of the Directive, however, to say that this result is actually prescribed. One of the main concerns of the Directive appears to be to disallow certain provisions of insolvency law, such as the preference avoidance mechanism contained in s 239 of the Insolvency Act 1986, that might cast doubt on the provision of top-up collateral and the substitution of collateral.[42] In the words of para 16 of the preamble:

---

39 See generally D Turing [2002] Financial Regulation International.
40 See J Coiley 'New Protections for Cross-Border Collateral Arrangements' [2001] JIBL 119 at 121–122:
   'Collateral providers are also required to register floating charges, and this head of charge would be potentially applicable where the security created is deemed to constitute a floating charge by virtue of a collateral provider's right of substitution.'
41 As Dr Joanna Benjamin explains in *Interests in Securities* (OUP, 2000) at p 108 substitution provisions are customary but 'if they are so drafted that the collateral taker can withdraw (interests in) securities from the collateral pool without restriction, this may render the security interest a floating charge, particularly in the light of the Court of Appeal judgment in *Re Cosslett (Contractors) Ltd* [1988] Ch 495.' See now, however, the decision of Lightman J in *Re Queen's Moat Houses plc* [2004] NPC 67 which suggests that there is a critical difference between the right of a corporate chargor to deal with and dispose of property free from a charge without reference to the charge holder and the right of the chargor to require the charge holder to release property from the charge and to substitute equivalent property of equal value. The existence of such a provision did not, in his view, transform what was otherwise a fixed charge into a floating charge.
42 Para 5 of the preamble and Article 8(3) of the Directive. The Directive, however, does introduce a welcome reform by permitting, to use the jargon of the financial markets, the rehypothecation or repledging of charged assets '[i]f and to the extent that the terms of a security financial collateral arrangement so provide'. In other words, where financial collateral is provided under a traditional security interest type collateral arrangement, the 'collateral taker is entitled to exercise a right of use' in relation to the financial collateral. Article 5 lays down that where a collateral-taker exercises a right of use, he thereby incurs an obligation to transfer equivalent collateral to replace the original financial collateral. The objective is that this proposal should increase liquidity in the market, with collateral-takers being able to generate income from the reuse of collateral and, consequently, enabled to offer better financing terms to the collateral-giver.

'The intention is merely that the provision of top-up or substitution financial collateral cannot be questioned on the sole basis that the relevant financial obligations existed before that financial collateral was provided, or that the financial collateral was provided during a prescribed period.'[43]

4.14   According to HM Treasury, the definition of 'security financial collateral arrangement' and of 'security interest' in the Regulations means that they do 'not apply to floating charges before the charge has crystallised and some control over the collateral has passed to the charge holder. Serious thought was given to extending the regulations to all floating charges. However, we have rejected this extension in the interests of providing appropriate protection for third parties, particularly unsecured creditors who appear after the floating charge has been taken.'[44] It is not clear how the Regulations, as drafted, accomplish this objective.[45] Security interest is defined as including:

> 'a charge created as a floating charge where the financial collateral charged is delivered, transferred, held, registered or otherwise designated so as to be in the possession or under the control of the collateral-taker or a person acting on its behalf; any right of the collateral-provider to substitute equivalent financial collateral or withdraw excess financial collateral shall not prevent the financial collateral being in the possession or under the control of the collateral-taker ...'[46]

Therefore, floating charges where the charge-taker has 'control' are included within the Regulations and the registration requirements laid down in Part XII of the Companies Act 1985 do not apply.[47] One interpretation would be to say that the essence of the floating charge is that the charge-giver and not the charge-taker should have control of the charged assets and therefore the Regulations only apply where the floating charge crystallises and control passes to the collateral-taker.

4.15   Another commentator has suggested, however, that the reference to control in the Regulations must be taken to mean either positive legal or operational control. In relation to floating charges, where the charge-taker has operational or legal positive control, Companies Act registration requirements are not applicable, and the protections under the UK Regulations are also available. In general, positive control is the ability to dispose of an asset. It is suggested that '[p]ositive control may be operational (ie the operational ability to dispose) or legal (ie the rights to do). Operational control will be present

---

43   For the position under current English law see J Benjamin *Interests in Securities* (OUP, 2000) at pp 92–93 who argues that the provision of top-up or substitute collateral should generally be safe from challenge as an improper preference or a transaction at an undervalue, though the avoidance (subject to validation by the court) of dispositions of property after the commencement of winding up proceedings under s 127 of the Insolvency Act 1986 may pose more problems; and see also D Turing [2002] Financial Regulation International.

44   'Implementation of the Directive on Financial Collateral Arrangements' (July 2003) at para 2.10

45   In fact the Financial Collateral Arrangements Regulations 2003 were withdrawn before they came into force and replaced by the Financial Collateral (No 2) Regulations 2003.

46   SI 2003/3226, reg 3.

47   Regulation 4.

where for example the chargee is also the custodian. Legal control in the absence of default may be present, for example where there is a right of use.'[48] On the other hand, some might argue that where the charge-taker has the ability to dispose of a charged asset this means that the charge is a fixed rather than a floating charge.[49]

INSURANCE POLICIES

4.16 Charges on insurance policies are not registrable under current English law. The leading case is *Paul and Frank Ltd v Discount Bank (Overseas) Ltd*[50] where a letter of authority authorised the payment of the proceeds of an insurance policy to the defendant and it was contended, unsuccessfully, that this letter amounted to a charge on book debts. There are two bases to the decision. First, Pennycuick J said that, in order to ascertain whether a particular charge constituted a charge on book debts, one had to scrutinise the units of property which formed the subject-matter of the charge at the date of its creation and to see whether any of those items represented a book debt. In a situation where the unit of property was the benefit of a contract and, at the date of the charge, the benefit of the contract did not encompass any book debt, the contract was not within the section merely by reason of the fact that it might ultimately result in a book debt. In common parlance, one would not depict as a 'book debt' a right under a contingency contract before the contingency occurs. Secondly, the test for book debts was whether they would be entered in the books of a company as an ordinary principle of account-ancy.[51] The accountancy evidence indicated that an insurance policy would not be so entered even after admission of the claim and ascertainment of the amount.

4.17 In the Diamond report it was suggested that, subject to an exception wide enough to cover certain policies of marine insurance and other policies on

---

48 See generally J Benjamin 'The Use of Securities as Collateral' in John De Lacy (ed) *The Reform of UK Credit and Security Law* (Cavendish, 2005 forthcoming) section 14. See also more generally Roy Goode *Legal Problems of Credit and Security* (3rd edn, 2003) at pp 230–231.

49 See the comments by D Turing 'New Growth in the Financial Collateral Garden' [2005] Butterworths Journal of International Banking and Financial Law 4 at 5:
> ' "Control" is a word which we all know describes the difference between a fixed charge and floating charge. If you have control, you have a fixed charge, if you don't you have a floater. But our knowledge is a dangerous thing in this case: ... floating charges are covered by the FCA Regulations, so some new meaning for "control" is needed. Unfortu-nately the FCA Regulations do not supply it ...'

See also the remarks by the Law Commission in its consultative report *Company Security Interests* (2004) at p 174, para 16:
> 'It is worth pointing out ... that the notion of "control" as used here ... is not the same as the "control" that must be exercised by a chargee under current law if the charge is to be fixed rather than floating ...'

50 [1967] Ch 348.

51 [1967] Ch 348 at 362.

goods, charges on insurance policies should become registrable.[52] The grounds advanced for the general recommendation seem fairly convincing in that a life or 'key person' insurance policy, for example, might well be a significant asset and persons dealing with a company might be interested to know whether it had charged the benefit of such a policy. The same considerations apply with respect to an insurance policy over property. Likewise, the Law Commission saw no reason why charges over insurance policies should be exempt from registration and suggested that the existing exclusion of insurance policies seemed to be based on political reasons rather than fully worked out legal or practical reasons.[53]

4.18   In general, security interests over insurance policies are not covered by Article 9 of the United States Uniform Commercial Code. Article 9–109(d)(8) renders Article 9 inapplicable to the transfer of an interest in, or the assignment of a claim under, a policy on insurance. This does not mean that it is impossible to create security interests or the functional equivalent of the same in insurance policies, but merely that the relevant law is not contained in Article 9. The Article 9 Reporters, Professors Harris and Mooney, attempted to bring insurance policies within the Article 9 framework, but their efforts were frustrated by opposition from within the insurance industry.[54] Insurers wanted to make certain determinations about whom to pay so as to discharge their obligations under insurance policies. Insurers did not wish to alter or change existing practices in making these determinations, though the revised Article 9 narrows the insurance exclusion somewhat by including health-care insurance receivables within its scope.[55] The inclusion of the latter is intended to facilitate health-care providers such as hospitals in obtaining finance.[56]

CHARGES OVER CASH DEPOSITS

4.19   The better view seems to be that charges over cash deposits created by companies do not require registration as charges over book debts or indeed

---

52   A Review of Security Interests in Property (HMSO 1989) at p 112.

53   Paragraphs 5.38–5.39 of the Consultation Paper.

54   See generally SL Harris and CW Mooney 'How Successful was the Revision of UCC Article 9?: Reflections of the Reporters' (1994) 74 Chicago-Kent L Rev 1357 at 1374–1376.

55   See also JO Honnold, SL Harris and CW Mooney *Security Interests in Personal Property: Cases, Problems and Materials* (Foundation Press, 3rd edn, 2001) at p 342.

56   In the United States hospitals often finance themselves by assigning to financiers monies owing to them under insurance policies for health-care goods and services provided. It was felt that bringing health-care insurance within the Article 9 framework would provide a more stable foundation for this form of financing. Nevertheless, the incorporation of health-care insurance within the Article 9 framework is only partial and, in particular, Article 9 does not override contractual and legal restrictions with respect to the rights and duties of the account debtor – Article 9–408(d). Consequently, other law, and not Article 9, must be consulted to ascertain whom an account debtor under a health-care insurance policy must pay before obtaining the discharge of its obligations under an insurance policy – Article 9–406.

under any other head of registrable charge.[57] The judgment of Lord Hoffmann, however, in *Re BCCI (No 8)* does admit the possibility of doubt. He said:[58]

> 'There is a suggestion ... that the banking community has been insufficiently grateful for being spared the necessity of registering such charges. In my view, this is a matter on which banks are entitled to make up their own minds and take their own advice on whether the deposit charged is a "book debt" or not.'

Reference was made by Lord Hoffmann to the judgment of Lord Hutton in the Northern Ireland Court of Appeal in *Northern Bank Ltd v Ross*[59] which suggests that, in the case of deposits with banks, an obligation to register is unlikely to arise. Lord Hoffmann could equally have invoked his own observations in *Re Brightlife Ltd*[60] which in fact formed the cornerstone of the decision in *Northern Bank Ltd v Ross*.

4.20 In *Re Brightlife Ltd*[61] Hoffmann J, as he then was, made the point that the relationship between banker and customer was one of debtor and creditor, so that it would not be legally inaccurate to describe a credit balance with a banker as a debt. It would not be normal usage, however, for an accountant or business person to describe a bank account in credit as a debt. Instead, it would be referred to as 'cash at bank'. It should be noted, however, that Hoffmann J's decision that the phrase 'debts' in one commercial debenture did not capture a bank account in credit is not conclusive as to the meaning of the phrase 'book debts' in the Companies legislation. In particular, the wording in the debenture was inappropriate to cover credit balances. The chargor was prohibited from dealing with its 'books or other debts' without the prior consent in writing of the charge holder 'otherwise than in the ordinary course of getting in and realising the same'. A credit balance at the bank could not sensibly be 'got in' or 'realised'.[62]

4.21 In *Northern Bank Ltd v Ross*[63] the question arose whether a sum of money paid into an account with Allied Irish Banks by the company before it went into liquidation was subject to a fixed charge over 'all book debts and other debts' previously executed by the company in favour of Northern Bank. Lord Hutton LCJ decided that 'cash at bank' was excluded from the expression 'book debts and other debts' and that 'cash at bank' meant money in a bank account whether or not the account was used as a trading account. There were three pillars to this conclusion. First, the wording of the specific debenture which referred to getting in or realising the debts; secondly, business and

---

57 See the comments by Sir Peter Millett at (1991) 107 LQR 679 reviewing Dr Fidelis Oditah's work *Legal Aspects of Receivables Financing* (Sweet & Maxwell, 1990).
58 [1998] AC 214 at 227.
59 [1990] BCC 883.
60 [1987] Ch 200.
61 [1987] Ch 200 at 209.
62 These comments were applied by Etherton J in *Quickson (South and West) Ltd v Katz* [2004] BPIR 1139 at [119].
63 [1990] BCC 883. The first instance judge had drawn a distinction between a trading account and a so-called special account and held that cash deposited in a special account came within the expression 'book debts and other debts'.

accountancy practice; and thirdly, Hoffmann J's observations in *Re Bright-life Ltd* and two poorly reported earlier cases. One of these cases is *Re Stevens*[64] where North J held that the balance at the bankers of a firm did not come within the term 'book debts'.

4.22   It should be remembered that again *Northern Bank Ltd v Ross* is tailored to the wording of a particular debenture and does not purport to provide a definitive interpretation of the phrase 'book debts' as used in the company charge legislation. In this connection, it should be noted that in *Re Permanent Houses (Holdings) Ltd*[65] Hoffmann J took the opportunity to say, if it was not sufficiently clear, that *Re Brightlife Ltd* did not decide that a credit balance at a bank could not in any context be a 'book debt' or 'other debt'. No opinion was expressed on whether a credit balance was a 'book debt' for the purposes of the company charge registration system.[66]

4.23   The potential registration problems are even more acute where the cash deposit is made with an institution or person other than a bank.[67] The example has been given of a situation where a client pays a margin deposit to his broker or to a clearing house in a securities or financial market to cover price swings, and his broker or clearing house becomes a debtor to the client in respect of the margin deposit.[68] Is the margin deposit made by a corporate customer registrable as a charge over book debts?

4.24   The same question arises with respect to the 'right of retention' of a factor of book debts. A factor, ie a purchaser of book debts, may not provide the full purchase price at the outset, but instead may retain a certain sum of money to cover the possibility that certain of the debts purchased may turn out to be bad. Essentially the factor is taking a security interest over money that it owes the assignor of the debts. The matter was discussed in *Re Charge Card*

---

64   [1888] WN 110 and 116. The second case, even more obscure, is referred to in *Dawson v Isle* [1906] 1 Ch 633.

65   [1988] BCLC 563 at 566–567.

66   See also *M O'Donnell & Sons (Huddersfield) Ltd v Midland Bank plc* 2001 WL 1676963 where it was held that a sum arising from the sale of all the company's assets was not a 'book debt' but came within the expression 'other debts' as used in a bank debenture. The Court of Appeal applied the general principles of interpretation set out by the House of Lords in *Investors Compensation Scheme Ltd v West Bromwich Building Society* [1998] 1 WLR 896 that interpretation is the ascertainment of the meaning which the document would convey to a reasonable person having all the background knowledge which would reasonably have been available to the parties in the situation in which they were at the time of the contract. The background included absolutely anything which would have affected the way in which the language of the document would have been understood by a reasonable man.

67   See, however, *Re SSSL Realisations (2002) Ltd Manning v AIG Europe (UK) Ltd* [2004] EWHC 1760 at [54] and [55] where Lloyd J suggested that it was possible to create a charge over a sum of money held by a person once it has been paid to him, without necessarily also creating a charge over the debt or other right in respect of which it may come to be paid. In the former case the charge over the sum of money would not be registrable as a charge over book debts.

68   See Philip Wood *Comparative Law of Security and Guarantees* (Sweet & Maxwell, 1995) at p 50.

Services Ltd.[69] In that case Millett J said that if the right of retention constitutes a charge, there was no doubt that it was a charge on book debts and so registrable. His reasons for concluding that the right of retention did not constitute a charge were twofold. First, there was the conceptual impossibility argument, ie that it was logically impossible to have a charge in favour of X over a debt owed by X. Secondly, however, he took the view that there was no relevant property capable of forming the subject matter of a charge. The only asset which the company could charge was its chose in action (ie the right to sue the factor for the sum due under the agreement), but this already contained within it the liability to suffer a retention. Under standard condition 3b of the factoring agreement the factor was to remit to the company or its order any balance for the time being standing to the credit of the current account less however, any amount which the factor in its absolute discretion decided to retain as security for, inter alia, any claims or defences against the company or any risk of non-payment by a debtor. Millett J said that the right of retention constituted a contractual limitation on the company's right to require repayment of the balance on the current account as a safeguard or security against overpayment by the other contracting party and not against default by the company. It was an essential safeguard against overpayment, since the balance on the current account, generally speaking, could never represent the true amount owing by the factor. Remittances from the account were in effect provisional payments only and represented the best estimate that could be made at the time of the true state of account between the parties. In his view, there were 'reciprocal obligations giving rise to credits and debits in a single running account, a single liability to pay the ultimate balance found due on taking the account and provisions for retention and provisional payment in the meantime.'[70]

4.25 The consequences of non-registration from the point of view of the charge-taker are draconian in that it is deprived of secured status if the charge-giver goes into liquidation. In the circumstances, the only safe advice would appear to be to submit details of the security interest to Companies House for registration. Under Part XII of the Companies Act 1985 a charge is not avoided if prescribed particulars of a registered charge are, in fact, delivered for registration within 21 days of the date of creation of the charge, irrespective of whether Companies House declines to register the particulars.[71] In fact, Companies House policy in relation to accepting details of purported charge-backs for registration has vacillated considerably.[72] The current policy seems to be that particulars will not be rejected merely because the charge-taker is a bank with whom a credit balance is held. This is part of a more general policy to accept details of charges over credit balances for registration notwithstanding the hesitation over the registration question that was manifested by Hoffmann J in *Re Brightlife Ltd.*

---

69   [1987] Ch 150 at 175.
70   [1987] Ch 150 at 174.
71   *Slavenburg's Bank NV v Intercontinental Natural Resources Ltd* [1980] 1 WLR 1076.
72   See generally R Goode *Legal Problems of Credit and Security* (Sweet & Maxwell, 2nd edn, 1988) at pp 130–131; and see now third edition at pp 99–100.

4.26   The Legal Risk Review Committee suggested that charge-backs of bank deposits should not become registrable for three reasons. First, charge-backs usually mirror the effect of a set-off and the latter did not require registration. Secondly, other creditors would not be caught by surprise if bank deposits were subject to a secret lien. Finally, registration of charges over quickly moving transactions and ephemeral or evanescent assets made registration too burdensome and also impeded commercial activity.[73] In the *Review of Security Interests in Property* conducted by Professor Diamond for the Department of Trade and Industry it was argued similarly that charges over cash deposits should not require registration. Diamond reasoned that prospective creditors of a company are not misled by the absence of any public acknowledgement of charges over bank balances. Bank accounts were generally conducted in secrecy and the amount a company was in credit was not visible to an outside creditor. In many cases the assumption was that the company, far from being in credit, had an overdraft.[74] Similarly, the Law Commission in the Consultation Paper *Registration of Security Interests* endorsed the viewpoint that registration of a security interest in a bank account was unnecessary to warn potential secured creditors and was equally unnecessary to warn potential investors.[75]

4.27   On the other hand, it has been argued that since intangibles of all types are such an important and growing form of collateral that one should be slow to dispense with registration requirements. Moreover, if there is little difference between charges strictly so-called and rights of set-off, why have banks agitated so vociferously in favour of being able to create charges in such circumstances? It should be noted, however, that security interests in cash deposits are not subject to any mandatory filing requirements under the revised Article 9 in the United States. Such security interests, to use the language of Article 9, may be perfected by control rather than by filing.[76]

---

73   For an analysis of the Legal Risk Review Committee's report see D Capper (1993) 44 NILQ 71.
74   A Review of Security Interests in Property (HMSO, 1989) at p 112.
75   (July 2002). At pp 142–143 of the Consultation Paper.
76   Prior to the 1998 revision, Article 9 excluded original security interests in deposit accounts as distinct from security interests in deposit accounts that represented the proceeds of other collateral. This limitation attracted criticism and led to a detailed report from the UCC Permanent Editorial Board Study Group *Use of Deposit Accounts as Original Collateral* (Philadelphia, American Law Institute, 1992) that recommended the extension of Article 9. The following reasons were given (at pp 333–334):
    '(1)   since depositories would retain their rights of set-off, their position would be strengthened, not weakened, by allowing them to hold a security interest;
    (2)   it would allow depository institutions to avoid the cumbersome and complex set off rules in s 553 of the United States Bankruptcy Code;
    (3)   it would avoid mutuality problems for depositories arising out of "special deposits" and parent/subsidiary relationships;
    (4)   it would avoid mutuality problems where the deposit is in a foreign currency; and
    (5)   it would give depository institutions stronger priority vis-à-vis federal tax liens.'
    The recommendations of the Study Group were substantially adopted by the drafters of the revised Article 9. Insofar as deposit accounts as original collateral are concerned, the revised Article 9 departs fairly radically from the traditional perfection and first-to-file-has-priority rules. Article 9–327 provides that a security interest held by a secured party having control of

4.28   In the case of a charge over a cash deposit the most likely beneficiary of the charge is the bank with whom the bank account is maintained, and prior to the decision of the House of Lords in *Re BCCI (No 8)* there was in fact a considerable question mark over whether such charges could legitimately be created. In the *BCCI* case the House of Lords upheld the legal effectiveness of 'charge-backs'.[77] In other words, the court held that it is possible for a debtor to take a charge over its own indebtedness to a creditor as security for the discharge of some reciprocal obligation, eg there is no conceptual impossibility in a bank having a charge over a cash deposit made with it by a customer that serves as security for a loan advanced to the customer. In reaching this conclusion, the House of Lords rejected the conceptual impossibility argument that found favour with the Court of Appeal in *Re BCCI (No 8)*[78] and also with Millett J in *Re Charge Card Services Ltd*.[79] Reciprocal indebtedness of this kind is a feature of many commercial transactions and the House of Lords decision has been welcomed by many in the commercial community as removing uncertainty and facilitating a form of transaction that is seen as highly beneficial, notwithstanding the probable availability of efficacious, legally acceptable alternatives. These alternatives encompass contractual rights of set-off[80] and making the deposit a 'flawed asset' which the depositor or third parties standing in the shoes of the depositor are not at liberty to withdraw.

4.29   These alternatives were accepted by Millett J in *Re Charge Card Services*,[81] the leading English decision prior to *Re BCCI (No 8)*, but, at the same time, the judge denied that a charge could be created in a situation of reciprocal indebtedness. Millett J said:

> 'It is true ... that no conveyance or assignment is involved in the creation of an equitable charge, but in my judgment the benefit of a debt can no more

---

the deposit account has priority over a conflicting security interest held by a secured party that does not have control.

77   [1998] AC 214.

78   The Court of Appeal decision is variously reported as *Morris v Agrichemicals Ltd* [1996] BCC 204 and *Re Bank of Credit and Commerce International SA (No 8)* [1996] Ch 245; [1996] 2 WLR 631; [1996] 2 All ER 121. For commentary on the case see Richard Millett (1996) 112 LQR 524 and A Berg [1996] LMCLQ 177.

79   [1987] Ch 150. This case has generated an enormous literature. For discussion of the case see generally R Goode *Legal Problems of Credit and Security* (Sweet & Maxwell, 2nd edn, 1988) at pp 124–129; and see now third edition at pp 93–94. Professor Goode is now of the view that:

> 'conceptual problems such as the blurring of the distinction between property and obligation, and policy problems such as the fact that the only method of distinguishing a charge-back from a contractual set-off is by the label given to the transaction by the parties, must yield to business practice and legislative developments designed to accommodate it.'

See also W Blair [1983] 1 FL Rev 14; W Blair *Butterworths' Banking & Financial Law Review 1987* at pp 173–176; F Neate [1981] Int Bus Lawyer 247; D Pollard [1988] JBL 127 and 219; T Shea [1986] 3 JIBL 192; P Wood (1987) 8 Co Law 262.

80   In other words, the secured party would have the right to apply the balance of the account towards the discharge of the secured obligations. The overall effect of a charge-back, a set-off and a flawed asset arrangement operating in tandem is referred to as a 'triple cocktail'.

81   [1987] Ch 150 at 176. Reference is made to the definition of an equitable charge given by Atkin LJ in *National Provincial and Union Bank of England v Charnley* [1924] 1 KB 431 at 449.

be appropriated or made available to the debtor than it can be conveyed or assigned to him. The objection to a charge in these circumstances is not to the process by which it is created, but to the result. A debt is a chose in action, it is the right to sue the debtor. This can be assigned or made available to a third party, but not to the debtor, who cannot sue himself. Once any assignment or appropriation to the debtor becomes unconditional, the debt is wholly or partially released. The debtor cannot and does not need to, resort to the creditor's claim against him in order to obtain the benefit of the security; his own liability to the creditor is automatically discharged or reduced.'

The judge also said:[82]

'It does not, of course, follow that an attempt to create an express mortgage or charge of a debt in favour of the debtor would be ineffective to create a security. Equity looks to the substance not the form, and while in my judgment this would not create a mortgage or charge, it would no doubt give a right of set off which would be effective against the creditor's liquidator or trustee in bankruptcy ...'

4.30   The view that it is a conceptual impossibility for a debtor to attempt to charge its own indebtedness to the bank creditor has also been upheld in Australia, where the leading decision is *Broad v Commissioner of Stamp Duties*[83] – a case in which the proper classification of a document was important for stamp duty purposes. It was decided by Lee J that what purported to be a mortgage or charge given by a bank customer over its account with the bank was not in fact what it purported to be. The judge referred approvingly to the following observations of Buckley LJ in *Halesowen Presswork and Assemblies Ltd v Westminster Bank Ltd*:[84]

'The money or credit which the bank obtained as the result of clearing the cheque became the property of the bank, not the property of the company. No man can have a lien on his own property and consequently no lien can have arisen affecting that money or that credit.'

Lee J adopted a similar approach, deciding the case on the simple footing that there can be no mortgage or charge in favour of oneself of one's own indebtedness to another.[85] *Broad v Commissioner of Stamp Duties* was followed by Yeldham J in *Estate Planning Associates v Commissioner of Stamp Duties*.[86]

4.31   The holding that there can be no charge in favour of oneself of one's own indebtedness to another has been subjected to strong criticism, particularly from the banking community. The 'anti' contingent argue that in some cases rights of set-off may not be available, such as with respect to a purely

---

82   [1987] Ch 150 at 177.
83   [1980] 2 NSWLR 40.
84   [1971] 1 QB 1 at 46; see also the statement of Lord Denning MR at 33–34. The observations of Buckley LJ were approved of by Viscount Dilhorne, Lord Simon and Lord Cross in the House of Lords, where the case is reported sub nom *National Westminster Bank v Halesowen*: see [1972] AC 785 at 802, 808, 810.
85   [1980] 2 NSWLR 40 at 46.
86   [1985] 2 NSWLR 495.

contingent liability and, in any event, a charge-back of the debt may be desirable to improve the priority of the set-off against assignees, garnishers, undisclosed principals and the like.[87] The legal objections could be summarised as follows:[88]

(1)   In one category of cases the protection afforded to a counterparty by set-off as judicially recognised and validated in *Charge Card* requires complex contractual provisions which may be either unnecessarily cumbersome or which are not feasible in the commercial world.

(2)   In the second set of cases, set-off may be prohibited or legally risky.

4.32   Moreover, on the conceptual level, it is claimed that the property in the deposit is held by the customer as the beneficial owner and the depositor may create security rights over this property in favour of anybody as over its other property.[89] The Court of Appeal in *Re BCCI (No 8)* was very conscious of practical realities and the criticisms of *Charge Card*. The court said:[90]

'It is important that ... routine financing arrangements should not be put at risk. If the reasoning in *Re Charge Card Services Ltd* led to the conclusion that charge-backs were invalid or ineffective to give security in the event of the chargor's insolvency, then that reasoning would be suspect and if it could not be faulted then we would be willing to sacrifice doctrinal purity on the altar of commercial necessity. But we are satisfied that neither conclusion would be justified.'

4.33   In other words, while the court was of the view that a charge-back did confer rights of property on the charge holder, at the same time a charge holder had powerful rights and remedies under a charge-back through the contractual set-off and flawed asset techniques. The Court of Appeal decision[91] led to a practice recommendation by the Financial Law Panel and a strengthening of resolve that the existing legal dispensation could be made to work satisfactorily without the need for legislative interventions.[92] The supplemental recommendation read as follows:

'1.   The use of a charge-back will be effective to confer on the chargee security over cash deposited with it, or otherwise over indebtedness which it owes.

2.   Appropriate restrictions should be included in the charge document to regulate the terms on which the deposit will be held and will become repayable. Although basic restrictions and contingencies may be implied merely by the use of the term "charge-back" or "charge" to

---

87   See P Wood (1987) 8 Co Law 262 at 266. Wood also argued that the methods of getting around *Re Charge Card Ltd* are sometimes commercially or legally unattractive; sometimes they are vitiated for regulatory or tax reasons, always they are a nuisance. Moreover, he suggests that there is no reason why the law should insist that business should adopt these contrivances when there is a perfectly acceptable alternative: see (1987) 8 Co Law 262 at 269.

88   Final Report of the Legal Risk Review Committee at p 42.

89   See W Blair Butterworths Banking & Financial Law Review 1987 at pp 173–174.

90   [1996] BCC 204 at 214.

91   [1996] 2 All ER 121; [1996] BCC 204.

92   Financial Law Panel Security over Cash Deposits: A supplemental practice recommendation (March 1996).

describe the contract between the depositor and the lender, it will almost always be preferable to set them out expressly.'

4.34 Notwithstanding the element of practical reassurance introduced by the Court of Appeal in *Re BCCI (No 8)*, the views of the court on charge-backs were rejected when the case went on appeal to the House of Lords. Lord Hoffmann, who spoke for a unanimous House of Lords, categorically rejected the proposition that it was conceptually impossible to create a charge in circumstances of reciprocal indebtedness.[93] His reasons for arriving at this decision may be summarised as follows:

(1)   The doctrine appeared to date from the judgment of Millett J in *Re Charge Card Services Ltd*.[94] The Legal Risk Review Committee had expressed disquiet about this ruling as a potential cause of obscurity and uncertainty in the law affecting financial markets.[95]
(2)   Documents purporting to create charge-backs have been used by banks for many years.
(3)   In many nineteenth century cases the possibility of a charge over a debt owed by the charge-taker caused no judicial surprise.
(4)   The depositor's right to claim payment of his deposit is a chose in action which the law has always recognised as property. A charge over such a chose in action could validly be granted to a third party. A charge is a security interest created without any transfer of title or possession to the beneficiary. The fact that the beneficiary of the charge was the debtor himself was not inconsistent with the transaction having some or all of the traditional features of a charge. It would be a proprietary interest because, subject to questions of registration and purchaser for value without notice, it would be binding upon assignees and a liquidator or trustee in bankruptcy. The depositor would retain an equity of redemption. There would be no merger of interests. The depositor would retain title to the deposit subject only to the bank's charge.[96]
(5)   A bank could obtain effective security in other ways such as contractual rights of set-off or combining accounts where the deposit was made by the principal debtor. Alternatively, it could make the deposit a 'flawed asset' by imposing contractual limitations on the right to withdraw the deposit. Nevertheless these were not good reasons for preventing banks and their customers from creating charges over deposits if, for reasons of their own, they wanted to do so.
(6)   Legislation reversing the effect of *Charge Card* had been passed in many

---

93   [1998] AC 214 at 225–228. For discussion of the case see R Calnan (1998) 114 LQR 174; G McCormack [1998] Company, Financial and Insolvency Law Review 111.
94   [1987] Ch 150.
95   The Legal Risk Review Committee that was appointed by the Governor of the Bank of England in April 1991 to ascertain the correct approach in tackling legal uncertainties that affected the United Kingdom's wholesale financial markets. The committee was chaired by Lord Alexander of Weedon, chairman of NatWest Bank and former practising QC.
96   The House of Lords considered that there was a slight difference between charge-backs and other charges in the manner of enforcement of the charge. According to Lord Hoffmann, '[t]he method by which the property would be realised would differ slightly: instead of the beneficiary of the charge having to claim payment from the debtor, the realisation would take the form of a book entry' ([1998] AC 214 at 226–227).

offshore banking jurisdictions such as Hong Kong, Singapore and the Cayman Islands.[97] In none of these jurisdictions did the statutes amend or repeal any rule of common law which would be inconsistent with the existence of a charge over a debt owed by the charge holder. The legislation simply said that such a charge could be created. If legislative simplicity of this kind was possible, then it was difficult, if not impossible, to detect conceptual impossibility.

(7)   The law should be slow to declare a practice of the commercial community to be commercially impossible given the fact that the law was fashioned to suit the practicalities of life.

PLEDGES

4.35   In general terms it is true to say that a pledge is not registrable under Part XII of the Companies Act 1985. Part IV of CA 1989 made this position explicit with a legislative restatement of the law relating to the registrability of pledges. First of all, a pledge came within the revamped definition of a charge as being any form of 'security interest (fixed or floating) over property other than an interest arising by operation of law ...' A pledge, however, in CA 1989, s 93 was declared not registrable as being a charge on goods or any interest in goods under which the chargee is entitled to possession either of the goods or of a document of title to them.

4.36   It might be argued that it is a misuse of language to use the word 'charge' to refer to possessory security. A charge is a non-possessory security under which the charge holder is not entitled either to the assets themselves or to documents of title pertaining to the same. The reason why a pledge falls outside the scope of the company charge registration system is simply because it is not a charge.

4.37   A pledge has been described as the actual or constructive delivery of possession of an asset to a creditor by way of security.[98] Another name for a pledge is a pawn, though the latter expression carries with it a somewhat pejorative resonance in popular parlance. The expression 'pawnbroker' connotes somebody who makes small advances against the pledge of domestic goods. The services of a pawnbroker were often availed of by persons denied conventional sources of credit, and in nineteenth-century literature a strong association was made between pawnbroking and the driving of harsh and unpopular bargains.[99] Recent times may have witnessed a revival of this rudimentary form of credit. Pawnbroking has long been subject to statutory

---

97   The Singapore legislation – now s 13 of the Civil Law Act – declares that it is possible, and always has been possible, for an obligor under a chose in action to take a mortgage or charge over that chose in action.

98   See generally R Goode *Legal Problems of Credit and Security* (Sweet & Maxwell, 3rd edn, 2003) at p 31; and see also E Sykes and S Walker *The Law of Securities* (Law Book Company, 5th edn, 1993) pp 734–737 and N Palmer *Bailment* (Law Book Company, 2nd edn, 1991) chapter 22.

99   See Charles Dickens *Sketches by Boz* and Kellow Chesney *The Victorian Underworld* (1970). See generally Palmer *Bailment* (2nd edn, 1992) at p 1380.

controls which contain a measure of consumer protection. The Pawnbrokers Acts 1872–1960 have now been replaced by the Consumer Credit Act 1974, ss 114–122 of which lay down various requirements that must be complied with in respect of transactions of pawn or pledge. This regime covers only 'articles taken in pawn under a regulated consumer credit agreement'.[100] So pledges or pawns securing an advance of more than £25,000 are generally not within the statutory controls, nor are cases where the pledgor is a body corporate. On the other side of the consumer-commercial coin, the trading practices of banks and finance houses depend heavily on pledges of bills of lading, bills of exchange, chattel paper and other similar documents.

Characteristics of a pledge

4.38   With a pledge the pledgee (lender) has possession of the items pledged, whereas ownership of the items remains with the pledgor (borrower). These factors were alluded to by Willes J in *Halliday v Holgate*:[101]

> 'There are three kinds of security: the first, a simple lien, the second, a mortgage, passing the property out and out; the third, a security interme-diate between a lien and a mortgage – viz, a pledge – where by contract a deposit of goods is made as security for a debt, and the right to the property vests in the pledge so far as necessary to secure the debt. It is true the pledgor has such a property in the articles pledged as he can convey to a third person but he has no right to the goods without paying off the debts, and until the debt is paid off the pledgee has the whole present interest.'

As possessor the pledgee is said to enjoy a 'special property', but the general property in the goods, however, or what might be termed ownership, still belongs with the pledgor.

4.39   There was much discussion on the nature of a pledge in *Donald v Suckling*.[102] Blackburn J referred to the observations of Lord Holt in *Coggs v Barnard*[103] that a pledgee has a 'special property, for the pawn is a securing to the pawnee that he shall be repaid his debt, and to compel the pawnor to pay him'. Blackburn J said that the contract of pledge, when perfected by delivery of possession, creates an interest in the pledgee, which interest may be assigned.[104] Mellor J talked about a well recognised distinction between a lien and a pledge, as regards the powers of a person entitled to a lien and the powers of the person who holds goods upon an agreement of deposit by way of pawn or pledge for the due payment of money. He went on:[105]

---

100   Under the new Consumer Credit Bill 2005 it is proposed to remove the financial limit for the regulation of consumer credit and consumer hire agreements under the 1974 Act so that in future all consumer credit and consumer hire agreements will be regulated by the 1974 Act unless specifically exempted, regardless of the amount of the credit.
101   (1868) LR 3 Ex 299 at 302.
102   (1866) LR 1 QB 585.
103   (1703) 92 ER 622; 2 Ld Raym 909 at 916.
104   (1866) LR 1 QB 585 at 613.
105   (1866) LR 1 QB 585 at 604.

'In the case of a simple lien there can be no power of sale or disposition of the goods, which is inconsistent with the retention of the possession by the person entitled to the lien; whereas in the case of a pledge or pawn of goods, to secure the payment of money at a certain day, on default by the pawnor, the pawnee may sell the goods deposited and realise the amount, and become a trustee for the surplus for the pawnor; or even if no day of payment be named, he may, upon waiting a reasonable time, and taking the proper steps, realise his debt in like manner.'

It is apparent from *Donald v Suckling*[106] that a lien may be transferred, but on the other hand a pledgee who sub-pledges the goods without the authority of the pledgor commits a breach of contract. The original pledgor may maintain an action against the repledgee if he tenders the amount due under the initial pledge agreement. The right of possession on the part of the pledgor revives if he tenders the sum of the original advance no matter how great the amount purportedly secured by the repledge agreement.[107]

4.40   The characteristics of a pledge were also elaborated upon in *Re Morritt ex parte Official Receiver*.[108] Cotton LJ observed that a pledge of personal chattels as a rule is and must be accompanied by delivery of possession. It was out of the possession given by the contract that the pledgee's rights spring. A contract of pledge carried with it the implication that the security may be made available to satisfy the obligation, and enabled the pledgee in possession (although he had not the general property in the thing pledged but a special property only) to sell on default in payment and after notice to the pledgor, although the pledgor could redeem at any moment up to sale.[109] He said a mortgage conveyed the whole legal interest in the chattels, whereas a pledge conveyed only a special property, leaving the general property in the pledgor.[110]

4.41   If the pledgor defaults in respect of the loan agreement, then the pledgee has authority to sell the goods pledged. This was made clear by Bowen LJ in *Re Hubbard ex parte Hardwick*.[111] If the sale is a provident one but nevertheless the proceeds of sale are insufficient to discharge the debt, then the pledgee has a right of action against the pledgor in respect of the balance. In *Jones v Marshall*[112] Lord Coleridge CJ explained that, in the case of a contract of pledge, if the article pawned does not realise the amount lent on it, the pledgee may bring an action for the deficit. The converse case was examined in *Matthew v TM Sutton Ltd*[113] and it was held that a pledgee who sells unredeemed chattels for more than the sum owed by the pledgor holds the surplus as a fiduciary on trust for the pledgor.

---

106   (1866) LR 1 QB 585.
107   (1866) LR 1 QB 585 at 610 per Mellor J and 611 per Blackburn J. See also *Sewell v Burdick* (1884) 10 App Cas 74.
108   (1887) 41 Ch D 222.
109   (1887) 41 Ch D 222 at 232.
110   (1887) 41 Ch D 222 at 234.
111   (1886) 17 QBD 690 at 698.
112   (1890) 24 QBD 269.
113   [1994] 4 All ER 793.

4.42   To constitute a pledge, delivery of possession need not be contemporaneous with the making of a loan. This was held in *Hilton v Tucker*.[114] It sufficed that possession was delivered within a reasonable time of the advance in pursuance of the contract to pledge. Kekewich J said:[115]

> 'My view of the law certainly is, that if money is advanced, as here, on a contract that goods shall be delivered and that then those goods are delivered in pursuance of that contract, the same legal results follow as if the money was handed over with one hand and the goods received with the other.'

4.43   It should be stressed that the actual or constructive delivery of possession is indispensable. The requirement of delivery means that the class of assets capable of forming the subject-matter of a pledge is confined to goods and to documentary intangibles which are 'documents embodying title to goods, money or securities such that the right to these assets is vested in the holder of the document for the time being and can be transferred by delivery with any necessary indorsement.'[116] Consequently, pledges may be created in respect of bills of lading and other documents of title to goods but not over common commercial contracts. The fact that a bill of lading may be pledged signifies the usefulness of pledges for the financing of international trade. The requirement, however, that a creditor take a pledge over a document which is actually a document of title suggests the limitations of the pledge as a security vehicle. Bills of lading are documents of title and so, too, are bearer share certificates, but not warehouse receipts nor certificates relating to registered shares.[117] On the other hand, the usefulness of the pledge mechanism has been extended by judicial validation of three techniques. The first is that of 'constructive delivery of possession'.[118] The second is that of attornment and the third technique is the 'trust receipt'.

Extensions of the pledge concept – constructive delivery of possession, attornment, trust receipts

4.44   The notions of 'constructive delivery of possession' and attornment were explained by the Privy Council in *Official Assignee of Madras v Mercantile Bank of India Ltd*.[119]

---

114   (1888) 39 Ch D 669.
115   (1888) 39 Ch D 669 at 677.
116   See also R Goode *Legal Problems of Credit and Security* (Sweet & Maxwell, 3rd edn, 2003) at pp 31–32. Professor Goode expresses the point in another way by saying that:
> 'the obligor's delivery or payment obligation is owed not to the original obligee as such but to whoever is the holder of the document and presents it for delivery or payment. Documentary intangibles are thus to be distinguished from pure intangibles, where the entitlement may be evidenced in or recorded in a document but it is not a document which represents the right.'

117   *Harrold v Plenty* [1901] 2 Ch 314.
118   The example was given in *Hilton v Tucker* (1888) 39 Ch D 669 of delivery of a key, as the symbol of possession, where the transfer of possession itself was practically impossible.
119   [1935] AC 53 at 58–59.

'At common law a pledge could not be created except by a delivery of possession of the thing pledged, either actual or constructive. It involved a bailment. If the pledgor had the actual goods in his physical possession, he could effect the pledge by physical delivery; in other cases he could give possession by some symbolic act, such as handing over the key of the store in which they were. If, however, the goods were in the custody of a third person, who held for the bailor so that in law his possession was that of the bailor, the pledge could be effected by a change of the possession of the third party, that is by an order to him from the pledgor to hold for the pledgee, the change being perfected by the third party attorning to the pledgee, that is acknowledging that he thereupon held for him; there was thus a change of possession and a constructive delivery; the goods in the hands of the third party became by this process in the possession constructively of the pledgee.'

4.45   As the judicial statement shows, where goods are in the possession of a third party rather than the debtor, the third party can 'attorn' to the creditor, ie undertake to hold the goods for the benefit of the creditor. Attornment is a technique that is often used in the art world:[120]

'If, for instance, the debtor is an art dealer who has deposited works of art with an auction house, the auction house can, by attorning in favour of the creditor (ie by confirming, at the request of the debtor, that it holds the works of art on behalf of the creditor), transfer constructive possession in the works of art to the creditor.'

4.46   On the third technique, the 'trust receipt' is a document which permits a pledgee to release goods to his pledgor as agent for sale and trustee of the proceeds but simultaneously maintaining his pledge interest.[121] The fact that goods are released back by the 'pledgee' to the 'pledgor' will not prejudice the claim to a pledge where the release takes place under the auspices of a trust receipt. Trust receipts received the approval of the House of Lords in *North Western Bank Ltd v Poynter, Son and Macdonalds*.[122] It was held that a pledgee

---

120   Richard Calnan 'Taking Security in England' in Michael Bridge and Robert Stevens (eds) *Cross-Border Security and Insolvency* (OUP, 2001) 17 at 19

121   See generally *North Western Bank Ltd v Poynter, Son and Macdonalds* [1895] AC 56; *Re David Allester* [1922] 2 Ch 211. Professor EP Ellinger suggests that to avoid any argument registration of the trust receipt should follow a few simple guidelines ('Trust Receipt Financing' [2003] JIBLR 305 at 306):

'First, it is imperative to avoid any language implying an intention to create a security in favour of the bank. The trust receipt seeks to extend the bank's special property obtained by it as pledge and should be formulated on this basis. Secondly, it is best to insist on the execution of a separate trust receipt in respect of every transaction. If commercial considerations dictate that only one global trust receipt be executed by the customer, the document should be phrased as a memorandum defining the nature of the contractual arrangement to be created between the parties where any goods pledged to the bank are to be released prior to its being reimbursed by the customer. Thirdly, the bank has to be constituted the cestui ... of the proceeds of the sale of the goods. Where the parties use a global trust receipt, care should be taken to avoid formulations indicative of the creation of a floating charge.'

122   [1895] AC 56.

may redeliver the goods to the pledgor for a limited purpose without thereby losing his rights under the contract of pledge. Pledgees of a bill of lading representing a specific cargo returned the bill of lading to the pledgors to obtain delivery of the merchandise and sell on the pledgees' behalf and account for the proceeds towards satisfaction of the debt. The House of Lords took the view that the pledgees' security was not affected and that they were entitled to the proceeds of the cargo as against the general creditors of the pledgors.

4.47   The same principle was applied in *Re David Allester Ltd*.[123] Here a company pledged bills of lading with a bank to secure an overdraft, but when it came to sell the goods the company, in accordance with long-standing mercantile practice, obtained the bills of lading from the bank. Realisation was on the terms stated in the usual letter of trust given by the company to the bank, ie that the company received the bills of lading in trust on the bank's account and undertook to hold the goods when received and the proceeds when sold as the bank's trustees and to remit the entire net proceeds as realised. The court held that the bank's previous rights as pledgee remained unaffected by this 'common and convenient mode of realisation'.[124]

Application of registration provisions to pledges

4.48   The application of the bills of sale legislation, and, by inference, the company charge registration provisions, to pledges has been considered on many occasions. In *Re Hardwick ex parte Hubbard*[125] the Court of Appeal held that where goods are pledged as security for a loan and delivered to the pledgee, a document signed by the pledgor that records the transaction and regulates the rights of the pledgee as to the sale of the goods was not a bill of sale and, hence, not registrable. Further explanation was provided by Lord Esher MR in *Johnson v Diprose*.[126] He said that a bill of sale was a document given with respect to the transfer of chattels, and was used in cases where possession was not intended to be given. Such a transaction was not a pledge, the conditions of which were entirely different. Davey LJ in *Ramsay v Margrett*[127] ventured a similar view. He said that the Bills of Sale Act does not apply to transactions in which the passing of property in goods is accompanied by the delivery of possession, but that the legislation only applies where the property passes without possession.

4.49   The matter is slightly more problematic if the pledgee is relying on constructive, rather than actual delivery of possession. In principle, however, there is neither a charge nor a bill of sale in this particular situation either. Authority for this proposition is found in *Wrightson v McArthur and*

---

123   [1922] 2 Ch 211.
124   If the company, however, fails to act in accordance with the bank's instructions, the bank may lose out to a third party to whom the company has sold the goods – see *Lloyds Bank Ltd v Bank of America* [1938] 1 KB 147.
125   (1886) 17 QBD 690.
126   [1893] 1 QB 513 at 515.
127   [1894] 2 QB 18 at 26.

Hutchisons (1919) Ltd,[128] though the court eschewed any talk of the expression 'constructive delivery of possession'. In the case, the defendant company, as security for the plaintiff, set aside certain specified goods in two rooms in the defendants' premises which were then locked up, and the keys handed over to the plaintiff. There were no other goods in those two rooms. The terms of the transaction were recorded in two letters written by the defendant company to the plaintiff. One letter was written before the keys were handed over, and the second letter subsequently. The last letter contained the words: 'The goods to be locked up, the keys in your possession, and you have the right to remove same as desired.' The company went into liquidation and the liquidator claimed that the transaction was invalid as being a charge created or evidenced by an instrument which if executed by an individual would require registration as a bill of sale. Rowlatt J rejected this submission. He held that possession of the goods passed to the plaintiff by the delivery of the keys of the rooms in which they were locked up, notwithstanding the fact that those rooms were on the defendants' premises.[129] The defendants had conferred upon the plaintiff a licence to make the necessary entry in order to use the keys, which licence could not be revoked. Rowlatt J referred to cases in which delivery of the key of a box in a house had been held to confer possession of the contents[130] and suggested that the principles enunciated in those cases could be extended somewhat to cover the facts of the instant case.

4.50 It is worth pointing out that there is no exception of pledges, using the specific language of pledges, from the legislation. This was stressed by Rowlatt J in *Wrightson v McArthur and Hutchisons*.[131] It is in a sense immaterial whether or not a pledge has been created for the purpose of application of the statutory provisions. The crucial question is whether or not possession has been conferred upon the creditor independently of any document recording the transaction. The leading case is *Dublin City Distillery v Doherty*.[132] Here the plaintiff advanced money to a distillery company on the security of whiskey manufactured by the company. The whiskey was stored by the company in a warehouse situated on the distillery premises in accordance with the Spirits Act 1880. The company could not obtain access to the warehouse without the assistance of the excise officer and vice versa. The whiskey could only be delivered out on presentation to the excise officer of a special form of warrant supplied by the Crown. When each advance was made the company entered the name of the plaintiff in their stock-book opposite the particulars of the whiskey intended to serve as security. They delivered to the plaintiff an ordinary trade invoice and, secondly, a document called a warrant which described the particulars of the whiskey and stated that it was deliverable to the plaintiff or his assigns and contained the words 'free storage'. The excise officer was given no notice of the transaction. The House of Lords held that the plaintiff was not entitled to a valid pledge on the whiskey comprised in the warrants. Lord Atkinson said that it was quite impossible to treat the delivery

---

128 [1921] 2 KB 807.
129 [1921] 2 KB 807 at 817.
130 *Jones v Selby* (1710) Prec in Ch 300; and *Mustapha v Wedlake* [1891] WN 201.
131 [1921] 2 KB 807 at 815–816.
132 [1914] AC 823.

warrants as the agreement or memorandum in writing was treated in *Re Hard-wick ex parte Hubbard*,[133] namely, as a document accompanying a pawn or pledge made independently of the document, and merely regulating the rights of the pledgee with regard to goods where possession had already been delivered to the pledgee.[134] In the present case there was not a particle of evidence, independently of the warrant and the entries in the books, to show that a single cask of whiskey was ever pledged to the plaintiff. It was the delivery of the warrants which constituted the plaintiff's security. According to Lord Sumner all that the plaintiff established was that he was a secured creditor, but how secured he left in doubt. In the judge's opinion, no valid pledge was created, since no change took place in the character of the company's possession. The company did not become a bailee for the plaintiff and consequently[135] any security in favour of the plaintiff was invalidated for want of registration.

4.51 The waters were muddied somewhat in the judgment of Lord Parker. At one point he stated:[136]

> 'The object of the [registration] section is to give notice to all who deal with a company of certain matters which vitally affect the company's credit. For this purpose no distinction can be drawn between a pledge at common law and a mortgage or charge.'

It seems, however, that Lord Parker contemplated a more expansive view of the concept of pledge than is commonly understood to be the case. He suggested that a person might obtain delivery sufficient to complete a common law pledge where there is some agreement between the parties the effect of which is to change the possession of the pledgor, from a possession on his own account as owner, into a possession as bailee for the pledgee. According to Lord Parker, such an agreement operates as a delivery of the goods to the pledgee and a redelivery of the goods by the pledgee to the pledgor as bailee for the purposes mentioned in the agreement.[137]

4.52 It may be that to bring such an agreement within the notion of a pledge is to stretch the notion almost to breaking point. It has been persuasively argued that it is better to treat such a security as an equitable charge which, as a security concept, postulates the transfer of neither property nor possession.[138] What is important to note is that even Lord Parker felt that a security interest

---

133 (1886) 17 QBD 690.

134 [1914] AC 823 at 848.

135 [1914] AC 823 at 865.

136 [1914] AC 823 at 854.

137 [1914] AC 823 at 852.

138 See WJ Gough *Company Charges* (2nd edn, 1996) at 668. Gough refers also to the Australian case *Askrigg Pty Ltd v Student Guild of the Curtin University of Technology* (1989) 18 NSWLR 738 and suggests:

> 'It is at least arguable whether "pledge" agreements with a debtor in actual possession should be treated as pledges or possessory security for the purposes of charges registration. A pledge in these circumstances is highly artificial and almost totally fictional. The security depends entirely on agreement with no independent possession held by the creditor. The reality and substance of the transaction is that the security is created,

dependent on a transfer of possession, and in no way reliant upon any written document, was not registrable. In *Dublin City Distillery Ltd v Doherty*, however, as Lord Parker observed, it would be hopeless to contend that, apart from the warrants, there was a good pledge at common law.[139]

CONCLUSION

4.53   There are a number of security interests in property properly categorisable as charges that fall outside the scope of the registration regime. Charges on bank accounts, for example, appear to be outwith the registration system since a bank account in credit is not considered to be a 'book debt' in terms of accountancy practice, even though, legally speaking, the banker-customer relationship is a debtor-creditor one. One might instance also charges on shares and charges on insurance policies. It has been suggested that the failure to make registrable charges on shares constitutes a significant lacuna in the legislation. There are, however, countervailing practical considerations that militate against extending the registration net more widely. Making fixed charges on charges registrable would be incompatible with the EC Financial Collateral Directive.

---

variously, by way of equitable mortgage, charge or hypothecation. In the context of the charges registration system, it should be treated as such.'
139   [1914] AC 823 at 855.

Chapter 5

REGISTRATION OF CHARGES AND RESERVATION OF TITLE CLAUSES

INTRODUCTION

5.1   One area where the question of whether or not a registrable charge has been created often arises is that of reservation of title. There are five different types of reservation of title clause. Some kinds of clause constitute a registrable charge, whereas others do not. In this chapter it is proposed to examine the interaction between the registration of company charge provisions and the reservation of title phenomenon.[1] In its Consultation Paper on *Registration of Security Interests* the Law Commission considered that all retention of title clauses should be registrable but, as a partly counterbalancing measure, the Commission canvassed the possibility that at least simple retention of title clauses should enjoy super-priority status, ie such clauses would rank ahead of pre-existing security interests granted by the debtor that extend to property afterwards acquired by the debtor.

TERMINOLOGY

5.2   The essence of the provision under consideration in this chapter is a clause in a sale of goods contract under which the seller keeps to itself title to goods, the subject-matter of the contract of sale, until some condition specified in the sales contract has been fulfilled. Such clauses are referred to as reservation of title clauses, or retention of title clauses, or *Romalpa* clauses and in this chapter the various expressions are used interchangeably. The seller is 'retaining' or 'reserving' title. The phrase 'reservation' comes from s 19 of the Sale of Goods Act 1979 which is headed 'reservation of a right of disposal'. The section provides that where there is a contract for the sale of specific goods or where goods are subsequently appropriated to the contract, the seller may, by the terms of the contract of appropriation, reserve the right to disposal of

---

1   For a comprehensive discussion of reservation of title clauses see G McCormack *Reservation of Title* (Sweet & Maxwell, 2nd edn, 1995); J Parris *Effective Retention of Title Clauses* (Blackwell, 1986); I Davies *Effective Retention of Title* (Fourmat Publishing, 1991); and for an empirical study of the operation of such clauses in practice see S Wheeler *Reservation of Title Clauses: Impact and Implications* (OUP, 1991). See also for a useful synthesis of the cases G McMeel 'Retention of Title: The Interface of Contract, Unjust Enrichment and Insolvency' in Francis Rose (ed) *Restitution and Insolvency* (Mansfield Press, 2000).

the goods until certain conditions are fulfilled: hence the expression 'reservation of title'. The popular shorthand expression for reservation of title clauses – *Romalpa* clauses – comes from the seminal case of *Aluminium Industrie Vaassen BV v Romalpa Aluminium Ltd*.[2] The concept of reservation of title is older than the Sale of Goods Act 1893; such a clause was used in the Irish case of *Bateman v Green and King*[3] in 1868. It was not until the mid 1970s, however, that the legal consequences of the concept began to be explored fully by the courts. The breakthrough came in the *Romalpa* case. Remarkably though, the insight offered by the decision proved unnoticed insofar as the compilers of the Official Series of Law Reports were concerned. *Romalpa* remain unreported in the Law Reports proper.

TYPES OF RESERVATION OF TITLE CLAUSE

5.3 As mentioned earlier, there are five different types of reservation of title clause, four of them purporting to go one step further than the original 'simple' clause. The objectives of each of these clauses may be summarised thus:

(1) *Simple clause*: the seller retains ownership in the goods delivered as against the buyer until the full purchase price for goods has been paid.

(2) *Current account clause*: the seller retains ownership in the goods delivered as against the buyer until all debts or other obligations owed by the buyer to the seller have been paid.

(3) *Extended (or 'continuing') clause*: the seller retains ownership in the goods delivered as against the buyer and any sub-buyer either until the full purchase price for goods has been paid or until all debts owed by the buyer to the seller have been paid.[4]

(4) *Tracing (or 'prolonged') clause*: the seller retains ownership in the goods delivered as against the buyer either until the full purchase price for those goods has been paid or until all debts owed by the buyer to the seller have been paid, but, if the goods are resold to a sub-buyer, then the seller acquires ownership either of the proceeds of sale or of the right to sue the sub-buyer for the proceeds of sale.

(5) *Aggregation (or 'enlarged') clause*: the seller retains ownership in the goods delivered as against the buyer either until the full purchase price for those goods has been paid, but, if the goods are manufactured into some other property, with or without the addition of other goods, then the

---

2 [1976] 1 WLR 676.

3 (1868) IR 2 Ch 607. There was a House of Lords appeal in the case – reported at (1871–72) LR 5 HL 591 – but the substantive reservation of title point was not considered on the appeal. The case is discussed by J Phillips and A Schuster 'Reservation of Title in the Commercial Laws of England and Ireland' [1978–1980] DULJ 1.

4 Extended reservation of title clauses are not much used in practice, for they are unlikely to be effective against sub-buyers. Section 25 of the Sale of Goods Act 1979 enables a buyer in possession to pass a good title to a sub-buyer even though the buyer may not itself have a good title; on which see generally *Forsythe International (UK) Ltd v Silver Shipping Co Ltd* [1993] 2 Lloyd's Rep 268 and *Re Highway Foods* [1995] 1 BCLC 209.

seller acquires ownership of the resulting property or of a proportionate part of it equal to the contribution made to the manufacturing process by the original goods.

As the wording of the summaries indicates, a current account clause (No 2) may be combined with an extended clause (No 3), a tracing clause (No 4) or an aggregation clause (No 5). In addition, an extended clause (No 3) or a tracing clause (No 4) may be added to an aggregation clause (No 5). However, No 3 and No 4 cannot be combined in the same clause. In the end, therefore, one might have a clause that represents No 2 and (No 3 or No 4) and No 5.

REASONS FOR THE USE OF RESERVATION OF TITLE CLAUSES

5.4   Why, one may ask, has 'reservation of a right of disposal' become a matter of great moment to business people and their advisors? Undoubtedly the principal reason underlying the insertion in a contract for the sale of goods of a term retaining title until certain requirements have been met is to provide security for payment of the purchase price. However, in *Clough Mill Ltd v Martin*[5] Oliver LJ questioned the correctness of the assumption that the whole purpose of a reservation of title condition is to give the seller security for the payment of the purchase price. Indeed, he suggested that the purpose of the clause goes well beyond a mere security for payment of the price. In more general terms its purpose was to protect the seller from the insolvency of the buyer in circumstances where the price remains unpaid.

5.5   The remedy of repossession is available against the goods, the subject-matter of the contract of sale. Alternatively, if the goods have been sold, the original seller's claim lies against the proceeds of sale. Where the goods have been incorporated into other products, or form part of the raw material for a process of manufacture, the seller may have an entitlement to the finished product, either alone or in common with others. The important point to note is that the seller is not left with an unsecured claim in respect of the purchase price in the event of the buyer's insolvency. There is often a jungle of competing claims in an insolvency and any device which puts a supplier of goods ahead of the queue is very much welcomed from the supplier's point of view.

COMPANY CHARGE REGISTRATION – SOME GENERAL OBSERVATIONS

5.6   Before discussing the application of the company charge registration provisions to the various individual types of reservation of title clause it is appropriate, perhaps, to make some general comments on company charge registration. Among the categories of registrable charge in s 396(1) of the Companies Act 1985 the most relevant in a reservation of title context are:

---

5   [1985] 1 WLR 111 at 122.

s 396(1)(c) – 'a charge, created or evidenced by an instrument which, if executed by an individual, would require registration as a bill of sale'; s 396(1)(c)(e) – a charge on book debts; and s 396(1)(f) – a floating charge on the whole or part of the company's property.

5.7   The law on bills of sale is contained in the Bills of Sale Acts 1878–1882, as amended, and the Companies Act provisions effectively incorporated into the Companies Code all the antique learning as to what constitutes a 'bill of sale'.[6] The Bills of Sale Acts are verbose and unclear, to say the least, and their application in the reservation of title context is not easy to discern.[7] Certainly they were not drafted with reservation of title clauses specifically in mind.

5.8   Bills of sale that fall within the Bills of Sale Acts are of two kinds: those which constitute absolute assurances of chattels and, secondly, bills of sale given by way of security. The former are regulated by the 1878 Act, whereas the latter are affected both by the 1878 and 1882 Acts. The 1878 Act has the long title 'An Act to consolidate and amend the law for preventing frauds upon creditors by secret Bills of Sale of Personal Chattels'. Section 3 of the Bills of Sale Act 1878 lays down that the Act shall apply to 'every bill of sale ... whereby the holder or grantee has power ... to seize or take possession of any personal chattels'. Section 4 of the same Act sets out three categories of bill of sale:

(i)   assignments, transfers, declarations of trust without transfer, inventories of goods with receipt thereto attached, or receipts for purchase monies of goods, and other assurances of personal chattels;

(ii)   powers of attorney, authorities or licences to take possession of personal chattels as security for any debt;

(iii) agreements by which a right in equity to any personal chattels or to any charge or security thereon shall be conferred.[8]

5.9   Aggregation clauses pose particular problems insofar as the application of the bills of sale legislation is concerned. The position is complicated by the fact that the first two categories of bills of sale – transfer of ownership and right to possession as security – apply only to property which the grantor owns at the time that the document is executed.[9] A document concerning after acquired property, such as an aggregation clause, is only a bill of sale if it comes within the third limb of the definition, ie an agreement conferring a right in equity to chattels or to any charge or security thereon. The precise scope of this third category of bill of sale was considered in *Reeves v Barlow*.[10] In this case a clause in a building contract whereby all building and other materials brought by the builder upon the land should become the property of the landowner was held not to constitute a bill of sale. The court held that the builder's agreement was not an equitable assignment of anything, but a mere

---

6   See generally on the Bills of Sale legislation chapter 8 of G McCormack *Reservation of Title* (2nd edn, 1995).

7   Diamond Report A Review of Security Interests in Property (HMSO, 1989), p 119.

8   The expression 'bill of sale' is accorded the same meaning in the 1882 Act – see s 3.

9   See B Allcock 'Romalpa Clauses and Bills of Sale' (1981) 131 New LJ 842.

10   (1884) 12 QBD 436.

legal contract that, upon the happening of a particular event, the legal property should pass in certain chattels. In its judgment, an agreement that created a legal right over future goods, without any preceding equitable right, was not a bill of sale.

5.10   Generally, however, assignments of future property, including manufactured goods not yet in existence at the time that a contract of sale is drawn up, only take effect in equity rather than at law. The leading case is *Holroyd v Marshall*[11] where it was held that an assignment of future property operates in equity by way of assignment, binding the conscience of the assignor, and so binding the property from the moment when the contract becomes capable of being performed, on the principle that equity regards as done that which ought to be done. A legal interest may pass, however, if the grantor is required to perform some new act manifesting an intention to pass the property. According to *Lunn v Thornton*[12] the act must be done for 'the avowed object and with the view of carrying the former grant or disposition into effect'. In *Reeves v Barlow* the taking of possession of goods by the transferee was held to be a new act within this doctrine. In practice, however, this option is not likely to be available to a seller where new products have been manufactured out of raw materials supplied subject to a reservation of title provision.[13]

5.11   Certain transactions that prima facie fall within the definition of a bill of sale are excluded from the ambit of the legislation. Section 4 of the Bills of Sale Act 1878 sets out a list of documents that are specifically exempted. The exceptions include transfer of goods in the ordinary course of any trade or calling. If what purports to be a reservation of title clause is held, in reality, to amount to a charge and the charge is neither a charge over book debts nor a floating charge over the undertaking or property of the company, then the charge will only be avoided if it comes within the statutory definition of a bill of sale. A fall-back position is for the seller of goods to argue that the charge, while prima facie a bill of sale, falls within one of the excepted categories such as the transfer of goods in the ordinary course of any trade or calling. At first, though, it appears a little incongruous to imagine how this provision might apply in a reservation of title context. The exception presupposes initially the transfer of title to the goods to the buyer, contrary to the express purpose of the reservation of title clause and, secondly the retransfer of rights back to the seller in the ordinary course of a trade or calling.[14] It has been suggested, however, that, in theory at least, there seems no reason not to apply the exception to retention of title clauses.[15] Most of the decided cases have covered letters of hypothecation and liens over trading stock executed by traders in

---

11   (1862) 10 HL Cas 191.

12   (1845) 1 CB 379.

13   See B Allcock (1981) 131 New LJ 842 at 843. Presumably one should insist that the new products be separated from the buyer's own goods. The courts, however, may not take the view that such separation is effected in the words of Tindal CJ 'for the avowed object and with the view of carrying the former grant or disposition into effect'.

14   See J Farrar and N Furey 'Reservation of Ownership and Tracing in a Commercial Context' (1977) 36 CLJ 27.

15   [1981] JBL 173 at 175.

need of short term finance, but the object is the same in this situation and the reservation of title sphere: namely, the regular use of trading stock as security for recurring obligations.

5.12   The leading case on the exception is *Re Young, Hamilton and Co ex parte Carter*.[16] The case concerned a textile partnership which required a bank loan and, to facilitate the borrowing, the partnership provided, in accordance with its business practice, letters of equitable charge over goods in its possession or in the possession of its bailees. The partnership went bankrupt and the trustee in bankruptcy claimed that the letters constituted bills of sale and, being unregistered, were void. The court rejected this contention on the ground, inter alia, that the letters amounted to a transfer of goods in the ordinary course of business.

5.13   The *Young* case was invoked unsuccessfully by a reservation of title claimant anxious to avoid registration requirements in *Ian Chisholm Textiles Ltd v Criffiths*.[17] The court said that the onus of proof was on the plaintiff to show that what was in effect a charge was created in the ordinary course of the buyer's trade. The plaintiff contended unsuccessfully that the absolute volume of cases on retention of title agreements was enough to discharge the onus of proof, with the court holding that it would require a very exceptional case before it was prepared to conclude, merely on the volume of reported cases on a particular topic, that something was 'in the ordinary course of business of any trade'. Moreover, the plaintiff did not normally deal with its customers, who were mostly in the same sort of business as the buyer, on the basis of reservation of title arrangements. Furthermore, it only entered into a reservation of title agreement with this particular buyer when the financial condition of the latter became parlous.

THE REGISTRATION MACHINERY AND COMPARISONS WITH THE POSITION IN THE UNITED STATES

5.14   It is fair to say that the registration of company charge provisions are not drafted adequately to deal with the reservation of title phenomenon. The particulars requiring registration cover the date of creation of a charge; the amount secured by the charge; short particulars of the property charged; and the persons entitled to the charge.

5.15   Difficulties arise in relation to the 'date of creation'. Take an 'aggregation clause', for instance. Such a clause gives the seller rights with respect to goods manufactured out of the original goods supplied. After *Clough Mill* the general view is that straightforward retention of title clauses are not registrable. What if a contract for the sale of goods includes an aggregation clause as well as a 'simple' reservation of title provision – is the 'date of creation' the date of the making of the original supply contract or the date of manufacture? If the latter is the date of creation, then it would be almost impossible for the seller to

---

16   [1905] 2 KB 772. See also *Re Slee ex parte North Western Bank* (1872) LR 15 Eq 69.
17   [1994] BCC 96.

fulfil the registration requirements, for he may not know the precise date when the goods supplied have become part of the process of manufacture. There may be other difficulties in meeting the letter of s 395 and succeeding sections. In practice, goods may be delivered on reservation of title terms over a prolonged period. It has been asked whether the 'date of creation' is every single invoice recording the delivery of goods subject to these conditions.[18] It is simply not feasible to expect a seller to register each contract of sale individually.[19]

5.16   In the United States, however, a supplier can take a security interest in the goods themselves, as well as proceeds and products, by filing a simple financing statement. The financing statement will expire at the end of five years unless renewed, but clearly can cover multiple deliveries of goods during that period. Therefore, there is no need to register each contract of sale individually. Transaction costs are kept to a minimum, but of course there is the initial filing expense. It should be noted, however, that a purchase money security interest (PMSI) in consumer goods is automatically perfected upon attachment.[20] In other words, it does not have to be filed to obtain effectiveness against third parties. A purchase money security interest arises where value is given to enable the debtor to acquire rights in or the use of collateral, if the value is in fact so used. This definition clearly covers the case of a simple reservation of title clause.

'SIMPLE' CLAUSES

5.17   The case law has affirmed the effectiveness of 'simple' reservation of title clauses. The principal authority is now the decision of the Court of Appeal in *Clough Mill v Martin*.[21] There the court rejected the notion, propounded by

---

18   See J Parris *Effective Retention of Title Clauses* (Basil Blackwell, 1986) at pp 129–130. See also the comment by the Law Commission at para 3.30 of their Consultation Paper *Registration of Security Interests* (2002):
   'each individual charge must be registered even when it is just one of a long series between the same parties. For example, the difficulty and expense this causes is the explanation usually given for suppliers not registering extended retention of title clauses even though these frequently create registrable charges.'

19   The Diamond report *Security Interests in Property* for the Department of Trade and Industry (February 1989), when suggesting that a supplier need file only one financing statement for each customer, was conscious of the burden even this requirement might impose. The work involved for a seller with thousands of customers would be enormous. See pp 89–90 of the Report.

20   Article 9–309(1) of the Uniform Commercial Code (2001 Revised version).

21   [1985] 1 WLR 111. It makes no difference that the buyer has been given a power of resale over the goods or a right to consume the goods in a process of manufacture. Robert Goff LJ was adamant on this point. He said:
   'I see nothing objectionable in an agreement under which A, the owner of goods, gives possession of those goods to B, at the same time conferring on B a power of sale and a promise to consume the goods in manufacture though A will remain the owner of the goods until they are either sold or consumed.'
   Furthermore, the fact that certain provisions of the contract of sale could only operate by way of charge did not warrant the conclusion that all efforts by the seller to obtain security for payment of goods must necessarily be by way of charge.

Judge O'Donoghue at first instance, that if the purpose of a reservation of title clause is to provide security for the payment of the purchase price, then the clause should be construed as creating a charge.[22] A charge on goods, if created by a company, must be registered under Part XII of the Companies Act 1985 for validity in the event of the company's liquidation.

5.18   One major hiccup occurred in *Re Bond Worth Ltd*[23] where a clause purported to reserve 'equitable and beneficial ownership'. It was held that legal and equitable title to the goods passed to the buyers and an equitable interest was granted back to the sellers by way of charge after a split second (scintilla temporis) had elapsed.[24] Clearly, the only safe course for a person drafting a reservation of title clause is to avoid use of the expression 'equitable and beneficial' ownership. The judgment of Slade J in *Re Bond Worth Ltd* may require reconsideration, however, in the light of the decision of the House of Lords in *Abbey National Building Society v Cann*.[25] Briefly stated, it was held in that case that where a purchaser relies on a loan for completion of the transaction, to be secured by a charge on the property, he could not be said to have acquired, even for a split second, the unencumbered interest in the property. Their Lordships were scathing of the legal fiction implied by the scintilla temporis notion. Despite the *Cann*[26] decision, *Re Bond Worth Ltd* was nevertheless followed in *Stroud Architectural Services Ltd v John Laing Contruction Ltd*.[27] This is a case where goods were supplied subject to a reservation of title clause which purported to retain in the seller the 'equitable and beneficial ownership in all or any goods supplied'. The court held that the clause necessarily involved the creation of a charge and, in its view, the status and authority of *Bond Worth* remained unaffected by *Cann*.[28]

---

22   The first instance decision is reported [1984] 1 WLR 1067.

23   [1980] Ch 228. See also *Coburn v Collins* (1887) 35 CPD 373.

24   The sellers argued that all they had passed to the purchasers was the shell of legal ownership from which the crabmeat of equitable ownership had been skilfully extracted. Slade J said:
   'However, no authority has been cited which satisfies me that on the transfer of the legal property in land or chattels, it is competent to a vendor expressly to except from the grant in favour of himself an equitable mortgage or charge thereon to secure the unpaid purchase price (in addition to or in substitution for any lien which may arise by operation of law), in such manner that the exception will take effect without any express or implied grant back of a mortgage or charge in the vendor's favour by the purchaser.'

25   [1991] 1 AC 56. *Cann*, however, enjoys a measure of support from the following observations of Lord Browne-Wilkinson in *Westdeutsche Landesbank Girozentrale v Islington Borough Council* [1996] AC 669 at 706:
   'A person solely entitled to the full beneficial ownership of money or property, both in law and in equity, does not enjoy an equitable interest in that property. The legal title carries with it all rights. Unless and until there is separation of the legal and equitable estates, there is no separate equitable title. Therefore, to talk about the bank "retaining" its equitable interest is meaningless.'

26   [1991] 1 AC 56. See generally J De Lacy 'The Purchase Money Security Interest: A Company Charge Conundrum' [1991] LMCLQ 531.

27   (1993) 35 Con LR 135.

28   Judge Newey said (at 145): 'Slade J did speak of the sale being "followed" by the giving back of security, but he described both events as occurring eo instanti. I think that the House of Lords and Slade J each envisaged transfers of title and grants of security occurring completely simultaneously.'

5.19 Other decided cases provide examples of clauses that have proved effective to reserve title and escaped judicial categorisation as charges. In *Hendy Lennox (Industrial Engines) Ltd v Grahame Puttick Ltd*,[29] for instance, it was provided that 'all goods ... shall be and remain the property of the [plaintiffs] until the full purchase price thereof shall be paid' and that the plaintiffs had the right to retake possession in the event of default. Staughton J referred to ss 16 and 17 of the Sale of Goods Act 1979 which stipulated basically that property passed when it was intended to pass. He could not see why the plain words of the contract should not mean what they say. The sellers retained the full rights of ownership, subject to contractual terms limiting the exercise of those rights and regulating how they might be transferred to others. The buyers did not 'confer' any proprietary rights in the goods to the seller: rather it was the sellers who retained proprietary rights.

5.20 *Re Peachdart Ltd*[30] is a case involving the supply of leather to a company which manufactured handbags. A receiver was appointed to the buyer company and it was held that a reservation of title clause in the supply contract was effective as regards unused leather in its possession at that time. The clause stipulated as follows:

'[T]he ownership of the products shall remain with the seller which reserves the right to dispose of the products until payment in full for all the products has been received by it in accordance with the terms of this contract or until such time as the buyer sells the products to its customers by way of bona fide sale at full market value.'

5.21 *Re Andrabell Ltd*[31] is a somewhat similar case. It concerned the supply of travel bags which were then resold. The buyer company went into liquidation but at that time all of the travel bags had been resold. The dispute in the case centred around a claim to the resale proceeds. It appears, however, that the reservation of title clause would have been effective as regards any travel bags still in the buyer company's possession at the commencement of liquidation. The clause contained the following provision:

'It is a condition of sale that ownership of the goods shall not pass to The Company until The Company has paid to Airborne the total purchase price including VAT.'

5.22 Retention of title clauses have been given the judicial imprimatur in the Republic of Ireland. The Irish cases provide further instances of clauses which are viewed as acceptable to reserve title:

'The ownership of the sugar ... shall only be transferred to the purchaser when the full amount of the purchase price has been discharged' (*Sugar Distributors Ltd v Monaghan Cash and Carry Ltd*).[32]

---

29 [1984] 1 WLR 485.
30 [1984] Ch 131.
31 [1984] 3 All ER 407.
32 [1982] ILRM 399.

'until all sums due to the seller shall have been fully paid to it, the plant, machinery and materials supplied by the seller herein shall remain the seller's personal property' (*Frigoscandia*).[33]

5.23   The impact of the EC Directive on late payment in commercial transactions should also be noted.[34] The Directive is designed to alleviate suppliers from the consequences of delayed receipt of payment for goods or services provided by introducing an entitlement to interest on overdue debts. As part of the overall package of 'pro-supplier' measures, however, it appears that Member States are obliged to recognise simple retention of title clauses throughout the EC. Article 4(1) of the Directive reads:

> 'Member States shall provide in conformity with the applicable national provisions designated by private international law that the seller retains title to goods until they are fully paid for if a retention of title clause has been expressly agreed between the buyer and the seller before the delivery of the goods.'

5.24   'Retention of title' is defined in Art 2 of Directive 2000/35/EC as meaning the contractual agreement according to which the seller retains title to the goods in question until the price has been paid in full. The most straightforward interpretation of the relevant provisions would be to say that if passing of property questions under a contract for the sale of goods are governed by the law of an EC Member State, then the Member State must recognise a simple reservation of title clause contained in the contract of sale. It is possible, however, to interpret the reference to private international law in Art 4 in such a way as to deprive the provision of substantive meaning. On such a construction, if the legal system invoked by the choice of law rules in a forum Member State does not recognise simple reservation of title clauses or requires observance of formalities for their enforcement, such as compliance with registration requirements, then the forum Member State is not compelled to recognise the clause. The so-called European rule would not be in accordance with the relevant national law whose application is dictated by the choice of law rules. In the case of an ordinary domestic sales contract governed by English law, then English law prevails over the European norm because English law is the governing law under the choice of law rules whose effect has not been altered by the Directive.[35] If this interpretation is correct, then the Late Payment Directive is devoid of much content because a reservation of title clause could

---

33   *Frigoscandia (Contracting) Ltd v Continental Irish Meat Ltd* [1982] ILRM 396. See generally on the Irish cases, RA Pearce 'Reservation of Title on the Sale of goods in Ireland' (1985) 20 Ir Jur (NS) 264.

34   Directive 2000/35/EC of the European Parliament and of the Council of 29 June 2000 on combating late payment in commercial transactions (OJ 2000 L2000/35); and see generally McCormack (2001) 1 Journal of Corporate Law Studies 501. For general background see G Monti, G Nejman and W Reuter 'The Future of Reservation of Title Clauses in the European Community' (1997) 47 ICLQ 866; J-H Dalhuisen 'The Conditional Sale is Alive and Well' in J Norton and M Andenas (eds) *Emerging Financial Markets and Secured Transactions* (Kluwer, 1998); and also E Kieninger 'Securities in Movable Property within the Common Market' (1996) 4 European Review of Private Law 41.

35   See G McCormack 'Retention of Title and the EC Late Payment Directive' (2001) 1 Journal of Corporate Law Studies at 505–506.

always be enforced according to the applicable law. If the governing law in a forum Member State recognises reservation of title, then, by that fact alone and without reference to the provisions of any EC Directive, reservation of title should be recognised in that forum.[36]

CURRENT ACCOUNT CLAUSES

5.25 Clauses which attempt to reserve ownership of the goods supplied in the seller until *all* obligations owed to the seller by the buyer have been discharged, and not just those flowing from the contract of sale, are slightly more problematic. The argument is that withholding ownership until a long overdue debt has been paid is creating something over and above what was in existence when the clause was first incorporated, unless it simply replaces another security right already provided for. Thus it is more difficult to disguise as something other than the creation of a security interest.[37] The reason for the use of 'all-liabilities' clauses is to circumvent problems of identification that arise if a buyer company has gone into liquidation receivership. Goods originally supplied by the seller are now in the buyer's warehouse. Some consignments have been paid for; others have not. The seller has a difficult task in identifying the goods actually unpaid for. Its task is easier when there are 'all-liabilities' reservation of title clauses in respect of all consignments, and it can therefore say to the buyer: 'You do not have title to any of the consignments in the warehouse because all of them have not been paid for.'

5.26 In *Romalpa* itself, an 'all-monies' or 'current account' clause had been inserted by the supplier. The clause provided that 'the ownership of the

---

36 In many EU Member States retention of title clauses are valid without registration. For a general discussion see the chapters on taking security in France and Germany in M Bridge and R Stevens (eds) *Cross-Border Security and Insolvency* (OUP, 2001) and note the following comment on German law (at p 94):

> 'Apart from charges on land which have to be registered in the land register, none of the security based on the BGB (namely the pledge over goods and rights, the transfer of title for security purposes, the security assignment, and the reservation of title) require registration against the asset.'

See also J-H Dalhuisen 'The Conditional Sale is Alive and Well' in J Norton and M Andenas (eds) *Emerging Financial Markets and Secured Transactions* (Kluwer, 1998) and *Dalhuisen on International Commercial, Financial and Trade Law* (Hart Publishing, 2002) pp 432–452 and 567–716.

37 What appears to have been a current account clause was upheld in *John Snow & Co Ltd v DBG Woodcroft & Co Ltd* [1985] BCLC 54 as not requiring registration under the Companies Act. The conditions of sale provided: 'The property in the goods agreed to be sold will only pass to the purchaser when the purchaser has met all the indebtedness to the seller ...' It has been suggested that in the absence of words expressly providing that indebtedness included indebtedness under other contracts it is arguable that 'all indebtedness' was limited to that under the particular contract and that the clause was in fact a single contract reservation of title clause. Boreham J, however, treated it as a current account clause and gave it the judicial imprimatur as such.

material to be delivered ... will only be transferred to the purchaser when he has met all that is owing' to the plaintiffs. The matter, however, occasioned no comment in the judgments.[38]

5.27   The House of Lords has upheld the effectiveness of 'all-liabilities' retention of title clauses in the Scottish case *Armour v Thyssen Edelstahlwerke AG*.[39] Here Lord Keith referred to s 17(1) of the Sale of Goods Act 1979 which provides that where there is a contract for the sale of specific or ascertained goods the property in them is transferred to the buyer at such time as the parties to the contract intend it to be transferred. Moreover s 19(1) stipulates that where there is a contract for the sale of specific goods the seller may reserve the right of disposal of the goods until certain conditions are fulfilled. In this particular case the sellers, by the terms of the contract of sale, had in effect reserved the right of disposal of the goods until fulfilment of the condition that all debts due to them by the buyer had been paid. The relevant clause read:

> 'All goods delivered by us remain our property (goods remaining in our ownership) until all debts owed to us including any balances existing at relevant times – due to us on any legal grounds – are settled.'

According to Lord Keith, such a provision did in a sense give the seller security for the unpaid debts of the buyer. It did so, however, by way of a legitimate retention of title, not by virtue of any right over his own property conferred by the buyer.

5.28   The *Armour* case did not involve a situation where the supplier recovered possession of goods because of the non-discharge of some indebtedness extraneous to the sales contract containing the reservation of title. It has been argued that if a seller retains legal and beneficial ownership in goods supplied, it must follow that if, after payment of the full purchase price of those goods, the seller recovers possession of them because of non-discharge of some other liability, the seller must refund the purchase price to the customer on the ground of total failure of consideration.[40] This would of course defeat the object of the clause. In almost all instances it would be the intention of the seller that he should be entitled to recover the goods and resell them elsewhere without having to refund the purchase price. It has been submitted that this can only be done if the clause is construed as creating a security for the payment of the customer's debts to the supplier and not as a condition that suspends the transfer of title. Another commentator contends that the treatment of an 'all

---

38   In *Clough Mill Ltd v Martin* [1985] 1 WLR 111 the Court of Appeal were faced with a contract to be performed in stages rather than an 'all-monies' clause stricto sensu. Nevertheless, there are some helpful dicta concerning 'all-monies' clauses by Robert Goff LJ at 117, Oliver LJ at 123 and Sir John Donaldson MR at 126.

39   [1991] 2 AC 339; the case is discussed by counsel for the suppliers, Jonathan Mance QC (now Mance LJ), in 'The operation of an "All Debts" Reservation of Title Clause' [1992] LMCLQ 35.

40   See the piece by Sir William Goodhart (1986) 49 MLR 96. See also the article by Goodhart and Professor Gareth Jones 'The Infiltration of Equitable Doctrine into English Commercial Law' (1980) 43 MLR 489 at 508; but cf McCormack [1989] Conv 92.

liabilities clause' as a charge is likely to be more beneficial to the seller than a retention of title clause. His argument continues as follows:[41]

> 'For example, if the supplier delivers goods under separate contracts and is paid in full under one contract but not the other, it follows that if the supplier repossesses the goods and sells them, he will have to account to the buyer for the sums the seller received under the first contract. This is pertinent when the price achieved in re-selling the goods is less than the combined value of the two contracts. The reason for this is that whereas a seller can treat non-payment of part of the purchase price under a single contract as a breach of the entire contract, a seller who has entered into several contracts cannot treat a failure to make payments under one contract as a breach of the other contracts.'

5.29   The whole argument is founded on the assumption that in a multiple contract situation a seller would be liable to refund the purchase price on grounds of total failure of consideration. It may be suggested, however, that there is not a total failure of consideration. After all, the buyer has had use of the goods for a certain time. Furthermore, in return for the buyer agreeing to a contract of sale which includes an 'all liabilities' reservation of title clause, the seller may have desisted from enforcing certain other obligations owed by the buyer.

5.30   The leading authority is *Rowland v Divall*[42] where it was held that under a sales contract the essential consideration for which the buyer pays the price is the transfer of ownership by the seller.[43] On this basis, where no title is transferred because of a defect in the seller's title, the buyer can recover the price on the grounds of total failure of consideration regardless of any use of the goods in the interim period. It is possible to argue, however, by relying upon the doctrine of set-off, that an all-liabilities reservation of title clause is of benefit to a supplier of goods. Set-off refers to a situation of reciprocal indebtedness, e g A owes X to B, but B owes Y to A. Set-off is compulsory in a liquidation under r 4.90 of the Insolvency Rules 1987 and its bankruptcy equivalent – Insolvency Act 1986, s 323. Set-off operates where, before the company goes into liquidation, there have been mutual credits, mutual debs or other mutual dealings between the company and any creditor of the company proving or claiming to prove for a debt in the liquidation. If B becomes insolvent, A is not required to pay to B's estate all that he owes and simply prove (submit a proof) in the bankruptcy for what he is owed by B. A can set-off the two amounts against each other and simply prove for the difference or pay the difference to B's estate, depending on the size of X compared with Y.

---

41   'The Trade Debtor and the Quest for Security' in Harry Rajak (ed) *Insolvency Law: Theory and Practice* (Sweet & Maxwell, 1993) 43 at 62.

42   [1923] 2 KB 500. See also *Butterworth v Kingsway Motors* [1957] 1 WLR 1286; *Warman v Southern Counties Car Finance Corpn* [1949] 2 KB 576; *Karflex Ltd v Poole* [1933] 2 KB 251 and *Linz v Electric Wire Co of Palestine* [1948] AC 371.

43   See R Bradgate (1991) 54 MLR 726.

Lord Hoffmann summarised the operation of the set-off provisions in *Re MS Fashions Ltd* in a commentary described by one leading commentator as 'masterly'.[44] He said:[45]

> 'First, the rule is mandatory ("the mandatory principle"). If there have been mutual dealings before the winding-up order which have given rise to cross-claims, neither party can prove or sue for his full claim. An account must be taken and he must prove or sue (as the case may be) for the balance. Secondly, the account is taken as at the date of the winding-up order ("the retroactivity principle"). This is only one manifestation of a wider principle of insolvency law, namely, that the liquidation and distribution of the assets of the insolvent company are treated as notionally taking place simultaneously on the date of the winding up order'.

5.31   If a repossessing supplier has to refund the purchase price on grounds of total failure of consideration, at the same time, however, the supplier has a claim against the buyer for non-payment of the outside indebtedness. The two claims should be set off against one another, assuming that the necessary element of 'mutuality' is present.[46] Thus an all-liabilities reservation of title clause *is* of benefit to the supplier of goods.

5.32   An 'all-liabilities' clause, in essence, purports to reserve title to the seller until all indebtedness arising between buyer and seller has been met, but there are theoretical difficulties if 'indebtedness' is construed as referring to future indebtedness. If there is a running account between buyer and seller that oscillates from debit to credit, the question arises whether property moves to and fro according to the momentary state of the account.[47] The better view seems to be that title passes when the account comes into credit and does not revert back to the seller when the account once again falls into debit. Consider also the situation where there is a continuous trading relationship between buyer and seller and the parties make it clear that title to a particular consignment of goods should only pass when all possible future debts between them have been met irrespective of the momentary state of the account. If the trading relationship between the parties may extend indefinitely into the future, clearly then it is impossible to say, at any particular point in time, that there will be no future debts owing from buyer to seller. This means that title will never pass to the buyer and seems to place the agreement between the parties outside the statutory definition of a contract for the sale of goods. A contract for the sale of goods is defined in s 2(1) of the Sale of Goods Act 1979 as a contract by which the seller transfer or agrees to transfer the property in goods to the buyer for a money consideration called the price. One approach by the courts to resolve this difficulty would be to say that the parties clearly intended a contract for the sale of goods and the surest way of ensuring this result and

---

44   See Roy Goode *Principles of Corporate Insolvency Law* (Sweet & Maxwell, 2nd edn, 1997) at p 185.

45   *MS Fashions Ltd v BCCI (No 2)* [1993] Ch 425 at 432–433.

46   See R Bradgate (1991) 54 MLR 726 at 735. See also on the conditions necessary to establish set-off *Smith v Bridgend County Borough Council* [2002] 1 AC 336.

47   See comments by Norman Palmer (1981) 1 Legal Studies 326 at 328 reviewing Professor TB Smith's book *Property Problems in Sales* (Sweet & Maxwell, 1978).

making sense of their agreement is to hold that title passes from seller to buyer on delivery of the goods. Such a construction of the agreement is not in the seller's interests and therefore it may be best to make it clear that the 'indebtedness' referred to in the sales contract is purely past indebtedness. On the other hand, it may be that the courts will brush aside as of no practical consequence theoretical problems stemming from potential future indebtedness. After all, disputes over reservation of title clauses only arise if the buyer has gone into liquidation/receivership. The seller will be endeavouring to repossess goods, not because some possible future indebtedness has not been cleared, but rather on account of an existing indebtedness.

RESALE PROCEEDS OR 'TRACING' CLAUSES

5.33 In many retention of title clauses a provision has been inserted conferring on the original supplier an entitlement to resale proceeds. This is referred to as a 'proceeds of sale' clause or 'tracing' clause and it seems clear that a tracing right arising by operation of law is not registrable. In this situation, the seller's 'security' rights have not been conferred or created by the buyer company. Similarly, where traceable funds have been mingled with other funds in a bank account, the courts may declare a charge on the mixed fund[48] but, again, since this charge has not been created by the buyer company, it is not registrable under Part XII of the Companies Act 1985. The courts, however, are loath to uphold a tracing claim in the reservation of title context.

5.34 It seems reasonably clear now from a series of decisions throughout the common law world that the mere fact that there is a reservation of title clause in a sale of goods contract does not give the seller an automatic claim against resale proceeds. The contrary derived some support from the seminal *Romalpa* case. Moreover, there was also some support for this proposition in Ireland in cases like *Re Stokes & McKiernan Ltd*[49] and *Sugar Distributors Ltd v Monaghan Cash and Carry Ltd*.[50] That view, however, is no longer in the ascendancy in Ireland and the prevailing judicial opinion is illustrated by the decision of Murphy J in *Carroll Group Distributors Ltd v Bourke*.[51] That decision followed the more recent English case law and rejected a claim to resale proceeds.[52]

---

48   See *Re Diplock* [1948] Ch 465; *Re Hallett's Estate* (1879) 13 Ch D 696; *Re Oatway* [1903] 2 Ch 356; *James Roscoe (Bolton) Ltd v Windsor* [1915] 1 Ch 62; *Re Tilley's Will Trusts* [1967] Ch 1179; *Boscawen v Bajwa* [1996] 1 WLR 328; *Foskett v McKeown* [2001] 1 AC 102.
49   [1978] ILRM 240.
50   [1982] ILRM 399.
51   [1990] ILRM 285.
52   See J De Lacy 'The Anglicisation of Irish Retention of Title?' (1990) 8 Irish Law Times (New Series) 279.

5.35 Claims to trace resale proceeds have been upheld in pre-PPSA New Zealand[53] and Australia,[54] with the courts not recognising or enforcing the limits placed on the *Romalpa* decision in England. In the leading New Zealand case of *Len Vidgen Ski & Leisure Ltd v Timaru Marine Supplies (1982) Ltd*[55] the plaintiffs supplied ski apparel and equipment to the defendant. The conditions of sale (clause 4) included the following retention of title clause:

> 'Risk in any goods supplied by the Company to a Customer shall pass when such goods are delivered to the Customer or into custody on the Customer's behalf but ownership in such goods is retained by the Company until payment is made or the goods and for all other goods supplied by the Company to the Customer. If such goods are sold by the Customer prior to payment therefore and if they shall become constituents of other goods then the proceeds of sale thereof shall be the property of the Company.'

There was also a period of credit in the following terms: 'Net Monthly Payment by 20th of month following invoice date.'

5.36 The judgment of the New Zealand High Court provides some support for the view that the mere presence of a reservation of title clause in a sale of goods contract per se constituted the buyer a fiduciary in relation to resale proceeds. It was said apropos clause 4 of the conditions of sale:[56]

> 'The first part of the clause states that the goods sold by the first defendant remain the property of the plaintiff, this indicates strongly that the parties did intend that the first defendant would be accountable to the plaintiff for the proceeds and would not receive them for its own account. It also provides a basis for implying into the agreement a duty on the part of the first defendant to keep the proceeds separate from its own moneys consistent with the obligations of a fiduciary.'

5.37 But of course there was more to the conditions of sale than the first part of clause 4. It was provided expressly that resale proceeds 'shall be the property of' the plaintiff. Moreover, the period of credit had to be reconciled with an accounting obligation. The court effected a reconciliation by suggesting the following:[57]

> 'The first defendant has had the benefit of the full term of credit in relation to any goods which it did not sell during the term or which it sold, but the proceeds of which it did not receive until after the period had expired; it would have enjoyed some advantge in relation to goods which it sold and for which it received the proceeds during the term of credit, because it would not be bound to pay for them immediately on delivery, but only after its own customers had paid it.'

---

53   See e g *Len Vidgen v Timaru Marine Supplies Ltd* [1986] 1 NZLR 349; *Bisley Ltd v Gore Engineering & Retail Sales Ltd* [1989] 2 NZBLC 103 at 593; *Peerless Carpets Ltd v Moorhouse Carpet Market Ltd* [1992] 4 NZBLC 102 at 747.

54   See *Puma Australia Pty Ltd v Sportman's Australia Ltd* [1994] 2 QD R 149; but c f *Chattis Nominees Pty Ltd v Norman Ross Homeoworks Pty Ltd* (1992) 28 NSWLR 338.

55   [1986] 1 NZLR 349.

56   [1986] 1 NZLR 349 at 364.

57   [1986] 1 NZLR 349.

On balance, the court concluded there was an obligation to account. In reaching this conclusion particular emphasis was placed on the express entitlement to resale proceeds conferred by the second sentence of clause 4 of the conditions of sale.

5.38 The leading authority in Australia is the decision of the High Court of Australia in *Associated Alloys Pty Ltd v ACN 001 452 106*.[58] This is a case where steel was supplied by the plaintiffs to the defendants and allegedly used in a complex manufacturing process so as to produce industrial equipment which was then sold to a third party. The defendants went into liquidation with substantial amounts owing to the plaintiffs remaining unpaid, and the latter claimed the proceeds of sale of the industrial equipment on the basis of a reservation of title clause in their invoices which provided inter alia:

'In the event that the [buyer] uses the goods/product in some manufacturing or construction process of its own or some third party, then the [buyer] shall hold such part of the proceeds of such manufacturing or construction process as relates to the goods/product in trust for the [seller]. Such part shall be deemed to equal in dollar terms the amount owing by the [buyer] to the [seller] at the time of the receipt of such proceeds.'

5.39 One of the questions the High Court of Australia had to decide was whether the clause in question constituted a charge requiring registration under the Australian Corporations Law. The majority took the view that the proceeds subclause was an agreement to constitute a trust of future-acquired property. It was not a charge within the meaning of the Corporations Law and the detailed provisions of the law pertaining to charges did not apply to it. The majority recognised that this holding had commercial significance and for third parties, such as financial institutions seeking to assess the creditworthiness of the buyer, the non-registration of the proceeds subclause on a public register could create practical difficulties. On the other hand, it was not for the courts to destroy or impair property rights, such as those arising under trusts, by supplementing the list of registrable interests. Moreover, reference was made to considerations that might militate against any extension of registration requirements:[59]

'The lack of any statutory obligation to register the proceeds subclause ... creates commercial incentives for entities, in the position of both the Buyer and the Seller, to incorporate clauses such as the proceeds subclause into their purchase agreements. These clauses reduce the risk of non-payment by the buyer. To the extent that this financial, or credit, risk is reduced, the commercial viability of the transaction for both parties may be increased. For example, the availability of this means of reducing credit risk for the seller may result in the seller accepting a lower cost price per unit of steel. Competitive pressures may thus operate upon the parties to incorporate clauses such as the proceeds subclause in their transactions.'

---

58 (2000) 202 CLR 588. The case is discussed, inter alia, by J De Lacy [2001] Insolvency Lawyer 64.

59 (2000) 202 CLR 588 at 611.

5.40   It should be noted that the original seller was only claiming a proportionate part of resale proceeds and not the entirety thereof. Whether such claim was sustainable, in the eyes of the court, is not entirely clear. Reference was made to the observations of Robert Goff LJ in *Clough Mill Ltd v Martin*[60] that it was a manifestly peculiar outcome to find that the parties intended that the seller should obtain the windfall of the full value of the newly manufactured products. Counterbalancing this, however, were the comments of Windeyer J in *Gurfinkel v Bentley Pty Ltd*[61] that the law ordinarily will take the parties at their word and the court will be slow to find that a bargain is not as the parties expressed it. The court appeared to lean in favour of this interpretation. There are some unsatisfactory features about the *Associated Alloys* decision, however, which, it is submitted, will reduce the possibility of it gaining judicial acceptance in England. First, as far the seller's claim is concerned, there was a break in the proprietary chain. The seller's steel was used in the manufacturing process and, at that point, according to the English authorities, title vested in the buyers. The latter, in selling the finished article, were selling their own goods and, consequently, the proceeds of sale of these goods belonged to them too. The original seller's claim against such proceeds amounted to a claim over the property of another and fell within the classic definition of a charge.[62] Secondly, in *Associated Alloys* the seller's claim fell on the facts, as the sellers failed to establish a necessary and direct link between particular unpaid invoices and payments received from the third party. Consequently, the views expressed on the permissible limits of proceeds of sale reservation of title clauses might be regarded as strictly obiter. It is submitted that, all in all, an English court is likely to be more persuaded by the strong dissent of Kirby J in the case:[63]

> 'The most that [the clause] can amount to for [the seller] is an unregistered charge on a "book debt". Any other construction ... would permit the easy defeat of the clear purpose of the Law, namely that creditors of companies which become insolvent must, unless they are secured creditors that are afforded priority, participate pari passu in the available assets of the company. It would be contrary to principle to adopt a restrictive or confined construction of the provisions of the Law, which is designed to ensure that a company's charges on book debts are registered and that those which are not registered are unenforceable against the administrator or liquidator of that company. In effect, [the seller] seeks   to have a priority by virtue of its own undisclosed contractual stipulation.'

5.41   *Aluminium Industrie Vaassen BV v Romalpa Aluminium Ltd* is the first of the modern English cases on proceeds of sale retention of title – indeed on any

---

60   [1985] 1 WLR 111 at 120.
61   (1966) 116 CLR 98 at 114.
62   See the comments by J De Lacy [2001] Insolvency Lawyer 64 at 65:
> 'should a seller seek to claim the proceeds of sub-sale resulting from the buyer's sale of manufactured/processed goods (including the seller's goods) then as the manufacturing process will cause the seller's title to be lost no claim can exist against the process. Any such claim will be dependent upon a contractual provision granting such an interest and will be construed as a registrable security interest.'
63   (2000) 202 CLR 588 at 626.

aspect of retention of title – and for this reason alone merits extended treatment, even though it has been almost distinguished to death in subsequent cases. In *Romalpa* the plaintiffs, a Dutch company, supplied aluminium foil to the defendants, an English company, and some of this foil had been resold in its original unprocessed state before a receiver was appointed to the defendant company. The conditions of sale gave the buyers a 75-day period of credit and also contained a current account retention of title clause. The buyers were required to store the goods separately from their own property and it was conceded that this provision rendered the buyers bailees of any foil in their possession while money was still owing to the suppliers. The courts upheld the suppliers' claim to resale proceeds even though there was no clause in the conditions of sale dealing expressly with the claim to resale proceeds where the goods had been resold in their original state. Roskill LJ said:[64]

> 'I see no difficulty in the contractual concept that, as between the defend-ants and their sub-purchasers, the defendants sold as principals, but that, as between themselves and the plaintiffs, those goods which they were selling as principals within their implied authority from the plaintiffs were the plaintiffs' goods which they were selling as agents for the plaintiffs to whom they remained fully accountable. If an agent lawfully sells his principal's goods, he stands in a fiduciary relationship to his principal and remains accountable to his principal for those goods and their proceeds.'

5.42   In subsequent English cases the *Romalpa* decision has been distin-guished almost out of existence with the courts disallowing successive claims to resale proceeds.[65] The decisions may be viewed in a very pragmatic light. It is almost as if the courts are drawing a line in the sand and saying to a supplier, 'You can have your simple and current account reservation of title clauses, but thus far and no further.' Some of the various strands of reasoning apparent in the different cases, however, seem mutually contradictory.

5.43   The courts have rejected resale proceeds claims on the basis that a charge has been thereby created which is void for want of registration. In *Hendy Lennox (Industrial Engines) Ltd v Grahame Puttick Ltd*[66] the court in rejecting such a claim, pointed to the absence of an express obligation on the buyers to store the goods in such a way that they were clearly the property of the seller. Moreover, there was no express mention of the buyers as 'fiduciary owner'. Similarly, in *Re Andrabell Ltd*[67] Peter Gibson J relied on the fact that the buyers were not bound to store the goods in such a way as to manifest the continued ownership of the sellers.

---

64   [1976] 1 WLR 676 at 690. For a full critical discussion of this area see J De Lacy (1995) 27 Anglo-American Law Review 327.

65   According to Phillips J in *Pfeiffer GmbH & Co v Arbuthnot Factors Ltd* [1988] 1 WLR 150 at 159 the normal implication is that when a buyer resells the goods he does so on his own account and will not hold any proceeds thereby received in a fiduciary capacity on behalf of the seller.

66   [1984] 1 WLR 485.

67   [1984] 3 All ER 407.

5.44 A person drafting a retention of title clause has, however, to steer a course between under-provision, which proved fatal in *Andrabell*, and the over-elaboration that was the supplier's undoing in *Tatung (UK) Ltd v Galex Telesure Ltd.*[68] Here the plaintiffs supplied goods to the defendants under two separate sets of conditions. The first set declared that the proceeds of resales of the goods belonged to the supplier absolutely. The second, and more elaborate, set of conditions obliged the defendants to keep the proceeds of resales in a separate account for the benefit of the plaintiffs. It was held that a charge had been created over the proceeds of sale.

5.45 Phillips J noted that in *Tatung* the contracts made express provision for the interest that the plaintiffs were to have in the proceeds of dealing with the goods. In these circumstances he considered that the source of the plaintiffs' rights was the contractual agreement between the parties and not equitable principles that might have applied in the absence of such agreement. In other words, the plaintiffs are being penalised for precision in their supply contracts – a somewhat strange result to say the least. Certainly the result is impossible to square with the decision of Barker J in *Len Vidgen Ski & Leisure Ltd v Timaru Marine Supplies (1982) Ltd*[69] which has been discussed earlier. Here, in concluding that the buyer was obliged to account for resale proceeds, the judge placed particular emphasis on the express entitlement to resale proceeds conferred on the seller by the proceeds of sale clause.

5.46 *Tatung (UK) Ltd v Galex Telesure Ltd* follows very much the pattern shown by Phillips J in *Pfeiffer Weinkellerei-Weineinkauf GmbH & Co v Arbuthnot Factors Ltd.*[70] In this case wine was supplied by Pfeiffer, a Germany company, to an English importer, Springfield, and then resold on credit terms. The question arose as to the nature of the interest which Pfeiffer had in the proceeds of the sub-sales. It was argued by the plaintiffs that their interest in the proceeds of sale of the wine did not constitute a charge over property owned by the importer. Rather, it amounted to an absolute beneficial interest in the proceeds of sale, albeit that the plaintiff would come under an implied contractual duty to account to Springfield to the extent that proceeds of sale ultimately recovered by the plaintiff were in excess of the debts owed by Springfield to it. The plaintiff's beneficial interest was not created by Springfield. Instead it arose by operation of law as a consequence of a sale by Springfield of property owned by the plaintiff. In support of this submission, reliance was predictably placed on *Romalpa*.

5.47 Phillips J found that this reliance was misplaced for two reasons. First of all, in *Romalpa* counsel for the defendants conceded that the relationship of the plaintiffs and defendants was that of bailor and bailee. Furthermore, the latter part of clause 13 in *Romalpa* expressly described the buyers as 'fiduciary owner' of mixed goods of which aluminium foil supplied by the plaintiffs formed part. The judge opined that it was inappropriate to describe the

---

68 (1989) 5 BCC 325.
69 [1986] 1 NZLR 349.
70 [1988] 1 WLR 150. See generally on these two cases G McCormack 'Reservation of title – the controversy continues' [1989] LMCLQ 198. See also S Wheeler (1989) 10 Co Law 151 and J De Lacy (1989) 10 Co Law 188.

relationship of a seller and a buyer in possession to whom title had not yet passed as that of bailor/bailee, for it would not normally have the same incidents as the classic bailment relationship. This conclusion may be questioned. The feeling of inappropriateness was obviously not experienced by the Court of Appeal in *Romalpa*. Moreover, such feelings were equally alien to the court in another common law jurisdiction, namely New Zealand, where *Motor Mart Ltd v Webb*[71] is a case in point.

5.48 It is respectfully submitted that Phillips J in *Pfeiffer* was guilty of over-simplification in dismissing the fiduciary relationship argument. He contented himself with the conclusion that there was no bailment in the present case, but proceeded on the basis of a limited conception of the nature of bailment. The fact, however, that there is a bailment does not necessarily mean that there is a fiduciary relationship between the parties.[72] In this particular case, nonetheless, the fiduciary relationship argument might be thought to have been strengthened by certain provisions in the contract between plaintiff and importer. The importer was subjected to a contractual obligation to separate the proceeds of cash sales from his other monies, book the sales accordingly, administer the funds until called for, notify the assignment of the seller's claim, and pass on all rights relating to the sub-sales to the seller.

5.49 An overarching reason why proceeds of sale retention of title clauses are not recognised flows from the fact that the original seller's interest or claim in resale proceeds comes to an end once the original purchase price, plus any outstanding expenses, have been discharged. For this reason, one might cynically observe that there is very little chance of a reservation of title clause receiving judicial approval. This view tends to be confirmed by *Compaq Computer Ltd v Abercorn Group Ltd*.[73] In this case the plaintiff sold computer equipment to the first defendant, Abercorn. The latter resold the equipment and also entered into a factoring arrangement with another company, Kellock. The factoring arrangement included debts arising from the resales of the computer equipment. The equipment had been sold subject to a reservation of title clause in favour of the seller. Resales, though, were permitted subject to the following qualification:

> 'Insofar as the dealer may sell or otherwise dispose of the Compaq products or receive any monies from any third party in respect of the Compaq products, he shall strictly account to Compaq for the full proceeds thereof (such monies as the dealer shall receive) as the seller's bailee or agent and shall keep a separate account of all such proceeds or monies for such purpose.'

5.50 The court held that the sub-sales claims and proceeds were effectively charged to the seller as security for the price of the goods. As the charge had not been registered, it became void when the buyer went into liquidation. The

---

71 [1958] NZLR 773.

72 It is important to bear in mind too the words of Robert Goff LJ in *Clough Mill Ltd v Martin* [1985] 1 WLR 111 at 116 that words like 'bailment' and 'fiduciary duty' are our tools and not our masters.

73 [1991] BCC 484.

court came to the conclusion that the buyer was not a trustee for the seller because the seller's interest in sub-sales and proceeds was not absolute but was defeasible on payment of the purchase price. In its view, analysing the contract in this way led inevitably to a charge construction. Once it was conceded that the beneficial interest in the proceeds of sale was determinable on payment of the debts, the seller had to confront the difficulty that the rights and obligations of the parties were in reality, and in substance, characteristic of those of the parties to a charge, and not of those in a fiduciary relationship. Reference was made to the following observations in *Re Bond Worth Ltd*:[74]

> '[A]ny contract which, by way of security for the payment of a debt, confers an interest in property defeasible or destructible upon payment of such debt, or appropriates such property for the discharge of the debt, must necessarily be regarded as creating a mortgage or charge, as the case may be.'

5.51   Reasoning by analogy, the buyer was empowered to redeem the charge in favour of the seller if the outstanding debts were paid, but the seller was not entitled to retain out of resale proceeds a sum that was more than sufficient to pay those debts. If the resale proceeds were deficient in this respect, the seller had a right of action against the buyer for the balance of the purchase price as a simple contract debt. It is submitted that this reasoning is open to criticism if one contrasts it with the judicial approach towards 'simple' reservation of title clauses, where the courts have brushed aside a charge construction notwithstanding the fact that the seller's interest in the goods comes to an end when the buyer pays the outstanding sums due. If the seller repossesses and realises the goods for less than the original purchase price, then the seller may sue the buyer for the balance. The analysis adopted in *Compaq Computer* is very much in line with the purposive approach towards 'simple' reservation that found favour at first instance,[75] but was decisively rejected by the Court of Appeal, in *Clough Mill Ltd v Martin*.[76]

5.52   It is by no means easy to state determinative principles on whether a tracing clause constitutes a registrable charge. The authorities speak with forked tongues, as it were. Certain commentators suggest that the following points should be borne in mind when drafting a proceeds of sale clause so as to avoid a charge construction:[77]

(1)   The buyer should be obliged to store the goods in a manner which manifests the seller's ownership.
(2)   There should be reference to the seller as 'fiduciary' in respect of the goods: further, that the seller retains full ownership rights over the goods although subject to some contractual restrictions. Also, that the seller should obtain the benefit of all claims against sub-buyers.
(3)   There should be an obligation to keep the proceeds of sub-sales in a separate account.

---

74   [1980] Ch 228 at 248.
75   The first instance decision is reported [1984] 1 WLR 1067.
76   [1985] 1 WLR 111.
77   See JH Farrar and Chiah Kim Chai [1985] JBL 160.

(4)   The contract should spell out that so long as the purchase price remains unpaid any sub-sales by the buyer would be on the seller's behalf as agent.

(5)   The contract should provide for immediate payment of the price upon delivery but that the seller may at its discretion not enforce it for a stated period.

(6)   It should be provided that so long as the purchase monies remain unpaid the proceeds of any resale should be held by the buyer as trustee for the seller.

5.53   It is worth developing some of these points. For instance, in relation to point (1), it appears from *Romalpa* that separate storage as such is not required but rather the duty to store separately if so required by the seller. With respect to (3) it is debatable whether the accounting obligation should extend to all resale proceeds or whether the buyer might safely be allowed to keep profits on resales.[78] In *Romalpa*[79] the supplier was entitled under the terms of the reservation of title clause to keep resale profits, whereas in *Re Andrabell Ltd*[80] the buyer was entitled to resale profits and this was taken as militating against a fiduciary relationship. The authorities, however, it must be admitted, are by no means unanimous on this score. In this respect there is a divergence between *Re Nevill ex parte White*[81] and *Re Smith ex parte Bright*,[82] or least a conflict between dicta in the two cases.

5.54   Take *Re Nevill* initially. For instance Sir George Mellish LJ said that if a consignee was at liberty, according to the contract between him and his consignor, to sell at any price he likes and receive payment at any time he likes, but was bound, if he sold the goods, to pay the consignor for them at a fixed price and a fixed time, the relationship between the parties was not that of principal and agent.[83] The contract of sale which the alleged agent makes with his purchasers was not a contract made on account of his principal. It was said that, in such a case, the alleged agent was making, on his own account, a contract of purchase with his alleged principal and again reselling.[84]

---

78   See the comments of the High Court of Australia in *Associated Alloys Pty Ltd v ACN 001 452 106 Pty Ltd* (2000) 202 CLR 588 at 607:

    'The present case is not an example of an arrangement whereby, upon its proper construction, proceeds subject to the trust in favour of the seller were defined otherwise than by reference to the state of indebtedness between the Buyer and the Seller, and the beneficial interest of the Buyer in a greater sum might have been appropriated by the Seller to give it a windfall. Equity favours the identification and protection of an equity of redemption and, in that regard, prefers substance to form ... [This] might have provided a footing for the treatment of the interest of the seller as no more than a charge upon the proceeds to secure the indebtedness of the Buyer. It is unnecessary to express any concluded view upon the matter.'

79   [1976 1 WLR 676.
80   [1984] 3 All ER 407.
81   (1871) LR 6 Ch App 397. The decision in this case was confirmed by the House of Lords, where it is reported sub nom *Towle & Co v White* (1873) 29 LT 78.
82   (1879) 10 Ch D 566.
83   (1871) LR 6 Ch App 397 at 403.
84   (1871) LR 6 Ch App 397 at 404.

5.55   James LJ was a party to the decision in *Re Nevill*. He was also party to the decision in *Re Smith* where he was at pains to relegate the earlier case to the realm of cases decided on their special facts. James LJ voiced the view that such cases when quoted and argued only tend to waste the time of the court and divert its attention from the principle upon which the case should be decided.[85] Jessel MR did not refer directly to *Re Nevill*. However, he enunciated the following principle:[86]

'There is nothing to prevent the principal from remunerating the agent by a commission varying according to the amount of the profit obtained by the sale. *A fortiori* there is nothing to prevent his paying a commission depending upon the surplus which the agent can obtain over and above the price which will satisfy the principal. The amount of commission does not, turn the agent into a purchaser.'

5.56   A 'del credere' agency was found to exist in *Re Smith*. The characteristic of a del credere agency is that the agent guarantees the performance of obligations by the third parties with whom he contracts on behalf of the principal.[87] *Re Smith* enjoys some support from the decision of the New Zealand Court of Appeal in *Westpac Banking v Savin*.[88] In this case two boat owners authorised Aqua Marine to sell their boats. Aqua Marine's commission was to be whatever price the company achieved above a certain stated sum. The court held that the company was a fiduciary in respect of the proceeds of sale and was not entitled to pay them into its overdrawn trading account.

5.57   The *Westpac* case also supports the proposition that if a particular relationship is deemed fiduciary, then the fiduciary comes under an obligation to segregate his assets from the principal's. It is a counsel of prudence, however, to spell this separation obligation out clearly. Such a statement will stiffen the resolve of the court in coming to a fiduciary relationship conclusion.[89]

5.58   A related question is whether a buyer may be allowed to use profits from resales in the ordinary course of its business. Clearly, the counsel of prudence is not to allow the buyer to use such resale proceeds in this way. The Court of Appeal in *Romalpa* seemed unperturbed that this permission was afforded. The subsequent course of judicial decisions suggests a stricter attitude, however. It would be unwise for any draftsperson of a reservation of title clause to assume a return to the halcyon days of *Romalpa*.

---

85   (1879) 10 Ch D 566 at 572.
86   (1879) 10 Ch D 566 at 570.
87   *Morris v Cleasby* (1816) 4 M & S 566; *Hornby v Lacy* (1817) 6 M & S 166.
88   [1985] 2 NZLR 41. See also *Fraser-Ramsay (NZ) Ltd v De Renzy* [1912] NZLR 553; *Re Conway (a bankrupt)* [1936] NZLR 334; and *Ticki Paaka v MacLarn* [1937] NZLR 369.
89   See generally *Henry v Hammond* [1913] 2 KB 515, particularly at 521 per Channell J. For valuable pointers for and against the existence of a fiduciary relationship in a particular case see the New Zealand case *Len Vidgen Ski & Leisure v Timaru Marine Supplies (1982) Ltd* [1986] NZLR 349. The case is fully discussed by P Watts 'Reservation of Title Clauses in England and New Zealand' (1985) 5 OJLS 456.

5.59 Points (4) and (5) (see **5.52**) link up with the notion whether the seller may afford the buyer a period of credit. In *Re Andrabell Ltd*[90] Peter Gibson J was very much against a period of credit. The judge reasoned that the 45-day credit period afforded the buyers in the particular case meant that the buyers were free to use resale proceeds in their business. In other words, the provision of credit was irreconcilable with the equitable duty to account and thus was incompatible with the existence of a fiduciary relationship between buyer and seller. Similar considerations moved the Australian Court in *Re Country Stores Pty Ltd*[91] and Mummery J in *Compaq Computer Ltd v Abercorn Group Ltd*.[92] Professor Goode has argued, however, that this is not necessarily so. In his view:[93]

'The sale agreement may, for example, be construed as providing that the buyer is to have 45 days' credit but subject to a duty to account for proceeds of sale on receipt, the transfer of such proceeds *pro tanto* reducing the buyer's price indebtedness. The duty to account thus cuts down the scope of the provision for credit but does not deprive it of effect, for the buyer remains entitled to avail himself of the full period of the credit except insofar as he receives proceeds of sale during that period.'

AGGREGATION CLAUSES AND THE MANUFACTURE OF 'NEW' GOODS

5.60 If goods supplied subject to a retention of title clause have been altered, mixed, or refined in some way, the question arises whether the claim by the supplier is still effective. In England the common law appears to distinguish between three basic situations.[94] The first is that of accession, which occurs

---

90 [1984] 3 All ER 407.
91 [1987] 2 Qd R 318.
92 [1991] BCC 484.
93 R Goode *Proprietary Rights and Insolvency in Sales Transactions* (Sweet & Maxwell, 2nd edn, 1989) p 100. For a somewhat similar interpretation see the views expressed by the High Court of Australia in *Associated Alloys Pty Ltd v ACN 001 452 106 Pty Ltd* (2000) 202 CLR 588 at 610:
    'The express term in the agreement ... which provides for a period of credit within which the debt need not be paid by the Buyer is, in turn, incorporated as an express term of the trust. This term thereby prescribes the period within which the Seller, as beneficiary, cannot call upon the trust property (if the trust is constituted during the credit period). The implied term thus provides one means of discharging the debt by performance. No relevant inconsistency arises between this implied term and the express term in the agreement providing for a period of credit for the Buyer.'
    See also *Len Vidgen v Timaru Marine Supplies* [1986] 1 NZLR 349 at 364.
94 See, however, the comments of Oliver LJ in *Clough Mill v Martin* [1985] 1 WLR 111 at 124:
    'English law has developed no very sophisticated system for determining title in cases where undistinguishable goods are missed or become combined in a newly manufactured article ...'

where one chattel is added to a more dominant chattel. The second involves the mixing of goods, and the third involves the manufacture of a 'new product' (nova species).[95]

5.61 It seems to be the rule under English law that where heterogeneous goods are mixed together in a manufacturing process so as to result in the manufacture of what might be called a 'new product', the manufacturer becomes the owner of the new product and the title of owners of the constituent items disappears.[96] This rule would apply unless the manufacturing work was done on a contract or agency basis for the owners of the raw materials. The question obviously arises as to what kind of 'process' goods must be subjected to before the title of the original owner disappears. The issue has been considered on a pragmatic basis by the courts and, while the general principle is clear, the detailed aspects of the issue are not. One may state a general rule of somewhat uncertain ambit that where substantial work is done on raw materials then the title of the supplier of the raw materials is extinguished. Certainly the courts in England have made it clear that where goods supplied under a reservation of title clause form part of a process of manufacture, then the supplier must make express contractual provision if it wishes to acquire rights in the finished product. It cannot simply rely on its ownership of the raw material. This proposition was enunciated in *Borden (UK) Ltd v Scottish Timber Products Ltd*.[97] Here the plaintiffs supplied resin to the defendants which, as the plaintiffs well knew, was to be mixed with certain hardeners, wax emulsion and wood chippings so as to manufacture chipboard. The defendants went into receivership owing the plaintiffs some £318,000. The resin was supplied subject to the following reservation of title clause:

'(2) *Risk and Property.* Goods supplied by the company shall be at the purchaser's risk immediately on delivery to the purchaser or into custody

---

95 For a comparison between English and Roman law in this area see Birks 'Mixtures' in N Palmer and E McKendrick (eds) *Interests in Goods* (Lloyds of London Press, 2nd edn, 1998), chapter 9; but see the comments by Lord Hope in *Foskett v McKeown* [2001] 1 AC 102 at 121–122 who points to uncertainties in the Roman law position (not easily resolved in the present day!):

'It is worth noting that even in the well known case of the picture painted by Apelles on someone else's board or panel differing views were expressed: see *Stair's Institutions* (1832, vol. 1, 11.1.39. Paulus thought that the picture followed the ownership of the board as accessory to the picture (*Digest*, 41.1.9.2). Justinian's view, following Gaius, was that the board was accessory to the picture, as the picture was more precious *(Institutes of Justinian*, 11.1.34).'

96 Subject to what was said in *Clough Mill Ltd v Martin* [1985] 1 WLR 111; and see also the judgment of Moore-Bick J in *Glencore v Metro Trading International* [2001] 1 Lloyds Law Reports 284 at 322 who was prepared to hold that:

'in a case where title to newly manufactured goods would otherwise vest solely in the manufacturer, there is no reason in principle why the manufacturer and a supplier should not by agreement cause title to vest originally in the supplier rather than the manufacturer. Other considerations would clearly arise if more than one supplier had entered into an agreement of that kind with the same manufacturer ...'

Moore-Bick J rejected the submission of counsel that in all cases title must necessarily vest for an instant in the manufacturer before passing to the supplier as 'contrary to both principle and authority'.

97 [1981] Ch 25.

on the purchaser's behalf (whichever is the sooner) and the purchaser should therefore be insured accordingly. Property in goods supplied hereunder will pass to the customer when:

(a) the goods the subject of this contract, and (b) all other goods the subject of any other contract between the company and the customer which, at the time of payment of the full price of the goods sold under this contract, have been delivered to the customer but not paid for in full, have been paid for in full.'

5.62 The plaintiffs made a claim in respect of chipboard manufactured with the resin or any money or property representing the proceeds of sale of such chipboard. *Romalpa* was invoked in support of this contention but the incantation of that case proved unavailing. The Court of Appeal held that the plaintiffs' title to the resin disappeared once it was used in the manufacturing process.[98] The tracing remedy recognised in *Romalpa* did not apply where there was a mixture of heterogeneous goods in a manufacturing process wherein the original goods lost their character and what emerged was a wholly new product.[99]

5.63 Bridge LJ said what had happened was fairly analogous to the instances where cattle cake was sold to a farmer, or fuel to a steel manufacturer, in each case with a reservation of title clause, but on terms which permitted the farmer to feed the cattle cake to his herd and the steelmaker to fuel his furnaces, before paying the purchase price. It was universally agreed that the seller could not trace into the cattle or the steel. The learned Lord Justice suggested that if the seller wished to acquire rights over the finished product, he could only do so by express contractual stipulation.[100] Templeman LJ was of the same opinion. He said the following:[101]

'When the resin was incorporated in the chipboard, the resin ceased to exist, the plaintiff's title to the resin became meaningless and their security vanished. There was no provision in the contract for the defendants to provide substituted or additional security. The chipboard belonged to the defendants.'

5.64 If title to the new products belongs to the buyer and is transferred to the seller as a means of security for the discharge of indebtedness, then the arrangement will probably be viewed as creating a charge over goods. This charge will then be void for non-registration in the event of the buyer's insolvency. An object lesson in this regard is provided by the decision of the Court of Appeal in *Specialist Plant Services Ltd v Braithwaite Ltd*.[102] The relevant provision was in the following terms:

---

98 [1981] Ch 25 at 41 per Bridge LJ and at 44 per Templeman LJ.
99 See Bridge LJ at 41.
100 [1981] Ch 25 at 42.
101 [1981] Ch 25 at 44.
102 [1987] BCLC 1.

'(b) Further, it is hereby agreed that if the said goods and materials, or any part thereof supplied hereunder in any way whatsoever become a constituent of another article or other articles the company shall be given the ownership of this (these) new article(s) as surety of the full payment of what the customer owes the Company … (c) The word "article" or "articles" contained in clause (b) above shall mean and include and be deemed to mean and include any building or part thereof, any structure of whatever description or part thereof, any machinery or part thereof, or any other object, goods or article of whatever description.'

The case concerned a contract for the repair of machinery. The repairer was claiming ownership of the entirety of the customer's machinery if any parts he supplied were incorporated therein. The provision was designed to afford security for payment of the repair bill. The Court of Appeal had no hesitation in holding that a charge had been created over the customer's assets and that this charge was void for want of registration.

5.65   The question arises when exactly title to goods is lost by incorporation in a new product or use in a manufacturing process. At what moment of time does the title of the supplier disappear? This question is by no means easily answered. Various tests have been applied in the decided cases, though often without clearly distinguishing between these tests. One test asks whether the goods have been 'appropriated' to the manufacturing process; another whether they have lost any significant value as raw material; and a third, whether they have been subjected to more than minor physical manipulation or alteration. The overwhelming tendency, however, is to hold that the title of the supplier is 'lost' in processed goods. A case in point is *Re Peachdart Ltd*[103] where leather was sold to a company which used it to manufacture handbags. The pertinent provision in the supply contract read:

'If any of the products [of the goods supplied] are incorporated in or used as material for other goods before such payment the property in the whole of such other goods shall be and remain with the seller until such payment has been made or the other goods have been sold as aforesaid and all the seller's rights hereunder in the products shall extend to those other goods.'

5.66   The supplier argued the analogy of a sportsperson who, having shot a rare animal, takes the skin to a leather worker and instructs him to make it into a game bag. According to this argument, the property in the skin would remain with the sports person notwithstanding the fact that the skin would undergo many operations and would have thread and other material added to it. *Borden (UK) Ltd v Scottish Timber Products Ltd* was distinguished on the basis that resin was inevitably consumed and destroyed as a separate substance if used in the manufacture of chipboard.

5.67   Vinelott J did not succumb to this line of reasoning. In his view, the parties must have intended that, at least after a piece of leather had been appropriated to be manufactured into a handbag and work had started on it (when the leather would cease to have any significant value as raw material), the

---

103   [1984] Ch 131.

leather would cease to be the exclusive property of the suppliers. Thereafter, the suppliers would have a charge on handbags in the course of manufacture and on the distinctive products which would come into existence at the end of the process of manufacture. The value of these products would be derived for the most part from the buyer's reputation and skill in design and the skill of its workforce.[104]

5.68   Some commentators would say that when a judge begins by saying what the parties must have intended, this is a sure sign that in reality he is substituting his own views for the views of the parties. *Peachdart* was nevertheless applied in *Modelboard Ltd v Outer Box Ltd*.[105] The case concerned cardboard sheets that were subjected to a 'process' by the buyer. The exact nature of this process was somewhat unclear, but at the end of it the cardboard sheets had lost any significant value as raw material. The judge reached the stark conclusion that the suppliers' interest in the goods was lost and their interest in the processed goods was in the nature of a charge. The crucial factor was the fact that they had ceased to have any significant value as raw material. On the other hand, some might say that the facts in *Modelboard* were more akin to the cutting of steel that occurred in *Armour v Thyssen Edelstahlwereke AG*[106] and which did not prejudice the title of the original supplier.

5.69   *Peachdart* was also applied in *Ian Chisholm Textiles Ltd v Griffiths*[107] – a case which concerned cloth that was sold for use in the manufacture of clothes. The court took the view that once the cloth was combined to any significant extent by the buyer with goods owned by the buyer or by a third party, the beneficial ownership of the seller in the cloth changed into that of a security interest holder over the clothes in the course of manufacture or the finished articles.

5.70   Moreover, *Peachdart* is in line with the proposition that where a party applies his own labour to another's raw materials in bringing out the formation of a new product, the worker, as it were, becomes the owner of the new product. A case in point is *Thorogood v Robinson*[108] where chalk was turned into lime. A dug chalk from B's land and burnt it, thereby leaving lime. The Court of Queen's Bench held that the limeburner rather than the landowner had a right to the goods.

5.71   In New Zealand the climate of judicial opinion seems more adverse to the notion that the title of a seller is easily lost where goods have been subjected by the buyer to certain operations. A case in point is *New Zealand Forest Products v Pongakawa Sawmill Ltd*[109] where Forest Products supplied a quantity of logs to a company, Pongakawa, which had now gone into receivership. At the time of receivership Pongakawa held a quantity of sawn timber on its

---

104   [1984] Ch 131 at 142–143.
105   [1993] BCLC 623.
106   [1991] 2 AC 339.
107   [1994] BCC 96.
108   (1845) 6 QB 769.
109   [1991] 5 NZCLC 67, 085; [1991] 3 NZLR 112.

premises which was identifiable as being the product of the Forest Product logs. These logs were supplied to Pongakawa subject to a retention of title provision which read as follows:

> 'The title to the logs and/or products made from those logs shall not pass to the purchaser until payment in full for the logs has been made.'

5.72   Essentially, the question that had to be determined was whether upon conversion from logs into sawn timber, Pongakawa became the owner of the sawn timber. It was contended that once processing commenced ownership then vested in Pongakawa and that the only effect of the reservation of title clause was to create a charge over the product. Reference was made to the now familiar English cases where title to goods had been lost by a process of manufacture. Examples include *Re Bond Worth Ltd*[110] (fibre for use in the manufacture of carpet); *Borden (UK) Ltd v Scottish Timber Products Ltd*[111] (resin which was used in manufacturing chipboard); *Re Peachdart Ltd*[112] (leather that was used to create handbags).

5.73   The New Zealand court took the view that, in the final analysis, it was a question of construction of the particular contract. It was in the contemplation of the parties that logs supplied would be processed by Pongakawa. The plain words of the clause were that title to products made from logs supplied was not to pass to Pongakawa until payment for those logs had been made. The sawn timber was identifiable as being a product made from logs supplied by Forest Products for which payment had not been received. Moreover, there had not been a mixture of the logs with other goods – simply a conversion of them by the process of sawmilling into a different form. These considerations moved the court towards the conclusion that no charge had been created and that the reservation of title clause was effective according to its terms.[113]

5.74   In Scotland there has also been more resistance to the notion that a new product has been formed and the title of the original supplier lost. An interesting case is *Kinloch Damph Ltd v Nordvik Salmon Farms Ltd*[114] where salmon smolts were supplied by the plaintiffs to the defendants subject to a reservation of title clause. The clause provided that until the price for the goods is paid for in full, the goods shall, notwithstanding delivery, remain the property of the seller. The contract went on to provide that the buyer should, so far as practicable, keep the goods in such a way that they were identifiable as the property of the supplier and, until property passed, the buyer would 'rear the goods in accordance with good husbandry as applicable to the farming of salmon in Scotland'. It was also stated that the buyer 'accepts that no amount of growth in the size of the fish or weight or change of growth class of any fish delivered under this contract shall prevent the operation of this condition nor shall it permit the buyer to make any claim that title to the fish has passed to him by such fact alone.'

---

110   [1980] Ch 228.
111   [1981] Ch 25.
112   [1984] Ch 131.
113   [1991] 5 NZCLC 67, 085 at 67, 089.
114   Ct Sess (OH), 30 June 1999 – available through www.scotcourts.gov.uk/.

5.75 Despite this clause, it was argued on the basis of the doctrine of specificatio that a fish farmer who feeds and husbands large numbers of *Salmo salar* while they develop from smolts into mature salmon creates a nova species ownership which vests in him. The court dismissed this contention, holding that the mere fact that the salmon are larger and more valuable than the smolts from which they have grown had no adverse effect on the validity of the retention of title clause. In its view the doctrine of specificatio was inapplicable to the process of growth of living creatures.

5.76 While the English case *Chaigley Farms Ltd v Crawford, Kaye & Grayshire Ltd*[115] raises broadly similar issues, it was not referred to by the Scottish Court of Session in *Kinloch Damph Ltd v Nordvik Salmon Farms Ltd* but perhaps the two cases are distinguishable on their facts. In *Chaigley Farms* a farmer supplied cattle to an abbatoir on credit terms retaining title to 'the goods' until paid for. The cattle were slaughtered and the question arose whether the retention of title clauses was effective vis-à-vis the dead animals – in particular, whether the carcasses could be classed as goods supplied under the contract of sale. The court said not, holding that there was 'an inescapable difference between a live animal and a dead one, particularly a dead one minus hide or skin, offal, etc not sold on as butcher's meat.'[116]

CONTRACTUAL RIGHTS IN THE FINISHED PRODUCT

5.77 A seller may have, by express contractual stipulation, conferred on himself rights in the product formed partly of the goods that he has supplied. Does such a stipulation constitute a charge? Robert Goff LJ considered the point in *Clough Mill Ltd v Martin*, a case where yarn was supplied for manufacture into fabrics. He said:[117]

'Now it is no doubt true that, where A's material is lawfully used by B to create new goods, whether or not B incorporated other material of his own, property in the new goods will generally rest in B, at least where the goods are not reducible to the original materials (see *Blackstone's Commentaries* (17th edn, 1830), Vol 2, pp 404–405). But it is difficult to see why, if the parties agree that the property in the goods shall vest in A, that agreement should not be given effect to. On this analysis the buyer does not confer on the seller an interest in property defeasible upon the payment of the debt; on the contrary, when the new goods come into existence the property in them *ipso facto* vests in the seller, and he thereafter retains his ownership in them, in the same way and on the same terms as he retains his ownership in the unused material.'

5.78 Oliver LJ was of the same opinion. He failed to see any reason in principle why the original legal title in a newly manufactured article composed

---

115 [1996] BCC 957, QBD.

116 As Moore-Bick J explained in *Glencore v Metro Trading International* [2001] 1 Lloyds Law Reports 284 at 325 the case turned essentially on whether the word 'goods' in the retention of title clause should (as the judge in fact held) be construed as referring only to livestock.

117 [1985] 1 WLR 111 at 119.

of materials belonging to A and B should not lie where A and B had agreed that it should lie.[118] Sir John Donaldson was more tentative. He said that if the incorporation of the yarn in, or its use as material for, other goods, left the yarn in a separate and identifiable state, there was no reason why the sellers should not be able to retain title in it. On the other hand, if the incorporation of the yarn created a situation in which it ceased to be identifiable, and a new product was created consisting of the yarn and the other material, it would be necessary to determine who owned that product. He made no pronouncement on the issue.[119]

5.79　The fourth condition of the reservation of title clause in *Clough Mill* provided that if any of the material supplied was incorporated in or used as material for other goods before payment, the property in the whole of such goods shall be and remain with the seller until such payment had been made. It was not strictly necessary to decide whether this condition created a registrable charge but nevertheless both Robert Goff LJ and Oliver LJ stated that it did.[120] This expression of opinion is quite surprising in light of the acknowledgement that where a new product had been formed consisting of material belonging to both A and B the parties could agree on the location of the title to the product.

5.80　Robert Goff LJ adduced two reasons for refusing fully to effectuate the logical consequences of his earlier argument. First, he found it impossible to believe that it was the intention of the parties that the seller would thereby gain the windfall of the full value of the new product. The new product might derive not merely from the labour of the buyer but also from materials that were his. There did not appear to be any duty to account to the buyer for any surplus of the proceeds of sale above the outstanding balance of the price due by him to the seller. There are two answers to this. Surely, the course of action available to the buyer in a situation like this is simple? He should sell the goods that incorporate his labour and use the proceeds to pay off the seller. Alternatively, it might be argued that an obligation to account arises from a general principle that no one should be unjustly enriched at another's expense. The windfall profit problem could be surmounted by holding that the seller is under a duty to account to the buyer for the surplus value based on the principles of unjust enrichment. The law of unjust enrichment has now been accepted at the highest judicial levels as an inherent feature of English law.[121]

5.81　Secondly, Robert Goff LJ talked about the prospect of two lots of material, supplied by different sellers, each subject to a *Romalpa* clause that vests in the seller the legal title in a product manufactured from both lots of material. Agreed, the scenario is not at all sensible, but an easy answer is to hold that a charge has been created in this situation. This conclusion does not

---

118　[1985] 1 WLR 111 at 124. Oliver LJ also adopted the words of Lord Moulton in *Sandeman & Sons v Tyzack & Branfoot Steamship Co* [1913] AC 680 at 695 that 'the whole matter is far from being within the domain of settled law'.

119　[1985] 1 WLR 111 at 125.

120　[1985] 1 WLR 111 at 120, 124.

121　See eg *Lipkin Gorman v Karpnale Ltd* [1991] 2 AC 548; *Westdeutsche Landesbank v Islington London Borough Council* [1996] AC 669. See also the comment of Moore-Bick J in *Glencore v Metro Trading International* [2001] I Lloyds Law Reports 284 at 322.

affect the view that no charge arises where an agreement vests title to a product composed of material belonging to the seller and buyer in the seller. A 'split' result like this, after all, corresponds to the Court of Appeal's conclusions in *Clough Mill*. It was held that the fact that condition four of the retention of title clause might constitute a charge did not mean that condition one was also a charge.

5.82 If supplier and buyer are free to agree where ownership of a new product shall lie, then they should be free to agree, at least in theory, that ownership should lie between them in whatever proportions they like. This obviates the problem of the large windfall profit element that arises if owner-ship of the entirety of the new goods is given to the supplier. In the Irish case *Kruppstahl AG v Quitmann Products Ltd*[122] the drafter of the reservation of title clause dealt with this problem by providing that the seller and buyer were to hold the new product jointly in the ratio of the invoice value of the seller's goods to those of the buyer's goods. Gannon J held that the provision constituted a registrable charge. He interpreted the contract as meaning that the accountability of the buyers was limited to the extent of their indebtedness. In consequence the agreement was construed as conferring on the suppliers a means of security for the discharge of an indebtedness. It may be that if accountability was not restricted to the amount of indebtedness on the original sales contract, the agreement would have been upheld.

5.83 In the New Zealand case *Coleman v Harvey*[123] there is strong support for the view that where the goods of two parties are mixed together so as to result in a loss of physical identity the parties should be free to decide about ownership of the new product. *Coleman v Harvey* is a case of consensual mixing where silver coins belonging to one Harvey were mixed with silver belonging to a company for whom Coleman acted as agent. The mass was mixed so as to produce ingots and the question arose whether Harvey could sustain an action in conversion against Coleman. The court held that the parties became tenants in common of the ingots and that a conversion action was maintainable.

5.84 Cooke P referred to the facts that there was an intended destruction of the coins by chemical means and an obligation to set aside ingots of specified weight.[124] He said, however, that neither consideration should be regarded as changing the essence of the transaction. In his view, the facts were analogous to an implied reservation of title which was merely an agreement between the parties as to when ownership transferred. Mention was made of the following passage from the judgment of Staughton J in *Indian Oil Corpn v Greenstone Shipping SA*:[125]

'[W]here B wrongfully mixes the goods of A with goods of his own, which are substantially of the same mixture and quality, and they cannot in

---

122 [1982] ILRM 551. See also R Goode *Proprietary Rights and Insolvency* (Sweet & Maxwell, 2nd edn, 1989) at pp 98–99.
123 [1989] 1 NZLR 723.
124 [1989] 1 NZLR 723 at 725–726.
125 [1987] 3 All ER 893.

practice be separated, the mixture is held in common and A is entitled to receive out of it a quantity equal to that of his goods which went into the mixture, any doubt as to that quantity being resolved in favour of A. He is also entitled to claim damages from B in respect of any loss he may have suffered, in respect of quality or otherwise, by reason of the admixture.'

5.85   Cooke P considered that the same should apply to a consensual refining, at least where the evidence did not point to an intention to part with ownership from the start.[126] It is certainly possible to read *Coleman v Harvey* as supporting the proposition that a change in physical properties does not preclude agreement between the parties as to where property in the new product shall lie. Such a change does not necessarily entail ownership on the part of the mixer or manufacturer.

ONE CHATTEL ATTACHED TO A DOMINANT CHATTEL

5.86   A not uncommon feature in the retention of title context is a provision to the effect that the goods supplied should not be attached to other chattels without the consent of the seller. The purpose clearly is to prevent the supplier from losing title to the goods by virtue of the doctrine of accession. Under this doctrine, where a subsidiary chattel is attached to a dominant chattel, ownership therein inheres in the owner of the dominant chattel.[127] If the goods are attached without the supplier's knowledge or consent, he might have a personal claim against the buyer for breach of contract, but this personal claim does not involve any right to priority in the event of the buyer's insolvency.

5.87   Another approach might be for the seller to state that any additions to the goods supplied become the seller's property. The danger here lies in the fact that if the additions are identifiably separate from the goods supplied, then the seller can only be regarded as transferring his own property to the buyer. If this is done for the purpose of ensuring payment of the purchase price, then the arrangement will probably be struck down by the courts as creating a registrable charge over goods.[128]

5.88   The principles of accession were applied in the reservation of title context in *Hendy Lennox (Industrial Engines) Ltd v Grahame Puttick Ltd*.[129] The case concerned diesel engines which had been incorporated into generating sets. Staughton J held that the proprietary rights of the sellers in the engines were not affected when the engines were wholly or partially incorporated into the generator sets. The title of the original seller remained because the diesel engines could be removed without serious injury to or destruction of the whole so formed. The judge explained that the engines were not like the acrilan which

---

126   [1989] 1 NZLR 723 at 727.
127   See generally G McCormack 'Mixture of Goods' (1990) 10 Legal Studies 293.
128   *Specialist Plant Services Ltd v Braithwaite Ltd* [1987] BCLC 1.
129   [1984] 1 WLR 485.

became yarn and then carpet (*Bond Worth*),[130] or the resin which became chipboard (*Borden*),[131] or the leather which became handbags (*Peachdart*).[132]

MIXING OF GOODS WITHOUT LOSS OF PHYSICAL IDENTITY

5.89   Where goods belonging to different parties are mixed together but not so as to affect the physical characteristics of the commingled goods, different rules may apply depending on whether one of the parties has been guilty of intentional wrongdoing in bringing about the mixing. In particular, there was some authority supporting the existence of a penal rule whereby a party who was guilty of intentional wrongdoing in bringing about the mixing forfeited his share in the resultant mixture.[133] More recently, however, in *Indian Oil Corpn v Greenstone Shipping SA (Panama)*[134] the existence of a penal rule was denied. The court held that where a party wrongfully mixed the goods of another with his own goods which were substantially of the same nature and quality, and they could not be separated for practical purposes, the mixture was held in common. The innocent party, however, could claim from the wrongdoer any loss sustained by reason of the admixture, whether in respect of quality or otherwise.[135]

5.90   Where commingling has been effected in good faith or with the consent of the respective owners, then the authorities suggest that the owners of the constituent items become tenants in common of the mass in proportion to their respective contributions.[136] Cases usually cited in this connection are *Buckley v*

---

130   *Re Bond Worth Ltd* [1980] Ch 228.
131   [1981] Ch 25.
132   [1984] Ch 131.
133   See *Lupton v White* (1808) 15 Ves 432 and *Sandeman & Sons v Tyzack and Branfoot Steamship Co Ltd* [1913] AC 680 at 695 where Lord Moulton said: 'If the mixing has arisen from the fault of "B", "A" can claim the goods.' See also the comments of Lord Millett in *Foskett v McKeown* [2001] 1 AC 102 at 132–133.
134   [1988] 1 QB 345.
135   See the statement of principle by Moore-Bick J in *Glencore v Metro Trading International* [2001] 1 Lloyds Law Reports 284 who concluded (at 330) that:
       'when one person wrongfully blends his own oil with oil of a different grade or specification belonging to another person with the result that a new product is produced, that new product is owned by them in common. In my view justice also requires in a case of this kind that the proportions in which the contributors own the new blend should reflect both the quantity and the value of the oil which each has contributed. As in other cases of mixing, any doubts about the quantity or value of the oil contributed by the innocent party should be resolved against the wrongdoer. The innocent party is also entitled to recover damages from the wrongdoer in respect of any loss which he has suffered as a result of the wrongful use of his oil.'
136   See the comments of Lord Millett in *Foskett v McKeown* [2001] 1 AC 102 at 141:
       'A mixed fund, like a physical mixture, is divisible between the parties who contributed to it rateably in proportion to the value of their respective contributions, and this must be ascertained at the time they are added to the mixture … If 20 gallons of A's oil are mixed with 40 gallons of B's oil to produce a uniform mixture of 60 gallons, A and B are entitled

Gross[137] and *Spence v Union Marine Insurance Co.*[138] In *Buckley v Gross*, tallow in a warehouse belonging to a number of persons flowed out as a result of a fire into a common sewer. Blackburn J said:[139]

> 'The tallow of the different owners was indeed mixed up into a molten mass, so that it might be difficult to apportion it among them ... Probably the legal effect of such a mixture would be to make the owners tenants in common in equal portions of the mass, but at all events they do not lose their property in it.'

In this case there was no proof of the respective contributions of the owners of the separate goods. Therefore, a tenancy in common in equal shares solution was adopted.

5.91   In *Spence v Union Marine Insurance Co* it was possible to quantify the contributions of each party to the mixture and, accordingly, a tenancy in common was declared in line with the contribution of each party to the whole. This was a case where a ship carrying a cargo of cotton from the American South to Liverpool became shipwrecked. Consequently, distinguishing marks on the bales of cotton were obliterated. The court took the view that:[140]

> '... by the mixture of the bales, and their becoming undistinguishable by reason of the action of the sea, and without the fault of the respective owners, these parties became tenants in common of the cotton, in proportion to their respective interests.'

More generally, the court said:[141]

> '(I)f ... separation is not practicable, then the former proprietors of the things now connected will be joint owners of the whole, whenever the mixture has been made with the consent of both parties, or by accident.'

5.92   The English authorities in this area are of respectable antiquity, to say the least, but were applied in a modern setting by the New Zealand Court of Appeal in *Coleman v Harvey*.[142] The New Zealand Court of Appeal accepted the view that where the goods of two persons are intermixed by consent or agreement, so that the several portions can no longer be distinguished, the proprietors have an interest in common in proportion to their respective shares. In principle, this body of doctrine should apply in the reservation of title context. Consequently, where goods supplied under a reservation of title

---

to share in the mixture in proportions of 1 to 2. It makes no difference if A's oil, being purchased later, cost £2 a gallon and B's oil cost only £1 a gallon, so that they each paid out £40. This is because the mixture is divisible between the parties ratably in proportion to the value of their respective contributions and not in proportion to their respective cost.'

For a somewhat more complicated analysis see Birks 'Mixtures' in N Palmer and E McKendrick (eds) *Interests in Goods* (Lloyds of London Press, 2nd edn, 1998) chapter 9.

137   (1863) 3 B & S 566; 122 ER 213.
138   (1868) LR 3 CP 427.
139   (1863) 3 B & S 566 at 574–575; 122 ER 213 at 216.
140   (1868) LR 3 CP 427 at 438–439.
141   (1868) LR 3 CP 427 at 438.
142   [1989] 1 NZLR 723.

clause have been mingled with other goods without resulting in a loss of physical identity, the supplier should be able to claim co-ownership of the mixture. Under English law, no security interest in the mixture has been created in favour of the supplier and, as a result, there are no registration requirements to fulfil before the supplier's co-ownership is recognised.

5.93 Some commentators distinguish between fluid mixtures and granular mixtures. For fluid mixtures the rule is co-ownership, whereas in the case of granular mixtures there is some conflict of authority.[143] *Spence v Union Marine Insurance Co*, however, seems to have set out deliberately to assimilate the two categories of case and there appears to be little policy for drawing a distinction.[144]

REFORM INITIATIVES

5.94 In Part II of the Diamond report on *Security Interests in Property* it was argued that the retention of title by the seller under a contract of sale of goods was in truth a security interest taken by the supplier.[145] As acknowledged in the report, there was nothing new in this observation. It formed the basis of the recommendation of the Crowther Committee in 1971 that a new scheme for security interests should apply to every agreement having as its true purpose the creation or retention of rights in property other than land for the purpose of securing payment of money or performance of an obligation, whatever the form of the agreement used by the contracting parties.[146] The Committee suggested that the retention of title for the purpose of security was in reality a chattel mortgage securing a loan.[147]

5.95 In the Diamond scheme of things reservation of title clauses in non-consumer contracts would be registrable in the new Register of Security Interests. Pending implementation of this fundamental recasting of personal property security law, the Diamond Report did not suggest any major changes in the way reservation of title clauses are treated by the company charge registration provisions. The proposal was for the statutory statement of the clauses which create a registrable charge.[148] It was suggested that a clause would be deemed to create a charge unless it did no more than retain title to goods sold under the contract while they remained in their original state in the buyer's possession, with or without a claim to be entitled to the proceeds of sale of such goods, for the purpose of obtaining the price of those goods. Initially the Department of Trade and Industry were enamoured with the Diamond idea.[149]

---

143 See chapter entitled 'Mixtures' by Peter Birks in N Palmer and E McKendrick (eds) *Interests in Goods* (Lloyds of London Press, 2nd edn, 1998) p 227. The distinction is based on Roman law, though the commentator does not advocate preservation of the distinction merely for the sake of antiquity (see p 239).

144 As Birks acknowledges at p 246.

145 At pp 11 and 87.

146 Cmnd 4596, para 5.2.8.

147 Paragraph 5.2.8.ii.

148 At p 114.

149 Letter of 2 September 1987, para 3.4(c).

Later, however, it recoiled from the recommendation.[150] The proposal did not find a place in the Companies Act 1989, the justification for this change of heart being that the legislation did not single out other examples of security which constituted a charge, but did not do so expressly and which were in fact registrable.

5.96   The issue of company charge registration and reservation of title clauses was also considered by the Company Law Review Steering Group. In its Final Report *Modern Company Law for a Competitive Economy* the Steering Group pointed out that:[151]

> 'the broad thrust of case law is that complex retention of title clauses, where the title protecting the indebtedness shifts from one good to another on transformation, are charges over the goods and thus registrable but that simple retention of title clauses, where the seller merely retains title on transfer, are not.'

The Steering Group suggested that 'such questions, which give rise to difficult issues in a developing area of commercial practice, are best left to the courts.'

5.97   A different tack was taken by the Law Commission, who recommended that all reservation of title clauses should be subjected to filing obligations.[152] The Law Commission suggested that even 'simple' retention of title clauses served a clear security purpose and it was pointed out that in the case of an 'all-monies' clause, security was effectively being taken over goods already delivered and paid for.[153] The Law Commission proposed in respect of the treatment of retention of title clauses a move over to a system modelled along the lines of Article 9 of the American UCC and the Personal Property Security Acts in the common law provinces of Canada and in New Zealand.[154]

5.98   Under English law, insofar as a simple reservation of title clause is recognised as being effective without registration, it will enjoy super-priority status.[155] In other words, it will outrank security interests strictly so-called that are subject to a requirement of registration. If a reservation of title clause is held to constitute a registrable charge, however, the position is much less favourable from the point of view of a seller. In practice, a registrable retention of title clause is unlikely to be registered and the claimant relying on such a clause will be reduced to the ranks of the unsecured creditors.

---

150   See heading 'Registrable charges' in the letter of 7 July 1988.

151   Final Report (July 2001) at p 265.

152   Paragraph 7.24 of the Consultation Paper.

153   At para 7.10 the Commission wondered 'whether there might be a risk that in time overseas investors may be hesitant before investing in United Kingdom companies if we persist in having a system that does not take a functional approach, instead retaining the application of any system only to charges.'

154   The Law Commission proposals on retention of title have attracted criticism for reasons discussed in Chapter 2. In short, registration would be required in all instances and not just for the more complicated manifestations of retention of title.

155   Put shortly, the property never comes into the beneficial ownership of the insolvent.

5.99 Superficially, the picture under Article 9 is more straightforward. What is important under Article 9 is the substantive purpose and effect of the agreement and not the label which has been applied to it by the parties. If the essence of the agreement is to secure payment or performance of an obligation, then Article 9 characterises it as a security interest and it will be governed by the Article 9 principles. Article 9 applies irrespective of the location of title to the secured property. Retention of title clauses are recharacterised as security interests and are subject to filing requirements, and this is coupled with a 'first to file' rule for determining priorities between competing security interests in the same property. There is, however, an exception in the case of purchase-money security interests (PMSIs). A purchase-money security interest will rank ahead of a prior security interest with an after-acquired property clause, and a retention of title clause may qualify as a PMSI. On the other hand, Article 9 undoubtedly weakens the position of a conditional seller as compared with the position prevailing in England. First, the seller has to file to protect its interest,[156] whereas, under the English position, simple and current account retention of title clauses are not the subject of any requirement of registration. Secondly, there are special perfection requirements that must be complied with so as to acquire PMSI status. In other words, a person who has bought goods that have been sold subject to a retention of title clause will have acquired sufficient rights in these goods so as to enable an earlier security interest given by the buyer in after-acquired property to attach. In consequence, a prior security interest holder will assume priority in the event that an unpaid seller fails to comply with the super-priority perfection requirements for PMSIs.[157]

5.100 The point is illustrated by *Hongkong and Shanghai Banking Corpn v HFH USA Corpn*[158] where a German company sold and shipped machinery to a US customer pursuant to a reservation of title clause. The supplier did not file a financing statement until becoming aware of the buyer's financial problems. At that time the grace period for filing had expired and so it was held that the supplier's purchase money security interest could not defeat the general security interest held by the buyer's principal financier. The sales contract contained a choice of law clause which subjected the contract including the reservation of title element to German law, but the New York court refused to enforce the provision. It said that if German law were applied under the present circumstances, it would violate a fundamental purpose of Article 9 'to create

---

156 By way of exception to the general rule, Article 9–309 provides for the automatic perfection of a purchase money security interest in consumer goods, ie the security interest is perfected automatically when it attaches. There is no need for filing or the creditor acquiring possession of the same. The principle of automatic perfection does not apply, however, in the case of consumer goods governed by certificate-of-title statutes like automobiles.

157 See generally K Meyer 'A Primer on Purchase Money Security Interests under Revised Article 9 of the Uniform Commercial Code' (2001) 50 Kansas LR 143; P Shupack 'Defining Purchase Money Collateral' (1992) 29 Idaho LR 767.

158 (1992) 805 F Supp 133. The case is discussed by J Hausmann in 'The Value of Public-Notice Filing Under Uniform Commercial Code Article 9: A Comparison with the German Legal System of Securities in Personal Property' (1996) 25 Georgia Journal of International and Comparative Law 427 at 477–478.

commercial certainty and predictability by allowing third party creditors to rely on the specific perfection and priority rules that govern collateral within the scope of Article 9.'[159]

5.101 The basic rationale for awarding the PMSI super-priority is that if an earlier creditor could rely on an after-acquired property clause to the prejudice of a purchase money security interest holder, the earlier creditor would obtain an unjustified windfall at the expense of the later creditor whose advance of funds enabled the additional property to be acquired.[160] Moreover, it is contended that the first creditor on the scene should not be permitted to obtain a security monopoly over the assets of the debtor.[161] The effect of this might be to preclude the debtor from procuring further credit elsewhere or to force later creditors to contract on a riskier basis, having to settle for lower ranking security or no security at all.[162]

5.102 A PMSI can only be created in goods or software, but Article 9 distinguishes between inventory and other goods for the purpose of conditioning entitlement to PMSI status. Article 9–324 states that a purchase-money security interest in inventory has priority over any other security interest in the same collateral. Purchase-money super-priority over the proceeds of inventory may also be established in certain circumstances. 'Inventory' is defined as meaning goods that are held by a person for sale or lease, or that have been leased, or that are to be furnished or have been furnished under a contract of service, or that are raw materials, work in progress, or materials used or consumed in a business with 'proceeds' defined as meaning whatever property, in any form, is derived, directly or indirectly, from any dealing with collateral, and including any payment representing indemnity or compensation for loss of, or damage to, the collateral. Article 9–324, however, lays down some conditions which must be met before a retention of title clause can qualify as a PMSI. During the five-year period before the debtor receives possession of the inventory, the purchase-money secured party must send an authenticated notification to the holder of a potentially conflicting security interest in the same collateral. The notification is required to state that the person giving it

---

159 (1992) 805 F Supp 133 at 141.
160 See also the justification offered at para 4.159 of the Law Commission Consultation Paper *Registration of Security Interests* (July 2002):
  'someone who simply advances further funds to a company, whilst providing new value in exchange for any security she takes, is not contributing to the property available to secured creditors: she is not making their position any better. In contrast, where the fresh finance was to enable the debtor to acquire further property, if the property subject to the purchase-money interest in favour of the second (or later) creditor was available to the earlier creditors, they would be better off as a result of that later creditor, who would probably lose out.'
  For a law and economics perspective on the issue see H Kanda and S Levmore 'Explaining Creditor Priorities' (1994) 80 Va LR 2103 at 2138–2141.
161 See generally T Jackson and A Kronman 'Secured Financing and Priorities Among Creditors' (1979) 88 Yale LJ 1143 at 1167: 'the purchase-money priority is best thought of as a device for alleviating the situational monopoly created by an after-acquired property clause'.
162 The Law Commission make the point at para 7.69 of their Consultation Paper that not having a concept of purchase money super-priority under a functional system would make it more difficult for a company to obtain vendor credit.

has, or expects to acquire, a purchase-money security interest in inventory of the debtor and to describe such inventory.[163] The Official Comment to Article 9–324 explains the purpose of the notification requirement as being to protect a non-purchase-money inventory secured party. The financing arrangement between an inventory secured party and its debtor may typically require the secured party to make periodic advances against incoming inventory. If the inventory secured party receives notification, it may decide not to make the advance, whereas if it does not receive notification it will ordinary have priority under the first-to-file priority rule of Article 9–322.

5.103   Where the retention of title clause relates to goods other than inventory (e g capital equipment), the qualifications necessary for gaining PMSI status are somewhat less demanding.[164] Essentially, automatic super-priority over prior secured lenders is gained if the PMSI is perfected within 20 days of the debtor obtaining possession of the collateral as a debtor. The risks to earlier creditors are supposed to be greater in the case of inventory financing, and this explains the stricter conditions applying to inventory. As certain commentators observe:

> 'The rules intimate that the acquisition of new inventory and its associated debt is more threatening to earlier creditors than the debt-financing of new equipment but that debt tied to new inventory is still less threatening than new money unlinked to particular assets.'[165]

CONCLUSION

5.104   As we have seen, there are at least five different types of reservation of title clause. Some of the kinds of clause are properly viewed as registrable charge, while others are not. It appears that neither 'simple' reservation of title clauses nor 'all-liabilities' clauses fall within the scope of the company charge registration provisions. The position with respect to 'all-liabilities' clauses is not completely free from doubt, however, despite the decision of the House of Lords in the *Armour*[166] case. Proceeds of sale clauses have been struck down by the English courts in recent cases despite valiant arguments in support of the

---

163   Article 9–324(b).
164   See generally K Meyer (2001) 50 Kansas LR 143 at 170 who argues that the relevant requirements are relatively easily satisfied. He states:
> 'It is probably easy for sellers to control when the debtor obtains possession and file before transferring the goods. Lenders, on the other hand, face some dangers. First, they must prove that the advance was in fact used to purchase the goods and that the loan enabled the debtor to buy the goods, which normally requires that the goods be purchased after the advance or substantially contemporaneously with it. Next, lenders must be certain when the debtor obtains possession of the goods and file within twenty days. The lender can avoid this issue by filing a financing statement before it releases any funds. Finally, another potential problem is the possibility that the previous secured creditor will declare the debtor in default when it learns of the lender's PMSI.'
165   See H Kanda & S Levmore 'Explaining Creditor Priorities' (1994) 80 Virginia Law Review 2103 at 2139; and see generally M Bridge, R Macdonald, R Simmonds and C Walsh 'Formalism, Functionalism and Understanding the Law of Secured Transactions' (1999) 44 McGill LJ at fns 99–108.
166   [1991] 2 AC 339.

efficacy of such clauses. Aggregation clauses as applied to the mixture of heterogeneous goods in the manufacturing process have also fallen foul of registration requirements. It has been submitted in this chapter, however, that the position is both more complex and more favourable towards aggregation clauses than a superficial reading of the case law might suggest. The case law continues to define the parameters of effective reservation of title clauses.

Chapter 6

MECHANICS OF REGISTRATION

INTRODUCTION

6.1 Previous chapters have discussed the objectives of the registration system as well as detailing the category of charges requiring registration. Brief reference has been made as well to the consequences of non-registration from the point of view of the charge holder, in particular the loss of priority suffered as a result. In this chapter it is intended to examine in detail the mechanisms of the registration system. Particular attention will be paid to the respective roles of the various parties to the process, namely the charge holder, the company granting the charge, other creditors of the company, and the court.

THE REGISTRATION OBLIGATION

6.2 The primary obligation to register particulars of charge is cast on the company. Section 399 of the Companies Act 1985 provides that it is the duty of a company to send to Companies House ('the registrar of companies') for registration particulars of every charge created by the company and of the issues of debentures or a series of debentures requiring registration under ss 395 to 398. This must be done within 21 days of the date of creation of the charge. The obligation applies to charges created by companies that are registered in England and Wales. The instrument (if any) by which the charge is created or evidenced must be delivered along with the prescribed particulars of the charge. This task may be carried out, however, by any person interested in the charge.[1] In such an eventuality the person is entitled to recover from the company the amount of any fees paid to Companies House in connection with the registration. If particulars are not submitted for registration within the 21-day period, then the company and every officer of it who is in default is liable to a fine and, for continued contravention, to a daily default fine.[2]

6.3 In practice, registration is effected on the application of the charge holder and it is unlikely that this practice will discontinue. The economic incentive is stronger from the point of view of the charge holder. Non-registration or, as more correctly stated, non-delivery of particulars for registration, will result in a loss of priority. Where a charge has been created by a company and particulars are not delivered within the 21-day period, the charge is, so far as it

---

1   CA 1985, s 399(2).
2   CA 1985, s 399(3).

confers any security over the company's property or undertaking, void against the liquidator or administrator and any creditor of the company.

6.4 It should be noted that while Companies Act 1985, ss 395–409 (Chapter I of Part XII) deal with the registration of charges created by companies registered in England and Wales, the provisions in Chapter II of Part XII of the Act (ss 410 to 424) deal with the registration of charges created by companies registered in Scotland.[3] The jurisdiction of an English court to deal with the consequences of a charge in Scotland under Chapter II of Part XII of the Companies Act 1985 was considered for the first time in *Arthur D Little Ltd (in Administration) v Ableco Finance LLC*.[4] It was held that Chapter II of Part XII was part of the law of England as well as that of Scotland. The two Chapters of Part XII were part of the law of both jurisdictions and were a complementary whole prescribing who was to register what and where:

> 'There is no provision exclusively and expressly making a Chapter applicable only to one jurisdiction. A Scottish company registered in Scotland may carry on business in England and grant a charge over English property. An English judge, for example, in possession of proceedings may need to ask himself where the charge is registered and has it been validly registered for the purpose of enforcement in England? He cannot, in my judgment, simply shut his eyes to each Chapter; each is complementary of the other and each provides the answer. Each is part of the uniform code marking out the process of registration.'[5]

The court decided that, applying s 410(4)(e) in Part II, a charge over shares in an English subsidiary did not have to be registered in Scotland.

ACCELERATION OF THE REPAYMENT OBLIGATION

6.5 Companies Act 1985, s 395(2) states that where a charge becomes void under s 395 the money secured by it immediately becomes payable. So it might be said that there is an acceleration of the repayment obligation insofar as the company is concerned.[6] There are some obscurities about the provision, however. It is, to an extent, unclear when the repayment obligation arises. Does it arise when the 21-day period for registration has elapsed? Or does it arise only when liquidation or administration supervenes, or upon a person acquiring an interest in or right over property subject to the charge? These doubts are

---

3   Sections 462–466 of the Companies Act 1985 deal with floating charges in Scotland.
4   [2003] Ch 217.
5   [2003] Ch 217 at [22].
6   For criticism of the equivalent Scottish provision – CA 1985, s 410(3) – see G Gretton 'Registration of Company Charges' (2002) 6 Edinburgh Law Review 146 at 164 165:

> 'The logic of this statutory acceleration is not obvious. It might be supposed to be intended to be a protection to the creditor, but it should be noted that (unlike most acceleration clauses in commercial loan agreements) this is not merely an option to accelerate but is an automatic acceleration. This may hurt the creditor. A carefully crafted loan agreement, involving phased drawdown and phased repayment schedules running over many years will be wrecked by this provision, and that fatal consequence ensues even if the problem is a minor one about which the creditor cares little.'

long-standing.[7] The better view appears to be that the money became repayable once the 21 days were up. It has been argued that it would defeat the whole purpose of the provision if the charge holder had no immediate right to repayment. The injustice from the point of view of the charge holder arises because its money remains its loan while, at the same time it is deprived of security.[8] The only 'let-out' is the possibility of making an application to the court for late registration of the charge.[9]

AVOIDANCE OF UNREGISTERED CHARGES – GENERAL PRINCIPLES

6.6 Under s 395 of the Companies Act 1985 the general principle is that unregistered security interests are invalid in the event of the company creating the charge going into liquidation or administration. In the United States, the same broad principle applies under the Uniform Commercial Code and the Federal Bankruptcy Code to security interests that have not been perfected by filing or some other permissible perfection method.[10] On the other hand, it has been argued that unsecured creditors gain an undeserved windfall if a security interest is held to be void for non-registration.[11] The argument proceeds on the basis that, by deciding not to require security, unsecured creditors are agreeing to be subordinated to later-in-time secured parties that have properly registered their security. Even if an unsecured creditor does search and rely upon the existing state of the register, subsequent events could render the information of little value. In other words, the registration system cannot possibly protect an unsecured creditor from having its claim primed by a secured party, because the day after the unsecured creditor's search is made, the debtor could grant a security interest that is later registered.

---

7   According to the unimplemented s 99 of the Companies Act 1989, where a charge became void to any extent by virtue of non-registration, the whole of the sum secured by the charge was payable forthwith on demand.

8   See WJ Gough *Company Charges* (Butterworths, 2nd edn, 1996) at p 733:
    'This saving and acceleration of the debt obligations reflect the statutory provision imposing the primary duty to register on the chargor. It would be unduly harsh on the chargee not only to invalidate the charge but also to leave the debt payable at a future date as a consequence of default in what is primarily a duty of the company charger.'

9   Under s 404 of the Companies Act 1985 and preceding legislation.

10 See the statement by J McCoid 'Bankruptcy, the Avoiding Powers, and Unperfected Security Interests' (1985) 59 American Bankruptcy Law Journal 175 at 190 that:
    'invalidation of unperfected security interests by the bankruptcy trustee takes from innocent secured parties to give to unsecured creditors who are not prejudiced by the failure to perfect. Even if avoidance did not take time and effort, one might seriously question this structure which requires those who meant no harm to compensate those who have not been injured, particularly when both bargained for the extension of credit on a different assumption.'

11 See E Smith 'Commentary' (1995) 79 Minn LR 715 at 718 and see also more generally C Scott Pryor 'Revised Uniform Commercial Code Article 9' (1999) 7 American Bankruptcy Institute Law Review 465.

6.7 Professor Sir Roy Goode accepts that the effect of avoidance is to give unsecured creditors who did not act in reliance on the want of registration an apparently unjustified windfall addition to the assets available for distribution. Nevertheless, in his view, there are sound policy reasons for the avoidance of unregistered securities:[12]

> 'In the first place, the avoidance rule reflects the law's dislike of the secret security interest, which leaves the debtor's property apparently unencumbered and at common law was considered a fraud on the general creditors. Secondly, the registration provisions help to curb the fabrication or ante-dating of security agreements on the eve of the winding-up. Thirdly, though unsecured creditors have no existing interest in the company's assets outside winding up, [upon winding-up] … their rights become converted from purely personal rights into rights more closely analogous to that of beneficiaries under an active trust. Fourthly, there may well be unsecured creditors who were misled by the want of registration into extending credit which they would not otherwise have granted. But it would be expensive and impracticable to expect the liquidator (or administrator) to investigate each unsecured creditor's claim to see whether he did or did not act on the assumption that the unregistered charge did not exist. So a broad brush approach which in effect assumes detriment to unsecured creditors at large is justified. Finally, the registration provisions serve a general public notice function as well as being a registration requirement …'

6.8 In New Zealand, however, these arguments were rejected and, in a conscious departure from the US Article 9 model, a notice-filing system was introduced without any invalidation of 'unperfected' security interests in liquidation.[13] It was suggested that the propositions advanced by Professor Goode rested on an outdated conception of how business was actually conducted.[14] The policy against secret security interests was misplaced because nowadays there was little danger of a creditor being induced to give credit on the assumption that goods in the debtor's possession are its own property.[15]

---

12   *Principles of Corporate Insolvency Law* (Sweet & Maxwell, 2nd edn, 1997) at pp 420–421.

13   See the New Zealand Law Commission Report No 8 *A Personal Property Securities Act for New Zealand* (1989) at p 115:
   'In practice, only two parties are possibly misled by the absence of a registration statement. The first is the prospective creditor who would normally advance credit only against a first ranking security in a debtor's goods. Under the proposed statute, if such a creditor files a registration statement, it is protected against any unperfected security interests … Creditors, who supply goods or funds on an unsecured basis are generally either not concerned about the presence of outstanding interests or assume that such interests exist. Prospective buyers and lessees, like prospective secured creditors, also rely heavily on the ostensible ownership of their transferor. Accordingly, they are protected from unperfected security interests … unless they have knowledge of the security interest.'

14   See DF Dugdale 'The Proposed PPSA' [2000] New Zealand Law Journal 383 at 384.

15   See generally on the New Zealand legislation L Widdup and L Mayne *Personal Property Securities Act: a conceptual approach* (2000) and see also D Webb 'The PPSA – A New Regime for Secured Transactions' [2000] New Zealand Law Review 175; D McLauchlan 'Fundamentals of the PPSA: An Introduction' (2000) 6 NZBLQ 166; R Scragg 'Personal Property Securities Law Reform in New Zealand' (1999) 7 Insolvency LJ 163.

6.9   Be that as it may, while an unsecured creditor may not actively seek a proprietary right against the company, the register provides important information about the existence of creditors who possess such rights.[16] A wider reliance interest is promoted in that the general credit assessment of the company would involve the receipt of such information. By making regular inspections of the register an unsecured creditor is enabled to police any negative pledge covenants that might exist in the loan agreement and also to police the borrower more generally.[17] The presence of a security interest on the register could cause an unsecured creditor to alter the conditions of the loan or the other terms of the business relationship with the debtor. The fact that that a particular individual unsecured creditor may not have relied on the register in this way is irrelevant. As Dr De Lacy comments:[18]

'The hypothetical nature of the unsecured creditor in this context is designed to remove complex factual inquiries that would otherwise occur at considerable expense to the liquidation process thereby prejudicing creditors as a whole. Indeed the concept of reliance in this context would be exceedingly difficult to establish or refute were it be made fact specific.'

6.10   The European Convention on Human Rights (now incorporated in domestic English law through the Human Rights Act 1998) provides a possible, though superficially unlikely, vehicle for challenging the legislative invalidation of unregistered security interests. Article 1 of Protocol 1 to the Convention provides:[19]

'Every natural or legal person is entitled to the peaceful enjoyment of his possessions. No one shall be deprived of his possessions except in the public interest and subject to the conditions provided for by law and by the general principles of international law.'

Article 1 adds, however, that the preceding prescriptions do not in any way impair the right of a State to enforce such laws as it deems necessary to control the use of property in accordance with the general interest or to secure the payment of taxes or other contributions or penalties.[20]

---

16   See J De Lacy 'Ambit and Reform of Part XII of the Companies Act 1985 and the Doctrine of Constructive Notice' in J De Lacy (ed) *The Reform of UK Company Law* (Cavendish, 2002) 333 at 362–363; but see D Baird 'Notice Filing and the Problem of Ostensible Ownership' (1983) 12 J Legal Stud 53 at 60.

17   On the possible prejudice that may be suffered by unsecured creditors through 'springing' security interests and so-called affirmative negative pledge clauses see Tan Cheng Han 'Charges, Contingencies and Registration' (2002) 2 Journal of Corporate Law Studies 191.

18   'Ambit and Reform of Part XII of the Companies Act 1985 and the Doctrine of Constructive Notice' in J De Lacy (ed) *The Reform of UK Company Law* (Cavendish, 2002) 333 at 356–357. De Lacy refers in this connection to the observations of Lord Wilberforce in *Midland Bank Trust Co Ltd v Green* [1981] AC 513 at 530.

19   See generally for an assessment of the implications of these provisions in the commercial law sphere A Dignam and J Allen *Company Law and Human Rights* (Butterworths, 2000) at pp 263–285.

20   For a discussion of the position in the United States under the Fifth Amendment ('no taking without due process') see J Rogers 'The Impairment of Secured Creditors' Rights in Corporate Reorganisation: A Study of the Relationship Between the 5th Amendment and the Bankruptcy Clause' (1983) 96 Harvard Law Review 973; D Baird and T Jackson 'Corporate

6.11　By analogy with *Wilson v First County Trust Ltd (No 2)*,[21] it has been argued that the sanction of invalidity for failure to register a security interest constitutes a disproportionate deprivation of property rights. In the *Wilson* case certain provisions of the Consumer Credit Act 1974 were held by the Court of Appeal to be contrary to the Human Rights Convention. On the other hand, there is a clear difference between the Consumer Credit Act provisions and the existing company charge registration provisions and any future notice filing regime. Under the Consumer Credit Act, an improperly executed regulated agreement is unenforceable as between the parties thereto and not just vis-à-vis certain named third parties and, moreover, there is no mechanism of application to the court whereby the defects can be cured.

6.12　Nevertheless, somewhat surprisingly, the Company Law Review Steering Group accepted the *Wilson* analogy at face value and suggested that the present avoidance power needed to be amended to reflect that decision.[22] Consequently, it suggested that the beneficiary of an unregistered security interest should be given the right to apply to a court for relief from the invalidity.[23] Implementation of this recommendation might create uncertainty and produce practical difficulties and it is submitted that the avoidance power does not fall foul of the Convention being legitimate, proportionate and justifiable in the public interest. The Law Commission has taken a more robust line than the Company Law Review Steering Group stating that the avoidance power was not incompatible with the European Convention because:[24]

'the provision merely invalidates the unregistered charge as against third parties in certain circumstances, not as between the parties themselves in all cases; because the sanction is imposed for the important purpose of securing publicity of charges that may have a serious effect on third parties; and because the sanction is easy to avoid by registration ...'

6.13　The Court of Appeal decision in the *Wilson* case was reversed by the House of Lords,[25] who held that the Consumer Credit Act 1974 was a proportionate regulation of property rights and served a legitimate social end. Lord Nicholls said:[26]

'The fairness of a system of law governing the contractual or property rights of private persons is a matter of public concern. Legislative provisions intended to bring about such fairness are capable of being in the public interest, even if they involve the compulsory transfer of property from one person to another.'

He added:

　　Reorganisation and the Treatment of Diverse Ownership Interests: A Comment on Adequate Protection of Secured Creditors in Bankruptcy' (1984) 51 University of Chicago Law Review 97.

21　[2002] QB 74.
22　Modern Company Law for a Competitive Economy: Final Report (July 2001) at para 12.16.
23　See generally J De Lacy *The Reform of UK Company Law* at pp 382–384.
24　Consultation Paper No 164 *Registration of Security Interests* (2002) at p 58.
25　*Wilson v First County Trust Ltd (No 2)* [2004] 1 AC 816; and see generally on this decision J De Lacy 'Company Charge Avoidance and Human Rights' [2004] JBL 448.
26　[2004] 1 AC 816 at [68].

'It is open to Parliament, when Parliament considers the public interest so requires, to decide that failure to comply with certain formalities is an essential prerequisite to enforcement of certain types of agreements. This course is open to Parliament even though this will sometimes yield a seemingly unreasonable result in a particular case. Considered overall, this course may well be a proportionate response in practice to a perceived social problem. Parliament may consider the response should be a uniform solution across the board. A tailor-made response, fitting the facts of each case as decided in an application to the court, may not be appropriate. This may be considered an insufficient incentive and insufficient deterrent.'

INVALIDITY AS AGAINST THE LIQUIDATOR, ADMINISTRATOR OR CREDITORS OF A COMPANY

6.14 It is clear from s 395(1) of the Companies Act 1985 that a registrable but unregistered charge is invalid as against the liquidator, administrator or creditors of a company. The meaning of this provision was considered by the House of Lords in *Smith v Bridgend County Borough Council*.[27] Lord Hoffmann observed that the plain intention of the legislature was that property subject to a registrable but unregistered charge should be available to the general body of creditors (or a secured creditor ranking after the unregistered charge) as if no such charge existed. He also said:

'When a winding-up order is made and a liquidator appointed, there is no divesting of the company's assets. The liquidator acquires no interest, whether beneficially or as trustee. The assets continue to belong to the company but the liquidator is able to exercise the company's right to collect them for the purposes of the liquidation. It must in my opinion follow that when section 395 says that the charge shall be "void against the liquidator" it means void against a company acting by its liquidator, that is to say, a company in liquidation.'[28]

Consequently, where proceedings are brought by a liquidator, or for that matter by an administrator, to challenge a charge for want of registration the proceedings should be brought in the name of the company notwithstanding the fact that the company is pleading its own failure to register.

6.15 Lord Hoffmann added, when the administration procedure for ailing companies was introduced by statute, that s 395 of the Companies Act 1985 was amended simply by adding the words 'or administrator' after the word 'liquidator' and this indicated that the section was to operate in relation to a company in administration exactly as it had in relation to a company in liquidation. In the Court of Appeal, Laws LJ described the right of an

---

27   [2002] 1 AC 336.
28   [2002] 1 AC 336 at [20].

administrator to 'take advantage' of the ineffectiveness of the floating charge as 'nothing but statutory serendipity'. Lord Hoffmann, however, was of a different view stating:[29]

> 'I see no reason to impute such whimsical intentions to the legislature. The purpose of section 395 as originally enacted was to protect the interests of the general body of creditors. The purpose of section 395 as extended to administrators is to protect the interests of the company in administration and, if it should subsequently go into liquidation, the interests of creditors. If, on the other hand, the company emerges solvent from the administration, the secured creditor will by definition obtain payment of his debt without recourse to the avoided security.'

6.16   The word 'creditors' has been interpreted as meaning secured creditors.[30] In *Re Ehrmann Bros Ltd*[31] Vaughan Williams LJ said 'the unsecured creditors who have acquired no rights of property as against the property which is the subject of the debentures do not come within those words' and Judge Micklem remarked in *Re Telomatic Ltd*[32] ' "creditor" means only a creditor who has acquired a property right to or an interest in the subject matter of the unregistered charge.' The issue would assume some practical importance if an unsecured creditor obtained judgment and tried to execute against property that was subject to an unregistered fixed charge. If the charge, though unregistered, is still valid vis-à-vis unsecured creditors, then the execution would be ineffective. Similar legislation has generated difficulties of interpretation in Singapore where the leading case is *Ng Wei Teck Michael v Oversea-Chinese Banking Corpn Ltd*.[33] In this case, for some unexplained reasons, there was a significant gap between the presentation of a winding up petition and the making of a winding up order. During this interval the unregistered chargee sold the charged property. The Singapore Court of Appeal took the view that the liquidator could not invoke the statutory equivalent of CA 1985, s 395. As against the liquidator the section only came into operation upon the appointment of the liquidator. On that date the charge had been realised and thus was spent. Consequently, there was nothing for the section to bite on. On the other hand, it was held that the unregistered charge was void as against the unsecured creditors. On the presentation of a winding up petition, an unsecured creditor acquired sufficient interest in the subject matter of the unregistered charge so as to qualify as a 'creditor' for the purposes of the statutory provision. At that time, a statutory scheme came into place to preserve the assets of the company for pari passu distribution among the unsecured creditors. The latter were in the nature of a cestui que trust with beneficial interests extending to all the company's property, including the subject matter of the unregistered charge.

---

29   [2002] 1 AC 336 at [33].
30   See generally E Ferran *Company Law and Corporate Finance* (OUP, 1999) at p 543.
31   [1906] 2 Ch 697 at 704.
32   [1994] 1 BCLC 90 at 95.
33   1998] 2 SLR 1; on which see Tan Cheng Han 'Unregistered Charges and Unsecured Creditors' (1998) 114 LQR 565.

6.17 It is submitted that the reasoning of the Singapore Court of Appeal cannot stand in the light of *Smith v Bridgend County Borough Council*.[34] An unregistered charge is void as regards a company in liquidation and the liquidator is simply acting on behalf of the company. Under the doctrine of 'relation back' the operation of the winding up order is backdated to the time when the petition for winding up was presented.[35] Therefore, an unregistered charge is invalid against the company from that date. Moreover, as Chadwick J pointed out in *Re Ayala Holdings Ltd*[36] the proper plaintiff in the proceedings to recover property or obtain reimbursement for the benefit of a company in liquidation is the company itself, acting through its liquidator.

POSITION OF AN UNREGISTERED CHARGE AS AGAINST THE RECEIVER AND PURCHASERS

6.18 There are certain doubts and difficulties about CA 1985, s 395. For instance, the question remains whether an unregistered but registrable charge is void against a receiver appointed by debenture holders.[37] No explicit guidance is provided on the point, so that one must look to the case law. In *Clough Mill Ltd v Martin*[38] Judge O'Donoghue held, at first instance, that since the receiver represented, as it were, the interests of the secured creditors who had appointed him, an unregistered charge was void against the receiver. The decision of Judge O'Donoghue was reversed on appeal, but no aspersions were cast on the decision in this respect.[39]

6.19 Section 44(1)(a) of the Insolvency Act 1986 deems an administrative receiver to be the company's agent, provided that the company has not gone into liquidation. This statutory declaration merely confirms what is stated to be the position in most commercial debentures. It has been argued that the receiver, as agent of the company, is estopped from pleading the company's

---

34 [2002] 1 AC 336.

35 Insolvency Act 1986, s 129.

36 [1993] BCLC 256. This case was distinguished in *Ng Wei Teck Michael v Oversea-Chinese Banking Corpn* [1998] 2 SLR 1 on the basis that the creditor in *Ayala Holdings* was not seeking a declaration that the unregistered charge was void against him as a creditor under s 395 of the Companies Act 1985. Rather, the applicant contended that he was entitled under the Insolvency Act 1986 to a declaration that the charge was void against the liquidator under CA 1985, s 395 and Chadwick J's judgment was confined to that issue: see [1993] BCLC 256 at 261.

37 The Enterprise Act 2002 in s 250 and Sch 16 abolishes the right to appoint an administrative receiver in the majority of cases, but there are still a substantial number of cases where the holder of a qualifying floating charge may still make such an appointment (now Insolvency Act 1986, s 72A). Moreover, the legislative restriction on the appointment of administrative receivers only applies with respect to floating charges created after the coming into force of the legislation on 15 September 2003.

38 [1984] 1 WLR 1067.

39 [1985] 1 WLR 111.

want of compliance with the statutory registration requirements.[40] In *Independent Automatic Sales Ltd v Knowles and Foster*[41] Buckley J noted that the statutory duty to register any registrable charge had been imposed upon the company. Ex hypothesi, where a charge had not been registered, the company was in default of the statutory obligation and in an action directed to avoid such charge for non-registration must necessarily plead its own default. Buckley J refused to allow it to do this.

6.20 Should the same position obtain in the case of a receiver who is appointed agent of the company? There is no reported judicial decision on the point save for *Clough Mill Ltd v Martin*, which implicitly rejects it.[42] The better view, it is submitted, is to regard the receiver as being invested with the same capacity to plead lack of registration as the appointing charge holders. After all, an administrator of a company is entitled to plead non-registration. It seems strange that a receiver should be any worse off, especially since the office of administrator was originally modelled on that of a receiver appointed by the holder of a floating charge.

6.21 Should a subsequent purchaser of charged assets be entitled to rely upon non-registration?[43] This assumption was made in *Pfeiffer-Weinkellerei Weineinkauf GmbH & Co v Arbuthnot Factors Ltd*[44] where Phillips J held that a right to proceeds of sub-sales conferred on the original supplier by a contract for the sale of goods constituted a charge on book debts arising from sub-sales. He reached the further conclusion that this charge, being unregistered, was void as against a subsequent factor of the debts. There is no discussion in the judgment of the scope of the invalidity provisions. It may be however, that, in some extended sense, a purchaser of charged assets is a 'creditor' of the company creating the charge.[45]

POSITION OF AN UNREGISTERED CHARGE AS AGAINST OTHER CHARGE HOLDERS

6.22 Under CA 1985 and preceding legislation, it appears that an unregistered charge is invalid only against subsequent charge holders who acquired their interest outside the 21 days allowed for registration of the first charge. Dicta to this effect in *Re Ehrmann Bros Ltd*[46] received the seal of approval from

---

40   J Parris *Effective Retention of Title Clauses* (Blackwell Publishing, 1986) at p 103.
41   [1962] 1 WLR 974.
42   See, however, the comments of Judge Newey QC in *Stroud Architectural Systems Ltd v John Laing Construction Ltd* [1994] BCC 18 at 24.
43   See, however, the statement by Howard Bennett in 'Registration of Company Charges' in J Armour and H Bennett (ed) *Vulnerable Transactions in Corporate Insolvency* (Hart Publishing, 2003) 217 at 276: 'Purchasers are clearly excluded from the benefit of section 395(1)'.
44   [1988] 1 WLR 150. See G McCormack [1989] LMCLQ 198 at 211–212.
45   Under the unimplemented s 95 of the Companies Act 1989 an unregistered charge was declared void against any person who for value acquired an interest in or right over property subject to the charge.
46   [1906] 2 Ch 697.

Templeman J in *Watson v Duff Morgan and Vermont (Holdings) Ltd.*[47] On this analysis a charge does not become void until the time for registration has elapsed. Until the expiry of the 21 days it is valid. Therefore it prevails over any charges created within that period, although such charges are not registered until after the 21 days. A subsequent chargee takes priority over an earlier, unregistered charge, however, only if particulars of the second charge have been submitted for registration within 21 days of its creation or before registration of the first charge.[48]

6.23 What if an interest in charged assets is acquired outside the 21-day period with the subsequent acquirer having actual notice of the prior unregistered charge? The Act does not address the issue that we are specifically concerned about here, so one must fall back on cases decided under earlier legislation. The leading case is *Re Monolithic Building Co*[49] where the Court of Appeal had no hesitation in deciding in favour of the subsequent charge holder. Lord Cozens-Hardy MR stated bluntly that notice was not material. He acknowledged that the doctrine of the court in case of fraud proceeds upon a different footing, and that any security may be postponed if one could find fraud in its inception. But he said that it was not fraud to take advantage of legal rights the existence of which may be taken to be known to both parties.[50] The other judges were equally forthright. Joyce J, for instance, said that he could not sanction the engrafting onto the plain words of the Act a very ingenious limitation, which in the result would render the section unworkable and absurd.[51]

---

47 [1974] 1 WLR 450; see D Bennett (1974) 118 SJ 286. The case was concerned with the meaning of the usual proviso attached to orders permitting late registration. The proviso: 'This order to be without prejudice to the rights of parties acquired prior to the time when such security shall be actually registered.'

48 This result seems to follow from the analysis in the *Watson* case. The Companies Act 1989 in s 99 proposed to make it explicit.

49 [1915] 1 Ch 643. Cf *Ram Narain v Radha Kishen Moti Lal Chamaria Firm* (1929) LR 57 Ind App 76. See also the Land Charges Act and Land Registration Act cases: *Midland Bank Trust Co Ltd v Green* [1981] AC 513; *Peffer v Rigg* [1977] 1 WLR 285; *De Lusignan v Johnson* (1973) 230 EG 499; and *Lyus v Prowsa Developments Ltd* [1982] 1 WLR 1044. In *Midland Bank Trust Co Ltd v Green* [1981] AC 513 at 530 Lord Wilberforce specifically approved the words of Lord Cozens-Hardy MR in *Re Monolithic Building Co* [1915] 1 Ch 643. Lord Wilberforce's speech has been subjected to some criticism by Kevin Gray and Susan Frances Gray in *Elements of Land Law* (Butterworths, 3rd edn, 2001) at p 1098. They say that the decision of the House of Lords in *Midland Bank Trust Co Ltd v Green* epitomises the traditional view of the busy property lawyer that there is much to be said in favour of trading off a little justice in return for enhanced security and certainty in commercial transactions. In their view, however, this pragmatic approach will never satisfy all of the people all of the time. They suggest that while it may well be that, in the eyes of the law, it is not fraud to take advantage of the folly of another, it remains an uncomfortable fact of life that most fraud consists in doing precisely that.

50 [1915] 1 Ch 643 at 663.

51 [1915] 1 Ch 643 at 672. In the United States, knowledge of a prior unperfected security interest will not deprive a perfected security interest holder of priority – See G McCormack *Secured Credit under English and American Law* (CUP, 2004) at pp 155–156:
    'Article 9 made a change to pre-existing law where actual notice of an earlier unperfected interest in the property would prevent the second interest from obtaining priority. The change in legislative policy reflects an assumption that making the issue of priorities turn

6.24   What if a subsequent charge holder acquires an interest in or right over property and the acquisition is expressly subject to the unregistered charge? In that event, the first charge, although it has not been registered, may take priority. In any event, the High Court in the Republic of Ireland in *Re Clarets Ltd*[52] reached such a result on the basis of statutory provisions which are the equivalent of the English legislation.[53] Costello J said that the second chargee's rights were at all times limited and qualified ones, namely the right to a second charge ranking after the first. While the case is not directly in point, the proposition advanced in the text also derives some support from the decision of Vinelott J in *Re Fablehill Ltd*.[54]

VALIDITY OF AN UNREGISTERED CHARGE AGAINST THE COMPANY

6.25   Is an unregistered charge valid as against the company? To this relatively simple inquiry it appears possible to provide only a 'yes' answer. The Companies Act 1985 and preceding legislation does not affect the position of an unregistered charge apropos the company creating it, and as regards the ordinary unsecured creditors of the company. One might cite a number of cases to illustrate this statement.

6.26   The first case that might be mentioned is *Re Ehrmann Bros Ltd*.[55] Here Romer LJ said that an ordinary creditor could not intervene in an action brought by debenture holders against the company where the debenture holders were seeking to enforce their security. This point was developed at some length as follows:[56]

> 'Now, in the absence of liquidation before the date of registration or of some charge acquired by a creditor, no ordinary creditor had a right which could have been enforced by him as against the debenture-holders, if the debenture-holders sought to get payment of their charge. The general avoidance of the debentures as charges as against the ordinary creditor prior to liquidation proceedings, and in the absence of any charge acquired

---

on factual inquiries based on the state of knowledge generates uncertainty and breeds litigation. For example, it may be difficult to determine what exactly happened before the event in question and this makes life more difficult for subsequent parties who may not know whether to negotiate subordination agreements or to adjust interest rates accordingly. Moreover, it could be argued that a system which makes priorities turn on knowledge tends to reward careless creditors who do not make inquiries about their debtors rather than the diligent creditor who examines a debtor's credit history and prior lending agreements before entering into the commitment to lend.'

52   (Unreported) 21 November 1978, on which see generally G McCormack (1984) 2 Irish Law Times 67 at 72.

53   Under Companies Act 1989, s 99 a charge was declared not to be void against a person acquiring an interest in or right over property where the acquisition was expressly subject to the charge.

54   [1991] BCLC 830. See also *Barclays Bank plc v Stuart Landon Ltd* [2001] 2 BCLC 316.

55   [1906] 2 Ch 697.

56   [1906] 2 Ch 697 at 708.

by him, would not entitle him to intervene as between the company and the debenture-holders if the company chose to pay the debenture-holders or to give other security to the debenture-holders; nor, in my opinion, could such a creditor apply or intervene in an action brought by the debenture-holders against the company where the debenture-holders were seeking to enforce the charge and to use its assets in paying those debentures off. An ordinary creditor could have no locus standi; if there was liquidation, of course different considerations would apply; he might then intervene, and I think his intervention would be accepted by the Court. But, as I have said, in the absence of liquidation and the absence of something in the nature of a charge acquired upon the security comprised in the debentures, a creditor could not intervene as against any property of the company or as against the debenture-holders in any way whatever. That being so, it appears to me, as I have said, that the only right protected is something which affects the property covered by the debentures.'

6.27   Another case in point is *Mercantile Bank of India Ltd v Central Bank of India, Australia and China*.[57] In this case Porter J held that letters of hypothecation over goods in India amounted to floating charges which should have been registered. But the charges remained valid against the company. Therefore the charge holder was able to convert the charges into fixed charges and perfect them by seizure prior to liquidation. This seizure was then good as against the liquidator.

6.28   To the same effect is *Saunderson & Co v Clark*.[58] This is a case where there was an unregistered charge over the debts of the company. Before winding up, the debtor, pursuant to an instruction from the company, paid the secured creditor as assignee of the company. It was held by Lush J that after the winding up the debtor was not liable to pay again to the liquidator, nor could the liquidator recover from the assignee.

6.29   The same points were driven home in *Re Monolithic Building Co.*[59] Phillimore LJ ventured the view that the relevant provision:

'makes void a security; not the debt, not the cause of action, but the security, and not as against everybody, not as against the company grantor, but against the liquidator and against any creditor, and it leaves the security to stand as against the company while it is a going concern. It does not make the security binding on the liquidator as successor of the company.'

Lord Cozens-Hardy MR was of the same opinion. He said:[60]

---

57   [1937] 1 All ER 231.
58   (1913) 29 TLR 579.
59   [1915] 1 Ch 643 at 667–668.
60   [1915] 1 Ch 643 at 667. See generally on this whole issue WJ Gough *Company Charges* (Butterworths, 2nd edn, 1996) chapter 30. In *Smith v Bridgend County Borough Council* [2002] 1 AC 336 at [66] Lord Scott said that the references in the *Monolithic Building Company* case to the unregistered security remaining enforceable while the grantor company was a going concern produced the same effect for companies pre liquidation as s 8 of the Bills of Sale Act 1878 produced for individuals pre bankruptcy:

'Until bankruptcy supervened the unregistered bill of sale was enforceable against the

'It is a perfectly good deed against the company so long as it is a going concern.'

An unregistered chargee is entitled with respect to the company to exercise all the remedies of a secured creditor, including sale. A purchaser from the chargee will get a good title. This is still the case even if liquidation of the company supervenes after completion of the sale. *Mercantile Bank of India Ltd v Central Bank India, Australia and China*[61] attests to this proposition.

6.30 *Re Row Dal Construction Pty Ltd*[62] may also be mentioned in this connection. The case indicates that it is too late for a liquidator to intervene if a charge holder has already been paid prior to liquidation. The case involved the loan of money by a bank to a company on the security of certain book debts which were assigned by the company to the bank. The book debtor duly paid the bank pursuant to the terms of the assignment, thereby discharging the company's indebtedness to the bank. All this happened before the company went into liquidation. Upon liquidation the bank sought to recover the proceeds of the assignment on the basis that the assignment was invalid against him for non-registration. The claim failed. The debt had been discharged prior to the appointment of the liquidator. Herring CJ in the Supreme Court of Victoria put the point cogently:[63]

'Had liquidation in this case intervened before the payment of the $6000 actually paid ... on 31 May, no doubt in that event there would have been a contest as to the destination of this sum, the liquidator claiming it as property of the company and relying upon non-registration of the assignment to defeat the bank's claim and the bank for its part claiming it as its property by reason of the absolute assignment. But as things are the liquidator can derive no assistance from the failure to register under s 72 [of the Victorian Companies Act 1958] when he was appointed on 6 July 1962 there was no property of the company upon which the bank claimed any security, and there was consequently no basis upon which he could call in aid s 72 to defeat the bank's assignment. These considerations are in my opinion sufficient to dispose of the point.'

6.31 Another case in point from an analogous context is *Mace Builders (Glasgow) Ltd v Lunn.*[64] The case concerned that section in the companies legislation which provides for the invalidation, except in certain circumstances, of floating charges granted within a prescribed period prior to the commencement of winding up. The provision was then s 322 of the Companies Act 1948

---

grantor. Thereafter it was not. Until a liquidator or administration intervenes, the unregistered charge is enforceable against the grantor company. Thereafter, or until the liquidator or administration comes to an end, it is not.'

61   [1937] 1 All ER 231. See also *NV Slavenburg's Bank v Intercontinental Natural Resources Ltd* [1980] 1 WLR 1076 at 1090 where the case was cited by Lloyd J as authority for the proposition that once a charge has been perfected by the seizure of the goods charged it is too late for the liquidator to intervene.

62   [1966] VR 249.

63   [1966] VR 249 at 258. See generally on this case WJ Gough *Company Charges* (2nd edn, 1996) at pp 738–739.

64   [1987] Ch 191.

and is now s 245 of the Insolvency Act 1986.[65] Scott J held that the section did not have retrospective effect so as to invalidate transactions by a debenture holder or receiver which predated the commencement of winding up. Accordingly, where a debenture holder or receiver sold charged assets and applied the proceeds towards repayment of the charged debt, the subsequent entry of the company into liquidation in circumstances where the invalidating rule applied did not enable the liquidator to require repayment of those proceeds of sale.[66]

CHARGES EXISTING ON PROPERTY ACQUIRED

6.32   It is important to note the distinction between charges created by a company and charges existing on property which has been acquired by the company. Both categories of charge are registrable, but the consequences of non-registration are fundamentally different in each case. Non-registration of a charge created by a company leads to avoidance of the charge against certain categories of persons.[67] Non-registration, on the other hand, of a charge which is already subsisting on property that is acquired by the company does not lead to invalidation of the charge. Rather, the consequence is simply the imposition of a fine and, for continued contravention, a daily default fine.[68] The distinction is a time-honoured one. The relevant provisions of the Companies Act 1985 mirror ones found in earlier companies legislation.[69] Of course, when a company acquires property that is subject to a charge, the charge will usually be discharged by the seller of the property out of the proceeds of sale of the property.

PARTICULARS REQUIRING REGISTRATION

6.33   Section 395(1) of CA 1985 talks about delivery to the registrar of 'prescribed particulars'. Section 744 of the Act refers us to the Companies (Forms) Regulations 1985, SI 1985/854 for an account of these prescribed particulars. According to reg 4 the particulars contained in Form 395 are the particulars prescribed for the purpose of s 395. Form 395 refers to the company's number, the name of the company, date of creation of the charge, description of the instrument (if any) creating or evidencing the charge, the amount secured by the mortgage or charge, names and addresses of the mortgagees or persons entitled to the charge, short particulars of the property mortgaged or charged and, finally, particulars as to commission allowance or discount. The prescribed particulars do not as a matter of law have to be on Form 395, though the Court of Appeal in *R v Registrar of Companies ex parte*

---

65   The relevant period is two years where a floating charge is granted in favour of a person connected with the company and 12 months in any other case.

66   In Companies Act 1989, s 99 there were some complicated provisions dealing with the avoidance of charges, on which see generally G McCormack [1990] LMCLQ 520 at 531–533.

67   CA 1985, s 395(1).

68   CA 1985, s 400(4).

69   CA 1985, s 400.

Central Bank of India,[70] interpreting earlier legislation in similar terms, made it clear that it would be unwise for a charge holder not to put the particulars on that form. In *Sun Tai Cheung Credits Ltd v AG*[71] the Privy Council emphasised the importance of achieving accuracy with respect to the prescribed particulars. Lord Templeman said that it was for the applicant to provide the prescribed particulars in the form and if he failed to do so the registrar was entitled to reject the application unless the registrar was able and willing to complete his register and to issue a certificate on the basis of the information available to him. The registrar was clearly not bound to analyse and understand a bundle of documents submitted by the applicant for registration and then to draft the necessary particulars himself.[72]

6.34 In *Grove v Advantage Healthcare (T10) Ltd*[73] Lightman J adopted a somewhat relaxed view as to the interpretation of CA 1985, s 395. In this case Advantage Healthcare borrowed monies from a bank secured by a mortgage. The Form 395 sent to Companies House for the purpose of registering the charge gave, however, the wrong registered number for the company, being the registered number of an associated company, Advantage Healthcare (T9) Ltd. The erroneous information led the registrar to believe that it was T9 which had granted the mortgage and the prescribed particulars were entered in T9's file rather than T10's file. The mistake was only discovered some years later when receivers were appointed to Advantage Healthcare (T10) Ltd and the receivers applied to the court for a declaration that the mortgage had been properly registered despite the mistake. In acceding to the application, Lightman J noted that under s 395 registration of a charge was not valid unless the 'prescribed particulars' were provided. In his view, provision of the correct registered number was not a 'prescribed particular' because it could not be categorised as a 'particular of the charge' within s 395. Instead, it constituted a particular of the mortgagor.[74] According to Lightman J s 401 implicitly made clear what was in the legislative mind when referring to the prescribed particulars, for it required the Registrar to enter in the register particulars as to the date of creation, the amount secured by the charge, short particulars of the property charged and the persons entitled to the charge.[75] On the other hand, the distinction drawn between particulars of the charge and particulars of the mortgagor may be difficult to justify. As Lightman J himself recognised, the most unfortunate sequence of events in this case, flowing from the failure to provide the correct registered number, could have led to the prejudice of third parties who dealt with the company. He went on to say:[76]

> 'For they could have so dealt on the basis of a search of the company's incomplete file which (by reason of the errors) did not disclose the grant by T10 of the mortgage. A remedy might in those circumstances have been available to the third party in the form of a claim to recover any loss

70   [1986] 1 QB 1114.
71   [1987] 1 WLR 948.
72   [1987] 1 WLR 948 at 954.
73   [2000] BCC 985; [2001] 1 BCLC 661.
74   [2000] BCC 985 at [9].
75   [2000] BCC 985 at [5].
76   [2000] BCC 985 at [10].

occasioned from the Registrar or the party who misinformed the Registrar as to the registered number of the company. But the failure to provide the correct registered number does not in my view constitute a failure to comply with section 395.'

6.35   There is no need to send to the registrar of companies the original instrument of charge where a charge has been created out of the United Kingdom that comprises property situated in the United Kingdom. In such a situation the delivery to and receipt by the registrar of a copy (verified in the prescribed manner) of the instrument by which the charge is created or evidenced has the same effect as the delivery and receipt of the instrument itself. There is a further provision to tackle the case where a charge has been created in the United Kingdom but comprises property outside the United Kingdom. Here the instrument creating or purporting to create the charge may be sent for registration under CA 1985, s 395 notwithstanding the fact that further proceedings may be necessary to make the charge valid or effectual according to the law of the country in which the property is situated.

6.36   Section 397 of the Companies Act 1985 deals with the situation where a series of secured debentures has been issued to which the holders are entitled pari passu. The section lays down that the following particulars must be delivered in the prescribed form together with the deed containing the charge or, if there is no such deed, one of the debentures of the series. The requisite particulars encompass

(a)   the total amount secured by the whole series; and
(b)   the dates of the resolutions authorising the issue of the series and the date of the covering deed (if any) by which the security is created or defined; and
(c)   a general description of the property charged; and
(d)   the names of the trustees (if any) for the debenture holders.

6.37   When an issue is made of particular secured debentures in a series there is an obligation to deliver to the registrar of companies, for entry in the register, particulars of the date and amount of each issue. The omission to do so does not affect, however, the validity of any of those debentures. Where an entire series of secured debentures is issued, the relevant form is Form 397, whereas Form 397a applies if an issue is made of secured debentures within the series.

DEFECTIVE PARTICULARS

6.38   Section 97 of the Companies Act 1989 purported to render a charge void to the extent that it confers rights on the charge holder in excess of those referred to in the particulars submitted for registration. This provision goes to the heart of the unimplemented changes contained in the 1989 Act.

6.39   Under CA 1985, the original instrument of charge, together with the requisite particulars, has to be submitted to Companies House. The registrar compares the charge document with the filed particulars and is required to issue a certificate of due registration. The task is an onerous, time-consuming one. There is a view that the burden imposed on the registrar is an unreasonable one and also that the system slows down the process of registration unduly. For instance, the Jenkins Committee on Company Law Reform stated:[77]

> 'We understand that the Registrar has been advised that the effect of these provisions is to impose upon him an absolute duty to enter on the register the effect of every instrument of charge delivered to him ... Thus, he may receive an instrument of charge which is extremely complicated or is obscurely drafted, but in fact creates both a specific charge on land and a floating charge over the remaining assets of the company, although the prescribed particulars furnished to him may mention only the fixed charge: if he fails to detect the existence of the floating charge and therefore omits any reference to it from his register, he may be liable to anyone who suffers loss in consequence of the omission.'

6.40   The certificate of due registration issued by the registrar is stated to be conclusive evidence that the requirements of the Act as to registration have been complied with.[78] The courts have held the certificate effective even where a false date had been inserted on the charge,[79] where the amount secured was misstated,[80] and where the particulars did not accurately represent the full coverage of the charge.[81] Indeed, in judicial review proceedings the Court of Appeal held that the 'conclusive evidence' formula precluded the reception of information to rebut the facts stated on the certificate.[82]

6.41   The Companies Act 1989 proposed to do away with the checking function on the part of the registrar and, consequently, the conclusive evidence certificate. To reduce the possibility of any consequent increase in the number of inaccuracies on the register, a charge holder was not allowed to assert rights conferred by the instrument of charge that were greater than those mentioned in the particulars delivered for registration. These changes have not been brought into force because of fears that they might compromise the marketability of debentures and also on account of practical difficulties arising out of the interrelationship between the company charge registration process and the Land Registry.[83] The old system therefore remains with us. This being so, it is useful to dwell a little on those decisions that capture the full spirit of the present regime.

---

77   Cmnd 1749, para 302. See also Professor Aubrey Diamond's report for the Department of Trade and Industry, *A Review of Security Interests in Property* (1989) at pp 98–101. The burden on the registrar would be eliminated if, as in some jurisdictions, the requirement to deliver the original instrument of charge was removed. The filer might be required simply to deliver the instrument of charge together with a statutory declaration that the filed particulars were in fact correct. See, for example, s 131 of the Singapore Companies Act.

78   CA 1985, s 401(2)(b), on which see generally G McCormack (1989) 10 Co Law 175. The certificate is required to be either signed by the registrar or authenticated by his official seal.

79   *Re Eric Holmes Ltd* [1965] 1 Ch 1052; *Re CL Nye Ltd* [1971] 1 Ch 442.

80   *Re Mechanisations Eaglescliffe Ltd* [1966] 1 Ch 20.

81   *National Provincial and Union Bank of England v Charnley* [1924] 1 KB 431.

82   [1986] QB 1114.

83   See generally Chapter 2.

6.42 One such case is *Yolland, Husson and Birkett Ltd*[84] where the company intended to issue a series of debentures in two separate rankings as regards priority. They were registered as a single ranking pari passu and the registrar gave a certificate of due registration. The liquidator of the company contended that the proper registration procedure had not been gone through. The Court of Appeal, however, refused to consider whether or not there was any mistake made by the registrar. Cozens Hardy MR in his opinion, stated that it would be almost shocking if the court were to hold that the certificate of the registrar, which was actually indorsed on each of the debentures, did not justify the debenture holders in saying that they had, as against the unsecured creditors represented by the liquidator, a perfectly good charge upon the assets of the company. He suggested that the legislature thought that it would be an unendurable state of affairs for the person entitled, or claiming to be entitled, to the charge, to have to prove compliance with all the requirements of the section.[85]

6.43 Another case in point is *National Provincial and Union Bank of England v Charnley*.[86] Here a company granted a mortgage to the bank of a certain leasehold factory together with all the movable 'plant used in or about the premises'. The bank sent the indenture to the Registrar of Companies for registration. The instrument was described as a mortgage of the leasehold premises, no mention being made of the chattels. The Registrar entered the description of the instrument in the register in similar terms, identifying it by date, and omitting all mention of any charge on the chattels. He also issued a certificate stating 'that a mortgage or charge dated [specifying the date and the parties to the instrument] was registered pursuant to s 93 of the Companies Act'.

6.44 A priority dispute subsequently arose between the bank and a judgment creditor of the company who had seized certain chattels on the mortgaged premises. The bank emerged victorious. The Court of Appeal held that as the certificate identified the instrument of charge, and stated that the mortgage or charge thereby created had been duly registered, it must be understood as certifying the due registration of all the charges created by the instrument, including that of the chattels. The fact that the register was defective and misleading to a potential creditor of the company did not sway the court. It is incumbent upon such a person to look at the charging instrument itself to discover the precise nature of the security granted by the company. The fact of registration only puts a person on notice that there is a charge.

6.45 Scrutton LJ talked about the rationale of the conclusive evidence provision. He raised the possibility, first, of the company making an error in delivering the particulars and secondly, of the registrar making an error either in omitting to enter something specified in the particulars or in misunderstanding the instrument of charge delivered to him with the particulars. Once the certificate was given, the grantees were safe. Although this might cause great

---

84 [1908] 1 Ch 152. See generally G McCormack (1989) 10 Co Law 175.
85 [1908] 1 Ch 152 at 158. See also *Cunard Steamship Co Ltd v Hopwood* [1908] 2 Ch 564; but cf *Esberger and Son Ltd v Capital and Counties Bank* [1913] 2 Ch 366.
86 [1924] 1 KB 431.

hardship to a person who gave credit to a company in reliance on a defective register, equal hardship, he said, would be caused to secured creditors if their security was to be upset for reasons connected with the actions of persons over whom they had no control.[87]

6.46 A slightly different situation arose in *Re Mechanisations (Eaglescliffe) Ltd.*[88] Here, in particulars supplied for registration, the amount secured was given as the principal sum only, no mention being made of the payment of interest. The registrar gave his certificate, again referring only to the principal sum. Buckley J held nevertheless that the charges constituted valid security for the full amount due under them. He said the certificate was not conclusive evidence that the amount thereby stated to be secured by the charge was in fact the amount secured by the charge. It was in fact only conclusive evidence that the requirements as to registration had been complied with. Although no doubt the legislature contemplated that when particulars were submitted they would be accurate and that when the registrar made entries in the register he would have checked the accuracy of such particulars against the instrument which he had for that purpose, the legislature had not made accuracy in that respect a condition of the validity of the charge.

6.47 In *Re Eric Holmes (Property) Ltd*[89] the court witnessed another variation on the same theme. The particulars delivered incorrectly stated the date of the charge. The registrar, however, unaware of this fact, gave a certificate of due registration. This was held to be conclusive evidence that the requirements of the Act as to registration had been complied with.

6.48 To the same effect is *Re CL Nye Ltd,*[90] where the facts are somewhat similar to those in *Eric Holmes*, with an incorrect date being inserted on the particulars delivered to the registrar. It was contended on behalf of the liquidator that while the certificate was conclusive as to the correctness of its contents, it was not conclusive as to the date of its creation. This argument was based, in part at least, on the view that where there was an instrument creating the charge that was available to the registrar, he could check the correctness of the particulars, but he had no such means insofar as the date of creation was concerned. Harman LJ, however, pointed out that the argument did not survive the test where the charge was created without any instrument at all and therefore where none could be delivered to the registrar. There could not be any bifurcation. The certificate was not merely conclusive in part, as was argued.[91]

6.49 In *Re CL Nye Ltd*[92] there is a fairly detailed discussion concerning the reasons why evidentiary conclusiveness was attributed to the registrar's certificate. Harman LJ explained that if it were possible to go behind the certificate and show that the date of the creation of the charge made it out of time, no lender on the faith of the charge could be secure and sure that it would not

---

87   [1924] 1 KB 431 at 447–448.
88   [1966] 1 Ch 20.
89   [1965] 1 Ch 1052.
90   [1971] 1 Ch 442.
91   [1971] 1 Ch 442 at 469.
92   [1971] 1 Ch 442 at 470.

thereafter be attacked by somebody who could successfully prove that there was in fact an interval of more than 21 days between the charge's creation and its registration. Russell LJ developed the same theme. He said that it was to be expected that the registration provisions should provide for a marketable security. This could not be achieved unless the certificate of the registrar was in every respect conclusive and unassailable.[93]

6.50 The *Re CL Nye Ltd* line of authorities was applied by the Court of Appeal in *Exeter Trust Ltd v Screenways Ltd*.[94] This is a case where a charge was not registered within 21 days of its creation but an order extending the time for registration was granted pursuant to CA 1985, s 404 Companies. Registration was effected within this extended time frame and the High Court registrar issued a certificate of due registration pursuant to s 401(2)(b). Later on the same day that the charge was registered the company went into liquidation. The liquidator then applied to the court to have the order permitting late registration set aside. The court set aside the order, but the charge holder appealed.

6.51 Nourse LJ, speaking for the Court of Appeal, felt unable to distinguish this case from the normal case where registration had occurred within 21 days from the date of creation of a charge. There was no reason why it should be possible to go behind the registrar's conclusive evidence certificate any more than in the normal case.[95] This conclusion was bolstered by reference to the decision of the High Court of Australia in *Wilde v Australian Trade Equipment Co Property Ltd*.[96] The Australian court stated:[97]

'We are unable to escape the conclusion that the order extending time was beyond recall so soon as registration had been effected in reliance upon it, and once those steps were taken the operation of the order could not be undone retrospectively. It follows that the validity of the registration was not dependent on the continued subsistence of the order extending time, and consequently the order setting aside the extension of time could not affect the registration that had already been concluded.'

6.52 It was also argued in *Exeter Trust Ltd v Screenways Ltd* that the court had an inherent power to rectify the register or to order the charge holder to procure the cancellation of the entry. Nouse LJ would have none of this idea.[98] He mentioned *Re CL Nye Ltd* where it was said that under CA 1985, s 404 the court may rectify an omission by adding, or rectify a misstatement by correcting. It could not, however, delete a whole registration.[99]

6.53 An attempt was made to sidestep the effect of *Re CL Nye Ltd* in *R v Registrar of Companies ex parte Central Bank of India*.[100] Here the prescribed particulars of the charge sent to Companies House for registration were

---

93 [1971] 1 Ch 442 at 474.
94 [1991] BCLC 888.
95 [1991] BCLC 888 at 893.
96 (1981) 5 ACLR 404.
97 (1981) 5 ACLR at 413.
98 [1991] BCLC 888 at 895.
99 [1971] Ch 442 at 474.
100 [1986] QB 1114.

defective. Companies House returned the form for amendment and later accepted a corrected form of the particulars after the 21-day period had elapsed. Use was made of the judicial review procedure and an order sought quashing the certificate of registration issued by Companies House. It was contended that an exercise of a statutory authority to make decisions affecting the rights and obligations of other persons was normally subject to review by way of certiorari. Reliance was placed on familiar administrative law cases like *Anisminic v Foreign Compensation Commission*[101] and *Re Racal Communications Ltd*.[102]

6.54   The Court of Appeal held, however, that while the jurisdiction of the court to grant judicial review had not been ousted, it was not permissible to adduce evidence to challenge the Registrar's certificate. What is now CA 1985, s 401 precluded the admission of evidence to rebut what was stated on the certificate. According to Lawton LJ, if an unsecured creditor sought judicial review solely on the ground that the charge holder did not deliver the prescribed particulars, he could not put the necessary evidence before the court. Therefore, his application was doomed to failure.[103] Dillon LJ advanced a similar proposition.[104]

6.55   Slade LJ was driven to the conclusion that the relevant provisions on their true construction conferred on the registrar the power to decide finally and conclusively all ancillary questions, whether they were questions of fact or law, or mixed fact and law, which fell to be decided in determining whether the registration requirements had been complied with.[105] The facts of the present case were quite different from those considered by the House of Lords in *Anisminic v Foreign Compensation Commission*. There a statutory provision that the 'determination by the commission of any application made to them under this Act shall not be called in question in any court of law' was held not to preclude an inquiry by the court whether a purported determination was in fact a 'determination' within the meaning of the relevant statute. That statute contained no 'conclusive evidence' provision.

LIMITS TO THE CONCLUSIVE EVIDENCE PROVISION

6.56   The Court of Appeal in *R v Registrar of Companies ex parte Central Bank of India* talked about a number of cases where a certificate of due registration issued by Companies House might be set aside. First, the certificate did not operate to confer validity on a charge which was invalid for reasons other than lack of registration. Secondly, the Companies Act was not expressed to bind the Crown. Therefore, it was possible that the Attorney-General was not constrained by the conclusive evidence provision if he were to seek judicial

---

101   [1969] 2 AC 147.
102   [1981] AC 374.
103   [1986] 1 QB 1114 at 1169–1170.
104   [1986] 1 QB 1114 at 1180.
105   [1986] 1 QB 1114 at 1176.

review so as to quash a certificate.[106] Thirdly, an applicant could conceivably increase his chances of success by demonstrating an error of law on the face of the certificate or by proving that it had been procured by fraud or duress.[107] Moreover, the Court of Appeal approved the revised practice of Companies House whereby it will not accept for registration particulars of charge, whether in original or revised form, submitted after the 21 days had elapsed, subject to the qualification that obvious clerical or typing errors could be corrected without recourse to the courts.[108]

OTHER CONSIDERATIONS THAT MAY LESSEN THE IMPACT OF THE CERTIFICATE

Fraud

6.57 In *Re CL Nye Ltd* it was suggested that creditors who had been damnified by fraud on the part of the charge holder might take proceedings in personam. Fraud surely arises in a situation where a charge holder deliberately leaves a charge unregistered, affixes a later date and then registers within 21 days of that. The right of action, however, would only appear to be available to somebody who advances money to the company in the interval between the time when the charge should have been registered and when the charge was actually registered and would not have advanced the money but for the fact of there appearing to be no such charge.

6.58 A more far-reaching and satisfactory remedy is hinted at in the *Central Bank of India* case. It was suggested that a certificate might be set aside where it had been procured by fraud.[109] If this happened, the charge holder guilty of fraud would be deprived of priority. The property which would otherwise fall within the scope of the charge becomes available for distribution among unsecured creditors.[110]

6.59 Another pitfall for a charge holder who inserts a later date on a charge is that he might bring himself within the reach of s 245 of the Insolvency Act 1986. This section invalidates floating charges created within 12 months of

---

106 Lawton LJ referred ([1986] 1 QB 1114 at 1169) to the Divisional Court decision in *R v Registrar of Companies ex parte Attorney-General* [1991] BCLC 476. Here the Attorney-General applied successfully for the registration of a company, Lindi St Claire (Personal Services) Ltd, to be quashed despite the provisions of what is now s 13 of the Companies Act 1985 that a certificate of incorporation shall be conclusive evidence that all the requirements of the Act as to registration have been complied with.

107 [1986] 1 QB 1114 at 1169, 1177.

108 [1986] 1 QB 1114 at 1171, 1178. Lawton and Slade LJJ issued a warning that copies of instruments will not be accepted.

109 See also *National Provincial and Union Bank of England v Charnley* [1924] 1 KB 431 at 454 per Atkin LJ.

110 There is of course the argument that it would come within the grasp of a duly registered floating charge.

the onset of insolvency. The period is two years in the case of charges granted in favour of a charge holder connected with the company.

Negligence

6.60 Matters are more problematic in a situation where the register is defective because of negligence on the part of the charge holder and/or Companies House.[111] First of all, take the situation where Companies House negligently mistranscribed the particulars submitted onto the register. There are a whole host of problems associated with the bringing of a negligence action. Who could sue? Presumably, somebody could sue if he was misled into advancing money to the company by reason of the defective state of the register. It may be very difficult to establish, though, that credit would not have been extended to the company if the register disclosed the true state of affairs concerning the nature and extent of security granted by the company. Secondly, the registrar might argue that the claimant should have apprised itself of the true facts by consulting the company's own register maintained at its registered office pursuant to s 407 of the Companies Act 1985.

6.61 CA 1985, s 407 obliges every limited company to keep at its registered office a register of charges and to enter on it all charges specifically affecting property of the company and all floating charges on the company's undertaking or property. The entry generally gives a short description of the property charged, the amount of the charge and the persons beneficially entitled thereto. Moreover, this register maintained by the company can be inspected by anyone for a small fee. Where it is Companies House who has blundered in transcribing particulars, the company's own register should reveal the proper position.

6.62 Thirdly, Companies House might argue that a person contemplating the giving of credit to a company should not rely on the register in any event. Companies House might refer to the long line of judicial decisions and say that the register does not provide an accurate pointer to the coverage of a charge.

6.63 These are formidable arguments and it is perhaps a testimony to their strength that no creditor has raised the issue in any reported case. Furthermore, the question arises whether Companies House is under any duty of care to potential plaintiffs. The leading case is *Yuen Kun Yeu v Attorney-General of Hong Kong*,[112] which is concerned with the statutory set-up surrounding the Commissioner of Deposit-taking Companies in Hong Kong. An ordinance of 1976 gave the Commissioner various functions in relation to deposit-taking business in Hong Kong, including the power to refuse or revoke the registration of any company he considered unfit for this purpose. The appellants brought an action against the Commissioner for negligence in the performance of his functions. They alleged that they had made deposits in reliance upon the Commissioner's representation and that he knew, or ought to have known, had he exercised reasonable care, that the company's affairs were being carried on in

---

111 Lightman J suggested the possibility of such an action in *Grove v Advantage Healthcare (T10) Ltd* [2000] BCC 985 at [10].

112 [1988] AC 175.

a fraudulent, speculative manner to the detriment of its depositors. Their contention was that the Commissioner should have suspended or revoked the registration of the company before they made their deposits, as he had cogent evidence to suspend it because of fraud and speculation.

6.64 The Privy Council denied that a duty of care existed. Lord Keith mentioned various factors which militated against the imposition of such a duty: the disastrous effects on existing depositors of de-registration; the fact that a duty of care, if it existed, would be owed to all would-be depositors; and the fact that the statutory regulatory system made no allowance for individual claims.[113]

6.65 Turning from *Yuen Kun-Yeu* to the present case one might draw certain parallels. Any duty of care would be owed to all would-be creditors of the company. Moreover, there is no specific statutory recognition of the possibility of individual claims against the registrar. Furthermore, there is an alternative means of ascertainment of a company's creditworthiness through inspection of the register of charges maintained by the company under CA 1985, s 407.

6.66 One notable omission from *Yuen Kun-Yeu* is any reference to *Ministry of Housing and Local Government v Sharp*.[114] The facts of that case are quite complicated, but basically they boil down to a situation where 'A' suffered loss through the negligence of 'B' in issuing a certificate to 'C'. There was really only one person, however, who had suffered loss through the negligent issuance of the certificate. In the company charges registration case the class of potential plaintiffs is far wider.[115] There are a number of persons who might claim that they would not have extended credit to a company had they been aware of the true extent of the company's secured indebtedness.

Negligence on the part of the chargee

6.67 At first sight, it would seem easier to argue that a charge holder who is guilty of negligence should be liable personally to a creditor who has been induced to give the company credit on the assumption that the register of charges kept by Companies House correctly states the position. The duty of care difficulties do not appear to arise. The charge holder, however, might say that all the blame does not fall on its shoulders. After all, the original instrument of charge has to be submitted to Companies House along with the requisite particulars. Companies House could easily verify the particulars by checking the instrument of charge.

---

113 [1988] AC 175 at 190. See also *Governors of Peabody Donation Fund v Sir Lindsay Parkinson and Co* [1985] AC 210; *Leigh and Sillivan Ltd v Aliakamon Shipping Co Ltd* [1986] AC 785; *Curran v Northern Ireland Housing Executive* [1987] AC 718; *Rowling v Takaro Properties Ltd* [1988] AC 473; *Caparo Industries plc v Dickman* [1990] 1 All ER 568; *Murphy v Brentwood District Council* [1990] 2 All ER 908; *Marc Rich & Co AG v Bishop Rock Marine Co Ltd (The Nicholas H)* [1996] AC 211; *White v Jones* [1995] 2 AC 207; *Stovin v Wise* [1996] AC 923.

114 [1970] QB 223.

115 See also *Business Computers International Ltd v Registrar of Companies* [1987] BCLC 621.

6.68 In addition, the charge holder has all the arguments against liability that are available to Companies House at its disposal, with the exception of the duty of care point. These considerations combine to make the prospects of success in any action brought against the charge holder rather remote.

CORRECTION OF MISTAKES

6.69 There is a mechanism under s 404 of the Companies Act 1985 whereby the court, on application by the company or any other interested party, may order that the register of charges be rectified to correct the omission or misstatement of any particular. Where, however, a certificate of due registration has been issued in respect of incorrect particulars, the charge holder can still rely on the full extent of his security to the detriment of third parties. Furthermore, as was pointed out in the Parliamentary debates on what became Part IV of the Companies Act 1989, the holder of a conclusive evidence certificate has no incentive whatever to tell the registrar of any changes in the charge.[116] Any variation in the terms of the charge providing that it does not amount to the creation of a fresh charge, can be made with impunity, even though it is not reflected on the register.

6.70 Section 403 of the Companies Act 1985 is concerned with entries of satisfaction and release. There is provision whereby, if the registrar of companies receives a statutory declaration in the prescribed form that the debt for which the charge was given has been paid or satisfied in whole or in part, or that part of the property or undertaking charge has been released from the charge or has ceased to form part of the company's property or undertaking, he may make appropriate entries to the relevant effect on the register. If the registrar has issued a memorandum of satisfaction in whole, he must, if so required, furnish the company with a copy of it.

6.71 In *Igroup Ltd v Ocwen*[117] it was held that the power of rectification granted to the court by CA 1985, s 404 is limited to correcting mistakes of omission or commission in the entry of any particular with respect to a mortgage or charge or in a memorandum of satisfaction made by the registrar on the register of charges maintained by the registrar under s 401. Lightman J said that the jurisdiction of the court did not extend to mistakes otherwise than in a particular entered on the register and accordingly does not extend to the information particulars entered on a Form 395 or a Form 403b by or on behalf of an applicant for registration under s 395(1).

---

116 See, for instance, the statement of the Parliamentary Under-Secretary of State for Industry and Consumer Affairs in the House of Commons, Standing Committee D, col 398 (20 June 1989).
117 [2004] 1 WLR 451.

LATE REGISTRATION

6.72 If a charge has not been registered as required under CA 1985, s 395 within the period of 21 days from the date of creation, s 404 gives the court jurisdiction to make an order sanctioning late registration. The discretion in the court arises if the omission to register on time was accidental, or due to inadvertence or to some other sufficient cause, or is not of a nature to prejudice the position of creditors or shareholders of the company, or that, on other grounds, it is just and equitable to grant relief.

6.73 The major change suggested by the 1989 Companies Act, Part IV apropos late registration is the abolition of the requirement of having to apply to the court. The idea was to cut down on a lot of court time and administrative inconvenience. In fact, at the moment, the court appears to have acceded to late registration applications almost as a matter of course, save where the company was in liquidation or, more controversially, where liquidation was imminent.[118]

6.74 A person seeking an order permitting late registration does not have a difficult first hurdle to clear. The words of the section are wide. A conveyancing muddle or an oversight on the part of solicitors is sufficient to elevate the applicant over the first obstacle. Even ignorance of the existence of the requirement of registration comes within the rubric of inadvertence. *Re Jackson & Co Ltd*,[119] while not exactly in point, does bring home the proposition. Kekewich J thought it a little disturbing that gentlemen engaged in business or, perhaps more accurately, their legal advisers, should not take the trouble to inquire about the provisions of the statutes which affect such dealings. Nevertheless, such lack of comprehension constituted inadvertence.

6.75 Bringing a case within the words of CA 1985, s 404 is a necessary condition of success. Once that is done, the charge holder has not a very onerous task to perform. The judge has a discretion to permit late registration, but such discretion is normally exercised in favour of the charge holder. To borrow Dworkinian phraseology, the discretion is 'weak' rather than 'strong'. One factor that has, however, exercised judicial minds over the years is the relevance of evidence concerning the solvency of the company.

Imminence of liquidation

6.76 *Re Bootle Cold Storage and Co*[120] is the first reported late registration application. In that case evidence was put forward that the company was still carrying on business, and that no petition to wind up the company had been presented, nor had notice of a meeting to pass a resolution to wind up the same been given, nor had any creditor recovered judgment against the company.

---

118 See G McCormack [1986] JBL 282 at 283–289.
119 *Re Jackson & Co Ltd* [1899] 1 Ch 348.
120 [1901] WN 54.

6.77   Thereafter, it became the custom for such evidence to be presented upon the making of a late registration application. In the 1930s and 1940s, judges differed about the propriety or rather the necessity for the practice.[121] Lord Denning and Davies LJ in 1967 in *Re Resinoid & Mica Products Ltd*[122] ventured the view that a late registration could be refused on the ground that a winding up of the company was imminent. Unfortunately, *Re Resinoid & Mica Products Ltd* remained unreported until 1982 when it was unearthed by counsel arguing the case of *Re Ashpurton Estates Ltd*[123] and the views expressed in *Re Resinoid* commended themselves to the Court of Appeal.

6.78   The leading case is *Re Ashpurton Estates Ltd*[124] where the facts are relatively straightforward. The charge holder discovered that the charge executed in its favour by the respondent company had not been registered with the Registrar of Companies due to some oversight. Instead of immediately seeking relief, the charge holder decided to stay its hand. Sales of the charged properties were then pending and it did not wish to alarm other creditors and so precipitate a collapse of the company. When, however, notice was given convening an extraordinary general meeting to consider a resolution to wind up the company, the charge holder decided to apply for an extension of time to effect registration. The application was refused on the basis, inter alia, that a winding-up of the company was imminent and an appeal to the Court of Appeal proved unsuccessful.

6.79   To mix metaphors, there seem to be three strings to the judicial broadside fired by the Court of Appeal. Lord Brightman, who delivered the collegiate judgment, laid particular stress on three points. One point related to the fact of liquidation when the application came before the judge. A second point was that the charge holder had deliberately chosen not to apply for an extension of time when the mistake of non-registration was first discovered. Lord Brightman said that when an unregistered charge holder discovers his mistake he should apply without delay for an extension of time if he desires to register.[125] The court should look askance at a charge holder who deliberately defers his application in order to see which way the wind is going to blow. In other words, having elected to play on under the offside rule, the charge holder could not now be heard to claim a foul.

6.80   A final point related to the likelihood of liquidation. A court was entitled to have regard to evidence concerning the solvency of the company when exercising its discretion. When the court makes an order permitting late registration it is customary to include a proviso protecting rights acquired before the time when particulars of the charge are actually registered. The proviso protects only proprietary rights.

---

121   Compare *Re MIG Trust Ltd* [1933] Ch 542 and *Re Kris Cruisers Ltd* [1949] Ch 138 with *Re LH Charles & Co Ltd* [1935] WN 15.
122   [1983] Ch 132: case decided in 1967.
123   [1983] Ch 110.
124   [1983] 1 Ch 110; on which see D Milman (1983) 4 Co Law 82; J Farrar [1983] JBL 253.
125   [1983] 1 Ch 110 at 132.

6.81 In *Re Cardiff Workmen's Cottage Co Ltd*[126] Buckley J discussed whether the court should, in granting an extension of time, impose any terms for the protection of unsecured creditors of the company. After a good deal of judicial soul-searching, he answered in the negative. The unsecured creditors may have given credit to the company on the footing that the registrable charges did not exist. A person who is an unsecured creditor of the company is, however, always exposed to the danger that the company may execute in favour of other creditors' incumbrances on its property and, unless these other securities can be attacked as improper preferences, they prevail. A proviso protecting unsecured creditors would effectively put the applicant in a worse position than if he took a new charge at the time when the order was made. If the applicant took that course, it would obtain priority over all existing unsecured creditors, subject only to questions of undue preference. The judge, nevertheless, left open the possibility that when a case of sufficient magnitude arises it may be advisable to give notice to some of the unsecured creditors of substantial amount so as to give them an opportunity of being heard, if they so desire, upon the question of what is 'just and expedient' in their interest.[127]

6.82 The admissibility of evidence apropos the solvency of the company signifies limited judicial recognition of the position of the unsecured creditor. Its interests are safeguarded when an order allowing late registration is refused on the ground that the company is likely to go into liquidation. In the Australian case of *Re Dudley Engineering Pty Ltd*[128] Street J said the solvency or insolvency of the company was not the governing consideration. It represented but one of the overall complex of facts upon which the court must exercise its discretion. The mere fact that the grant of an extension of time would prejudice unsecured creditors was not sufficient either to require a refusal of the extension or the insertion of a condition protecting the rights of unsecured creditors. The position of unsecured creditors is also protected by orders of the kind made in *Re LH Charles & Co Ltd*.[129]

Re Charles-type orders

6.83 In *Re LH Charles & Co Ltd* Clauson J extended the time for registration, but as a quid pro quo the charge holder was required to give an undertaking that if winding up became effective on or before a certain date, and the liquidator should apply to the court within 21 days thereafter to discharge the order, then the charge holder would submit to the court's jurisdiction. The charge holder should also comply with any order the court might make for rectification of the register by the removal of any registration effected under the order. In *Re Braemar Investments*[130] Hoffmann J approved the procedure

---

126 [1906] 2 Ch 627.
127 [1906] 2 Ch 627 at 630. See also *Re Chantry House Developments plc* [1990] BCLC 813.
128 [1968] 1 NSWLR 483 at 486. See also the useful analysis by Somers J in *Re Jack Harris Ltd* [1977] 1 NZLR 141. Note too *Re Dalgety & Co Ltd* [1928] NZLR 731 and *Westpac Finance Ltd v Tahuna No 23 Ltd* [1992] 3 NZLR 222.
129 [1935] WN 15; and see generally on this procedure WJ Gough *Company Charges* (2nd edn, 1996) at pp 782–787.
130 [1989] Ch 54. See also *Exeter Trust Ltd v Screenways Ltd* [1991] BCLC 888 at 896 where

outlined by Clauson J in *Re LH Charles & Co Ltd*. He said that an order in this form met the difficulty caused by the fact that applications to extend time for registration were essentially ex parte in nature. Creditors who may be affected were not respondents to the summons, and the company did not necessarily have an interest in protecting their position.

6.84   The same theme was developed by Scott J in *Re Chantry House Developments plc*.[131] In this case a charge holder, the Halifax, agreed to advance money to the company to finance the development of a particular site. By an oversight, the charge was not registered. Additional funding was needed to complete the development of the site and the Halifax was willing to provide it if it succeeded in having its charge registered under CA 1985, s 404. Scott J took the view that it was just and equitable that an order should be granted under s 404 to restore to the Halifax the security that it had contracted for and to enable the site to be completed. However, if the Halifax charge were to be registered, it would reduce the amount payable to the unsecured creditors in a winding up from approximately 9p in the pound to 3p. Furthermore, the company's unsecured creditors had not had an opportunity to be heard on the motion. Accordingly, Scott J made an order under s 404, but only on the back of an undertaking by the Halifax that, within a timetable laid down by the court, it would arrange for the company's substantial unsecured creditors to be informed of the s 404 order and of their right to apply to have it discharged. Moreover, the Halifax must submit to the jurisdiction of the court should such an application be made.[132]

Actuality of liquidation

6.85   Since *Re Joplin Brewery Co Ltd*[133] it is customary in an order extending the time to include a proviso preserving rights acquired against the property of the company, the subject-matter of the charge, before particulars of the charge are actually registered. When a company goes into liquidation, the liquidator is obliged to administer the assets of the company for the benefit of its creditors. The unsecured creditors acquire rights against the property of the company.[134] As a necessary consequence, a s 404 order with the usual proviso attached would be worthless from the point of view of the unregistered charge holder. It does not facilitate the applicant in jumping the queue of creditors.[135] Instead, it seeks a s 404 order minus the proviso and the applicant faces an uphill task in trying to persuade the court to come to this conclusion, having regard to the mischief which the registration sections are designed to avoid.

Nourse LJ said that the standard practice in London is to adopt that form unless there is evidence from a director or the secretary of the company stating that a liquidation is not imminent.

131   [1990] BCLC 813.
132   [1990] BCLC 813 at 823.
133   [1902] 1 Ch 79.
134   *Re Spiral Globe Ltd* [1902] 1 Ch 396; *Re Abrahams & Sons Ltd* [1902] 1 Ch 695; *Re Anglo-Oriental Carpet Manufacturing Co Ltd* [1903] 1 Ch 914; *Re Ehrmann Bros Ltd* [1906] 2 Ch 697.
135   Such an order was refused on the basis of futility in *Re Abrahams & Sons Ltd* [1902] 1 Ch 695.

6.86 The decision of the Court of Appeal in *Re Ashpurton Estates Ltd*[136] fortifies principle with authority. In that case, the company was free of liquidation at the time of the application to extend time and at the date of the unsuccessful hearing before the High Court Registrar. Liquidation had, however, supervened when the matter reached the judge on appeal from the registrar. Lord Brightman advanced the view that the judge was therefore almost precluded from granting an extension of time. Save in a wholly exceptional instance such as fraud, time should not be extended if the company has gone into liquidation.[137] From the approach adopted by the court, it seems that the judge's function is not merely to review the exercise of the High Court Registrar's discretion but to exercise an independent judgment in the light of the facts then currently available.

6.87 The case has been criticised on this score. Priority disputes in the event of corporate insolvency depend on crystallisation of rights at precise dates, and rights should not be jeopardised by matters happening after the case first reaches the judicial forum.[138] It must be remembered, however, that Lord Brightman entered a caveat to his judgment. He reserved for future consideration what the position might be if (i) the registrar refused an extension of time without justification when liquidation was not a foreseeable event but (ii) subsequently the company's fortunes dramatically deteriorated so that liquidation came about before an appeal inevitably succeeded.[139] This judicial straw in the wind suggests that any differences between the respective approaches are more apparent than real.

6.88 Only in the most exceptional instances will time be extended after the commencement of a winding-up. In *Re Ashpurton Estates Ltd* Lord Brightman highlighted fraud as an example. *Re Arnold & Co Ltd*[140] throws further light on the subject. Here Lloyds Bank plc held a debenture containing a fixed charge on any land that might be acquired by the company. Canada Permanent Trust agreed to make a loan to the company to enable it to purchase certain land. Lloyds Bank expressly consented to Canada Permanent having a fixed legal charge on the land to be acquired with the advance of monies from Canada Permanent. The land was acquired and a legal charge executed in favour of Canada permanent, but owing to a conveyancing muddle the charge was never registered within the prescribed period. Canada Permanent also had a fixed equitable charge of an earlier date on any land acquired or to be acquired by the company, which was properly registered. An application for late registration of the legal charge was made at a time when liquidation of the company was a highly probable event. The application was heard after a petition for the winding-up of the company had been presented. Under the doctrine of relation back it was very likely that commencement of the winding-up would date back to the presentation of the petition. There was evidence indicating that there was an almost total deficiency as regards the claims of unsecured creditors, probably a very serious deficiency as regards the claims of preferential creditors

---

136 [1983] 1 Ch 110.
137 [1983] 1 Ch 110 at 131.
138 See D Milman (1983) 4 Co Law 82 at 84.
139 [1983] 1 Ch 110 at 130.
140 [1984] BCLC 535; on which see D Milman (1985) 6 Co Law 128.

and possibly a deficiency with respect to the claims of the secured creditors. Lloyds Bank did not object to late registration and the judge commended them for this.

6.89 In Harman J's opinion, this was a very unusual case. If an order was refused, Canada Permanent could fall back on its properly registered equitable charge under the debenture and so defeat the claims of unsecured creditors.[141] The only real contention arose between Canada Permanent and Lloyds Bank. The latter, however, had decided not to upset the order of priorities expressly agreed upon between the parties. In the exceptional circumstances Harman J made an order permitting late registration with the normal proviso attached. An insertion was made to cover the unlikely possibility of any creditor having acquired a legal interest in the land between the time of its acquisition by the company and the registration of the charge.

6.90 The upshot of *Re Arnold & Co Ltd* was that Canada Permanent achieved late registration notwithstanding liquidation. An attempt was made to emulate their success in *Re John Bateson & Co Ltd*.[142] Here the company had bought an hotel and a portion of the purchase price was immediately, after a notional split second of time (scintilla temporis), lent back by the vendor to the company and secured by a mortgage. The charge was never registered. Finally, after notices convening a meeting to consider a resolution for the voluntary winding-up of the company had been sent out, a summons was issued seeking an order allowing an extension of time. Three days after issue of the summons, the company went into voluntary liquidation.

6.91 Before Harman J, counsel for the charge holder tried to rely on the rule in *Condon ex parte James*.[143] The rule really amounts to a discretionary power in the court to prevent a form of enrichment of the assets of a bankrupt or insolvent company at the expense of the person seeking recoupment.[144] The rule operates on the basis of ethical considerations. An officer is not permitted to avail of a legal technicality where it would be dishonourable so to do. There is of course the difficulty whether a liquidator in a voluntary winding-up is an officer of the court. Counsel contended that compulsory liquidators are undoubtedly officers and it would be invidious if liquidators in a voluntary winding-up were treated differently. A simple solution would be not to apply the principle in *Ex parte James* to a liquidation. Harman J, however, tackled the case on another basis. First, he doubted if the rule applied to cases where there had been dealing between the parties well before the inception of the bankruptcy or liquidation. Secondly, he found no trace of dishonourable conduct on the part of the liquidator. There was a clear statutory obligation to register charges created by a company. The primary duty to register was on the

---

141 [1984] BCLC 535 at 538.
142 [1985] BCLC 259.
143 (1874) LR 9 Ch 609; for an examination of the rule see *Re Clark* [1975] 1 WLR 559. In a liquidation the rule seems to be the last refuge of despairing counsel. *Condon ex parte James* is used as justification for a conclusion already reached, as it appears to have been used in *Re Wyvern Developments* [1974] 1 WLR 1097. For another application of *Ex parte James* in the corporate context see *Re Regent Finance and Guarantee Corpn Ltd* [1930] WN 84.
144 See the observations of Lord Keith in *Government of India v Taylor* [1955] AC 491 at 513.

company. If, nevertheless, the charge holder wished to effect registration, he could do so. In this case there was a tacit understanding that the charge holder would send the particulars of charge for registration. There was nothing which smacked of sharp practice on the part of the company. Therefore, there was no room for the application of the rule in *Ex parte James*.

6.92   What if the company had given the charge holder an express undertaking to register the charge, yet failed to do so? Might the charge holder invoke the principle in *Ex parte James* in that situation, or would the court tell him that he was, in effect, obliged to check the register? Much depends on the detailed facts of a particular case. *Ex parte James*, if it is regarded as applicable at all, does little more than emphasise the discretionary nature of the court's power to sanction late registration.

Late registration and administration orders

6.93   The Insolvency Act 1986 introduced the concept of administration primarily as a mechanism for the rescue or rehabilitation of ailing companies, though that was not the only purpose for which an administration order might be made. Section 8 of the Insolvency Act 1986 invested the court with jurisdiction to make an administration order if it was likely to achieve one or more of the following objectives:

(a)   the survival of the company, and the whole or any part of its undertaking as a going concern;
(a)   the approval of a voluntary arrangement;
(c)   the sanctioning of a compromise or arrangement between the company and its creditors or members;
(d)   a more advantageous realisation of the company's assets than would be effected on a winding up.

6.94   The Enterprise Act 2002, by inserting a new Sch B1 into the Insolvency Act 1986 enlarges the scope of administration enormously. As well as retaining the facility for court appointment, the Enterprise Act now permits out-of-court appointments of administrators to be made by a qualifying floating charge holder or by the company itself, though a qualifying floating charge holder has an effective veto on the identity of a person appointed. There is now a clear statutory hierarchy of objectives that administration is supposed to serve. Trying to rescue the business of the company comes first, followed by achieving a better return for company creditors than could be achieved on a winding-up and then, finally, making distributions to secured and/or preferential creditors.

6.95   The question arises how the jurisdiction to extend time for registration should be exercised once the company is in administration. In *Re Barrow Borough Transport Ltd*[145] Millett J took the view that, once an administration order had been made and it had become clear that administration would result in insolvent liquidation of the company, the discretion of the court should be

---

145   [1990] Ch 227.

exercised against granting an extension of time for registration of charges.[146] The judge looked in detail at the administration order procedure and said that if the rescue or rehabilitation of the company and its business as a going concern is one of the statutory purposes inserted in the order and is still capable of achievement, there may be no reason why the order should not be made. But if that purpose was not included in the order, or if it had already proved incapable of achievement, then simple justice required that no extension of time should be made. During the period while a company is in administration, no resolution may be passed nor order made for the winding up of the company. It would not be consonant with principles of justice to unsecured creditors to grant an extension of time, on the ground that the creditors' rights had not yet crystallised by liquidation, when that was because the court by the making of an administration order had prevented the creditors from taking the necessary steps to obtain those rights. Millett J referred also to considerations of policy. Administration procedure was an alternative to liquidation. In the judge's view, it would be most unfortunate if the presence of an unregistered charge, and the possibility that the creditor might obtain an extension of time to register, should tip the scales against the making of an administration order and in favour of liquidation.[147]

The proviso

6.96   Reference has already been made to the proviso accompanying orders which allow late registration of charges. The wording of the proviso has changed somewhat over the years.[148] An order permitting late registration is now usually made without prejudice to the rights of the parties acquired during the period between the date of creation of the charge and the date of its actual registration. The normal proviso protects only proprietary rights, and this aspect of the matter has not changed.[149] On occasions judges will vary the wording of the normal proviso.

6.97   This occurred in *Re Fablehill Ltd.*[150] This is a case where a company executed a charge in favour of its bank in February 1988. On 6 March 1990 it executed a second charge over the same property in favour of two directors of the company, T and D. The charge was not made subject to the charge in favour of the bank. On 19 March 1990 the company executed a third charge in favour of I and that charge was not made subject to any prior charges. Both the

---

146   The judge also held that a late registration application could not be described as 'proceedings against the company or its property' within s 11(3)(d) of the Insolvency Act 1986 (see now Insolvency Act 1986, Sch B1, para 43(6) as inserted by Enterprise Act 2002). Therefore, the leave of the court was not necessary in the making of a late registration application. Otherwise there would be an absurdity. The leave of the court would be necessary to bring an application to seek leave.

147   [1990] Ch 227 at 235.

148   See *Watson v Duff, Morgan and Vermont (Holdings) Ltd* [1974] 1 WLR 450, on which see Bennett (1974) 118 SJ 286. See also Chapter 7.

149   A homely example was given by Cozens-Hardy LJ in *Re Ehrmann Bros Ltd* [1906] 2 Ch 697 at 709–710.

150   [1991] BCLC 830.

second and third charges were duly registered with the Registrar of Companies. The bank sought to have its charge registered out of time. Vinelott J said that in deciding whether to grant an extension of time under CA 1985, s 404 the overriding principle was whether for any reason it would not be just and equitable to grant the extension. The judge pointed out that T and D were the only directors of the company and it was the responsibility of the company under s 395 to register the charge. This being so, it would be plainly inequitable to include in any late registration order a proviso protecting the rights of directors who, when they learned that the company had failed in its duty to register a charge, took advantage of it by registering a charge in their own favour.[151] Despite the long delay in seeking a s 404 order, the bank had not acted unreasonably in the circumstances. Thus, a late registration order was made without a proviso making the charge subject to the charge in favour of T and D. A proviso was, however, inserted making it subject to the charge in favour of I. Accordingly, the order of priority was as follows: (i) the bank to the extent of T and D's charge, (ii) I who was the holder of the third charge, (iii) the bank for the balance of the sums owing on its charge less the sum paid to I, (iv) T and D, and (v) the bank.[152]

A COMPANY'S OWN REGISTER OF CHARGES

6.98 A company is required to keep at its registered office a register of all charges specifically affecting property of the company and all floating charges of the company's undertaking or any of its property. The obligation encompasses all charges and not just those charges requiring registration with the Registrar of Companies. Failure to abide by the obligation does not result in invalidation of the charge, but leaves an officer who knowingly and wilfully authorises or permits the omission of an appropriate entry liable to a fine. The register is open to inspection by members and existing creditors (not prospective creditors) free of charge, and by any other person on payment of a fee. The register is required to contain entries for each charge, giving a short description of the property charged, the amount of the charge and (except in the case of securities to bearer) the names of the persons entitled to it.

6.99 A company is also required to keep at its registered office a copy of every instrument creating a charge that needs to be registered with the registrar of companies under CA 1985, s 395 and succeeding sections. Likewise, such copies of charging instruments are open to inspection by existing members and creditors free of charge and by other persons on payment of a fee. There is no statutory definition of the word 'charge', so the reader might refer back to the discussion in Chapter 1 for guidance.

---

151 [1991] BCLC 830 at 841.

152 The judge drew inspiration for this course of action from the practice adopted in *Re Woodrof-fes (Musical Instruments) Ltd* [1986] Ch 366; but cf *Re Portbase Clothing Ltd* [1993] Ch 388.

CONCLUSION

6.100   The whole company charge registration process is something of an administrative chore for Companies House. The original instrument of charge is submitted to Companies House along with prescribed particulars and the particulars have to be cross-checked against the instrument. This function of scrutiny adds to the time lag between submission of particulars and the actual appearance of details of a charge on the register. Failure to comply with the registration obligation within 21 days of the creation of a charge results in invalidation of the security thereby granted, but only as against a liquidator, administrator or secured creditors of the company. There is a facility for late registration in cases of inadvertence etc, but this necessitates an application to the court. Late registration applications are generally granted, save where liquidation or administration of the company is imminent or has already occurred. Orders permitting late registration are usually accompanied by a provision containing a saver for rights acquired to the time when particulars of the charge are actually registered. The Companies Act 1989 proposed a number of changes in relation to the mechanics of registration. Under the proposed new regime there was no longer any need to submit an instrument of charge to Companies House for registration. All one needed to do was to submit the prescribed particulars. The time-consuming process whereby the registrar checked the instrument of charge against the prescribed particulars was therefore ended. On the other hand, it was in a charge holder's interest to ensure that accurate particulars were delivered, for it could not claim rights to security greater than those outlined in the filed particulars. Given the cessation of the scrutiny function on the part of Companies House, it made sense to abolish, as the legislation did, the certificate of due registration issued by Companies House. The certificate with its stamp of evidentiary conclusiveness is a key feature, however, of the present regime governing the registration of company charges.[153]

6.101   The Company Law Review Steering Group has also made a number of recommendations to address the problem of the delivery of defective particulars.[154] It proposed, first, to make it an offence knowingly or recklessly to deliver false information to the registrar; secondly, that while filing of defective particulars should not invalidate the charge as a whole, a charge should only be valid as to the property or classes of property properly included in the particulars; thirdly, the charge holder should be under civil liability with respect to the accuracy of the particulars, irrespective of who actually filed the particulars; fourthly, the registrar should not be liable for any inaccuracy in the information filed. The Law Commission was more tentative on some of these points, but its general approach was somewhat similar.[155] In the Consultative Report on *Company Security Interests* it provisionally recommended that the

---

153   There is also the possibility of liability on the part of the registrar for mistakes made in the registration process – see the comments of Lightman J in *Grove v Advantage Healthcare (T10) Ltd* [2000] 1 BCLC 661 at 665.

154   See pp 255–256 of Modern Company Law for a Competitive Economy: Final Report (July 2001).

155   See pp 72–76 of Consultation Paper No 164 *Registration of Security Interests* (July 2002).

effectiveness of a filing should not be affected by a defect, irregularity, omission or error in the financing statement, unless it would have the result that a reasonable search conducted in accordance with the requirements of the draft regulations and the Rules relating to searches would not reveal the financing statement. It was suggested that an error in the collateral description would result in the security interest remaining unperfected in relation to collateral that was omitted, but would not affect it as regards other collateral that was described in the financing statement.[156]

---

156 Consultative Report at p 109. The Law Commission also made reference at p 73, fn 67 of its Consultation Paper No 164 *Registration of Security Interests* (July 2002) to the following statement of principle from the Supreme Court of British Columbia in *Coates v General Motors Acceptance Corporation of Canada Ltd* (1999) 10 CBR (4th) 116 at para 17:
'1. The test of whether a registration is seriously misleading is an objective one, independent of whether anyone was or was not misled by the search, or whether a search was in fact conducted. 2. Total accuracy in registration by name or registration by serial number is not necessary. 3. A seriously misleading description of either the name or the serial number in the registration will defeat the registration. 4. A seriously misleading registration is one that, (a) would prevent a reasonable search from disclosing the registration or, (b) would cause a reasonable person to conclude that the search was not revealing the same chattel (in the case of a serial number search) or the same debtor (in the case of a name search). The obligation is on the searcher to review the similar registrations to make this determination. 5. Whether a registry filing and search program is reasonable in the sense that its design will reveal simple discrepancies without arbitrary distinction, will not be assessed in determining if a reasonable search would disclose a registration. The only question to be answered is whether a registry search will reveal the incorrect registration.'

Chapter 7

REGISTRATION AND PRIORITIES

INTRODUCTION

7.1   There is a complex interaction between the provisions of the law governing registration of company charges and the issue of priorities between
competing charges over the same property. The question is a multi-faceted one
and raises a number of different issues.[1] In this chapter an attempt will be made
to tease out the problems and perhaps to offer some solutions.

AN OVERVIEW ON EXISTING PRIORITY RULES

7.2   Under current English law the question of priorities between competing
security interests is a fairly difficult one. One must make do with a system that
consists of a mixture of inherited common law and equity, occasionally
supplemented by statute. The existing priority rules have been succinctly
summarised in the Diamond Report,[2] which states:

> 'Fixed legal charges which are registered within 21 days of creation rank
> with one another according to the time of creation and fixed legal charges
> created before a floating charge crystallises have priority over the floating
> charge, but subject to this the rules are complicated, resting on the
> distinction between legal and equitable charges and involving questions of
> notice.'

7.3   There appears to be some practitioner dissatisfaction with the existing
priority rules.[3] A focal point for the criticism lies in the fact that there is no
single reference point for determining priorities. Unlike the position in the US
under Article 9 of the UCC, registration is not per se a priority determinant
between competing security interests in the same property. Under English law,
interests that involve the use of absolute title by way of security, such as
interests under trusts and 'simple' retention of title clauses,[4] enjoy super-
priority status and, moreover, they are not subject to any requirement of

---

1   For a brief thumbnail sketch see G McCormack [1990] LMCLQ 520 at 537–539; and see also
     WJ Gough *Company Charges* (2nd edn, 1996) chapter 37.
2   A Review of Security Interests in Property (HMSO, 1989) at p 124.
3   See Richard Calnan 'Taking Security in England' in Michael Bridge and Robert Stevens (eds)
     Cross-Border Security and Insolvency (OUP, 2001).
4   Put shortly, the property never comes into the beneficial ownership of the insolvent.

registration.[5] As far as charges, strictly co-called, are concerned, while failure to register a registrable charge will result in the invalidation of the charge in the event of the corporate debtor going into liquidation, once registration has been duly effected, then priority among competing charges turns on the date of creation. In other words, fixed charges rank amongst themselves according to the order of creation but, on the other hand, a floating charge is postponed, priority-wise, to a fixed charge, irrespective of the order in which the two charges were created.[6]

7.4 If, however, a floating charge instrument contains a 'negative pledge' or 'restrictive clause', ie a clause forbidding the creation of any subsequent security having priority to the floating charge and a subsequent fixed charge holder has actual notice, not just constructive notice, of the restrictive clause, then the floating charge holder will be paid out of the assets in question in priority to the floating charge holder.[7] It appears that the practice of submitting details of a negative pledge clause among the particulars of a charge delivered for registration does not automatically infect a chargee with notice of the negative pledge clause, though notice might be inferred in the particular context.[8] Registration of negative pledge clauses is not required by statute. In practice, though, a bank which is thinking about making a secured loan to a corporate borrower will consult the register of charges and, in this way, previous secured borrowings by the company will come to light.[9]

7.5 The complexities in the law governing priorities has led to calls for legislation that clarifies the position, or at least for private law solutions negotiated amongst secured parties. As one commentator has said:[10]

> 'The priority rules are a potential minefield for secured creditors. The rules vary depending on the nature of the assets concerned, floating charges are governed by a different set of rules altogether, and there is yet another set of rules for money lent after the creditor has received notice of a subsequent charge ... For all these reasons, it is common practice for secured creditors to enter into a priority agreement with any other secured creditor of which they become aware.'

---

5   The registration obligation contained in Part XII of the Companies Act 1985 only applies to charges created by a company.

6   See G McCormack 'Priority of Charges and Registration' [1994] JBL 587.

7   See *G & T Earle Ltd v Hemsworth Rural District Council* (1928) 44 TLR 605; and see also *Re Standard Machine Co Ltd* (1906) 95 LT 829 and *Wilson v Kelland* [1910] 2 Ch 306.

8   But cf J Farrar (1976) 40 Conv (NS) 397 who argues for the existence of inferred actual knowledge rather than constructive knowledge. The argument seems inconsistent, however, with *Re Valletort Sanitary Steam Laundry Co* [1903] 2 Ch 654 and *Welch v Bowmaker (Ireland) Ltd* [1980] IR 251. For a discussion of the priority position in Australia in this context see P Ali *The Law of Secured Finance* (OUP, 2002) at pp 152–153.

9   For possible circularity problems see *Re Portbase Clothing Ltd* [1993] Ch 388 and *Re Woodroffes (Musical Instruments) Ltd* [1986] Ch 366; and see generally P Ali *The Law of Secured Finance* (OUP, 2002) at pp 242–247.

10 See Richard Calnan 'Taking Security in England' in Michael Bridge and Robert Stevens (eds) *Cross-Border Security and Insolvency* (OUP, 2001) 17 at 33.

SPELLING OUT THE PRIORITY RULES

7.6 In painting a comprehensive account of the present priority picture, perhaps the best approach is to state the rules in point form and then to elaborate upon such points at a later stage. The following is an attempt to expound the priority rules.

(1) A duly registered charge (charge A) takes priority over a previously or subsequently created unregistered charge (charge B).

(2) There is an exception to the foregoing rule if charge B is prior in point of time to charge A and charge B was duly registered within 21 days of its creation even though in actual fact it was registered after the registration of particulars of charge A. This is despite the fact that chargee A may have relied on the absence of any charges appearing on the register when advancing his money. Therefore it is clear that registration is not a reference point for determining priorities.

(3) A registered charge ranks after a prior unregistered chargee over the same property where the registered chargee takes expressly subject to the first unregistered charge.[11]

(4) Where particulars of a charge (charge A) are delivered for registration outside the 21-day period from the date of the charge's creation and a second charge (charge B) is created before actual registration of charge A, charge B takes priority over charge A, irrespective of whether charge B was created within or without the period of 21 days from the date of creation of charge A.[12]

(5) While the statement of the foregoing four rules was premised on the assumption that all the charges were fixed legal charges, in fact there is little modification of the priority rules if a later legal charge is competing against an equitable fixed charge which is prior in point of time. A holder of a legal estate in land or goods takes free from the holder of an earlier equitable interest in the same property, provided that the subsequent holder of the legal estate is bona fide, has paid value, and is without notice, actual or constructive of the earlier equitable interest. Since registration is deemed to constitute notice, the holder of the subsequent legal interest will be postponed to the holder of the prior equitable interest.[13]

(6) In certain circumstances an earlier chargee may be able to make subsequent advances that rank in priority to any loans made by intervening charge holders.

(7) A subsequent assignee of property, the subject-matter of a registered charge, takes subject to the rights of the chargee where particulars of the charge have been delivered for registration within 21 days of the date of

---

11   This point had been made explicit in the unimplemented s 99 of the Companies Act 1989, where it is provided that a charge is not void as against a person acquiring an interest in or right over property where the acquisition is expressly subject to the charge.

12   In the Companies Act 1989 the issue was specifically addressed in s 95.

13   The position was made even more explicit in the Companies Act 1989 where it is provided that a person taking a charge over a company's property shall be taken to have notice of any matter requiring registration and disclosed on the register at the time the charge is created: s 103.

the charge's creation. The assignee, however, has to be a person who might reasonably have been expected to search the register, whether by reason of prior dealings between the parties or otherwise. If the subsequent assignee is not such a person and the buyer of goods in the ordinary course of business does not come within the category, then the assignee ranks ahead of the prior security interest.

(8)   There are specialist registers concerned with land, ships or aircraft, and a charge affecting any of these must be registered under the other appropriate registration system to enjoy priority over an absolute assignment or another charge registered under the companies legislation.[14]

(9)   As a general rule a duly registered floating charge ranks after a duly registered fixed charge irrespective of the respective dates of creation of the two charges.[15]

(10)   However, a floating charge has priority over a subsequent fixed charge (assuming due registration in both cases) where the subsequent fixed chargee has actual notice of a restrictive clause in the earlier floating charge.[16] A restrictive clause (sometimes called a negative pledge clause) is a provision in the debenture containing the floating charge which prohibits the creation of subsequent fixed charges ranking prior to, or pari passu with the earlier floating charge.

(11)   Actual, not just constructive notice of a restrictive clause in the debenture is required before the priority of a fixed charge holder is displaced in favour of a floating charge holder.

(12)   Under the Companies Act 1985 the practice of submitting details of a negative pledge clause among the particulars of a charge delivered for registration does not, it is argued, automatically fix the subsequent fixed chargee with notice of the negative pledge clause, though it is something from which notice may be inferred.[17] Floating charge holders have invariably submitted these particulars and then tried to rely on the constructive notice doctrine. The better view, however, regards registration under the existing dispensation as constituting constructive notice of

---

14   See Professor Diamond's report for the Department of Trade and Industry in February 1989 *A Review of Security Interests in Property* at p 125.

15   A floating charge permits a company to carry on business in the ordinary way insofar as the class of assets charged is concerned. This would include the creation of fixed charges in the ordinary course of business. For statements on the ingredients of a floating charge see the judgment of Romer LJ in *Re Yorkshire Woolcombers Association Ltd* [1903] 2 Ch 284 and 285 and the famous 'ambulatory' metaphor employed by Lord MacNaghten in the appeal in that case which is reported under the name *Illingsworth v Houldsworth* [1904] AC 355 at 358.

16   See generally *Wilson v Kelland* [1910] 2 Ch 306; *Cox v Dublin City Distillery Co* [1906] IR 446; *Coveney v HS Perse Ltd* [1910] 1 IR 194; *G and T Earle Ltd v Hemsworth Rural District Council* (1928) 44 TLR 605.

17   But cf Farrar (1976) 40 Conv (NS) 397 who argues for the existence of inferred actual knowledge rather than constructive knowledge. He suggests that the failure on the part of a subsequent chargee to inspect the register might give rise to an inference of actual knowledge, particularly since restrictive clauses are so common. The argument seems inconsistent, however, with *Re Valletort Sanitary Steam Laundry Co* [1903] 2 Ch 654 and *Welch v Bowmaker (Ireland) Ltd* [1980] IR 251. Farrar has previously suggested that restrictive clauses may be inconsistent with the nature of a floating charge, but reaches the conclusion that 'it would now seem too late for the point to be raised': (1974) 38 Conv (NS) 315 at 318.

matters in relation to which registration is required rather than of optional extras.[18] In *G & T Earle Ltd v Hemsworth Rural District Council*[19] Wright J said:

> '... the debentures having been duly registered ... the plaintiffs, like all the world, are deemed to have constructive notice of the fact that there are debentures. But it has never been held that the mere fact that persons in the position of the plaintiffs have constructive notice of the existence of debentures also affects them with constructive notice of the actual terms of the debentures or that the debentures are subject to the restrictive condition to which these debentures were subject. No doubt it is quite common for debentures to be subject to this limiting condition as to further charges, but that fact is not enough in itself to operate as constructive notice of the actual terms of any particular set of debentures.'[20]

(13) There was provision under the Companies Act 1989 for details of a negative pledge clause to become compulsorily registrable and this could have affected the issue of priorities. Section 94 of the Companies Act 1989 provided that the register shall be made up of particulars and other information delivered to the registrar under Part IV. The implications of making a negative pledge clause compulsorily registrable were made manifest in s 103 of the Companies Act 1989. The section stipulated that a person taking a charge over a company's property shall be taken to have notice of any matter requiring registration and disclosed on the register at the time the charge is created.

(14) If a fixed charge holder has priority over a floating charge holder in a particular case because the fixed charge holder has actual notice of a restrictive clause, then this gives rise to a circularity problem that also implicates the preferential creditors who, in terms of priorities, are in between the fixed and floating charges. The issue has provoked judicial disagreement, with one view suggesting that, by coming after the floating charge, the fixed charge should therefore come after the preferential

---

18   See the statement by Handley JA in the Australian case *Fire Nymph Products Ltd v Heating Centre Pty Ltd* (1992) 7 ACSR 365 at 377:

> 'In order to protect unsecured creditors in the event of winding up from the prejudice of undisclosed charges over the company's assets the legislature as early as 1900 in England required particulars of the floating charge (but not the charge itself) to be registered in a public registry. The courts refused to extend the doctrine of constructive notice to include a restrictive clause in the charge. It was held that registration of particulars of a floating charge, although constituting constructive notice of the existence of the charge itself, did not constitute constructive notice of a restrictive clause contained within the floating charge ... Registration was constructive notice of the existence but not the contents of the charge.'

19   (1928) 44 TLR 605.

20   See also *Re Standard Machine Co Ltd* (1906) 95 LT 829 and *Wilson v Kelland* [1910] 2 Ch 306. See also the decision of the Hong Kong High Court in *ABN AMRO BANK NV v Chiyu Banking Corpn Ltd* [2000] 3 HKC 381, which holds that registration of a floating charge constitutes constructive notice of the charge but not of any restrictive provision therein contained, since particulars of such a provision are not required to be registered under the Hong Kong Companies Ordinance.

creditors.[21] On the other hand, it was also suggested in this case that a different result would follow if the respective secured parties had agreed to exchange their proprietary rights. Another possible solution is to apply the doctrine of subrogation and to hold that, by virtue of the altered priorities between them, the floating charge holder stands in the shoes of the fixed charge holder to the extent of the amount secured by the fixed charge and therefore the floating charge holder will be paid ahead of preferential creditors by the degree to which liabilities are secured by a fixed charge.[22]

(15) A crystallised floating charge takes priority over a subsequently created equitable fixed charge (assuming both charges have been duly registered within the 21-day period from the date of creation. A floating charge is taken to be a fixed equitable charge from the moment of crystallisation.

(16) The priority rules are further complicated by apparent judicial acceptance of the proposition that where a second floating charge covers only part of the assets covered by a prior floating charge, then the second floating charge will have priority, provided that the first instrument of charge authorises the creation of subsequent charges having this effect.[23]

(17) In certain circumstances a creditor who has made a loan that enables the debtor to acquire property may outrank an earlier creditor with a security interest that includes property afterwards acquired by the debtor. Basically, for this to happen the property must be fettered at the outset by the security interest in favour of the enabling or purchase money lender. There cannot be a moment of time in which the debtor is the unencumbered owner of the property, for if this were to happen the earlier creditor's afterwards acquired property clause would bite and therefore trump the purchase money security interest.

(18) Charge holders over property can agree to alter the priority between them, but such an agreement does not affect the rights or entitlements of a person who is not party to the agreement.

(19) Where there is more than one assignment of the same debt, then priority among competing assignments is determined by the order in which notice of the assignments is given to the debtor, save where a subsequent assignee has actual or constructive notice of an earlier assignment at the time that the subsequent assignment is made.[24] In the latter situation priority is governed by a simple 'first-in-time-has-priority' rule.

---

21 *Re Portbase Clothing Ltd* [1993] Ch 388. For criticism of the reasoning in *Portbase* see R Goode *Principles of Corporate Insolvency Law* (Sweet & Maxwell, 2nd edn, 1997) at pp 170–171 and *Legal Problems of Credit and Security* (Sweet & Maxwell, 3rd edn, 2003) at pp 188–189.

22 See *Re Woodroffes (Musical Instruments) Ltd* [1986] Ch 366.

23 *Re Automatic Bottle Makers* [1926] Ch 412; *Re Benjamin Cope & Co* [1914] 1 Ch 800. See also *Griffiths v Yorkshire Bank plc* [1994] 1 WLR 1427; *Re H & K Medway Ltd* [1997] 1 WLR 1422. Surely the question should be, however, whether the first floating charge authorises the creation of superior ranking subsequent floating charges, and not whether the second floating charge is over part only of the assets covered by the first – see generally R Goode *Principles of Corporate Insolvency Law* (Sweet & Maxwell, 2nd edn, 1997) at p 208, fn 14; and see also R Goode *Legal Problems of Credit and Security* (Sweet & Maxwell, 3rd edn, 2003) at p 178.

24 This is known as the rule in *Dearle v Hall* (1828) 3 Russ 1 and see generally J De Lacy 'The Priority rule of *Dearle v Hall* Restated' [1999] Conv 311. For a discussion of whether the principle applies to competing fixed charges over receivables as distinct from competing

EXPOUNDING THE BASIC RULES

7.7 Section 395 of the Companies Act 1985 supplies statutory reinforcement to proposition (1). The provision requires that the prescribed particulars of the charge, together with the instrument (if any) by which the charge is created or evidenced, must be delivered to or received by the Registrar of Companies within 21 days after the date of creation of the charge. if this is not done, the charge is void against the liquidator and any creditor of the company insofar as any security on the company's property or undertaking conferred by the charge is concerned.

7.8 Proposition (2) would have been affected by the system of provisional registration canvassed in the Diamond Report but rejected by Parliament. This system assumes the submission of a form of particulars to the registrar without any date thereon. This form secures priority for 21 days. The system means that if the company or prospective charge holder named in the form applies for registration of a freshly-created charge before the provisional registration period expires, the date of registration of the charge would be the date of provisional registration. If the provisional registration period expires without a full registration, the form is simply removed from the register.[25]

7.9 The official reasons for refusing to embrace the idea of provisional registration have been articulated as follows:[26]

'A charge that had been created but did not yet appear on the register would still take priority over a provisionally registered charge, just as it takes priority over a subsequently created charge ... Provisional registration would protect a prospective chargee during the period between his search and the date on which the charge is created. He would not run the risk that someone else might get in before him and take a charge over the same property during that period. But this problem is best dealt with by chargees ensuring that they leave as little time as possible between their search and the creation of the charge.'

7.10 Professor Diamond also suggested the notion of an official certificate of search procedure but likewise Parliament was oblivious to the attractions of this idea. This procedure revolves around an official certificate being issued by the registrar which is permanent evidence that the register contains no relevant charge. The issue of the certificate is itself recorded, so that it gives priority to applications made pursuant to it within a prescribed period.[27] Laying down a procedure for an official certificate of search would undoubtedly have added to the administrative burden on the registrar. It is not surprising therefore that the seed of provisional registration sown by Professor Diamond failed to germinate

---

assignments see L Smith *The Law of Tracing* (OUP, 1997) at p 359. The Privy Council answered this question in the affirmative in *Colonial Mutual Central Insurance Co Ltd v ANZ Banking Group* [1995] 1 WLR 1140.

25   Security Interests in Property (HMSO, 1989) at p 129.

26   *Hansard*, HC Deb, vol 504, col 135 (14 February 1989).

27   Diamond A Review of Security Interests in Property (HMSO, 1989) at p 104.

in governmental circles as the aim of successive administrations has been to ease the workload on the Registrar of Companies.[28]

7.11   Proposition (3) is somewhat controversial insofar as it purports to be a statement of existing law. In *Re Monolithic Building Co*[29] the Court of Appeal held that even though a subsequent registered chargee had actual notice of an earlier unregistered charge, the subsequent chargee still took free of it. The court was adamant in its views. Lord Cozens-Hardy MR, while acknowledging that any security may be postponed if one could find fraud in its inception, said that it was not fraud to take advantage of legal rights the existence of which may be known to both parties. It was the state of the register that was decisive.

7.12   There has been a lot of policy and academic discussion about the relevance of the 'knowledge' criterion in this context in the United States. The consensus view is that to make the issue of priorities turn on factual inquiries based on the state of knowledge generates uncertainty and breeds litigation. For example, it may be difficult to determine what exactly happened before the event in question and this makes life more difficult for subsequent parties, who may not know whether to negotiate subordination agreements or to adjust interest rates accordingly. Moreover, it could be argued that a system which makes priorities turn on knowledge tends to reward careless creditors who do not make inquiries about their debtors, rather than the diligent creditor who examines a debtor's credit history and prior lending agreements before entering into the commitment to lend. The Article 9 progenitor, Grant Gilmore, has pointed out that a good faith or knowledge requirement creates evidentiary problems:[30]

> '[T]he presence or absence of "knowledge" is a subjective question of fact, difficult to prove. Unless there is an overwhelming policy argument in favor

---

28   It should be noted that s 265 of the Australian Corporations Law 2001 permits a system of provisional registration, though in a slightly different context. Provisional registration is possible in two circumstances. The system is operated through the Commission (equivalent to the registrar) entering the word provisional next to an entry. It is done either when the prescribed particulars contained in the notice lodged with the Commission are incomplete or where the document accompanying the notice of charge lodged with the Commission has not been duly stamped.

29   [1915] 1 Ch 643. Cf *Ram Narain v Radha Kishen Moti Lal Chamaria Firm* (1929) LR 57 Ind App 76. See also the Land Charges Act and Land Registration Act cases: *Midland Bank Trust Co Ltd v Green* [1981] AC 513; *Peffer v Rigg* [1977] 1 WLR 285; *De Lusignan v Johnson* (1973) 230 EG 499; and *Lyus v Prowsa Developments Ltd* [1982] 1 WLR 1044. In *Midland Bank Trust Co Ltd v Green* [1981] AC 513 at 530 Lord Wilberforce specifically approved the words of Lord Cozens-Hardy MR in *Re Monolithic Building Co* [1915] 1 Ch 643. Lord Wilberforce's speech has been subjected to some criticism by Kevin Gray and Susan Frances Gray in *Elements of Land Law* (Butterworths, 3rd edn, 2001) at p 1098. They say that the decision of the House of Lords in *Midland Bank Trust Co Ltd v Green* epitomises the traditional view of the busy property lawyer that there is much to be said in favour of trading off a little justice in return for enhanced security and certainty in commercial transactions. In their view, however, this pragmatic approach will never satisfy all of the people all of the time. They suggest that while it may well be that, in the eyes of the law, it is not fraud to take advantage of the folly of another, it remains an uncomfortable fact of life that most fraud consists in doing precisely that.

30   *Security Interests in Personal Property* (Boston, Little Brown, 1965) at p 902.

of using such a criterion, it is always wise to discard it and to make decision turn on some easily determinable objective event – as, for example, the date of filing.'

7.13 The statement from Grant Gilmore was approved by the United States District Court in *Re Smith*.[31] This is a case where a second lender advanced credit and perfected a security interest at the time that it had knowledge of a prior unperfected security interest. The court held that Article 9 did not make good faith a requirement for obtaining priority. The provision legislated for a race to the filing office with actual knowledge of a prior unperfected security interest being irrelevant if one perfected first by filing. Knowledge of an earlier unperfected interest had no bearing on priority. The court suggested that there were good reasons for disregarding knowledge and creating a race to file situation. The integrity of the filing system was protected only if perfection of interests took place promptly. It was appropriate therefore that a secured party who failed to file promptly should run the risk of subordination to a later, more diligent, party. Stepping back from the case for a minute, one might say that the law rewards diligence and punishes indolence in many different contexts and this situation is fundamentally no different.

7.14 Leading scholars, writing more recently, have also endorsed this proposition. Professors Baird and Jackson suggest:[32]

'First, even if there are advantages from insisting that subsequent [security interest holders] meet the traditional requirement of being without knowledge, these advantages seem to pale beside the costs they impose. Any inquiry into knowledge is likely to be expensive and time consuming. It is simply much easier to live in a world in which everyone knows that he must comply with a few simple formalities or lose than to live in a world where the validity of someone's property rights turns on whether certain individuals had knowledge at some particular time in the past. Those who are required to make appropriate filings, in the main, either are professionals or engage the services of professionals. We think it likely that everyone is ultimately better off with a clear rule than with a legal regime that is somewhat more finely tuned but much more expensive to operate. Ferreting out those who took with knowledge despite a defective filing generally is not worth the uncertainty and the litigation it generates.'

7.15 But what if the subsequent chargee not only had notice but took expressly subject to the prior unregistered charge? How does this affect the priority picture? There does not appear to be a reported case on the point in the United Kingdom, but in Ireland *Re Monolithic Building Co* was distinguished in such a situation. The court held in one case that the second chargee's rights were at all times limited and qualified rights, namely the right to a second charge ranking after the first.[33]

---

31   (1971) 326 F Supp 1311.

32   (1984) 13 J Legal Stud 299 at 314 and see also D Carlson 'Rationality, Accident and Priority under Article 9 of the Uniform Commercial Code' (1986) 71 Minn LR 207.

33   *Re Clarets Ltd* (unreported) High Court, 22 November 1978 on which see G McCormack (1984) 2 Irish Law Times 67 at 72.

7.16 The unimplemented s 99 of the Companies Act 1989 confirmed that interpretation and put the position beyond doubt. The section of course cannot be regarded as a definitive statement of the existing position. The statement in the text derives, however, some support from the decision and observations of Vinelott J in *Re Fablehill Ltd.*[34] In fact, the decision goes somewhat further. The facts of the case in a truncated form are as follows. A company executed a charge in favour of its bank but the company solicitors failed to register the charge although they had accepted responsibility for so doing. Some two years later the company executed a second charge over the same property in favour of two directors of the company. This charge was not made subject to the charge in favour of the bank. A late registration application was made by the bank pursuant to CA 1985, s 404 for an order extending the time for registration of its charge. Vinelott J granted the order but refused to include a proviso safeguarding the rights of the second chargees. In his view, it would be plainly inequitable to include a proviso protecting the rights of directors who, when they learned that the company had failed in its duty to register the bank's charge, took no steps to remedy the company's breach of duty by applying to register the charge out of time, but created and registered a charge in their own favour.[35] The overriding question was whether it was just and equitable to grant relief by acceding to the late registration application.[36] The attitude of the court in hearing this application was conditioned by the fact the second charge holder consisted of the only directors of the company and it was the responsibility of the company under CA 1985, s 395 to register the charge.

7.17 Proposition (4) is based on the practice of the court in acceding to late registration applications. Orders of the court permitting late registration of charges were accompanied by a proviso,[37] but the wording of the proviso has changed over the years. Originally the proviso stated that the order extending the time was without prejudice to the rights acquired against the holders of the charge in question prior to the time when particulars of the charge shall be actually registered. It was clear from the authorities that the wording protects only proprietary rights,[38] and this aspect of the matter did not change.

7.18 It was also held that the wording protected only rights which intervene between the end of the 21 days within which the statute requires registration and the time of registration under the order for extension of the time. Dicta to this effect in *In re Ehrmann Bros Ltd*[39] received the seal of approval from Templeman J in *Watson v Duff, Morgan and Vermont (Holdings) Ltd.*[40] On the learned judge's analysis a charge did not become void until after the time for registration has elapsed. Until the expiry of the 21 days it is valid. Therefore it

---

34 [1991] BCLC 830.
35 [1991] BCLC 830 at 841.
36 Reference was made to the comments of Lord Hanworth MR in *Re MIG Trust Ltd* [1933] Ch 542 at 560 and Hoffmann J in *Re Braemar Investments Ltd* [1988] BCLC 556 at 561.
37 See generally McCormack 'Extension of time for Registration of Company Charges' [1986] JBL 282 at 290.
38 See the homely example used by Cozens Hardy LJ in *Re Ehrmann Bros Ltd* [1906] 2 Ch 697 at 709–710.
39 [1906] 2 Ch 697.
40 [1974] 1 WLR 450.

prevails over any charges created within that period, although such charges are not registered until after the 21 days. This conclusion produces anomalous results. The order of priorities varies according to whether a later registered charge was created before or after 21 days from the date of creation of the first unregistered charge. In the aftermath of *Watson* the wording of the proviso was changed,[41] though there are references to the old form of working in *Re Ashpurton Estates Ltd*.[42] After *Watson* the order was usually made without prejudice to the rights of the parties acquired during the period between the date of creation of the charge and the date of its actual registration.

TACKING OF FURTHER ADVANCES

7.19 Proposition (5) is also the subject of a lot of complicated law which is centred around, first, the so-called 'tabula in naufragio doctrine' and, secondly, the right to tack further advances. The tabula in naufragio principle allows the holder of a later equitable interest who has made his advance without notice of an earlier equitable interest to achieve a tabula in naufragio by acquiring the legal title. This affords priority even though at the time of acquiring the legal title he may have notice of the prior equitable interest.[43]

7.20 Often a mortgage or charge is taken to secure further advances, such as a mortgage to secure a bank account.[44] The question arises whether a mortgagee may make further advances ranking in priority to a subsequent mortgagee. The ability of a mortgagee to make such further advances depends on whether the mortgage relates to land, registered or unregistered, or to personal property.[45] Section 94 of the Law of Property Act 1925 deals with mortgagees of unregistered land. The section gives a prior mortgagee a right to make further advances which rank in priority to subsequent mortgages (whether legal or equitable) in three situations:

---

41 See Bennett (1974) 118 SJ 286.

42 [1983] 1 Ch 110.

43 *Taylor v Russell* [1892] AC 244; *Bailey v Barnes* [1894] 1 Ch 25. See generally RM Goode *Legal Problems of Credit and Security* (Sweet & Maxwell, 3rd edn, 2003) at pp 160–161. In *Taylor v Russell* [1892] AC 244 at 253 Lord Herschell spoke thus, quoting from the words of Lord Selborne in *Blackwood v London Chartered Bank of Australia* LR 5 PC at p 111:

> 'It is not disputed that the doctrine of equity is well settled that a man who has bona fide paid money without notice of any other title, though at the time of payment he as purchaser gets nothing but an equitable title, may afterwards get in a legal title if he can and may hold it, though during the interval between the payment and the getting in of the legal title he may have had notice of some prior dealing inconsistent with the good faith of the dealing with himself.'

Lord MacNaghten said [1892] AC 244 at 259 that the mere fact that the subsequent encumbrancer has notice of the prior incumbrance when he gets n the legal estate counts for nothing.

44 In this case the security will have to be expressed to be a continuing security. Otherwise, under the rule in *Chyton's case* (1816) 1 Mer 572 and the principle of 'first in, first out' in relation to bank amounts, the security becomes discharged on repayment of the amount of the initial advance.

45 See generally Goode *Legal Problems of Credit and Security* (3rd edn, 2003) at pp 163–167; WJ Gough *Company Charges* (Butterworths, 2nd edn, 1996) at pp 941–947.

(a)   where an arrangement has been made to that effect with the subsequent mortgagees;

(b)   if the prior mortgagee had no notice of the subsequent mortgages at the time that the further advance was made;

(c)   where the mortgage imposes an obligation on him to make further advances.

This section applies regardless of whether a mortgage was made expressly for securing further advances.

7.21   Second mortgages of unregistered land are usually registrable in the Land Charges Register as Class C land charges. They may be registrable either as a puisne mortgage, ie a legal mortgage which is not protected by a deposit of documents relating to the legal estate affected, or as general equitable charges. Section 198 of the Law of Property Act 1925 provides that the registration of any instrument or matter in any register kept under the Land Charges Act shall be deemed to constitute actual notice of such instrument or matter, and of the fact of such registration, to all persons and for all purposes connected with the land affected.

7.22   There are obvious difficulties with the operation of this section in the case of a mortgage taken to secure a current account. A prior mortgagee can hardly be expected to search the Land Charges register every time it honours a drawing, yet s 198 would appear to fix him with actual notice of any subsequent mortgage registered therein. To tackle this problem, s 94(2) of the Law of Property Act 1925 provides that a mortgagee is not deemed to have notice of a mortgage merely by reason that it was registered as a land charge, if it was not so registered at the time when the original mortgage was created, or when the last search (if any) by the prior mortgage was made, whichever last happened.

7.23   Where registered land is concerned, notice of the second mortgage, whether actual or constructive, puts an end to the right to tack.[46] It appears that entry of the second mortgage on the register, whether as a registered charge or by way of notice or caution, constitutes notice for this purpose. Section 30 of the Land Registration Act 1925 provides partial protection for the first mortgagee. The section stipulates that where a registered charge is made for securing further advances the registrar, before making any entry which would prejudicially affect the priority of any further advance, must give notice to the proprietor of the charge, who is not in respect of any further advance to be affected by such entry unless the advance is made after the date when the notice ought to have been received in due course of post. Once such notice has been received, the charge holder should close the debtor's account and credit later payments to a new account.[47] If such steps are not taken, then the amount of the debt which enjoys priority over a subsequent mortgagee will become progressively eroded by the operation of the rule in *Clayton's Case*.[48]

---

46   *Hopkinson v Rolt* (1861) 9 HLC 514.
47   See R Goode *Legal Problems of Credit and Security* (3rd edn, 2003) at p 165.
48   (1816) 1 Mer 572.

7.24 Section 30 has now been replaced by s 49 of the Land Registration Act 2002, which enables the proprietor of a registered charge to make a further advance ranking in priority to a subsequent charge if:

(a)   he has not received from the subsequent charge holder notice of the creation of the subsequent charge; or

(b)   the further advance is made pursuant to an obligation which was entered in the register at the time of creation of the subsequent charge; or

(c)   the parties to the prior charge have agreed a maximum amount for which the charge is security and such agreement was entered in the register at the time of creation of the subsequent charge.

7.25 Professor Goode has been very critical of limb (c) of the new statutory provision, suggesting that effectively it enables the first charge holder to obtain a monopoly of the debtor's non-purchase-money financing by the simple device of specifying a maximum sum well beyond any amount that the charge holder is likely to lend or the asset given in security is likely to be worth.[49]

7.26 In relation to mortgages of pure personal property, the provisions of s 94 of the Law of Property Act 1925 govern a mortgagee's right to tack, save, of course, for those provisions relating to land charge registration. Notice, whether it be actual or constructive, of any subsequent mortgage puts an end to the right to tack, except in situations where the further advance is made by arrangement with the subsequent mortgagee or the first mortgagee is obliged to make it by the terms of the mortgage.

7.27 As we have seen, there is still a lot of complication and obfuscation with respect to the priority of subsequent advances over later mortgages. There are many interlocking statutory provisions with no clear indication of the relationship between them. There is much to be said for a comprehensive statutory scheme along Australian lines setting out priorities.[50] In Australia a distinction is drawn between present liabilities and prospective liabilities. A 'present liability' is defined as meaning a liability that has arisen, being a liability the extent or amount of which is fixed or capable of being ascertained, whether or not the liability is immediately due to be met. A 'prospective liability' is defined as any liability that may arise in the future, or any other liability that does not include a present liability.[51]

7.28 Priority in respect of future advances or what might be termed 'prospective liabilities' depends on a number of factors. A registered charge holder making further advances will enjoy priority over intervening charge holders if the case can be accommodated within one of the following circumstances:[52]

(a)   If the registered charge covers unlimited present and future liabilities (or

---

49   See R Goode *Legal Problems of Credit and Security* (3rd edn, 2003) at p 166.

50   See generally WJ Gough *Company Charges* (Butterworths 2nd edn, 1996) at pp 943–947.

51   Section 261 of the Corporations Law.

52   Section 282 of the Corporations Law.

future liabilities only), priority is enjoyed if the charge holder had no actual knowledge of another charge at the time when the future liability is incurred.

(b)   Where a charge secures present and future liabilities (or future liabilities only) up to a specified amount and this amount is stated in the notice of charge, the chargee has priority in respect of advances up to that limit irrespective of notice of other charges.

(c)   Where a charge covers present and future liabilities (or future debt only) up to a specified amount but the notice fails to state that amount, the charge holder has priority with regard to further advances actually made before the first charge holder has actual knowledge of any other charge, or even after such knowledge if the charge holder was bound to make further advances.

(d)   Where a charge covers unlimited prospective liabilities, priority is enjoyed in respect of future advances actually made before knowledge is had of another charge or even advances made subsequently if the charge holder was bound to make such further advances.

PRIORITY OF BUYERS OF GOODS IN THE ORDINARY COURSE OF BUSINESS

7.29   Proposition (6) merits a little exploration. The proposition is stated in Gough in the following, somewhat different, terms:

'A registered charge takes priority from the date of its registration (by virtue of constructive notice) against a subsequent absolute assignment.'[53]

7.30   An example may serve to illustrate the distinction between the two statements. Say a charge has been created on day one and registered on day 20. But meantime there has been an absolute assignment of the property, the subject-matter of the charge, on day 10. On my formulation the registered charge takes priority over the subsequent absolute assignment. In Dr Gough's, however, the situation is different, with the absolute assignment ranking ahead of the registered charge.

7.31   The two formulations lead to the same result where the state of affairs is as follows:[54] a charge is created on day one, registered on day 20, and there is an absolute assignment of the property, the subject-matter of the charge, on day 25. There is no doubting that here the registered charge has priority.

---

53   *Company Charges* (Butterworths, 1978) at p 401. See now the second edition (1996) at p 907 where the point is formulated slightly differently:

    'A registered charge, duly registered through initial compliance or pursuant to a court extension order, takes priority from the date of its registration through constructive notice based on that registration as against ... (c) an absolute interest, created subsequent to that registration.'

    Nevertheless the meaning of the revised formulation seems to be essentially the same as the earlier one.

54   *Security Interests in Property* (HMSO, February 1989) at p 120.

7.32   It is also clear that if particulars of a charge have not been delivered for registration within 21 days from the date of the charge's creation and there has been an assignment of the property which constitutes the subject-matter of the charge within that 21-day period, then the assignee ranks before the charge holder. This is clear from ss 395 of the Companies Act 1985 and the terms of the normal proviso accompanying orders that permit the late registration of charges.

7.33   But the most fundamental question that derives from proposition (6) relates to the position of the purchaser of goods in the ordinary course of business. It is argued that such a person cannot reasonably be expected to search the register of charges and should take free from an equitable charge over the goods. The issue warrants further discussion. The first thing that one might say is that a purchase of goods is bound to operate at law rather than in equity. In sale of goods law there has been strong resistance to the introduction of equitable proprietary notions. This resistance was manifested in *Re Wait*.[55] Atkin LJ spoke of the codification of sale of goods law as reflected in the Sale of Goods Act 1893. He went on to say:[56]

> It would have been futile in a Code intended for commercial men to have created an elaborate structure of rules dealing with rights at law, if at the same time it was intended to leave, subsisting with the legal rights, equitable rights inconsistent with, more extensive, and coming into existence earlier than the rights so carefully set out in the various sections of the Code.'

7.34   The second point to make is that a security interest in goods will normally be equitable rather than legal.[57] In elaborating upon this argument it is necessary to draw a distinction between a mortgage and a charge. Slade J explained in *Re Bond Worth Ltd*[58] that the technical difference between a 'mortgage' and a 'charge' lies in the fact that a mortgage involves a conveyance of property subject to a right of redemption, whereas a charge conveys nothing and merely gives the charge holder certain rights over the property as security for the loan. To repeat, a mortgage involves the transfer of rights of ownership, whereas a charge entails merely a right of resort to the property for security purposes. In practice, though, the two terms are often used interchangeably in statutes.

7.35   It is perfectly possible to create a legal mortgage over personalty by assignment of the property with a provision for reassignment on repayment of the debt.[59] The common law, however, does not recognise certain types of property. For instance, a mortgage of future property is void at common law.[60] Therefore any security interest in future personalty must be equitable in nature.

---

55   [1927] Ch 606.

56   [1927] Ch 606 at 635–636.

57   See generally AP Bell *Modern Law of Personal Property in England and Ireland* (1989) chapter 8; MJ Bridge *Personal Property Law* (Clarendon Press Oxford, 3rd edn, 2002) chapter 7.

58   [1980] Ch 228 at 250.

59   Though this is no longer possible in the case of land: see ss 85–86 Law of Property Act 1925.

60   See *Lunn v Thornton* (1845) 1 CB 379; *Tailby v Official Receiver* (1888) 13 App Cas 523; and *Holroyd v Marshall* (1862) 10 HLC 191.

It is not strictly speaking possible to have a legal charge on personalty, though statute in the shape of ss 85–86 of the Law of Property Act 1925 permits the creation of a charge by way of legal mortgage over land. All this tells us that a security interest in goods is more likely to be equitable rather than legal. If that is in fact the case, then a subsequent assignee should take free of the earlier security interest. The old bona fide purchaser for value without notice principle should come into play here. Does registration in the company charges register constitute notice? The answer would appear to be 'no'. Professor RM Goode has observed:[61]

'What can be said with some confidence, having regard to the underlying purpose of the doctrine of notice, is that registration is notice only to those who could reasonably be expected to search. This would normally exclude a buyer in ordinary course of business, for it would be quite impracticable to expect a purchaser from a manufacturer or dealer to search in the Companies Registry every time he wishes to consummate a purchase ...'

7.36 The celebrated comments of Lindley LJ in *Manchester Trust v Furness*[62] also spring to mind in this connection. His dicta bear extensive quotation:

'The equitable doctrines of constructive notice are common enough in dealing with land and estates, with which the Court is familiar; but there have been repeated protests against the introduction into commercial transactions of anything like an extension of those doctrines, and the protest is founded on perfect good sense. In dealing with estates in land title is everything, and it can be leisurely investigated; in commercial transactions possession is everything and there is not time to investigate title; and if we were to extend the doctrine of constructive notice to commercial transactions we should be doing infinite mischief and paralysing the trade of the country.'

7.37 These dicta were applied by Neill J in *Feuer Leather Corp v Johnstone & Sons*[63] who held that a purchaser will not be affected in a commercial transaction by constructive notice. He emphasised the fact that there was no general duty on a buyer of goods in an ordinary commercial transaction to make inquiries as to the right of the seller to dispose of the goods.[64]

7.38 It must be said, however, that there is a paucity of authority, still less modern authority, on this particular point, but such authority as there is tends to restrict the ambit of the doctrine of constructive notice to subsequent security interest holders and not to extend it to trade purchasers. For instance,

---

61   *Legal Problems of Credit and Security* (3rd edn, 2003) at p 83; and for a forthright attack on the doctrine of constructive notice in this context see John De Lacy 'Constructive Notice and Company Charge Registration' (2001) 65 Conv 122.

62   [1895] 2 QB 539.

63   [1981] Com LR 251.

64   See also *Greer v Downs Supply Co* [1927] 2 KB 28; *Goodyear Tyre & Rubber Co (GB) v Lancashire Batteries* [1958] 1 WLR 857; *Wilts United Dairies v Robinson (Thomas) Sons & Co* [1957] RPC 220; *Panchaud Frères SA v Etablissements General Grain Co* [1970] 1 Lloyds Rep 53; *Worcester Works Finance v Cooden Engineering Co* [1972] 1 QB 210.

in *Channel Airways Ltd v Manchester Corpn*[65] Forbes J said: 'I do not find that the mere registration of a debenture ... amounts to notice to all the world ...' As Dr De Lacy argues, the effects of applying a doctrine of constructive notice to 'all the world' are not edifying, for we cannot really expect purchasers in the ordinary course of business to search the register prior to dealing.[66]

7.39 If a buyer of goods is competing against an earlier legal mortgage over the goods, then there are two legal interests in conflict. The later assignee may be able to rely on s 24 of the Sale of Goods Act 1979, though this is by no means certain.[67] The section tackles the situation where a seller of goods continues in possession after the sale. If the goods are then sold a second time to someone who does not know of the first sale, and the goods are delivered to the second buyer, the second buyer gets a good title and the first buyer is left to his personal rights against the seller. So equating a legal mortgage of goods with a sale, as it is in formal legal terms, the purchaser acquires a good title, whereas the mortgagee is left with a personal remedy. This view, however, runs into the problem of s 62(4) of SGA 1979 which says that the provisions of the Act relating to contracts of sale do not apply to a transaction in the form of a contract of sale which is intended to operate by way of mortgage, pledge, charge or other security. As Professor Diamond has pointed out, s 62(4) is comprehensible insofar as it excludes the seller's obligations to the 'buyer' (secured party) with respect to implied terms as to quality, but since the effect of s 24 is to safeguard innocent purchasers, there is no policy reason why it should not operate.[68] If, however, s 24 does not apply, one is left with the basic nemo dat principle, with the result that the trade purchaser does not obtain a good title to the goods free from the security interest.

7.40 In Professor Diamond's view, an important aspect of any reform of the law is to make the position of an innocent purchaser the same, whatever the nature of the security interest and without regard to whether the security interest might be said to be legal or equitable. He argued:[69]

'The main consideration is that it would be an unacceptable hindrance to trade if buyers from dealers in such goods, whether at the manufacturing, wholesale or retail level were expected to search in the register of security interests. It follows that buyers of goods sold in the course of the seller's business would take free of any security interest whether or not perfected.'

7.41 In the United States, Article 9–317 of the Uniform Commercial Code deals with the position of buyers and unperfected security interests. According to the provision, a buyer takes free of a security interest if the buyer gives value and receives delivery of the collateral without knowledge of the security

---

65 [1974] 1 Lloyds Rep 456 at 459; and see also the statement of Slade J in *Siebe Gorman & Co v Barclays Bank Ltd* [1979] 2 Lloyds Rep 142 at 160 that registration 'may by itself serve to give subsequent mortgages constructive notice ...'

66 See J De Lacy 'Ambit and Reform of Part XII of the Companies Act 1985' in J De Lacy (ed) *The Reform of UK Company Law* (Cavendish, 2002) at p 376.

67 See generally Diamond *A Review of Security Interests in Property* (HMSO, 1989) at p 75.

68 Diamond Report at p 72.

69 Diamond Report at p 75.

interest and before it is perfected. Article 9–320 deals with the position of buyers and perfected security interests and provides that a buyer in ordinary course of business takes free of a security interest created by the buyer's seller, even if the security interest is perfected and the buyer knows of its existence. The effect of Article 1–201 is, however, to limit the apparent protection afforded by Article 9–320. 'Buyer in ordinary course of business' is defined as meaning a person that buys goods in good faith and without knowledge that the sale violates the rights of another person in the goods, and in the ordinary course from a person, other than pawnbroker, in the business of selling goods of that kind. The end result of these somewhat convoluted definitions is that a buyer takes free of an existing security interest if the buyer merely knows that a security interest covers the goods, but takes subject to the same if the buyer knows additionally that the sale violates a term in the agreement with the secured party. There are also special provisions in Article 9–320 to protect buyers of consumer goods.

7.42   Just to summarise, a buyer in an Article 9 context takes free of a security interest unless it knows that the sale contravenes the terms of the security agreement. The situation in England is more or less the same. Buyers take free of floating charges and also of fixed charges, provided that they do not actually know of the latter's existence. The fixed charge is essentially a security agreement that prohibits the disposition of assets subject to it in the ordinary course of business. It is not clear whether the move to an Article 9 regime would be beneficial to this jurisdiction, apart from the clarity of having the law set out in statutory form.[70]

FLOATING CHARGES AND CRYSTALLISATION

7.43   The current of English authority is that actual rather than just constructive notice of a restrictive clause in a debenture is required before the priority of a subsequent fixed charge holder is displaced in favour of a floating charge holder. In *English and Scottish Mercantile Investment Co Ltd v Brunton*[71] the solicitor acting for the subsequent mortgagee actually knew of the existence of the earlier floating charge, but was misled by the managing director of the company granting the charge into believing that there was nothing in it to affect his client's security. The subsequent mortgagee obtained priority. Lord Esher MR said:

> 'At the time they took it ... there were in existence debentures issued by that company, and there were things stated in those debentures which, if the plaintiffs had known, would have prevented them in equity from saying

---

70   See generally pp 112–118 of the Law Commission Consultation Paper No 164 *Registration of Security Interests* (July 2002) and pp 131–134 of the Consultative Report (No 176) *Company Security Interests* (September 2004). The Law Commission provisionally recommended that a buyer of goods from a seller who normally sells goods of that kind, or a lessee from a lessor who normally leases goods of that kind, should take free of any perfected security interest created by the seller or lessor unless the buyer or lessee knows that the sale or lease is in violation of the security agreement(Consultative Report, para 3.260).

71   [1892] 2 QB 700 at 707.

that their mortgage could be enforced in priority to the debentures. If they had known what was in the debentures they would, in equity, have taken the mortgage with notice of prior charges on the subject-matter of it. It is admitted that the plaintiffs did not in fact know that there was that in the debentures which would prevent them, in equity, from having the full benefit of the mortgage which they took; but it is said that they had what in equity is termed constructive notice of what was in the debentures.'

7.44   The facts were somewhat similar in a later case, *Re Standard Rotary Machine Co.*[72] There was a floating charge debenture containing a restrictive clause and a subsequent fixed charge. The fixed charge holder actually knew of the existence of the earlier floating charge but did not know of the restrictive clause. In the circumstances it was held that the fixed charge holder was entitled to priority. Kekewich J said:

'By having notice of the debentures the bank did not obtain notice of this particular provision of the debenture or of any other particular provision – only notice that there were debentures which charged the property of the company; and not being affected with notice, they were innocent holders of their own charge and they are entitled to the priority which that charge gives them.'

7.45   *Re Standard Rotary Machine Co* was cited with approval by Eve J in *Wilson v Kelland*,[73] where the judge took the view that registration of the particulars of a charge pursuant to the company charge registration provisions amounted to constructive notice of a charge affecting the property, but not of any special provisions in the charge that restrict the company from dealing with their property in the usual manner when the subsisting charge is a floating security. The same view was clearly articulated by Wright J in *G & T Earle Ltd v Hemsworth Rural District Council*[74] who said:

'[T]he debentures having been duly registered ... the plaintiffs, like all the world, are deemed to have constructive notice of the fact that there are debentures. But it has never been held that the mere fact that persons in the position of the plaintiffs have constructive notice of the existence of debentures also affects them with constructive notice of the actual terms of the debentures or that the debentures are subject to the restrictive condition to which these debentures were subject. No doubt it is quite common for debentures to be subject to this limiting condition as to further charges, but that fact is not enough in itself to operate as constructive notice of the actual terms of any particular set of debentures.'[75]

---

72   (1906) 95 LT 829.
73   [1910] 2 Ch 306.
74   (1928) 44 TLR 605.
75   See also the decision of the Hong Kong High Court in *ABN AMRO BANK NV v Chiyu Banking Corpn Ltd* [2000] 3 HKC 381 which holds that registration of a floating charge constitutes constructive notice of the charge but not of any restrictive provision therein contained, since particulars of such a provision are not required to be registered under the Hong Kong Companies Ordinance.

7.46   Perhaps the fullest discussion of the authorities in modern times comes from the Irish Supreme Court in *Welsh v Bowmaker (Ireland) Ltd*.[76] In this case the floating charge holder argued that the subsequent fixed charge holder should be fixed with constructive notice of the provision in the floating charge, precluding the company from creating a mortgage that would have priority over the floating charge. Henchy J said that since such a prohibition was more or less common form in modern debentures, there was much to be said for applying the doctrine of constructive notice in such a situation were it not settled law that there was no duty on the bank in these circumstances to seek out the precise terms of the debenture.[77] Actual or express notice of the prohibition in the floating charge must exist before the subsequent mortgagee could be deprived of priority.[78]

7.47   A floating charge may be described as exemplifying the imagination and business awareness of nineteenth century equity practitioners.[79] Moreover, as well as being the subject of continued judicial scrutiny, floating charges have also engaged the attention of Parliament over the years. Hoffmann J in *Re Brightlife Ltd*[80] traced the history of legislative intervention.[81] Legislation in 1897 afforded priority to preferential debts and provision was made by the Companies Act 1907 for the invalidation of floating charges granted within three months prior to the commencement of winding up, which period has since been extended. The Companies Act 1900 introduced the requirement of registration of floating and certain other types of charge. Traditionally, the floating charge has been enforced through the mechanism of the appointment of a receiver over the assets covered by the charge and the Companies Act 1907 laid down that the appointment of a receiver be registered.

7.48   What has more recently prompted parliamentary intervention is the increasing use of so-called automatic crystallisation clauses.[82] As traditionally understood, a floating charge crystallised (or, to use non-technical terminology, converted into a fixed charge) where the debenture-holder appointed a receiver, or upon the commencement of winding up. In *Re Woodroffes (Musical*

---

76   [1980] IR 251.

77   [1980] IR 251 at 256. The judge went on to say that whatever attractions there may be in the proposition that priority should be deemed lost because a duty to inquire further was called for but ignored, and that such inquiry would have shown that the company was debarred from entering into a mortgage which would have priority over the debenture, it would be unfair to single out the bank for condemnatory treatment because of their failure to ascertain the full terms of the debenture when what they did was in accord with judicially approved practice and where such a precipitate change in the law would undermine the intended validity of many other transactions.

78   See generally WJ Gough *Company Charges* (Butterworths, 2nd edn, 1996) at pp 225–228 and 808–815.

79   For initial judicial recognition of the floating charge see the decision of the Court of Appeal in Chancery in *Re Panama, New Zealand and Australian Royal Mail Co* (1870) 5 Ch App 318.

80   [1987] Ch 200.

81   [1987] Ch 200 at 214–215. See also *Re Permanent Houses (Holdings) Ltd* [1988] BCLC 563.

82   See the discussion under the heading 'Crystallisation of a floating charge' in the DTI Consultative Letter of 7 July 1988.

Instruments) Ltd[83] Nourse J decided that the cessation of a company's business brought about the crystallisation of a floating charge. This occurred because cessation removed the raison d'être of the floating charge, which was to permit the company to carry on business in the ordinary way insofar as the class of assets charged was concerned. Then, in *Re Brightlife Ltd*[84] Hoffmann J held that notice given by the charge holder to the chargor could convert a floating charge into a fixed charge. He said it was not open to the courts to restrict the contractual freedom of parties to a floating charge. He pointed to the limited and pragmatic interventions by the legislature in the area and suggested that these rendered it wholly inappropriate for the courts to impose additional restrictive rules on grounds of public policy. In this respect he preferred the views of Speight J in the New Zealand case *Re Manurewa Transport Ltd*[85] to those of Berger J in the Canadian case *British Columbia v Consolidated Churchill Copper Corpn Ltd.*[86]

7.49 The decision *Re Brightlife Ltd* opens the door for clauses that stipulate for crystallisation on the occurrence of events such as the borrowing of the company exceeding a certain level or its assets falling below a stated sum. These events may take place at a time unknown to the chargee, so that he is not aware that crystallisation has occurred.

7.50 The objective of widely drafted crystallisation clauses is to secure the chargee as prominent a place as possible in the queue of creditors. The Insolvency Act 1986 has, however, reduced the attractions of automatic crystallisation clauses in this respect. According to ss 40 and 175, preferential debts are payable in priority to the claim secured by a floating charge in a receivership or liquidation. A floating charge is defined in s 251, for the purpose, inter alia, of these provisions, as a charge which, as created, was a floating charge.[87] So even if a floating charge has crystallised automatically prior to receivership or liquidation, it still ranks after the preferential creditors. A crystallised floating charge will still, however, take priority over a prior ranking floating charge, a subsequently created equitable fixed charge and execution creditors.

7.51 The effect of crystallisation is to terminate the company's management authority, ie its freedom to dispose of assets in the ordinary course of business clear of the security interest.[88] It seems, however, on the basis of normal agency

---

83 [1986] Ch 366.
84 [1987] Ch 200.
85 [1971] NZLR 909. See also *Deputy Commissioner of Taxation v Horsburgh* [1983] 2 VR 591; *Re Obie Pty Ltd (No 2)* (1984) 2 ACLC 69; and McLaughlan [1972] NZLJ 300.
86 (1978) 90 DLR (3d) 357. Pre-PPSA, Canadian courts took the view that floating charge holders were required to intervene in an overt fashion so as to give public notice to other creditors that the debtor's freedom of dealing with its assets in the ordinary course of business had been terminated: *Esket Wood Products Ltd v Starline Lumber Inc* (1991) 61 BCLR (2d) 359. See also WJ Gough *Company Charges* (Butterworths, 2nd edn, 1996) at pp 408–431 and AJ Boyle 'The Validity of Automatic Crystallisation Clauses' [1979] JBL 231.
87 See also the Insolvency Act 1986, s 29(2).
88 For a discussion of more convoluted concepts like selective crystallisation, de-crystallisation and reflotation of crystallised floating charges see C Rickett 'Automatic Reflotation of a

principles that a third party who is unaware that crystallisation has occurred pursuant to an automatic crystallisation is entitled to assume the continuance of a company's managerial authority implied by the floating charge until cessation of that authority has been brought explicitly to its attention.[89]

7.52 Part IV of the Companies Act 1989 represented another legislative intervention. The relevant provision is s 100. The section was an enabling one and gave the Secretary of State power to make various regulations:

'(1) The Secretary of State may by regulations require notice in the prescribed form to be given to the registrar of –

(a) the occurrence of such events as may be prescribed affecting the nature of the security under a floating charge of which particulars have been delivered for registration, and

(b) the taking of such action in exercise of powers conferred by a fixed or floating charge of which particulars have been delivered for registration, or conferred in relation to such a charge by an order of the court, as may be prescribed ...

(3) As regards the consequences of failure to give notice of an event causing a floating charge to crystallise the regulations may include provision to the effect that the crystallisation –

(a) shall be treated as ineffective until the prescribed particulars are delivered, and

(b) if the prescribed particulars are delivered after the expiry of the prescribed period, shall continue to be ineffective against such persons as may be prescribed subject to the exercise of such powers as may be conferred by the regulations on the court.'

7.53 This section which, along with the rest of CA 1989, Part IV of course has never been implemented, may be regarded as recognising the existence of an issue but not deciding how that issue might be resolved. In *Re Bright-life Ltd*[90] Hoffmann J said that the public interest requires a balancing of the advantages to the economy of facilitating the borrowing of money against the

---

Crystallised Floating Charge' (1992) 22 UWALR 430; Tan Cheng Han 'Automatic Crystallisation, De-Crystallisation and Convertibility of Charges' [1998] CFILR 41; and see generally P Ali *The Law of Secured Finance* (OUP, 2002) at pp 127–129.

89 See R Goode *Legal Problems of Credit and Security* (Sweet & Maxwell, 3rd edn, 2003) at pp 180–181. Dr Gough in *Company Charges* (2nd edn, 1996) at p 255 states:

'The chargee under the floating charge which has crystallised into a specific charge may in the event still lose priority to a subsequent specific charge on the grounds of estoppel. To retain priority the floating chargee needs to prove that the subsequent fixed chargee knew of the existence of a previous specific charge, ie prove knowledge by the subsequent chargee of the circumstances in which the prior floating charge would crystallise and that those circumstances had eventuated by the time that he took his charge.'

See also the comments of McGarvie J in the Australian case *Horsburgh v Deputy Commissioner of Taxation* (1984) 54 ALR 397 at 413 who doubted whether 'modern equity would be forced to run in such established grooves that if employees received pay and customers bought goods from a company, while reasonably unaware that the property of the company, had become subject to a fixed equitable charge, they would be losers.'

90 [1987] Ch 200 at 215.

possibility of injustice to unsecured creditors. Parliament seemed unsure as to where the scales should fall. Any regulations were likely to cut down even more on the advantages bestowed by automatic crystallisation clauses, thus making them less attractive to lenders. However, in an earlier consultation exercise, the Department of Trade and Industry pointed out:[91]

> 'Such clauses may often be inserted precisely because neither the chargee nor the company will know at the time that the crystallising event has occurred. A requirement to notify could undermine the reason for such clauses, and, in doing so, prevent potential lenders from offering loans where they might do so now given the protection conferred by automatic crystallisation. Lenders could be deprived of the opportunity for profitable business and companies could be deprived of a means of raising finance.'

PURCHASE MONEY SECURITY INTEREST

7.54 Proposition (17) on the purchase money security interest requires some elucidation. There has been judicial recognition of the concept of a purchase money security interest in England, but this recognition in the main has been confined to cases involving land, although the reasoning employed in the cases is, in principle, applicable in other contexts.[92] The leading authority is now the decision of the House of Lords in *Abbey National v Cann*,[93] but this decision is best understood in the light of the earlier authorities such as *Re Connolly Bros Ltd (No 2)*[94] and *Wilson v Kelland*.[95]

7.55 In *Re Connolly Bros Ltd (No 2)*[96] a company issued debentures creating a floating charge upon their undertaking and all their property, including both present and future property. The debentures contained a condition that the company should not be at liberty to create any other mortgage or charge in priority to the debentures. A couple of years later the company wished to purchase premises but did not have the money for that purpose. Consequently, it borrowed a sum from a purchase money lender to facilitate the acquisition upon terms that the lender should have a charge upon the premises when purchased. The Court of Appeal held that the debenture holders ranked after the purchase money lender on the basis that when the company purported to purchase the premises it, in fact, acquired only an equity of redemption subject to the equitable charge of the purchase money lender. The full ownership of the premises never constituted part of the company's assets insofar as the charge in

---

91 Letter of 7 July 1988.
92 See generally J De Lacy 'The Purchase Money Security Interest: A Company Charge Conundrum?' [1991] LMCLQ 531; 'Retention of Title, Company Charges and the Scintilla Temporis Doctrine' [1994] Conv 242.
93 [1991] 1 AC 56; on which see generally G Goldberg 'Vivit ac Vivat Scintilla Temporis' (1992) 108 LQR 380.
94 [1912] 2 Ch 25.
95 [1910] 2 Ch 306.
96 [1912] 2 Ch 25.

favour of the debenture holders was concerned, for the purchase money lender acquired an interest in the property coincident with its acquisition by the company.[97]

7.56   Another case in point is *Wilson v Kelland*[98] where a vendor of land gave up the lien in respect of the unpaid purchase price in return, inter alia, for a contractual promise of an equitable charge over the property. The subsequently created charge was held to prevail over a floating charge over all the assets, present and future of the company, which was prior in point of time. The raison d'être of the decision was that the company had only acquired an equity of redemption in the property. Any equity which attached to the purchased property in favour of the debenture holders was subject to the paramount equity of the unpaid vendors.

7.57   The problem with many of these old cases is that they turn on quite narrow distinctions rather than on the underlying economic realities.[99] The courts have scrutinised the facts quite minutely to determine whether or not there has been a split second of time (scintilla temporis) in which it could be said that a borrower has been the unencumbered owner of property. If there is such a period of time, however minute, then an earlier security interest extending over the borrower's after-acquired assets will have time to bite and consequently outrank a secured lender whose advance enabled the property in question to be acquired. As Professor Goode has stated:

> '[T]he courts have examined the sequence of operations with meticulous detail to find out whether the debtor's interest in the asset was encumbered at the outset by the purchase-money mortgage (in which case A's after acquired property clause can attach to the asset only in its encumbered form, so that B wins, even if taking with notice of A's security interest) or whether on the other hand there was a moment of time (*scintilla temporis*) in which B was the unincumbered owner of the asset before granting the purchase-money security interest, in which event A's after acquired property clause flashes in to catch the asset seconds before the purchase-money security interest takes effect.'[100]

7.58   In *Abbey National Building Society v Cann*[101] the House of Lords appeared to give wider scope for the recognition of purchase money security interests and by rejecting the doctrine of scintilla temporis. In other words, a purchaser of domestic property who relied on a bank or building society mortgage for completion could not be said to be the unencumbered legal and equitable owner of the property for a split second of time. In the court's view, the acquisition of the legal estate and the charge were not only precisely simultaneous but indissolubly bound up together.[102] In *Cann* it was held that

---

97   [1912] 2 Ch 25 at 31.
98   [1910] 2 Ch 306.
99   But for recognition of the purchase money security interest in Malaysia on the basis of the old English authorities see *United Malayan Banking Corpn v Aluminex* [1993] 3 MLJ 587.
100   *Legal Problems of Credit and Security* (Sweet & Maxwell, 3rd edn, 2003) at p 190.
101   [1991] 1 AC 56.
102   [1991] 1 AC 56 at 92. Lord Oliver pointed out that in many, if not most, cases of building

the interest of a mortgagee whose advance of funds financed the acquisition of the property prevailed over the beneficial interest of somebody who was in actual occupation of the property for a mere half an hour before completion took place. The actual result in the case is hardly surprising, but it is not entirely clear how far the *Cann* case signifies any wider recognition of the purchase money security interest outside the important, but still relatively narrow, confines of domestic conveyancing.[103] All is plain sailing where a purchaser needs a 100% mortgage or a mortgage approaching that level and the reality clearly is that the advance is necessary for completion of the purchase. Different questions arise, however, if the loan is in the nature of a top-up; perhaps the purchaser has ample funds to complete out of his own resources but wishes to obtain a loan merely to smooth over potential financial difficulties. Does the purchase money financier prevail even in this case? The recent decision of the Court of Appeal in *Whale v Viaystems Ltd*[104] does not provide precise answers to these questions, but the case does signify a wider recognition of the concept of a purchase money security interest. Speaking for the Court of Appeal, Jonathan Parker LJ said:[105]

> 'it must now be taken as settled law that, in the context of an issue as to priorities between equitable interests, the court will have regard to the substance, rather than the form of the transaction or transactions which give rise to the competing interests; and in particular that conveyancing technicalities must give way to considerations of commercial and practical reality ... [T]his approach is not limited to cases involving the purchase of a property coupled with the grant of a mortgage or charge to secure repayment of the funds which were required to enable completion of the purchase to take place ... [I]t falls to be adopted generally, in every case where an issue arises as to priority as between equitable interests.'

The court endorsed the sentiments expressed by Professor Goode about 'the inequity that would result in allowing the prior chargee a windfall increase in his security brought about not with the debtor's money or new funds injected by the prior chargee but with financing provided by a later incumbrancer.'[106]

---

society mortgages there will have been formal offer of acceptance of an advance which will ripen into a specifically enforceable agreement immediately the funds are advanced, which will normally be a day or so before completion. Furthermore, under the Land Registration Rules the registrar was entitled to register the charge even before registration of the transfer to the charger if he was satisfied that both were entitled to be registered. In registered land cases the expression 'the legal estate' is used in the sense of an estate which will become legal when registered. See also the comments of Lord Jauncey at 101.

103 According to Professor Goode in *Legal Problems of Credit and Security* (3rd edn, 2003) at p 192 both Lord Jauncey and Lord Oliver seemed to be in no doubt that the priority of the purchase-money charge resulted from the pre-completion agreement for a charge, which fettered the property at the moment of its acquisition. Professor Goode suggests that to secure priority a purchase-money financier must get an agreement for a charge before exchange of contracts.

104 [2002] EWCA Civ 480.

105 [2002] EWCA Civ 480 at [72].

106 *Legal Problems of Credit and Security* (2nd edn, 1988) at pp 99–100; and see now the third edition at pp 190–193.

7.59 There has been a lot of discussion about the theoretical basis for recognising purchase money security interests (PMSIs) in the United States. It has been suggested that the super priority of the PMSI can be thought of as a mechanism which alleviates the situational monopoly created by an after-acquired property clause.[107] The debtor is in a better position to access alternative lending streams and any dependence on the original lender for additional funds is lessened. Another justification rests on the fact that the release of funds by the purchase money creditor increases the debtor's total pool of assets.[108] The debtor is enabled in consequence to acquire new assets as distinct from merely rolling over existing debt. Whereas a security interest granted by the debtor over property that it already owns is potentially harmful to existing creditors, a security interest granted over newly acquired property to secure the price paid for that property is neutral in its effect on existing creditors. The debt incurred to pay for the property is offset by the addition of the property. Moreover, if an earlier creditor could rely on a provision in the instrument of charge that catches after-acquired property to the prejudice of a PMSI holder, the earlier creditor would gain an undeserved windfall, for it was the advance of funds by the later creditor that enabled the property to be acquired.[109] On the other hand, providing privileges to the holder of a PMSI in this manner seems premised on the assumption that the release of funds to facilitate the acquisition of new assets is more valuable to a debtor's business than making advances which enable existing employees to be paid, for example. There is a question mark about whether one of these advances is necessarily of greater social benefit than the other.[110]

7.60 In the United States, under the Uniform Commercial Code, Article 9, there is an exception to the general first to file has priority rule in the case of purchase-money security interests (PMSIs).[111] A purchase-money security interest will rank ahead of a prior security interest with an after-acquired property clause. If a debtor has granted an all-assets security interest that extends over future property then, notwithstanding the general first-to-perfect priority rule, a creditor whose advances funded the acquisition of 'new

---

107   T Jackson and A Kronman 'Secured Financing and Priorities among Creditors' (1979) 88 Yale LJ 1143 at 1171–1178.

108   See also A Schwartz 'The Continuing Puzzle of Secured Debt' (1984) 37 Vanderbilt Law Review 1051 who argues that whereas a general financier takes account of average risk, the PMSI lender may have particular skills and is able to lend on particularly advantageous terms because of its special knowledge of the collateral.

109   See the discussion at para 17.7 of the Diamond report *A Review of Security Interests in Property* (HMSO, 1989); and for a law and economics perspective see H Kanda and S Levmore 'Explaining Creditor Priorities' (1994) 80 Virginia Law Review 2103 at 2138–2141.

110   See WJ Gough *Company Charges* (Butterworths 2nd edn, 1996) at p 436 who argues that credit, as a matter of business need, is 'indivisible in the sense that all business inputs, including wages, overheads, equipment and supplies are all vital to an ongoing business.'

111   Article 9–324 deals with the priority of purchase-money security interests. See generally on this area P Shupack 'Defining Purchase Money Collateral' (1992) 29 Idaho Law Review 767; K Meyer 'A Primer on Purchase Money Security Interests Under Revised Article 9' (2001) 50 Kan LR 143. For an argument against the PMSI super-priority rules see A Schwartz 'A Theory of Loan Priorities' (1989) 18 J Legal Stud 209 at 250–254 who would limit super-priority in inventory and prevent PMSI super-priority in other collateral from trumping secured parties who do not have blanket liens.

property' in the debtor's hands will outrank the earlier financier in respect of the collateral represented by the new property.[112] There is a fairly convoluted definition in Article 9–103 which requires a close nexus between the acquisition of the collateral and the security interest. Basically what is required is the giving of value 'to enable the debtor to acquire rights in or the use of the collateral if the value is in fact so used.' There are, however, special perfection requirements applicable to PMSIs under Article 9 and compliance with these requirements is necessary to obtain super-priority status. Article 9–324 distinguishes between inventory and other goods with a claim to PMSI status in inventory being more difficult to establish. 'Inventory' is defined as meaning goods that are held by a person for sale or lease or that have been leased or that are to be furnished or have been furnished under a contract of service, or that are raw materials, work in progress or materials used or consumed in a business or profession. Article 9–324 lays down quite onerous conditions which must be satisfied before a security interest in inventory can qualify as a PMSI. Basically, before the debtor receives possession of the inventory, the purchase-money secured party must give notice in writing to every other secured party who has already registered a financing statement over the same collateral. The notice is required to state that the person giving it has, or expects to acquire, a purchase-money security interest in inventory of the debtor and also the notice is required to describe the inventory.[113]

7.61   Where capital equipment rather than inventory is concerned, the qualifications necessary for obtaining PMSI status are somewhat less demanding, with automatic super-priority over prior secured lenders gained if the PMSI is registered within 20 days of the debtor acquiring possession of the collateral.[114] In the view of certain commentators:

> 'The rules intimate that the acquisition of new inventory and its associated debt is more threatening to earlier creditors than the debt-financing of new equipment but that debt tied to new inventory is still less threatening than new money unlinked to particular assets.'[115]

---

112 Under Article 9–324(g) the holder of a purchase money security interest that secures the unpaid purchase price of collateral will prevail over the holder of a conflicting purchase money security interest that enables the collateral to be acquired. Translated into English law terms, this means that a retention of title seller has priority over a lender that makes an enabling loan. For criticism of this rule see K Meyer (2001) 50 Kan LR 143 at 188 who points to some possible inconsistency with Article 9–328, which deals with investment property. Priority in investment property is given to the secured party who has control. Article 9–328(2) provides that if two or more secured parties have control, priority is determined by who obtained control first.

113 Article 9–324 Official Comment explains the purpose of the notification requirement as being to protect a non-purchase money inventory secured party which, under an arrangement with the debtor, is typically required to make periodic advances against incoming inventory or periodic releases of old inventory as new inventory is received. If the inventory secured party receives notice it may not make an advance. While the notification requirement is not the same as imposing a consent requirement before a PMSI over inventory can take priority, through the mechanism of an inventory secured party exerting pressure on the debtor it may function in roughly the same way.

114 Article 9–324(a).

115 See H Kanda & S Levmore 'Explaining Creditor Priorities' (1994) 80 Virginia Law Review

SUBORDINATION AGREEMENTS

7.62 Proposition (18) derives from the judgment of the Privy Council in *Cheah v Equiticorp Finance Group Ltd.*[116] Lord Browne-Wilkinson made it clear that where there were two charges over the same property, the chargees could agree to alter the priority of their security interests without the consent of the debtor. He pointed out that in the ordinary case a mortgagor was not affected by the order in which the debts were satisfied. A mortgagor was bound to satisfy all the debts secured on the property before the property could be recovered, and priority of mortgages affected only the rights of the mortgagees inter se, in particular where the security was inadequate to pay all the secured debts in full. Lord Browne-Wilkinson added:[117]

> 'There may be cases (for example where the successive mortgages carry differing rates of interest) where the mortgagor has a genuine interest in ensuring that the debts are satisfied in a particular order. In such a case it will be for the mortgagor to insist upon a specific contractual provision precluding the alteration of the priorities of the mortgages.'

7.63 More generally, there has been an argument that agreements among creditors for the subordination of one debt to another, in particular debt subordination trusts, fall foul of the pari passu principle as applied by the House of Lords in *British Eagle International Airlines Ltd v Cie Nationale Air France.*[118] In *British Eagle* the relevant parties were both members of the International Air Transport Association (IATA), which is an organisation originally incorporated in 1945 by an Act of the Canadian Parliament. IATA operated a clearing-house system for ticket sales by member airlines with all payments being channelled through IATA, so that if one company sold a ticket for a journey but another actually carried the passenger, the former would reimburse the latter through the clearing house. In fact, at the end of an accounting period, all the debits and credits due to transactions during that period were totalled, to arrive at a net figure for the debit or credit of the individual airline as against IATA, in order to avoid multiplicity of payments. British Eagle went into liquidation, being net debtors towards IATA in respect of services provided by the other airlines to them, but in credit as against Air France. The liquidator was of the opinion that the clearing house arrangements were not binding on him. Air France, on the other hand, claimed that by virtue

---

2103 at 2139; and see generally M Bridge, R Macdonald, R Simmonds and C Walsh 'Formalism, Functionalism and Understanding the Law of Secured Transactions' (1999) 44 McGill LJ at fns 99–108.

116 [1992] 1 AC 472. See generally E Ferran 'Subordination of Secured and Unsecured Debt' in *Company Law and Corporate Finance* (OUP, 1999) chapter 16; R Nolan 'Less Equal than Others' [1995] JBL 485. Under Article 9, however, there is nothing to prevent a secured party from giving up priority, whether voluntarily or in a contractual arrangement. Indeed, Article 9–339 expressly validates subordination agreements, stating that this Article does not preclude subordination by a person entitled to priority. As the Official Comment points out, however, only the person entitled to priority may make such a subordination agreement – a security interest holder's rights cannot be adversely affected by an agreement to which the person is not a party.

117 [1992] 1 AC 472 at 477.

118 [1975] 1 WLR 758; [1975] 2 All ER 390.

of the clearing house they owed nothing to the British Eagle liquidator. Air France contended that any net balances owed by airlines in respect of services provided for them by British Eagle should be applied in reduction of the net amount owed by British Eagle in respect of services provided by other airlines for it and that it was for the clearing house to submit a proof in the liquidation for the net deficiency.

7.64   The House of Lords, by a majority, held that Air France was bound to pay the British Eagle liquidator. It was held that for Air France to pay money to IATA for distribution to airlines that were creditors of British Eagle under the IATA scheme was repugnant to the principle of pari passu distribution of an insolvent's property. This would have result in making the airlines owed money by British Eagle into secured creditors; to the extent that the money paid by Air France could satisfy their debts they would be paid in full, instead of being obliged to prove in British Eagle's liquidation and receive the same dividend as other unsecured creditors. The provisions of the IATA scheme were contrary to public policy and it was irrelevant that the parties to the clearing house arrangements had sound business reasons for entering into them and did not direct their minds to the question how the arrangements might be affected by the insolvency of one or more of the parties.[119]

7.65   Lord Cross cited the observations of James LJ in *Ex parte Mackay*[120] to the effect that a man is not allowed, by stipulation with a creditor, to provide for a distribution of his effects in the event of bankruptcy different from that which the law provides. According to Lord Cross, the 'clearing house' creditors were clearly not secured creditors. They were claiming nevertheless that they ought not to be treated in the liquidation as ordinary unsecured creditors, but that they had achieved by the medium of the 'clearing house' agreement a position analogous to that of secured creditors without the need for the creation and registration of charges on the book debts in question.[121] Lord Cross rejected the proposition that the power of the court to go behind agreements, the results of which were repugnant to the insolvency legislation, was confined to cases in which the parties' dominant purpose was to evade its operation. Of course, as Professor RM Goode has pointed out,[122] the crucial question in *British Eagle* was whether its debtor was Air France or IATA. If IATA was creditor of the debtor airlines and the debtor of the creditor airlines,

---

119   [1975] 2 All ER 390 at 411 per Lord Cross. The majority in *British Eagle* consisted of Lords Cross, Diplock and Edmund-Davies. There were strong dissents from Lords Morris and Simon. Lord Morris said that because of the terms of the contracts British Eagle had no claims against, and no rights to sue, other individual members of the clearing house. It was a general rule that a liquidator takes no better title to property than that which was possessed by the insolvent company. The liquidator in the present case could not be allowed to remould contracts that had been validly made. Lord Simon suggested that British Eagle had long since deprived itself of the right to claim from Air France payment for the interline services which British Eagle had performed for Air France. No party to the interline agreement had any right to claim direct payment for interline service. It merely had the right to have the value of such service respectively credited and debited in the monthly IATA clearing house settlement account.

120   (1873) 8 Ch App 643 at 647.

121   [1975] 2 All ER 390 at 410–411.

122   *Principles of Corporate Insolvency Law* (Sweet & Maxwell, 2nd edn, 1997) at p 182.

then it would have been entitled to combine British Eagle's credit balance on the Air France account with its debits on the account with the creditor airlines. If, however, IATA acted merely as an agent of the airlines in operating a clearing mechanism, then, at the commencement of winding up, British Eagle had a claim against Air France which could not legitimately be the subject of a set-off with regard to claims by other airlines against British Eagle.

7.66   Peter Gibson J in *Carreras Rothmans Ltd v Freemans Mathews Treasure Ltd*[123] suggested that *British Eagle* was authority for a wide proposition, namely that:[124]

'... where the effect of a contract is that an asset which is actually owned by a company at the commencement of its liquidation would be dealt with in a way other than in accordance with [the pari passu principle], then to that extent the contract as a matter of public policy is avoided, whether or not

---

123   [1985] Ch 207.
124   [1985] Ch 207 at 226. In *Money Markets International Stockbrokers Ltd v London Stock Exchange Ltd* [2002] 1 WLR 1150 at [118] Neuberger J suggested that one could extract the following rather limited propositions from the cases:
   '1. A person cannot validly arrange his affairs so that what is already his own property becomes subject to being taken away in the event of his insolvency;
   2. Subject to [1] ..., the transfer of an asset for an interest coming to an end on the transferee's insolvency (or on some other event) is apparently effective even if the transferee is insolvent;
   3. Subject to [4–10] ..., the transfer of an asset on the condition that the asset will revest in the transferor in the event of the transferee's insolvency is generally invalid;
   4. A proviso in a lease for determination, ie for forfeiture or re-entry, even in the event of the lessee becoming insolvent, is enforceable where the lessee is insolvent;
   5. In deciding whether a deprivation provision exerciseable other than on insolvency offends against the principle, one is primarily concerned with the effect of the provision and not with the intention of the parties, but it may be that, if the deprivation provision is exerciseable for reasons which are not concerned with the owner's insolvency, default or breach, then its operation will not be within the principle;
   6. However, if the intention of the parties when agreeing the deprivation provision was to evade the insolvency rules, then that may invalidate a provision ..., and if the intention of the parties was not to evade the insolvency laws, the court will be more ready to uphold the deprivation provision if it provides for compensation for the deprivation;
   7. The court will scrutinise with particular care a deprivation provision which would have the effect of preferring the person to whom the asset reverts or passes, as against other unsecured creditors of the insolvent person whose estate is deprived of the asset ...;
   8. Where the deprivation provision relates to an asset which has no value, or which is incapable of transfer, or which depends on the character or status of the owner, then it will normally be enforceable on insolvency;
   9. A deprivation provision ... may be held to be valid if the asset concerned is closely connected with or, more probably, subsidiary to, a right or other benefit in respect of which a deprivation provision is valid;
   10. If the deprivation provision does not offend against the principle then [generally] ... it will be enforceable against a trustee in bankruptcy or on a liquidation just as much as it would have been enforceable in the absence of an insolvency.'
See also *Fraser v Oystertec* [2004] BPIR 486; on which see Look Chan Ho [2004] JIBLR 54.

the contract is entered into for consideration and for *bona fide* commercial reasons and whether or not the contractual provision affecting that asset is expressed to take effect only on insolvency.'

7.67 Debt subordination agreements were, however, upheld by Vinelott J in *Re Maxwell Communications Corpn plc (No 2)*.[125] Here a company, Maxwell Finance Jersey (MFJ), issued convertible bonds which were guaranteed by another company, MCC, under a guarantee which provided that MCC's liability to the bondholders was subordinated to MCC's liabilities to other unsecured creditors. In other words, if MCC became insolvent, the rights of the bondholders to the MCC were subordinated to all other unsecured liabilities owed by MCC. The guarantee stipulated that payments under the guarantee were to be made to a Swiss bank, SBC, on behalf of the MFJ bondholders. The guarantee and the subordination agreement were expressed to be subject to Swiss law, which did not recognise trusts. Vinelott J held that the subordination agreement was a valid contract. He took the view that since a creditor could waive his debt or decline to submit to proof, there was no reason why he should not, prior to any insolvency proceedings, agree to subordinate his claim to that of other creditors in the event of the debtor company's insolvency. On this analysis, the pari passu principle precluded a creditor from obtaining some advantage in the winding up of a company to which insolvency principles did not entitle him. Subordination, however, did not undermine that principle in any way. The *British Eagle* decision was read restrictively. Essentially, it was relegated to the realm of cases decided on its special facts.[126] This is in line with the view of one commentator that all that the *British Eagle* case decided was that a creditor cannot, after the insolvency, walk into the insolvent's house and help himself to the furniture. This proposition is as ancient as the bankruptcy laws themselves.[127]

7.68 Reference was made by Vinelott J to the decision of Southwell J in the Australian case *Horne v Chester & Fein Property Developments Pty Ltd*,[128] where it was held that the legislative provisions governing distribution of a company's assets on insolvency did not require that, in all cases, a liquidator must distribute assets pari passu amongst creditors. The liquidator might distribute in accordance with an agreement between the parties where to do so could not adversely affect any creditor not a party to the agreement. Southwell J recognised that it was a general principle of insolvency law that the whole of a debtor's estate should be available for distribution to all creditors and that

---

125 [1994] 1 All ER 737. On this decision see R Nolan [1995] JBL 485. See also *Re SSSL Realisations (2002) Ltd* [2004] EWHC 1760 where Lloyd J suggested that the effect of a subordination agreement did not involve the diversion of an asset of the junior creditor, but rather its suppression by subordination. Note too the comments of Look Chan Ho on this case in 'A Matter of Contractual and Trust Subordination' [2004] JIBLR 494 at 499: 'Decades of concern over the British Eagle/pari passu violation is in fact a schism over an ism that is now an anachronism.'

126 [1994] 1 All ER 737 at 749.

127 See P Wood *The Law of Subordinated Debt* (1990) at 25.

128 [1987] VR 913; [1987] ACLR 245.

no one creditor or group of creditors could lawfully contract in such a manner as to defeat other creditors not parties to the contract. This principle was not contravened, however, where the performance of an agreement between various parties could not affect the entitlement of creditors who were not parties to the agreement.[129]

7.69   Vinelott J in *Maxwell* considered the House of Lords decision in *National Westminster Bank Ltd v Halesowen Presswork and Assemblies Ltd*,[130] where it was held that the statutory regime of set-off applicable to insolvent companies was imperative. In other words, persons who had dealing dealings with an insolvent company could not validly contract out of the statutory set-off provisions. Vinelott J distinguished this case on the basis that the rationale underlining the set-off regime was one of public policy rather than private rights which, in his view, was the basis of the pari passu doctrine. The judge drew attention to the inconvenience and potential unfairness to the liquidator and to other creditors that might arise if a creditor was entitled either to exercise or, at his option, not to exercise the right of set-off. He said:[131]

> 'An agreement between the debtor and the creditor excluding the creditor's right of set-off, or the waiver by the creditor of his right of set-off, even after the commencement of the bankruptcy or winding up, might thus equally hinder the rapid, efficient and economical process of bankruptcy.'

7.70   More recently, the House of Lords in *Stein v Blake*[132] echoed the same view and endorsed the observations of Lord Simon in *National Westminster Bank Ltd v Halesowen Presswork and Assemblies Ltd*[133] that bankruptcy set-off was part of a 'code of procedure whereby bankrupts' estates ... are to be administered in a proper and orderly way.' In other words, the statutory regime of set-off, unlike the pari passu principle, is based on considerations of public policy rather than on private rights that parties are competent to waive.

---

129   See also the observations of FB Adams J in the New Zealand Supreme Court case *Re Walker Construction Co Ltd* [1960] NZLR 523 at 536:
> '[A]s the statutory requirement of pari passu payment does not rest on considerations of public policy, but is a matter of private right to which the maxim quilibet potest renunciare juri pro se introducto [anyone may, at his pleasure, renounce the benefit of a stipulation or other right introduced in his own favour] may properly be applied.'

130   [1972] AC 785. Note the following less than prophetic observations of RM Goode in *Legal Problems of Credit and Security* (2nd edn, 1988) at 96–97 on the Australian *Horne* decision:
> 'English courts, however, will almost certainly consider that priority agreements are governed by the same principles as agreements excluding set-off and that they are bound by the House of Lords decisions to rule that such agreements must be disregarded by a trustee or liquidator in distributing the assets.'

See now Legal Problems of Credit and Security (3rd edn, 2003) at p 187.

131   [1994] 1 All ER 737 at 746.
132   [1996] AC 243.
133   [1972] AC 785 at 809.

COMPETING ASSIGNMENTS OF RECEIVABLES

7.71 Priorities between competing assignments of receivables is determined by the application of the rule in *Dearle v Hall*,[134] which states that if a second or subsequent assignee has no notice of a prior assignment at the time of the second or subsequent assignment,[135] then the subsequent assignee can gain priority by being the first to notify the debtor of the assignment. If, however, the second assignee has notice, whether actual or constructive, of the earlier assignment at the time of the second assignment, then the first assignment has priority on a first-in-time basis.[136] It appears that the rule applies to assignments by way of charges but, in this context, the fact of registration should give the second chargee constructive notice of the earlier charge and thus determine the priority question.

7.72 Two rationales have been stated for the rule and both of these rationales derive a measure of support from the case itself. One view sees the giving of notice as tantamount to taking possession of a tangible asset. Another view sees the rule as being based on the prevention of fraud. In *Dearle v Hall* Plumer MR suggested that the omission to give notice enabled the assignor to 'carry the same security repeatedly into the market' and thereby to induce 'third persons to advance money upon it in the erroneous belief that it continues to belong to him absolutely, free from encumbrance.'

7.73 The rule has been widely condemned as an unsatisfactory determinant of priorities in the context of receivables financing.[137] Non-notification factoring is quite common and the priority principle in *Dearle v Hall* works to the

---

134 (1828) 3 Russ 1. See R Goode *Commercial Law* (Penguin, 3rd edn, 2004) at pp 652–653:
'It is high time that the rule in *Dearle v Hall* was abolished ... [It] is quite impracticable when applied to a continuous flow of dealings in receivables involving a substantial number of debtors ... The rule is effectively displaced where the previous security or assignment is registrable and is duly registered, for the second assignee is then fixed with notice of the previous assignment, and if registration were to be extended to cover all assignments of pure intangibles, whether outright or by way of security, *Dearle v Hall* would de facto become obsolete.'

135 According to Cotton LJ in *Mutual Life Assurance Society v Langley* (1886) 32 Ch D 460 at 468: 'It is not a question of what a man knows, when he does that which will better or perfect his security, but what he knows at the time when he took his security and paid his money.'

136 J De Lacy, however, argues in (1999) 28 Anglo-American Law Review 87 at 130 that:
'the courts should now reject the existence of the second limb to the rule in *Dearle v Hall*. There is neither principle nor, substantive precedent, in the way of acting on this conclusion. Although it is possible that a court of first instance might not find this recommendation at all palatable, given the long history of the second limb, the Appeal Courts should not entertain similar reservations. In future *Dearle v Hall* should be confined to a simple priority rule according to the dates upon which notice of assignments is received by a fund holder.'

137 See Report of the Crowther Committee on Consumer Credit (1971) Cmnd 4596, vol 2 at p 579; J Ziegel 'The Legal Problems of Wholesale Financing of Durable Goods in Canada' (1963) 41 Canadian Bar Review 54 at 109–110; R Goode (1976) 92 LQR 528 at 566; F Oditah (1989) 9 OJLS 521 at 525–527.

disadvantage of this form of business arrangement. Moreover, the rule transforms notice of the assignment to the debtor into a priority point, but the debtor is not a publicly commissioned official charged with the task of receiving and tracking notices.[138] It may be argued that requiring notice to be filed in a public register is a more logically coherent way of sorting out priorities.[139] Determining the rank of assignments according to the order in which each is publicised by registration would enable the later assignees to work out more efficiently a fair purchase price for the receivables, or the legal and operational risks of the transaction, as the case may be.[140]

CONCLUSION

7.74 It has been suggested that the question of priority between competing security interests over the same property is the area of the law of security interests that is most in need of reform.[141] A number of factors bear on the priority question, including time of registration, fact of registration, notice or otherwise of prior security interests and whether or not the security interest is fixed or floating. Nevertheless, the basic principle is that the first to be created has priority, and not the first to be registered, although non-registration of most charges renders them void. Moreover, registration can impart notice to subsequent interest holders and in this way bring an exception to the first in time principle into play. While the priority principles may be complicated, and seem to lack a rational economic basis, they are generally understood by practitioners and any adverse effects can always be mitigated by a priority agreement amongst charge holders. Practitioners have cautioned against assuming that it is easy to provide a better alternative to the current system:

---

138 F Oditah (1989) 9 OJLS 521 at 525–527 advances eight considerations in support of the proposition that the rule is harsh, hard to justify and decidedly inconvenient.

139 J De Lacy comments in (1999) 28 Anglo-American Law Review 197 at 214 that:
'the rule in *Dearle v Hall* is no longer suitable to meet the requirements of information and priority in an efficient or satisfactory manner. The only effective solution to this problem is to replace the fund holder with a centralised public register onto which information regarding assignments could be stored. This would solve the problem relating to the quality and objectivity of a fund holder that, at present, besets the operation of the rule. The establishment of a centralised register should also be coupled with a priority rule according to the date that assignments are registered. This would produce a simple and readily ascertainable priority point free of any issue relating to the doctrine of notice.'

140 See C Walsh 'Registration, Constructive Notice and the Rule in *Dearle v Hall*' (1997) 12 Banking & Finance Law Review 129; and see also M Bridge, R Macdonald, R Simmonds and C Walsh 'Functionalism, Formalism and Understanding the Law of Secured Transactions' at fns 49–56; and D Baird 'Security Interests Reconsidered' (1994) 80 Virginia Law Review 2249 at 2267–69.

141 See 'Registration of Security Interests' – response of the City of London Law Society to the Law Commission on their Consultation Paper No 164 (*Registration of Security Interests: Company Charges and Property other than Land*) at p 19.

'There is no straightforward answer to the question of which of ... two innocent parties should take priority; and the paucity of recent cases on priorities is some evidence of the fact that these problems do not arise very frequently in practice.'[142]

---

142 'Registration of Security Interests' at p 20.

Chapter 8

COMPANY CHARGE REGISTRATION AND OVERSEAS COMPANIES

INTRODUCTION

8.1   Section 409 of the Companies Act 1985 applies the provisions of the Act relating to registration of charges on property in England and Wales to charges created by a company incorporated outside Great Britain which had an established place of business in England and Wales. What is the rationale for requiring registration of charges created by overseas companies? The following justification was proffered by Stephen J in an Australian case *Luckins v Highway Motel Pty Ltd.*[1] He said:[2]

> 'It is not unreasonable that a mortgagee relying for his security on a floating charge over movables or over assets to be acquired by the mortgagor in the future should ensure that whatever State in the future those assets move to or be located in his charge is there registered so that those who may deal with the mortgagor can ascertain its true position as to encumbrances over assets.'

THE RELATIONSHIP BETWEEN REGISTRATION UNDER CA 1985, s 409 AND UNDER s 691

8.2   Section 691 of the Companies Act 1985 provides that where a company incorporated outside Great Britain establishes a place of business in Great Britain, it shall within one month of doing so deliver various documents to the registrar of companies for registration. Such a company incorporated outside Great Britain is referred to in the legislation as an oversea company. If an oversea company fails to comply with the obligation contained in s 691, the company, and every officer or agent of the company who knowingly and wilfully authorises or permits the default is liable to a fine.[3] The relationship (or lack of relationship) between ss 409 and 691 was considered by Lloyd J in *NV Slavenburg's Bank v Intercontinental Natural Resources Ltd.*[4]

---

1   (1975) 50 ALJR 309; on which see D Milman (1979) 123 Solicitors' Journal 560.
2   (1975) 50 ALJR 309 at 318.
3   Section 697. Sections 691 and 697 are in Part XXIII of the Companies Act 1985.
4   [1980] 1 WLR 1076. On this decision see generally D Milman (1981) 125 Solicitors' Journal 294.

8.3   *Slavenburg* was concerned with a company incorporated in Bermuda that dealt in oil and petroleum products. The company was not registered as an overseas company in England but had an established place of business there. The company went into liquidation and the Bermuda liquidators claimed a floating charge over assets in England was void because particulars had not been submitted to the registrar for registration. The assets had only been brought to England subsequent to the creation of the charge. Moreover, the charge, written in the Dutch language, had been granted to a Dutch bank and was governed by Dutch law. Nevertheless Lloyd J held that the charge was caught by the avoidance provisions in the Companies Act. The fact that the Bermudan company had not been registered in England as an oversea company under s 691 was immaterial. Reference was made in *Slavenburg* to the Companies House practice of not accepting particulars of a charge submitted for registration under s 407 unless the company itself had registered as an oversea company under s 691. Were charge holders to be penalised for this practice on the part of the registrar? Lloyd J felt, however, that there was nothing in the submission. The crucial fact was delivery of particulars of a charge for registration rather than actual registration. Once particulars had been delivered, the charge holder escaped the clutches of the avoidance machinery.[5] In support of this conclusion the learned judge cited dicta from *National Provincial and Union Bank of England v Charnley*.[6] In the latter case Scrutton LJ said, after looking at the language of the section: 'That makes the avoidance depend on the neglect to send in the particulars. The neglect to register the charge will not make it void.'[7]

8.4   Some criticism has been levelled at the *Slavenburg* decision. The judgment may have been in line with decided cases on an analogous point but, nevertheless, one might ask, what is the raison d'être in establishing a public registration system for company charges when the law recognises that a charge remains valid when details of it have been incorrectly recorded or even not recorded at all? It is harsh to expect a searcher to go to the trouble of checking the instrument of charge at the company's own registered office, and this is not easily done in the case of an overseas company. Although the *Slavenburg* decision may be correct as a matter of statutory interpretation, it has generated a number of difficulties.[8] As one commentator remarks:[9]

> 'Because it is difficult – if not impossible – to be certain that a given charger does or does not have an established place of business in England, the usual practice is to seek to register all "registrable" charges given by non-UK companies ... Any such attempted registration will be rejected by a polite letter from Companies House which will nevertheless record the particulars of the "*Slavenburg* registration" in a special register!'

---

5   [1980] 1 WLR 1076 at 1086.

6   [1924] 1 KB 431.

7   [1924] 1 KB 431 at 447.

8   See generally Howard Bennett 'Registration of Company Charges' in J Armour and H Bennett (eds) *Vulnerable Transactions in Corporate Insolvency* (Hart Publishing, 2003) 217 at pp 268–272.

9   See M Hughes 'Taking Security: Some Dilemmas and Dichotomies' [2001] 16 Butterworths Journal of International Banking and Financial Law 498 at 502.

8.5   The Companies House practice is not to enter on the charges register details of charges created by overseas companies that have failed to fulfil their obligation to register under CA 1985, s 691. On the other hand, Companies House will acknowledge delivery of particulars and then enter these in the so-called Slavenburg index which is an alphabetical list of companies that have delivered particulars in this way.

ESTABLISHED PLACE OF BUSINESS

8.6   In determining whether or not CA 1985, s 409 applies it is necessary to ascertain in a particular case whether a company has an 'established place of business' within the jurisdiction. The legislation talks about an 'established place of business' rather than carrying on business. Some early guidance as to the meaning of the phrase an 'established place of business' was provided by Lord Dunedin in the Scottish case of *Lord Advocate v Huron and Erie Loan and Savings Co.*[10] He said:[11]

> 'The expression "carrying on business" is so wide that it would really touch all persons having business in the United Kingdom – a result from which the Legislature may well have shrunk ... I therefore, in my judgment, merely look at the expression as it is used. That expression seems to me clearly to point to this, that the Company must have what I may call a local habitation of its own. I do not wish to say more, because I do not think that exact definition is at all a profitable pursuit; in fact, it always leads one into this trouble that one deserts the words which Parliament has used and substitutes others ...'

8.7   More light on the issue was shone by Oliver LJ in *Re Oriel Ltd.*[12] He suggested that 'when the word "established" is used adjectively ... it connotes not only the setting up of a place of business at a specific location but a degree of permanence or recognisability as being a location of the company's business.'[13] He also said that carrying on business was not synonymous with having an established place of business. The latter implied something more. A company, however need not necessarily own or even lease its 'established place of business'. The case concerned an Isle of Man company which had established seven petrol stations in Lancashire and then created charges over thee properties in favour of an oil company. The Court of Appeal held that three of the seven charges were registrable since it was only when they had been created that the company had an 'established place of business' in England. There was then in existence a permanent location at least associated with the company and from which habitually or with some degree of regularity business was conducted.[14]

---

10   1911 SC 612.
11   1911 SC 612 at 616.
12   [1986] 1 WLR 180.
13   [1986] 1 WLR 180 at 184.
14   See also *Deverall v Grant Advertising Inc* [1955] Ch 111.

8.8 Another case in point is *Cleveland Museum of Art v Capricorn International SA*.[15] Here Hirst J applied *Re Oriel Ltd* and held that, to show an established place of business, there had to be a specific location associated with the company from which it habitually or regularly carried on business. He also said that a visible sign or physical indication of a connection was not necessary but was simply a factor to be brought into the reckoning. Moreover, the learned judge stated that the section assumes that there is going to be some readily identifiable point of view at which it can be said that a company has established a place of business in the jurisdiction, because of the obligations imposed to deliver documents and make returns by a specified date.

8.9 In its reference to establishing a place of business, the wording of CA 1985, s 691 is practically identical to that of s 409. In *Rakusens Ltd v Baser* Arden LJ said:[16]

'It is important to note that section 691 uses the words establishes a place of business. It does not impose obligations on an overseas company which simply carries on business here. That the obligations are hinged upon establishing a place of business, and not on the carrying on of business, must be seen as a deliberate choice by Parliament. If Parliament had imposed the obligations in section 691 on an overseas company which merely carried on business here, the registration obligations would have been extremely wide in their applicaton.'

8.10 Ferris J amplified these points in *Matchnet plc v William Blair & Co Llc*.[17] He stated:[18]

'it is demonstrated that the question whether a company has established a place of business in Great Britain is essentially one of fact. The authorities also show that it is not enough that the company carries on business in the United Kingdom: it is possible for a company to carry on business in the United Kingdom without having a place of business here. Nor is it enough for the company to carry on business through an agent or subsidiary. Normally an agent or subsidiary is carrying on its own business. What has to be shown in every case is that the business which is carried on at the relevant location is the business of the company itself.'

STANDING TO INVOKE CA 1985, s 395 ON THE NON-REGISTRATION POINT

8.11 A second issue arising from *NV Slavenburg's Bank v Intercontinental Natural Resources Ltd* concerned the entitlement of the liquidator in a foreign winding up to plead the non-registration point. Lloyd J accepted that the primary meaning of the phrase 'liquidator' in the company charge registration provisions was a liquidator in an English winding up. Nevertheless, the term

---

15   [1990] BCLC 546.
16   [2002] 1 BCLC 104; [2001] EWCA Civ 1820 at pp 6–7 of the transcript.
17   [2003] 2 BCLC 195; [2002] EWHC 2128.
18   [2002] EWHC 2128 at p 2 of the transcript.

could be applied to a liquidator in a foreign winding up where those proceedings were conducted on similar lines to a winding up in this jurisdiction. The judge surmised that it could not be the intention of parliament that there should always be an English winding up before the charge avoidance provisions were operable for the benefit of unsecured creditors.[19] Viewed in the light of *Smith v Bridgend County Borough Council*,[20] the *Slavenburg* decision means that an overseas company in foreign insolvency proceedings that are the equivalent of liquidation or administration is entitled to invoke s 395. What foreign proceedings may be regarded as the equivalents of liquidation or administration may present problems in a particular case, though these difficulties are alleviated in the case of EC countries that are subject to the European Regulation on Insolvency Proceedings,[21] where Appendix 3 of the Regulation sets out a list of equivalent procedures.

ASSETS BROUGHT TO THE JURISDICTION AFTER THE CREATION OF THE CHARGE

8.12   Another problem with the *Slavenburg* judgment is the little matter of after-acquired assets or assets brought to the jurisdiction after a charge has been created. If an overseas company with an established place of business in the jurisdiction creates a charge, but there are no assets subject to the charge in the jurisdiction, then it appears the charge is not registrable. If, however, the company acquires assets subject to the charge in the jurisdiction more than 21 days after the date of creation of the charge or such assets are brought here after that time, it seems that the charges become registrable. But the time for registration – 21 days from the date of the charge's creation – has long since expired, so that the obligation is one impossible of fulfilment, though an application might be made to the court under CA 1985, s 404 for late registration of the charge. Another commentator suggests, however, that:

> 'all requirements for the application of section 409(1) to a charge must be considered by reference to the time of creation of the charge. A company that establishes a place of business in England and Wales after the creation of a charge on property in England and Wales does not have to register that charge under section 395(1). Similarly, whether the charge falls within section 409(1) by reason of the location of charged property should also be judged at the time of creation of the charge.'

REFORM PROPOSALS

8.13   The Companies Act 1989 contained a new set of provisions dealing with the registration of charges created by oversea companies. The 1989 Act also

---

19   [1980] 1 WLR 1076 at 1086–1087. The judge pointed out that there was nothing express to that effect and there was no reason why any such limitation should be implied.
20   [2002] 1 AC 336.
21   Council Regulation (EC) 1346/2000, OJ L160/1.

proposed far more detailed measures dealing with charges on assets of oversea companies. These provisions may be summarised as follows:[22]

(1)   Charges were registrable only if the company had registered as an oversea company under CA 1985, s 691 and has not given notice under s 696(4) that it has ceased to have a place of business in either part of Great Britain. Thus, the so-called 'Slavenburg register' was scrapped.

(2)   When a company registered under s 691, it was obliged to submit details of registrable charges over any of its assets in the jurisdiction to the registrar. Failure to do so, however, did not result in the avoidance of the charge, but only gave rise to the possibility of a fine.

(3)   The obligation to register applied only where a company created a charge on property (including future property) within the jurisdiction or acquired property subject to a registrable charge. Moreover, the obligation did not apply if the property at the end of the 21-day period was no longer within the jurisdiction. It is questionable whether many lenders would have availed of this exception given the fact that the property may still be within Great Britain at the expiry of the 21-day period but the time for registration has expired. Failure to register a charge created by a company means avoidance of the charge as well as a fine. Failure to register a charge on property acquired means only a fine. Some guidance is provided in the legislation as to the situation of property. A charge on future property is treated as situated in Great Britain unless it related exclusively to property of a kind which could not, after being acquired or coming into existence, be situated here. A ship, aircraft or hovercraft were treated as being located in Great Britain if registered in Great Britain. Other vehicles were regarded as being situated in Great Britain if the management of the vehicle is directed from a place of business of the company in Great Britain.

(4)   Where a registered oversea company brought property subject to a registrable charge to the jurisdiction and kept it there for a continuous period of four months, there was a duty to submit particulars for registration. The omission to do so had as its consequence avoidance of the charge as well as a fine.[23] It should be stressed that the period for registration was four months from the arrival of the property rather than 21 days from the date of creation of the charge.

8.14   The Department of Trade and Industry recognised that the proposed legislative reforms were not a perfect solution to the issues brought into focus by the *Slavenburg* judgment.[24] In particular, a company which had failed to register under CA 1985, s 691, or which traded here but had no established place of business, was outside the ambit of the registration system. As Professor Diamond pointed out, while this might be a regrettable gap in the registration provisions, if it was known to exist it could be taken into account by those concerned.[25]

---

22   The suggested charges are contained in Companies Act 1989, s 105, Sch 15, which proposed to insert a new Chapter III into Part XXIII of the Companies Act 1985.
23   CA 1985, s 703D(3) and (5), and s 703F(3).
24   Consultative letter of 2 September 1987, para 4.2.
25   A Diamond *A Review of Security Interests in Property* (HMSO, 1989) p 133, fn 3. It should be

8.15   Where the Companies Act departed dramatically from the Diamond scheme was in relation to assets of a registered oversea company subject to a registrable charge brought to the jurisdiction after the creation of a charge. Professor Diamond reasoned that the charge would have to remain valid to prevent prejudice to a foreign creditor who might be quite unaware that property subject to the charge had been brought into the country.[26] He mentioned the possibility of a fine on the company, but on the other hand since the bringing of foreign property into Great Britain would be regarded as a commercial activity, not a legal one, it was unlikely that lawyers would be consulted. Initially, the view favoured by the Department of Trade and Industry was to render the company concerned liable to criminal sanctions,[27] but in the legislation the civil sanction of voidness was added.[28] Certain other impracticalities and incongruities in the new legislative machinery proposed in the Companies Act 1989 have been pointed out.[29] It is submitted that the legislation did not achieve the desirable goals of equity, clarity, efficiency and ease of operation, and for these reasons its non-implementation in its original form was no bad thing.

8.16   More recently, the Law Commission have returned to the fray and recommended that security interests created by foreign companies over their assets in England and Wales should be subject to the proposed notice filing regime.[30] This recommendation is highly controversial, for in the initial 2002 Consultation Paper it was suggested limiting the scheme to those companies

---

noted that a registered oversea company was defined in the new s 703A(3) as an oversea company which had duly delivered documents to the registrar of companies under s 691 (s 703A(3)). Therefore, a person taking a charge over property from a company which would be registrable if that company was a registered oversea company had to be conscious of the fact that a company search might not be conclusive. The charge might in fact be registrable because of the time lag between the delivery of documents and actual registration of the company as an oversea company.

26   Diamond Report at p 134.
27   Consultative letter of 2 September 1988, para 4.1.
28   It has been strongly argued that the four-month rule is a major difficulty for a lender taking security over movable property of a registered oversea company situated outside Great Britain: see E Ferran and C Mayo [1991] JBL 152 at 168. The lender might require the company to covenant not to bring the property into Great Britain, or at least to notify the lender if it does so. Alternatively, the company might be required to move the property back outside Great Britain before the fourth-month period has elapsed. Apart from this, however, there is little that a lender can do to protect itself. The possibility of precautionary filing appears to have been foreclosed by the pertinent provisions which stipulated for the avoidance of a charge if the prescribed particulars are not delivered within the continuous period of four months when the property is in Great Britain. Delivery of particulars before the outset of this four-month period might have been ineffectual.
29   For a development of these points see G McCormack *Registration of Company Charges* (1st edn, 1994) at pp 155–156.
30   *Company Security Interests: A consultative report* (TSO, 2004) at para 3.372.

that had registered a place of business.[31] Consultees were unanimously in favour of this approach, but the Law Commission had a subsequent change of heart stating:[32]

> 'We do not think that a scheme that applied only to companies with places of business here would offer sufficient protection to buyers or potential secured parties. We also suspect that modern business methods may enable companies to operate in the UK on quite a large scale without having a "place of business" here, for example, if their goods are stored with third parties.'

---

31   *Registration of Security Interests* (Consultation Paper No 164) at pp 152–154, where there is a justification of the original proposals.
32   *Company Security Interests* at para 3.367.

Appendix 1

COMPANIES ACT 1985, PART XII

Part XII
Registration of Charges

Chapter I
Registration of Charges (England and Wales)

395 Certain charges void if not registered

(1) Subject to the provisions of this Chapter, a charge created by a company registered in England and Wales and being a charge to which this section applies is, so far as any security on the company's property or undertaking is conferred by the charge, void against the liquidator and any creditor of the company, unless the prescribed particulars of the charge together with the instrument (if any) by which the charge is created or evidenced, are delivered to or received by the registrar of companies for registration in the manner required by this Chapter within 21 days after the date of the charge's creation.

(2) Subsection (1) is without prejudice to any contract or obligation for repayment of the money secured by the charge; and when a charge becomes void under this section, the money secured by it immediately becomes payable.

396 Charges which have to be registered

(1) Section 395 applies to the following charges—

    (a)   a charge for the purpose of securing any issue of debentures,
    (b)   a charge on uncalled share capital of the company,
    (c)   a charge created or evidenced by an instrument which, if executed by an individual, would require registration as a bill of sale,
    (d)   a charge on land (wherever situated) or any interest in it, but not including a charge for any rent or other periodical sum issuing out of the land,
    (e)   a charge on book debts of the company,
    (f)   a floating charge on the Company's undertaking or property,
    (g)   a charge on calls made but not paid,
    (h)   a charge on a ship or aircraft, or any share in a ship,
    (j)   a charge on goodwill.

(2) Where a negotiable instrument has been given to secure the payment of any book debts of a company, the deposit of the instrument for the purpose of securing an advance to the company is not, for purposes of section 395, to be treated as a charge on those book debts.

(3)   The holding of debentures entitling the holder to a charge on land is not for purposes of this section deemed to be an interest in land.

(4)   In this Chapter, 'charge' includes mortgage.

397 Formalities of registration (debentures)

(1)   Where a series of debentures containing, or giving by reference to another instrument, any charge to the benefit of which the debenture holders of that series are entitled pari passu is created by a company, it is for purposes of section 395 sufficient if there are delivered to or received by the registrar, within 21 days after the execution of the deed containing the charge (or, if there is no such deed, after the execution of any debentures of the series), the following particulars in the prescribed form—

(a)   the total amount secured by the whole series, and
(b)   the dates of the resolutions authorising the issue of the series and the date of the covering deed (if any) by which the security is created or defined, and
(c)   a general description of the property charged, and
(d)   the names of the trustees (if any) for the debenture holders,

together with the deed containing the charge or, if there is no such deed, one of the debentures of the series:

Provided that there shall be sent to the registrar of companies, for entry in the register, particulars in the prescribed form of the date and amount of each issue of debentures of the series, but any omission to do this does not affect the validity of any of those debentures.

(2)   Where any commission, allowance or discount has been paid or made either directly or indirectly by a company to a person in consideration of his—

(a)   subscribing or agreeing to subscribe, whether absolutely or conditionally, for debentures of the company, or
(b)   procuring or agreeing to procure subscriptions, whether absolute or conditional, for such debentures,

the particulars required to be sent for registration under section 395 shall include particulars as to the amount or rate per cent of the commission, discount or allowance so paid or made, but omission to do this does not affect the validity of the debentures issued.

(3)   The deposit of debentures as security for a debt of the company is not, for the purposes of subsection (2), treated as the issue of the debentures at a discount.

398 Verification of charge on property outside United Kingdom

(1)   In the case of a charge created out of the United Kingdom comprising property situated outside the United Kingdom, the delivery to and the receipt by the registrar of companies of a copy (verified in the prescribed manner) of the instrument by which the charge is created or evidenced has the same effect for purposes of sections 395 to 398 as the delivery and receipt of the instrument itself.

(2)   In that case, 21 days after the date on which the instrument or copy could, in due course of post (and if despatched with due diligence), have been received in the United Kingdom are substituted for the 21 days mentioned in section 395(2) (or as the case may be, section 397(1)) as the time within which the particulars and instrument or copy are to be delivered to the registrar.

(3)   Where a charge is created in the United Kingdom but comprises property outside the United Kingdom, the instrument creating or purporting to create the charge may be sent for registration under section 395 notwithstanding that further proceedings may be necessary to make the charge valid or effectual according to the law of the country in which the property is situated.

(4)   Where a charge comprises property situated in Scotland or Northern Ireland and registration in the country where the property is situated is necessary to make the charge valid or effectual according to the law of that country, the delivery to and receipt by the registrar of a copy (verified in the prescribed manner) of the instrument by which the charge is created or evidenced, together with a certificate in the prescribed form stating that the charge was presented for registration in Scotland or Northern Ireland (as the case may be) on the date on which it was so presented has, for purposes of sections 395 to 398, the same effect as the delivery and receipt of the instrument itself.

399 Company's duty to register charges it creates

(1)   It is a company's duty to send to the registrar of companies for registration the particulars of every charge created by the company and of the issues of debentures of a series requiring registration under sections 395 to 398; but registration of any such charge may be effected on the application of any person interested in it.

(2)   Where registration is effected on the application of some person other than the company, that person is entitled to recover from the company the amount of any fees properly paid by him to the registrar on the registration.

(3)   If a company fails to comply with subsection (1), then, unless the registration has been effected on the application of some other person, the company and every officer of it who is in default is liable to a fine and, for continued contravention, to a daily default fine.

400 Charges existing on property acquired

(1)   This section applies where a company registered in England and Wales acquires property which is subject to a charge of any such kind as would, if it had been created by the company after the acquisition of the property, have been required to be registered under this Chapter.

(2)   The company shall cause the prescribed particulars of the charge, together with a copy (certified in the prescribed manner to be a correct copy) of the instrument (if any) by which the charge was created or is evidenced, to be delivered to the registrar of companies for registration in manner required by this Chapter within 21 days after the date on which the acquisition is completed.

(3)   However, if the property is situated and the charge was created outside Great Britain, 21 days after the date on which the copy of the instrument could in due course of post, and if despatched with due diligence, have been received in the United Kingdom is substituted for the 21 days above-mentioned as the time within which the particulars and copy of the instrument are to be delivered to the registrar.

(4)   If default is made in complying with this section, the company and every officer of it who is in default is liable to a fine and, for continued contravention, to a daily default fine.

401 Register of charges to be kept by registrar of companies

(1)   The registrar of companies shall keep, with respect to each company, a register in the prescribed form of all the charges requiring registration under this Chapter; and he shall enter in the register with respect to such charges the following particulars—

(a)   in the case of a charge to the benefit of which the holders of a series of debentures are entitled, the particulars specified in section 397(1),

(b)   in the case of any other charge—
    (i)   if it is a charge created by the company, the date of its creation, and if it is a charge which was existing on property acquired by the company, the date of the acquisition of the property, and
    (ii)   the amount secured by the charge, and
    (iii)   short particulars of the property charged, and
    (iv)   the persons entitled to the charge.

(2)   The registrar shall give a certificate of the registration of any charge registered in pursuance of this Chapter, stating the amount secured by the charge.
    The certificate—

(a)   shall be either signed by the registrar, or authenticated by his official seal, and

(b)   is conclusive evidence that the requirements of this Chapter as to registration have been satisfied.

(3)   The register kept in pursuance of this section shall be open to inspection by any person.

402 Endorsement of certificate on debentures

(1)   The company shall cause a copy of every certificate of registration given under section 401 to be endorsed on every debenture or certificate of debenture stock which is issued by the company, and the payment of which is secured by the charge so registered.

(2)   But this does not require a company to cause a certificate of registration of any charge so given to be endorsed on any debenture or certificate of debenture stock issued by the company before the charge was created.

(3)   If a person knowingly and wilfully authorises or permits the delivery of a debenture or certificate of debenture stock which under this section is required

to have endorsed on it a copy of a certificate of registration, without the copy being so endorsed upon it, he is liable (without prejudice to any other liability) to a fine.

403 Entries of satisfaction and release

(1)   The registrar of companies, on receipt of a statutory declaration in the prescribed form verifying, with respect to a registered charge,—

    (a)   that the debt for which the charge was given has been paid or satisfied in whole or in part, or

    (b)   that part of the property or undertaking charged has been released from the charge or has ceased to form part of the company's property or undertaking,

may enter on the register a memorandum of satisfaction in whole or in part, or of the fact that part of the property or undertaking has been released from the charge or has ceased to form part of the company's property or undertaking (as the case may be).

(2)   Where the registrar enters a memorandum of satisfaction in whole, he shall if required furnish the company with a copy of it.

404 Rectification of register of charges

(1)   The following applies if the court is satisfied that the omission to register a charge within the time required by this Chapter or that the omission or mis-statement of any particular with respect to any such charge or in a memorandum of satisfaction was accidental, or due to inadvertence or to some other sufficient cause, or is not of a nature to prejudice the position of creditors or shareholders of the company, or that on other grounds it is just and equitable to grant relief.

(2)   The court may, on the application of the company or a person interested, and on such terms and conditions as seem to the court just and expedient, order that the time for registration shall be extended or, as the case may be, that the omission or mis-statement shall be rectified.

405 Registration of enforcement of security

(1)   If a person obtains an order for the appointment of a receiver or manager of a company's property, or appoints such a receiver or manager under powers contained in an instrument, he shall within 7 days of the order or of the appointment under those powers, give notice of the fact to the registrar of companies; and the registrar shall enter the fact in the register of charges.

(2)   Where a person appointed receiver or manager of a company's property under powers contained in an instrument ceases to act as such receiver or manager, he shall, on so ceasing, give the registrar notice to that effect, and the registrar shall enter the fact in the register of charges.

(3)   A notice under this section shall be in the prescribed form.

(4) If a person makes default in complying with the requirements of this section, he is liable to a fine and, for continued contravention, to a daily default fine.

406 Companies to keep copies of instruments creating charges

(1) Every company shall cause a copy of every instrument creating a charge requiring registration under this Chapter to be kept at its registered office.

(2) In the case of a series of uniform debentures, a copy of one debenture of the series is sufficient.

407 Company's register of charges

(1) Every limited company shall keep at its registered office a register of charges and enter in it all charges specifically affecting property of the company and all floating charges on the company's undertaking or any of its property.

(2) The entry shall in each case give a short description of the property charged, the amount of the charge and, except in the case of securities to bearer, the names of the persons entitled to it.

(3) If an officer of the company knowingly and wilfully authorises or permits the omission of an entry required to be made in pursuance of this section, he is liable to a fine.

408 Right to inspect instruments which create charges, etc

(1) The copies of instruments creating any charge requiring registration under this Chapter with the registrar of companies, and the register of charges kept in pursuance of section 407, shall be open during business hours (but subject to such reasonable restrictions as the company in general meeting may impose, so that not less than 2 hours in each day be allowed for inspection) to the inspection of any creditor or member of the company without fee.

(2) The register of charges shall also be open to the inspection of any other person on payment of such fee, not exceeding 5 pence, for each inspection, as the company may prescribe.

(3) If inspection of the copies referred to, or of the register, is refused, every officer of the company who is in default is liable to a fine and, for continued contravention, to a daily default fine.

(4) If such a refusal occurs in relation to a company registered in England and Wales, the court may by order compel an immediate inspection of the copies or register.

409 Charges on property in England and Wales created by oversea company

(1) This Chapter extends to charges on property in England and Wales which are created, and to charges on property in England and Wales which is

acquired, by a company (whether a company within the meaning of this Act or not) incorporated outside Great Britain which has an established place of business in England and Wales.

(2) In relation to such a company, sections 406 and 407 apply with the substitution, for the reference to the company's registered office, of a reference to its principal place of business in England and Wales.

Chapter II
Registration of Charges (Scotland)

410 Charges void unless registered

(1) The following provisions of this Chapter have effect for the purpose of securing the registration in Scotland of charges created by companies.

(2) Every charge created by a company, being a charge to which this section applies, is, so far as any security on the company's property or any part of it is conferred by the charge, void against the liquidator and any creditor of the company unless the prescribed particulars of the charge, together with a copy (certified in the prescribed manner to be a correct copy) of the instrument (if any) by which the charge is created or evidenced, are delivered to or received by the registrar of companies for registration in the manner required by this Chapter within 21 days after the date of the creation of the charge.

(3) Subsection (2) is without prejudice to any contract or obligation for repayment of the money secured by the charge; and when a charge becomes void under this section the money secured by it immediately becomes payable.

(4) This section applies to the following charges—

 (a) a charge on land wherever situated, or any interest in such land (not including a charge for any rent or other periodical sum payable in respect of the land, but including a charge created by a heritable security within the meaning of section 9(8) of the Conveyancing and Feudal Reform (Scotland) Act 1970),
 (b) a security over the uncalled share capital of the company,
 (c) a security over incorporeal moveable property of any of the following categories—
  (i) the book debts of the company,
  (ii) calls made but not paid,
  (iii) goodwill,
  (iv) a patent or a licence under a patent,
  (v) a trade mark,
  (vi) a copyright or a licence under a copyright,
 (d) a security over a ship or aircraft or any share in a ship, and
 (e) a floating charge.

(5) In this Chapter 'company' (except in section 424) means an incorporated company registered in Scotland; 'registrar of companies' means the registrar or other officer performing under this Act the duty of registration of companies in Scotland; and references to the date of creation of a charge are—

(a)   in the case of a floating charge, the date on which the instrument creating the floating charge was executed by the company creating the charge, and

(b)   in any other case, the date on which the right of the person entitled to the benefit of the charge was constituted as a real right.

411 Charges on property outside United Kingdom

(1)   In the case of a charge created out of the United Kingdom comprising property situated outside the United Kingdom, the period of 21 days after the date on which the copy of the instrument creating it could (in due course of post, and if despatched with due diligence) have been received in the United Kingdom is substituted for the period of 21 days after the date of the creation of the charge as the time within which, under section 410(2), the particulars and copy are to be delivered to the registrar.

(2)   Where a charge is created in the United Kingdom but comprises property outside the United Kingdom, the copy of the instrument creating or purporting to create the charge may be sent for registration under section 410 notwithstanding that further proceedings may be necessary to make the charge valid or effectual according to the law of the country in which the property is situated.

412 Negotiable instrument to secure book debts

Where a negotiable instrument has been given to secure the payment of any book debts of a company, the deposit of the instrument for the purpose of securing an advance to the company is not, for purposes of section 410, to be treated as a charge on those book debts.

413 Charges associated with debentures

(1)   The holding of debentures entitling the holder to a charge on land is not, for the purposes of section 410, deemed to be an interest in land.

(2)   Where a series of debentures containing, or giving by reference to any other instrument, any charge to the benefit of which the debenture-holders of that series are entitled pari passu, is created by a company, it is sufficient for purposes of section 410 if there are delivered to or received by the registrar of companies within 21 days after the execution of the deed containing the charge or if there is no such deed, after the execution of any debentures of the series, the following particulars in the prescribed form—

(a)   the total amount secured by the whole series,

(b)   the dates of the resolutions authorising the issue of the series and the date of the covering deed (if any) by which the security is created or defined,

(c)   a general description of the property charged,

(d)   the names of the trustees (if any) for the debenture holders, and

(e)   in the case of a floating charge, a statement of any provisions of the charge and of any instrument relating to it which prohibit or restrict or regulate the power of the company to grant further securities ranking in priority to, or pari passu with, the floating charge, or which vary or otherwise regulate the order of ranking of the floating charge in relation to subsisting securities,

together with a copy of the deed containing the charge or, if there is no such deed, of one of the debentures of the series:

Provided that where more than one issue is made of debentures in the series, there shall be sent to the registrar of companies for entry in the register particulars (in the prescribed form) of the date and amount of each issue of debentures of the series, but any omission to do this does not affect the validity of any of those debentures.

(3) Where any commission, allowance or discount has been paid or made, either directly or indirectly, by a company to any person in consideration of his subscribing or agreeing to subscribe, whether absolutely or conditionally, for any debentures of the company, or procuring or agreeing to procure subscriptions (whether absolute or conditional) for any such debentures, the particulars required to be sent for registration under section 410 include particulars as to the amount or rate per cent of the commission, discount or allowance so paid or made; but any omission to do this does not affect the validity of the debentures issued.

The deposit of any debentures as security for any debt of the company is not, for purposes of this subsection, treated as the issue of the debentures at a discount.

414 Charge by way of ex facie absolute disposition, etc

(1) For the avoidance of doubt, it is hereby declared that, in the case of a charge created by way of an ex facie absolute disposition or assignation qualified by a back letter or other agreement, or by a standard security qualified by an agreement, compliance with section 410(2) does not of itself render the charge unavailable as security for indebtedness incurred after the date of compliance.

(2) Where the amount secured by a charge so created is purported to be increased by a further back letter or agreement, a further charge is held to have been created by the ex facie absolute disposition or assignation or (as the case may be) by the standard security, as qualified by the further back letter or agreement; and the provisions of this Chapter apply to the further charge as if—

(a) references in this Chapter (other than in this section) to the charge were references to the further charge, and

(b) references to the date of the creation of the charge were references to the date on which the further back letter or agreement was executed.

415 Company's duty to register charges created by it

(1) It is a company's duty to send to the registrar of companies for registration the particulars of every charge created by the company and of the issues of debentures of a series requiring registration under sections 410 to 414; but registration of any such charge may be effected on the application of any person interested in it.

(2)   Where registration is effected on the application of some person other than the company, that person is entitled to recover from the company the amount of any fees properly paid by him to the registrar on the registration.

(3)   If a company makes default in sending to the registrar for registration the particulars of any charge created by the company or of the issues of debentures of a series requiring registration as above mentioned, then, unless the registration has been effected on the application of some other person, the company and every officer of it who is in default is liable to a fine and, for continued contravention, to a daily default fine.

416 Duty to register charges existing on property acquired

(1)   Where a company acquires any property which is subject to a charge of any kind as would, if it had been created by the company after the acquisition of the property, have been required to be registered under this Chapter, the company shall cause the prescribed particulars of the charge, together with a copy (certified in the prescribed manner to be a correct copy) of the instrument (if any) by which the charge was created or is evidenced, to be delivered to the registrar of companies for registration in the manner required by this Chapter within 21 days after the date on which the transaction was settled.

(2)   If, however, the property is situated and the charge was created outside Great Britain, 21 days after the date on which the copy of the instrument could (in due course of post, and if despatched with due diligence) have been received in the United Kingdom are substituted for 21 days after the settlement of the transaction as the time within which the particulars and the copy of the instrument are to be delivered to the registrar.

(3)   If default is made in complying with this section, the company and every officer of it who is in default is liable to a fine and, for continued contravention, to a daily default fine.

417 Register of charges to be kept by registrar of companies

(1)   The registrar of companies shall keep, with respect to each company, a register in the prescribed form of all the charges requiring registration under this Chapter, and shall enter in the register with respect to such charges the particulars specified below.

(2)   In the case of a charge to the benefit of which the holders of a series of debentures are entitled, there shall be entered in the register the particulars specified in section 413(2).

(3)   In the case of any other charge there shall be entered—

    (a)   if it is a charge created by the company, the date of its creation, and if it was a charge existing on property acquired by the company, the date of the acquisition of the property,

    (b)   the amount secured by the charge,

    (c)   short particulars of the property charged,

    (d)   the persons entitled to the charge, and

    (e)   in the case of a floating charge, a statement of any of the provisions of the charge and of any instrument relating to it which prohibit or restrict or regulate the company's power to grant further securities ranking in priority to, or pari passu with, the floating charge, or which vary or otherwise regulate the order of ranking of the floating charge in relation to subsisting securities.

(4)   The register kept in pursuance of this section shall be open to inspection by any person.

418 Certificate of registration to be issued

(1)   The registrar of companies shall give a certificate of the registration of any charge registered in pursuance of this Chapter.

(2)   The certificate—

(a)   shall be either signed by the registrar, or authenticated by his official seal,

(b)   shall state the name of the company and the person first-named in the charge among those entitled to the benefit of the charge (or, in the case of a series of debentures, the name of the holder of the first such debenture to be issued) and the amount secured by the charge, and

(c)   is conclusive evidence that the requirements of this Chapter as to registration have been complied with.

419 Entries of satisfaction and relief

(1)   The registrar of companies, on application being made to him in the prescribed form, and on receipt of a statutory declaration in the prescribed form verifying, with respect to any registered charge,—

(a)   that the debt for which the charge was given has been paid or satisfied in whole or in part, or

(b)   that part of the property charged has been released from the charge or has ceased to form part of the company's property,

may enter on the register a memorandum of satisfaction (in whole or in part) regarding that fact.

(2)   Where the registrar enters a memorandum of satisfaction in whole, he shall, if required, furnish the company with a copy of the memorandum.

(3)   Without prejudice to the registrar's duty under this section to require to be satisfied as above mentioned, he shall not be so satisfied unless—

(a)   the creditor entitled to the benefit of the floating charge, or a person authorised to do so on his behalf, certifies as correct the particulars submitted to the registrar with respect to the entry on the register of a memorandum under this section, or

(b)   the court, on being satisfied that such certification cannot readily be obtained, directs him accordingly.

(4)   Nothing in this section requires the company to submit particulars with respect to the entry in the register of a memorandum of satisfaction where the company, having created a floating charge over all or any part of its property, disposes of part of the property subject to the floating charge.

(5)   A memorandum or certification required for the purposes of this section shall be in such form as may be prescribed.

420 Rectification of register

The court, on being satisfied that the omission to register a charge within the time required by this Act or that the omission or mis-statement of any particular with respect to any such charge or in a memorandum of satisfaction was accidental, or due to inadvertence or to some other sufficient cause, or is not of a nature to prejudice the position of creditors or shareholders of the company, or that it is on other grounds just and equitable to grant relief, may, on the application of the company or any person interested, and on such terms and conditions as seem to the court just and expedient, order that the time for registration shall be extended or (as the case may be) that the omission or mis-statement shall be rectified.

421 Copies of instruments creating charges to be kept by company

(1)   Every company shall cause a copy of every instrument creating a charge requiring registration under this Chapter to be kept at the company's registered office.

(2)   In the case of a series of uniform debentures, a copy of one debenture of the series is sufficient.

422 Company's register of charges

(1)   Every company shall keep at its registered office a register of charges and enter in it all charges specifically affecting property of the company, and all floating charges on any property of the company.

(2)   There shall be given in each case a short description of the property charged, the amount of the charge and, except in the case of securities to bearer, the names of the persons entitled to it.

(3)   If an officer of the company knowingly and wilfully authorises or permits the omission of an entry required to be made in pursuance of this section, he is liable to a fine.

423 Right to inspect copies of instruments, and company's register

(1)   The copies of instruments creating charges requiring registration under this Chapter with the registrar of companies, and the register of charges kept in pursuance of section 422, shall be open during business hours (but subject to such reasonable restrictions as the company in general meeting may impose, so that not less than 2 hours in each day be allowed for inspection) to the inspection of any creditor or member of the company without fee.

(2)   The register of charges shall be open to the inspection of any other person on payment of such fee, not exceeding 5 pence for each inspection, as the company may prescribe.

(3) If inspection of the copies or register is refused, every officer of the company who is in default is liable to a fine and, for continued contravention, to a daily default fine.

(4) If such a refusal occurs in relation to a company, the court may by order compel an immediate inspection of the copies or register.

424 Extension of Chapter II

(1) This Chapter extends to charges on property in Scotland which are created, and to charges on property in Scotland which is acquired, by a company incorporated outside Great Britain which has a place of business in Scotland.

(2) In relation to such a company, sections 421 and 422 apply with the substitution, for the reference to the company's registered office, of a reference to its principal place of business in Scotland.

Appendix 2

DEFINITION OF BILL OF SALE IN BILLS OF SALE ACT 1878, SECTION 4

4 Interpretation of terms

In this Act the following words and expressions shall have the meanings in this section assigned to them respectively, unless there be something in the subject or context repugnant to such construction; (that is to say),

The expression 'bill of sale' shall include bills of sale, assignments, transfers, declarations of trust without transfer, inventories of goods with receipt thereto attached, or receipts for purchase moneys of goods, and other assurances of personal chattels, and also powers of attorney, authorities, or licences to take possession of personal chattels as security for any debt, and also any agreement, whether intended or not to be followed by the execution of any other instrument, by which a right in equity to any personal chattels, or to any charge or security thereon, shall be conferred, but shall not include the following documents; that is to say, assignments for the benefit of the creditors of the person making or giving the same, marriage settlements, transfers or assignments of any ship or vessel or any share thereof, transfers of goods in the ordinary course of business of any trade or calling, bills of sale of goods in foreign parts or at sea, bills of lading, India warrants, warehouse-keepers' certificates, warrants or orders for the delivery of goods, or any other documents used in the ordinary course of business as proof of the possession or control of goods, or authorising or purporting to authorise, either by indorsement or by delivery, the possessor of such document to transfer or receive goods thereby represented:

The expression 'personal chattels' shall mean goods, furniture, and other articles capable of complete transfer by delivery, and (when separately assigned or charged) fixtures and growing crops, but shall not include chattel interests in real estate, nor fixtures (except trade machinery as herein-after defined), when assigned together with a freehold or leasehold interest in any land or building to which they are affixed, nor growing crops when assigned together with any interest in the land on which they grow, nor shares or interests in the stock, funds, or securities of any government, or in the capital or property of incorporated or joint stock companies, nor choses in action, nor any stock or produce upon any farm or lands which by virtue of any covenant or agreement or of the custom of the country ought not to be removed from any farm where the same are at the time of making or giving of such bill of sale:

Personal chattels shall be deemed to be in the 'apparent possession' of the person making or giving a bill of sale, so long as they remain or are in or upon any house, mill, warehouse, building, works, yard, land, or other premises occupied by him, or are used and enjoyed by him in any place whatsoever, notwithstanding that formal possession thereof may have been taken by or given to any other person:

'Prescribed' means prescribed by rules made under the provisions of this Act.

Appendix 3

COMPANIES FORMS 395, 397, 403A AND 403B

M

CHWP000

Please do not write in this margin

Please complete legibly, preferably in black type, or bold block lettering

* insert full name of Company

COMPANIES FORM No. 395

Particulars of a mortgage or charge

395

A fee of £10 *(£13 for forms delivered on or after 1 February 2005)* is payable to Companies House in respect of each register entry for a mortgage or charge.

Pursuant to section 395 of the Companies Act 1985

To the Registrar of Companies
(Address overleaf - Note 6)

For official use

Company number

Name of company

*

Date of creation of the charge

Description of the instrument (if any) creating or evidencing the charge (note 2)

Amount secured by the mortgage or charge

Names and addresses of the mortgagees or persons entitled to the charge

Postcode

Presentor's name address and reference (if any) :

For official Use (02/00)
Mortgage Section

Post room

Time critical reference

Page 1

Short particulars of all the property mortgaged or charged

Particulars as to commission allowance or discount (note 3)

Signed   Date

On behalf of [company][mortgagee/chargee]†

Notes

1 The original instrument (if any) creating or evidencing the charge, together with these prescribed particulars correctly completed must be delivered to the Registrar of Companies within 21 days after the date of creation of the charge (section 395). If the property is situated and the charge was created outside the United Kingdom delivery to the Registrar must be effected within 21 days after the date on which the instrument could in due course of post, and if dispatched with due diligence, have been received in the United Kingdom (section 398). A copy of the instrument creating the charge will be accepted where the property charged is situated and the charge was created outside the United Kingdom (section 398) and in such cases the copy must be verified to be a correct copy either by the company or by the person who has delivered or sent the copy to the registrar. The verification must be signed by or on behalf of the person giving the verification and where this is given by a body corporate it must be signed by an officer of that body. A verified copy will also be accepted where section 398(4) applies (property situate in Scotland or Northern Ireland) and Form No. 398 is submitted.

2 A description of the instrument, eg "Trust Deed", "Debenture", "Mortgage", or "Legal charge", etc, as the case may be, should be given.

3 In this section there should be inserted the amount or rate per cent. of the commission, allowance or discount (if any) paid or made either directly or indirectly by the company to any person in consideration of his:
(a) subscribing or agreeing to subscribe, whether absolutely or conditionally, or
(b) procuring or agreeing to procure subscriptions, whether absolute or conditional,
for any of the debentures included in this return. The rate of interest payable under the terms of the debentures should not be entered.

4 If any of the spaces in this form provide insufficient space the particulars must be entered on the prescribed continuation sheet.

5 A fee of £10 *(£13 for forms delivered on or after 1 February 2005)* is payable to Companies House in respect of each register entry for a mortgage or charge.
Cheques and Postal Orders are to be made payable to **Companies House**.

6 The address of the Registrar of Companies is: Companies House, Crown Way, Cardiff CF14 3UZ   Page 2

M

CHWP000

Please do not
write in
this margin

*Please complete
legibly, preferably
in black type, or
bold block lettering*

* insert full name
of Company

COMPANIES FORM No. 397

Particulars for the registration of a charge to secure a series of debentures

397

A fee of £10 *(£13 for forms delivered on or after 1 February 2005)* is payable to Companies House in respect of each register entry for a mortgage or charge.

Pursuant to section 397 of the Companies Act 1985

To the Registrar of Companies
(Address overleaf - Note 7)

For official use

Company number

Name of company

*

Date of the covering deed (if any) (note 2) _____

Total amount secured by the whole series _____

_____

_____

Date of present issue _____

Amount of present issue (if any) of debentures of the series _____

Date of resolutions authorising the issue of the series _____

Names of the trustees (if any) for the debenture holders

General description of the property charged

Continue overleaf as necessary

Presentor's name address and reference (if any) :

For official Use (02/00)
Mortgage Section

Post room

Time critical reference

Page 1

General description of the property charged (continued)

Particulars as to commission, allowance or discount (note 3)

Signed _____ Date _____

On behalf of [company] [mortgagee / chargee]†

Notes

1 Particulars should be given on this form of a series of debentures containing (or giving by reference to any other instrument) any charge to the benefit of which the debenture holders of the series are entitled pari passu. This form is to be used for registration of particulars of the entire series, and may also be used when an issue of debentures is made at the same time as the series of debentures is created. All issues of debentures made after the registration of the series with the Registrar of Companies should be notified to the Registrar on Form No. 397a.

2 The date should be given of the covering deed (if any) by which the security is created or defined.

3 In this section there should be inserted the amount or rate per cent of the commission, allowance or discount (if any) paid or made either directly or indirectly by the company to any person in consideration of his
(a) subscribing or agreeing to subscribe, whether absolutely or conditionally, or
(b) procuring or agreeing to procure subscriptions, whether absolute or conditional,
for any of the debentures included in this return. The rate of interest payable under the terms of the debentures should not be entered.

4 The deed (if any) containing the charge must be delivered with these particulars correctly completed, to the Registrar within 21 days after it's execution. If there is no such deed, one of the debentures must be so delivered within 21 days after the execution of any debenture of the series.

5 If the spaces in this form are insufficient, the particulars may be continued on a separate sheet.

6 A fee of £10 *(£13 for forms delivered on or after 1 February 2005)* is payable to Companies House in respect of each register entry for a mortgage or charge. Cheques and Postal Orders are to be made payable to **Companies House**.

7 The address of the Registrar of Companies is: Mortgage Section, PO Box 716, Companies House Crown Way, Cardiff CF14 3YA

M

CHWP000

COMPANIES FORM No. 403a

**Declaration of satisfaction
in full or in part
of mortgage or charge**

403a

Please do not
write in
this margin

Pursuant to section 403(1) of the Companies Act 1985

*Please complete
legibly, preferably
in black type, or
bold block lettering*

To the Registrar of Companies
(Address overleaf)

Name of company

For official use   Company number

* insert full name
  of company

*

I, _____

of _____

† delete as
appropriate

[a director][the secretary][the administrator][the administrative receiver]† of the above company, do

solemnly and sincerely declare that the debt for which the charge described below was given has been

insert a description
of the instrument(s)
creating or
evidencing the
charge, eg
'Mortgage',
'Charge',
'Debenture' etc

paid or satisfied in **[full][part]**†

Date and description of charge # _____

Date of registration ø _____

Name and address of [chargee][trustee for the debenture holders]† _____

ø the date of
registration may be
confirmed from the
certificate

_____

Short particulars of property charged § _____

§ insert brief details
of property

_____

And I make this solemn declaration conscientiously believing the same to be true and by virtue of the

provisions of the Statutory Declarations Act 1835.

Declared at _____

Declarant to sign below

Day   Month   Year

on   [| | | |]

before me _____

A Commissioner for Oaths or Notary Public or Justice of
the Peace or a Solicitor having the powers conferred on a
Commissioner for Oaths.

Presentor's name address and
reference (if any) :

For official Use (02/00)
Mortgage Section

Post room

Notes

The address of the Registrar of Companies is:-

The Registrar of Companies
Companies House
Crown Way
Cardiff
CF14 3UZ

M

CHWP000

Please do not
write in
this margin

COMPANIES FORM No. 403b

**Declaration that part of the
property or undertaking charged
(a) has been released from the
charge; (b) no longer forms part of
the company's property or undertaking**

403b

Pursuant to section 403(1) (b) of the Companies Act 1985

*Please complete
legibly, preferably
in black type, or
bold block lettering*

To the Registrar of Companies
(Address overleaf)

For official use   Company number

Name of company

* insert full name
of company

*

I, _____

of _____

† delete as
appropriate

[a director][the secretary][the administrator][the administrative receiver]† of the above company, do

solemnly and sincerely declare that with respect to the charge described below the part of the property

insert a description
of the instrument(s)
creating or
evidencing the
charge, eg
'Mortgage',
'Charge',
'Debenture' etc

or undertaking described [has been released from the charge][has ceased to form part of the

company's property or undertaking]†

Date and description of charge # _____

Date of registration ø _____

ø the date of
registration may be
confirmed from the
certificate

Name and address of [chargee][trustee for the debenture holders]† _____

_____

§ insert brief details
of property or
undertaking no
longer subject to
the charge

Short particulars of property or undertaking released or no longer part of the company's property or

undertaking § _____

_____

And I make this solemn declaration conscientiously believing the same to be true and by virtue of the

provisions of the Statutory Declarations Act 1835.

Declared at _____   Declarant to sign below

_____

	Day	Month	Year
on			

before me _____

A Commissioner for Oaths or Notary Public or Justice of
the Peace or a Solicitor having the powers conferred on a
Commissioner for Oaths.

Presenter's name address and
reference (if any) :

For official Use (02/00)
Mortgage Section

Post room

Notes

The address of the Registrar of Companies is:-

The Registrar of Companies
Companies House
Crown Way
Cardiff
CF14 3UZ

Appendix 4

THE LAW COMMISSION
CONSULTATION PAPER NO 176
COMPANY SECURITY INTERESTS
A CONSULTATIVE REPORT

London: TSO

PART 6
LIST OF PROVISIONAL RECOMMENDATIONS
AND CONSULTATION QUESTIONS

6.1 We set out below a summary of our provisional recommendations and questions on which we invite the views of consultees. We would be grateful for comments not only on the matters specifically listed below, but also on any other points raised by this consultative report. It would be very helpful if, when responding, consultees could indicate either the paragraph of the summary that follows to which their remarks relate, or the paragraph of this consultative report in which the issue was originally raised.

PART 2 – CRITICAL ISSUES

Replacing the scheme of registration and priority for company charges

6.2 We provisionally conclude that there are significant weaknesses in the way the current company charge registration system operates. (Paragraph 2.6.)

6.3 We provisionally recommend that a wholly electronic notice-filing scheme for company charges, and an associated scheme of priorities, should be introduced. (Paragraph 2.68.)

6.4 We would welcome consultees' estimates of the costs and benefits of introducing the scheme as set out in the draft regulations, but limited to 'traditional' securities. (Paragraph 2.69.)

Unincorporated businesses

6.5 We provisionally recommend that the notice-filing scheme for companies should be extended to SIs created by other business debtors as soon as possible. (Paragraph 2.79.)

6.6 We would welcome consultees' estimates of any additional costs and benefits of extending the companies scheme as set out in the draft regulations to all business debtors. (Paragraph 2.80.)

Quasi-security devices

6.7 We provisionally recommend that even at the companies-only stage:

(1) sales of receivables should be brought within the notice-filing scheme for the purposes of perfection and priority (but not the statement of remedies); and

(2) title-retention devices that have a security purpose should be brought within the scheme (including the statement of remedies).

If consultees do not agree with these recommendations we ask whether they think that the relevant SIs should be brought into the scheme:

  (a) only at an 'all business debtors' stage, or
  (b) not at all. (Paragraph 2.135.)

6.8 We ask consultees whether they agree that operating leases of over one year and commercial consignments that do not have a security purpose should be brought within the scheme for the purposes of perfection and priority:

  (c) at the 'companies-only' stage (our provisional recommendation), or
  (d) only at an 'all business debtors' stage, or
  (e) not at all. (Paragraph 2.136.)

6.9 We would welcome consultees' estimates of any additional costs and benefits of including (a) sales of receivables, and (b) title retention devices in the scheme as set out in the draft regulations. If it is possible, it would be helpful if consultees were to give separate estimates for both a companies-only scheme and one for all business debtors. (Paragraphs 2.137.)

Financial collateral

6.10 We provisionally recommend that SIs over investment property should be brought within the scheme, and that it should be possible to perfect such SIs by 'control'. (Paragraph 2.148.)

6.11 We provisionally recommend that SIs over bank accounts should be brought within the scheme; and that it should be possible to perfect such SIs by control. (Paragraph 2.157.)

6.12 We would welcome consultees' estimates of the costs and benefits of our provisional recommendations for financial collateral. (Paragraph 2.159.)

A statement of the parties' rights and obligations

6.13 We provisionally recommend that any scheme of rights and remedies should not contain a general reference to 'good faith', nor a general requirement that either party exercise its rights or perform its obligations in a commercially reasonable manner. Instead there should be specific requirements when these are necessary. (Paragraph 2.182.)

6.14 We provisionally recommend the inclusion of a statement of rights and remedies in the 'companies-only' scheme. (Paragraph 2.190.)

6.15 We would welcome consultees' estimates of the costs and benefits of our provisional recommendations for including a statement of rights and remedies. (Paragraph 2.191.)

PART 3 – THE SCHEME IN FULL

Scope of the scheme

6.16 We would welcome views on whether the scheme we provisionally propose should be limited to registered companies and LLPs, or should apply also to other corporate bodies; and, if so, as to which corporate bodies should be included. (Paragraph 3.8.)

6.17 We would welcome advice on whether we should continue to use a definition of 'debtor' that may refer to either the party creating the SI or the party whose obligation is secured, where they are not the same person, or both.[1] If not, should we refer to the first as 'the debtor' and the second as 'the obligor', as does the UCC; or do consultees have other suggestions? (Paragraph 3.14.)

Security interests

'In-substance' SIs

6.18 On the assumption that the scheme should apply to quasi-securities, we provisionally recommend that the definition of 'security interest' should encompass all those transactions that have a security purpose, irrespective of the form of the transaction or who has title to the collateral. (Paragraph 3.33.)

'Deemed' SIs

6.19 We provisionally recommend that leases for over one year that do not have a security purpose should be brought within the definition of 'security interest' for the purposes of perfection and priority. (Paragraph 3.38.)

6.20 We ask whether consultees agree with the way 'lease for a term of more than one year' has been defined in the draft regulations.[2] (Paragraph 3.40.)

6.21 We provisionally recommend that commercial consignments that do not secure payment or performance of an obligation should nonetheless be 'deemed' to be SIs. (Paragraph 3.43.)

6.22 We provisionally recommend that sales of accounts should be treated as SIs for the purposes of perfection and priority. (Paragraph 3.48.)

---

1   As set out in DR 5.
2   DR 8.

6.23   We ask consultees whether, for the purposes of priority, sales of promissory notes should also be treated as SIs that are automatically perfected. We also ask consultees whether sales of bills of exchange should be treated as SIs in the same way as sales of promissory notes. (Paragraph 3.49.)

Supporting obligations

6.24 We provisionally recommend that:

(1)   where an SI attaches to a monetary obligation, an SI attaches automatically to any supporting obligation for the collateral;
(2)   perfection of an SI in the collateral also perfects an SI in the supporting obligation. (Paragraph 3.57.)

Partial and total exclusions from the overall scheme

6.25 We ask consultees whether there are there other interests that should be wholly or partially excluded from the application of the draft regulations. (Paragraph 3.66.)

6.26 We provisionally recommend that the interests listed in DR 12 should be excluded from the scheme. We provisionally recommend that SIs over insurance policies and tort claims should be within the scheme. (Paragraph 3.67.)

Attachment of SIs

6.27 We provisionally recommend that for a non-possessory SI to attach there should be no requirement that a security agreement should be, or be evidenced, in writing (whether signed or not), and that the Law of Property Act 1925, section 53(1)(c) should, so far as it would otherwise apply, cease to apply to SIs under our scheme. (Paragraph 3.81.)

6.28   We ask whether the scheme should contain a provision dealing with the reattachment of an SI to goods which have been returned or repossessed. (Paragraph 3.85.)

Methods of perfection in detail

Perfection by filing

6.29 We provisionally recommend that the filing of a financing statement should be capable of perfecting an SI that has attached (whether before or after filing) over any type of collateral. (Paragraph 3.94.)

Automatic perfection

6.30 Should the scheme provide that an assignment which does not by itself or in conjunction with other assignments to the same assignee transfer a significant part of the assignor's outstanding accounts will be automatically perfected on attachment? (Paragraph 3.98.)

Perfection by possession and goods in the possession of bailees

Possession by secured party

6.31 We provisionally recommend that actual possession of collateral by the secured party (or its agent) should perfect an SI in goods, an instrument, a negotiable document of title or money. (Paragraph 3.100.)

6.32 We provisionally recommend that where the goods are in the possession of the debtor or its agent, attornment to the secured party will not amount to possession by the secured party. (Paragraph 3.102.)

Possession by bailee

6.33 We provisionally recommend that, where the goods are in the possession of a bailee other than the debtor, the SI may be perfected in three ways:

(1)   by the bailee attorning to the secured party;
(2)   by the bailee issuing a document of title in the name of the secured party;
(3)   or by the secured party perfecting an SI in a negotiable document of title to the goods, where the bailee has issued one. (Paragraph 3.104.)

Seized or repossessed goods

6.34 We provisionally recommend that a secured party who has not perfected its SI by filing but who has seized or repossessed the goods should not be excluded from having possession of them for the purposes of perfection. (Paragraph 3.107.)

Trust receipts and temporary perfection

6.35 We provisionally recommend that where an SI over instruments or certificated securities has been perfected by possession, or one over goods in the possession of a bailee has been perfected by the bailee issuing a negotiable document of title or otherwise, if the collateral or document of title is returned for specified purposes, the SI should remain perfected for a limited time thereafter. We ask whether 15 business days is an appropriate period. (Paragraph 3.112.)

Filing: financing statement

6.36 We would welcome views on whether the financing statement should record that the debtor is a trustee and, if so, whether the beneficiary of a bare trust should also be identified. (Paragraph 3.121.)

6.37 We provisionally recommend that the financing statement should contain:

(1)   the name of the debtor and its registered number (if any);
(2)   the name and address of the secured party or its agent;
(3)   a description of the collateral;
(4)   whether the filing is to continue indefinitely or for a specified period; and
(5)   such other matters as may be prescribed by the Rules.

We ask consultees to identify any additional information that they consider should be provided or any information that should not be required. (Paragraph 3.134.)

Who files?

6.38   We provisionally recommend that any person should be able to file a financing statement. (Paragraph 3.137.)

Filing for future SIs

6.39   We provisionally recommend that it should be possible to file before or after a security agreement has been made. (Paragraph 3.139.)

Consent of the debtor to filing

6.40   We provisionally recommend that a financing statement that is filed before a security agreement is made should be ineffective if it is made without the debtor's consent (whether before or after the filing). (Paragraph 3.140.)

6.41   We ask consultees whether they think a power should be taken to impose a criminal sanction on those who file without the debtor's consent when there is no security agreement in existence. (Paragraph 3.141.)

'Last-minute' filing

6.42   We provisionally recommend that, when our scheme is introduced, section 245 of the Insolvency Act 1986 be amended to apply to any SI in favour of the persons mentioned in that section that is filed within the times stated before the onset of insolvency, save when new value is given or the company is not insolvent at the time, as provided in section 245(3) and (4). (Paragraph 3.146)

Verification statement

6.43   We provisionally recommend that, when a financing statement has been filed, the Registrar must send the secured party a verification statement. The secured party must then send a copy of the statement to the debtor within 10 business days, unless the debtor has waived the right to receive a copy. (Paragraph 3.150.)

Effect of failure to file or perfect by other means

6.44   We provisionally recommend that it should not be compulsory to perfect an SI by filing or any other means; but that an unperfected SI should be:

(1)   at risk of losing priority to one that has been perfected;
(2)   ineffective against a liquidator or administrator on insolvency and other secured parties;
(3)   ineffective against an execution creditor who completes execution before the SI is perfected;
(4)   ineffective against some purchasers (whether a buyer or subsequent secured party) in certain circumstances. (Paragraph 3.153.)

Financing change statements

6.45 We provisionally recommend that the creditor should be able to make amendments to the financing statement by means of a financing change statement. The debtor should be able to demand that an incorrect or out of date financing statement is, as appropriate, corrected or removed. (Paragraph 3.162.)

Errors in the financing statement

6.46 We provisionally recommend that the effectiveness of a filing should not be affected by a defect, irregularity, omission or error in the financing statement unless it would have the result that a reasonable search, conducted in accordance with the requirements of the draft regulations and the Rules relating to searches, would not reveal the financing statement. An error in the collateral description will result in the SI remaining unperfected in relation to collateral that was omitted but will not affect it as regards other collateral that is described in the financing statement. (Paragraph 3.168.)

Effect of unauthorised or accidental discharge

6.47 We provisionally recommend that where there has been mistaken or unauthorised lapse or discharge of a financing statement, the secured party should be able to re-activate the financing statement within 30 days of the lapse or discharge. Where this is done, the lapse or discharge should not affect the priority ranking of the SI as against those SIs which, prior to the lapse or discharge, were subordinate in priority to it. However, this should not be the case as against SIs that are perfected by filing after the lapse or discharge but before the financing statement was re-activated, nor to the extent that the competing SI secures advances made or contracted for in that period. The Rules should deal with the procedure for re-activation of the financing statement. (Paragraph 3.170.)

Searching

6.48 We provisionally recommend that it should be possible to search the register online by the company name; the company registered number (where it has one – overseas companies may not be registered at Companies House); the financing statement number (the number allocated by the registry on filing); and (for collateral prescribed in the Rules) the unique identifying number. (Paragraph 3.174.)

System failure

6.49 We ask consultees whether there should be a statutory, no-fault compensation fund for system failures; and fault-based liability for loss caused by errors in the system. (Paragraph 3.175.)

SIs over vehicles

6.50 We provisionally recommend that where goods are of a type that is designated by the Rules as having a unique serial number, the financing statement may include that serial number. If it does not, a buyer of the goods who does not know of the SI will normally take free of it, and, where the goods are equipment, the SI will not be treated as perfected for the purposes of priority as against other SIs over the same goods. (Paragraph 3.180.)

Proceeds

Right to proceeds of disposition

6.51 We provisionally recommend that where collateral is disposed of by the debtor, unless the secured party has authorised the dealing free of the SI or the case is one in which the buyer will take free of the SI, the SI should continue in the collateral and attach to the proceeds. (Paragraph 3.183.)

6.52 We ask consultees whether the scheme should include a provision to limit the secured party's recovery from original collateral and proceeds to the market value of the collateral. (Paragraph 3.184.)

6.53 We provisionally recommend that whether proceeds are identifiable and traceable should not depend on the presence of a fiduciary relationship. (Paragraph 3.185.)

Perfection of right over proceeds

6.54 We provisionally recommend that an SI in proceeds should be continuously perfected if the SI in the original collateral is perfected by filing, and

(1)   the financing statement contains a description of the proceeds that would be sufficient to perfect an SI in original collateral of the same kind; or
(2)   the financing statement covers the original collateral, if the proceeds are of a kind within the description of the original collateral; or
(3)   the proceeds consist of money, cheques, deposits in or money credited to a bank account or insurance payments.

In other cases, the secured party should have a short period in which to perfect against the proceeds. (Paragraph 3.187.)

Obtaining additional information about the SI

6.55 We conclude from the point of view of obtaining information about security that there is little point in maintaining the company's own register of charges. We ask whether the scheme should contain a provision enabling the debtor to require the secured party to supply information relating to the amount owing and the collateral subject to the SI. In particular, we seek views on whether:

(1)   only the debtor should be entitled to make an 'information request',
(2)   the secured party should be obliged, at the debtor's request, to supply the information to a named third party,
(3)   the court should be able to order the sanctions set out in DR 18, including extinguishing the SI. (Paragraph 3.197.)

Priority between competing SIs

'Residual' priority rules

6.56 We provisionally recommend the following residual rules:

(1) Perfected SIs take priority over unperfected ones.
(2) As between secured parties with perfected SIs, priority is determined by whoever was first to file or perfect.
(3) As between unperfected SIs, priority is determined by date of attachment.
(4) The priority that an SI has under the rules above applies to all advances, including future ones, whether or not made under an obligation. (Paragraph 3.201.)

Specific priority rules

Purchase-money SIs

6.57 We provisionally recommend that an SI in collateral, to the extent that it secures all or part of the collateral's purchase price, and an SI taken by a person who gives value for the purpose of enabling the debtor to acquire rights in the collateral, to the extent that the value is applied to acquire those rights, should have priority over any other SI given by the debtor in the same collateral. Interests of lessors and consignors of goods should have the same priority. (Paragraph 3.208.)

6.58 We ask consultees whether our scheme should limit PMSIs to SIs over goods or whether it should include an SI over any type of collateral other than investment property. (Paragraph 3.209.)

6.59 We provisionally recommend that for an SI over inventory to have PMSI status, it must be perfected, and a notice must have been given to any other secured party who has filed a financing statement covering the same type of collateral, before the debtor (or another person on its behalf, if earlier) obtains possession of the collateral. The notice must state that the person giving the notice expects to acquire an SI in inventory, and describe the inventory by item or kind. (Paragraph 3.214.)

6.60 We provisionally recommend that a PMSI over goods that are not inventory should have priority over any other conflicting SI provided that it is perfected not later than 10 days after the debtor obtains possession of the collateral. In the case of a PMSI over intangibles, the 10 day period should date from attachment. (Paragraph 3.219.)

6.61 We provisionally recommend that PMSI status in one piece of inventory should extend to other inventory supplied by the same supplier, even if the particular item claimed has been paid for. (Paragraph 3.220.)

6.62 We provisionally recommend that where two PMSIs in goods or proceeds conflict, a PMSI taken by a seller, lessor or consignor has priority over any other PMSI, providing that it is perfected, in the case of non-inventory, within 10 days of the debtor obtaining possession of the collateral or, in the case of inventory, at the time the debtor obtains possession of the collateral. (Paragraph 3.221.)

6.63 We provisionally recommend that a secured party claiming an account as original collateral should have priority over a secured party claiming the account as the proceeds of a PMSI, provided that the receivables financier perfected its SI by filing before the PMSI secured party supplied the goods in question or filed in respect of its SI. (Paragraph 3.223.)

6.64 For the purposes of the priority rules, should the scheme provide that a PMSI in livestock be treated in the same way as a PMSI in inventory? (Paragraph 3.226.)

6.65 We ask whether the scheme should provide that an SI taken by a secured party who effectively enables a crop to be produced should have priority over competing SIs in the resulting crop or its proceeds. If so, should there be time limits or notice requirements in relation to this? (Paragraph 3.228.)

Protection of transferees of 'negotiable' collateral

6.66 We provisionally recommend that a purchaser of an instrument for value, without knowledge of the SI, and who takes possession of the instrument should have priority over any SI in the instrument, whether or not the SI was perfected, unless the purchaser not only knew of the SI but knew that the transaction would violate the terms of the security agreement. (Paragraph 3.231.)

6.67 We provisionally recommend that:

(1) holders of money (that is, notes and coins in any currency) which is subject to an SI, whether perfected or not, should have priority over that SI if the holder acquired the money without knowledge that it was subject to an SI, or is a holder for value, whether or not the holder acquires the money without knowledge of the SI;

(2) a creditor who has received payment of a debt owing to it by the debtor other than by payment in cash, should have priority over an SI in the funds, intangible or instrument used to effect the payment, whether or not it knew of the SI at the time of payment. (Paragraph 3.235.)

6.68 We provisionally recommend that a holder to whom a negotiable document of title is negotiated, and who gave value, should have priority over an SI in the document of title, whether or not the SI was perfected, unless the holder not only knew of the SI but knew that the transaction would violate its terms. (Paragraph 3.236.)

Priority in transferred collateral

6.69 We provisionally recommend that if collateral is transferred by the debtor to a party who takes subject to the SI, then provided the secured party's interest was perfected at the time of transfer and has remained so, it should have priority over any SI created by the transferee. This is so whether the SI created by the transferee was created or filed before or after the SI created by the transferor. (Paragraph 3.246.)

Liens

6.70 We provisionally recommend that where a person in the ordinary course of business supplies materials or services with respect to goods which are subject to an SI, a lien that that person has with respect to those services and materials has priority over the SI (unless the lien is a statutory lien which expressly provides otherwise). (Paragraph 3.249.)

Priority as against execution creditors

6.71 We provisionally recommend that execution creditors should have priority over unperfected SIs[3] and over a perfected SI in respect of further advances made after the secured party knows of the execution creditor's interest, unless the secured party was under an obligation to make the advance. (Paragraph 3.252.)

Priority as against buyers or lessees

Unperfected SIs

6.72 We provisionally recommend that a buyer or lessee of collateral should take free of an unperfected SI unless it had knowledge of the existence of the SI. (Paragraph 3.256.)

Sales in the ordinary course of business

6.73 We provisionally recommend that a buyer of goods from a seller who normally sells goods of that kind, or a lessee from a lessor who normally leases goods of that kind, should take free of any perfected SI created by the seller or lessor unless the buyer or lessee knows that the sale or lease is in violation of the security agreement. (Paragraph 3.260.)

Low price goods bought for private purposes

6.74 We ask consultees whether a person who

(1) buys goods for a purchase price of, say, £1000 or less (or leases them where they have that market value),
(2) does so primarily for personal, family or household purposes,
(3) and does not know that the goods are subject to an SI, should take free of any perfected or unperfected SI in the goods. If so, is the figure of £1000 appropriate? (Paragraph 3.262.)

Other priority situations

Fixtures

6.75 We ask whether consultees agree that specific rules dealing with fixtures are not needed. (Paragraph 3.268.)

---

3   DR 20(3).

Crops

6.76 We provisionally recommend that a perfected SI in growing crops (whether planted or natural) should have priority over a conflicting interest in the land, if the debtor has an interest in or is in occupation of the land. (Paragraph 3.272.)

6.77 We ask consultees whether growing trees should be treated like other crops or should be left outside the scheme. (Paragraph 3.273.)

Accessions, commingled goods and processed goods

6.78 We provisionally recommend that specific rules on accessions are not needed. (Paragraph 3.277.)

6.79 We provisionally recommend that there is no need for our scheme to include special rules to deal with commingled goods. (Paragraph 3.278.)

6.80 We provisionally recommend that there is no need for our scheme to include specific provisions on processed goods. (Paragraph 3.282.)

Liability in damages

6.81 Do consultees agree with the approach we have set out in DR 71 of permitting damages for reasonably foreseeable loss? If not, what sanctions should exist for failing to carry out any obligation imposed by the draft regulations? Should the availability of damages be limited to those to whom the duty or obligation is owed? If damages are an appropriate sanction, should there be provision for fixed-sum awards for breach of particular provisions? (Paragraph 3.286.)

6.82 Should there be a provision effectively limiting any duty of a secured party towards debtors and other secured parties unless the secured party knows that the person is a debtor or secured party as appropriate, and their identities? (Paragraph 3.288.)

SIs and the 'specialist' registries

Land

6.83 We provisionally recommend that the creation and transfer of interests in land should be excluded from the scope of the draft regulations. Arrangements should be made to make available on or via the Companies House register information about charges over a company's land that are registered at the Land Registry. (Paragraph 3.309.)

6.84 We provisionally recommend that interests over rights to payment arising from an interest in land should not be excluded from the scheme. (Paragraph 3.312.)

Aircraft

6.85 We provisionally recommend that SIs over aircraft registered in the UK or anywhere else in the world should be excluded from our scheme. (Paragraph 3.322.)

Ships

6.86 We provisionally recommend that any SI over a ship that is registered in the UK and to which the 'private law provisions' apply, or over a ship registered anywhere else in the world, should be outside our scheme. (Paragraph 3.333.)

6.87 For those SIs in ships that fall within the scope of the draft regulations, we provisionally recommend that the statement of rights and remedies contained in Part 5 of the draft regulations should be made without prejudice to current Admiralty practice relating to the enforcement of charges and mortgages in ships. (Paragraph 3.336.)

Intellectual property

6.88 We provisionally recommend that SIs over registered designs, patents and trade marks should be excluded from our scheme. (Paragraph 3.342.)

SIs over assets abroad or created by 'foreign' companies

Companies registered in England and Wales

6.89 We provisionally recommend that the scheme should apply to SIs created by companies registered in England and Wales over assets outside the UK. (Paragraph 3.363.)

Companies incorporated outside the UK

6.90 We provisionally recommend that SIs created by foreign companies over their assets in England and Wales, or to which the law of England and Wales would apply for the purposes of determining questions of perfection and priority, should be subject to the scheme. (Paragraph 3.372.)

Scotland

6.91 We provisionally recommend that an SI created by an English company over assets in Scotland should be subject to the scheme, including the normal rules of perfection. An SI created by a company registered in Scotland over assets in England and Wales, or to which the law of England and Wales would apply for the purposes of determining questions of perfection and priority, should also be subject to the scheme. (Paragraph 3.383.)

Transitional provisions

6.92 We provisionally recommend that pre-commencement registrable charges that were registered before commencement should be treated as perfected under the scheme. They should retain their existing priority as against other precommencement SIs. As against post-commencement SIs their priority should depend on the normal rules of priority of the new scheme. (Paragraph 3.393.)

6.93 We ask consultees whether there should be a transitional period during which pre-commencement charges that are not registrable under current law should have to be registered. (Paragraph 3.397.)

6.94 We provisionally recommend that:

(1) Pre-commencement sales of receivables should retain their existing effectiveness and priority for a transitional period of [five] years. If they are
perfected by filing within that period they will retain their priority (as
from the date of creation). If by the end of that period they have not been
perfected by filing they will cease to be effective in insolvency and will
lose their priority as against other post-commencement SIs.

(2) We ask consultees whether they agree with our conclusion that a similar
scheme should apply to post-commencement title-retention transactions
and, if so, how long the transitional period should be. (Paragraph 3.409.)

PART 4 – FINANCIAL COLLATERAL AND PROCEEDS OF LETTERS OF CREDIT

Basic principles

6.95 We provisionally recommend that our scheme for financial collateral
should adopt as basic principles that:

(1) a secured party, or with investment property an outright buyer, should be
treated as having sufficient 'control' to perfect its SI if it has taken all the
steps that it reasonably can to give itself the right to realise the collateral,
or to appropriate it in order to satisfy the secured obligation, without any
further act on the part of the debtor or any court order;

(2) a secured party who perfects by control should take priority over an SI
perfected by any other method (or that is unperfected);

(3) a bona fide purchaser for value who takes control of investment property
in such a way that no one else can also have control of it should take free
of other SIs; and

(4) otherwise, as between SIs perfected by control, priority should (unless
agreed otherwise) be in the order that the secured parties obtained
control. (Paragraph 4.29.)

Investment property

6.96 We provisionally recommend the definitions explained in the paragraphs
shown of:

(1) investment property (paragraph 4.31);
(2) security (paragraph 4.32);
(3) securities accounts (paragraph 4.34); and
(4) financial assets (paragraph 4.35). (Paragraph 4.37.)

Investment securities

Control

6.97 Do consultees agree that it is unnecessary for the draft regulation dealing
with control to refer to someone 'holding on behalf of' the purchaser?
(Paragraph 4.48.)

6.98 Do consultees agree that an agreement between the intermediary and the secured party, rather than simply a notice of assignment, should be a condition of 'control' and its consequences? (Paragraph 4.54.)

6.99 We provisionally recommend that with investment securities, a secured party or other purchaser will have control:

(1)   With a certificated security in bearer form, if it takes possession of the certificate;

(2)   With a certificated security which is in registered form if it:
      (a)   takes delivery of the certificate with a signed transfer form made out to him or in blank, or
      (b)   is registered with the issuer as the holder;

(3)   With an uncertificated security if:
      (a)   in systems in which it is entry in the register of the operator of the settlement system that determines legal title, either –
            (i)   the purchaser is entered in the register of the operator as the holder, or
            (ii) the operator, on the instructions of the registered holder, has placed the security into a sub-account in the holder's own name but has given the purchaser a power of attorney over the security, or
      (b)   in systems in which it is entry in the register of the issuer that determines legal title, either –
            (i)   the purchaser is entered in the register of the issuer as the holder, or
            (ii) the issuer has entered into a control agreement with the purchaser;

(4)   With a security entitlement, if it –
      (a)   becomes the entitlement holder; or
      (b)   has entered into a control agreement with the intermediary; or
      (c)   is the entitlement holder's own securities intermediary, to whom the entitlement holder has granted an SI.

Control over a securities account amounts to control over the security entitlements carried in the securities account. (Paragraph 4.57.)

6.100 We ask whether the issuer or intermediary should be obliged to disclose what control agreements exist if required to do so by the registered holder or entitlement holder. (Paragraph 4.58.)

6.101 We provisionally recommend that an SI in investment property created by a securities intermediary is treated as perfected when it attaches, without further steps being required. (Paragraph 4.61.)

6.102 We provisionally recommend that a secured party may have control of indirectly held securities whether or not the entitlement holder retains the right to deal with the entitlement. (Paragraph 4.64.)

6.103 We provisionally recommend that control over uncertificated securities or indirectly held securities (that is, those covered by the FCAR) should not be effective to perfect an SI unless the security agreement is evidenced in writing. (Paragraph 4.67.)

6.104 We provisionally recommend that a secured party that has control of investment property should have the right to create a further SI in it and, if agreed, to sell it. (Paragraph 4.68.)

6.105 We provisionally recommend that an SI that is perfected by control should remain perfected even though the secured party itself relinquishes control, until such time as the debtor recovers the equivalent of control. (Paragraph 4.69.)

Priority as between competing SIs over investment securities

6.106 We provisionally recommend that a secured party who takes control of a certificated or uncertificated security or, in the case of a security entitlement, has the entitlement transferred into its own name, for value and without knowledge that the sale or acquisition constitutes a breach of the security agreement creating or providing for a competing SI, should take free of that SI. (Paragraph 4.73.)

6.107 Do consultees agree that an SI held by an intermediary in an entitlement or account maintained by the intermediary should have priority over any other SI over the same assets? (Paragraph 4.75.)

6.108 We provisionally recommend that where competing SIs granted by securities intermediaries are perfected otherwise than by control they should rank equally. (Paragraph 4.76.)

Buyers of investment securities

6.109 We provisionally recommend that a buyer who takes control of a certificated or uncertificated security or, in the case of a security entitlement, has the entitlement transferred into its own name, for value and without knowledge that the sale or acquisition constitutes a breach of a security agreement creating or providing for a competing SI, should take free of that SI. (Paragraph 4.81.)

6.110 We ask whether the draft regulations should include a provision to the effect that where a security is certificated, an SI is treated as temporarily perfected, without filing or taking possession, for 20 days, provided that new value was given. (Paragraph 4.83.)

The 'broker's lien'

6.111 Do consultees think that it is necessary or desirable for the scheme we propose to include an automatic SI in favour of a securities intermediary who has credited the entitlement holder's account before receiving payment? (Paragraph 4.87.)

Commodities

6.112 We provisionally recommend that the scheme for SIs over investment property should cover commodity contracts and commodity accounts. We ask whether these should be treated separately, as in the draft regulations, or should simply be brought within the definition of a financial asset and thus within the rules governing SIs over what is currently termed a 'security entitlement'. (Paragraph 4.92.)

Bank accounts

6.113   We provisionally recommend that SIs created over a bank account should in principle be within the proposed scheme of notice-filing (though filing would not necessarily be required in all cases) and priority of SIs. (Paragraph 4.105.)

6.114   We provisionally recommend that SIs created over bank accounts should be brought within the provision for perfection by control and the associated priority rules. (Paragraph 4.110.)

What amounts to control of a bank account

6.115   We provisionally recommend that a secured party should be able to perfect an SI over a bank account by 'control', by:

(1)   becoming the account holder; or
(2)   entering an agreement with the debtor and the bank that the bank will accept directions from the secured party without further reference to the debtor; or
(3)   where the secured party is the bank at which the account is held, without any further steps being required.

There may be perfection by control even though the debtor retains the right to dispose of funds in the account. (Paragraph 4.119.)

6.116   We ask whether a bank that has entered a control agreement with a secured party should have to disclose it to a third party if required to do so by the customer/debtor. (Paragraph 4.121.)

Priority

6.117   We provisionally recommend that as between competing SIs over a bank account:

(1)   an SI perfected by control should take priority over one perfected by other means;
(2)   as between SIs perfected by control, priority should depend on the date of control, except that where one of the secured parties is the bank itself, the bank should have priority unless the other secured party has become the account holder. (Paragraph 4.126.)

Transferability of funds

6.118   Should a transferee be protected:

(1)   unless it did not give value or it knew that the transfer was in breach of the security agreement, or, alternatively,

(2)   whether or not it gave value or had knowledge, unless it colluded with the debtor? (Paragraph 4.129.)

Bank's right of set-off

6.119 We provisionally recommend that the existence of a control agreement with a third party secured party should not prevent the bank exercising defences and set-offs that it has against the debtor, but it should not be able to raise or exercise a right of set-off that it has against the debtor against a secured party who has taken control by becoming the customer of the bank. (Paragraph 4.130.)

Bank's obligations to debtor

6.120 We ask whether consultees consider it necessary or desirable to include a provision in the draft regulations providing that, unless agreed otherwise, the bank will continue to have its normal obligations to the debtor despite an SI in the bank account perfected by control. (Paragraph 4.132.)

Proceeds of letters of credit

6.121 Do consultees agree that:

(1)   an SI over the proceeds of a letter of credit should be regarded as perfected by control if the SP has obtained the bank's agreement to the assignment, and

(2)   an SI over the proceeds of a letter of credit that is perfected by control should take priority over one that is not, and that SIs perfected by control should rank according to priority in time of obtaining control? (Paragraph 4.150.)

PART 5 – A STATEMENT OF THE RIGHTS AND REMEDIES UNDER A SECURITY AGREEMENT

Scope of the statement of rights and remedies

6.122 We provisionally recommend that the statement of rights and remedies should not, in general, apply to 'deemed' SIs. (Paragraph 5.11.)

Limitations on the scope of the statement

SIs over both personal property and land

6.123 We ask whether the scheme should provide that, if the same obligation is secured by an interest in land and an SI to which the draft regulations apply, the secured party may either proceed under Part 5 as to the collateral, as to both the land and the personal property. (Paragraph 5.16.)

Essential provisions: surplus and deficit

6.124 We provisionally recommend that the draft regulations contain a provision setting out expressly how, unless otherwise provided by law or the agreement of all interested parties, the secured party must apply the proceeds of any disposition of the collateral. (Paragraph 5.21.)

6.125 We provisionally recommend that any surplus be accounted for and paid over in the following order:

(1) to a person who has a subordinate SI in the collateral and who has given written notice of the interest to the secured party prior to the distribution, and
(2) to the debtor or any other person known by the secured party to be an owner of the collateral. (Paragraph 5.26.)

6.126 We ask consultees whether the secured party should have to pay any surplus proceeds only to those subordinate secured parties who have given it a written notice of their interests, or also to any subordinate creditor who has filed against the collateral before the date of distribution. (Paragraph 5.27.)

6.127 We provisionally recommend that, as an alternative to paying over any surplus in the order specified in the draft regulations, the secured party should have an unqualified right to pay it into court. (Paragraph 5.28.)

6.128 We provisionally recommend that our scheme should provide that, unless otherwise agreed or provided for by statute, the debtor is liable to pay the amount of any deficiency to the secured party. (Paragraph 5.29.)

Desirable provisions

Effect of prohibition on assignment

6.129 We provisionally recommend that in a contract between a company and a third party creating an account payable to the company, a term that purports to prohibit or restrict assignment of the account should be of no effect against a third-party assignee. (Paragraph 5.39.)

Duties of parties under the security agreement but before default

Care in custody and preservation of collateral

6.130 We provisionally recommend that the secured party who has possession of the collateral should be under a duty to take reasonable care of it and should be able to insure it at the debtor's expense. (Paragraph 5.41.)

6.131 We provisionally recommend that an outright buyer of accounts or of a promissory note should be under a duty to take necessary steps to preserve rights against other parties unless the sale was on a non-recourse basis. (Paragrap 5.42.)

Income, etc from collateral

6.132 We provisionally recommend that the secured party who has possession or control of collateral should apply any money received from the collateral to reduction of the obligation secured or remit it to the debtor; and in the case of other proceeds should be entitled to hold them as additional collateral. (Paragraph 5.43.)

Right of use

6.133 We provisionally recommend that, unless otherwise agreed, the secured party who has possession of collateral should be permitted to use it for the purpose of preserving the collateral or to the extent authorised by the security agreement or the court; may create an SI in it, and, where the secured party has possession or control of collateral that is investment property, and the parties so agree, sell it. (Paragraph 5.46.)

Rights and remedies on default

Collection rights

6.134 We provisionally recommend that the statement of rights and remedies provide that where the collateral is an account and the debtor defaults, the secured party may:

(1) notify the account debtor to make payment to the secured party, whether or not the secured party was making collections on the collateral before the notification by the secured party;
(2) take any proceeds of collateral to which it is entitled; and
(3) apply the money received, or any account, instrument or security in the form of a debt obligation taken as collateral to the satisfaction of the secured obligation.

There should be similar provisions for bank accounts. (Paragraph 5.51.)

6.135 We provisionally recommend that a secured party who buys receivables on a recourse basis should be required, if it collects on the receivables, to proceed in a commercially reasonable manner. (Paragraph 5.52.)

6.136 We provisionally recommend that the secured party should be able to defer applying or paying over non-cash proceeds, provided that it is not commercially unreasonable; and that where a secured party does apply or pay over non-cash proceeds, it must do so in a commercially reasonable manner. (Paragraph 5.53.)

Taking possession on default

6.137 We provisionally recommend that the secured party should have an implied right to enter the debtor's premises in order to repossess collateral on the debtor's default, but should have to obtain a court order to enter the premises of a third party. (Paragraph 5.57.)

6.138 We provisionally recommend that on default the secured party should have the right to disable equipment collateral that is on the debtor's premises and to sell it from there, provided that the secured party does not cause the person in possession of the premises any greater inconvenience and cost than is necessary. (Paragraph 5.60.)

6.139 We ask whether the secured party should be able to require the debtor to assemble the collateral and make it available to the secured party at a place to be designated by the secured party which is reasonably convenient to both parties. (Paragraph 5.61.)

Power of sale

6.140 We provisionally recommend that the secured party should have the power to dispose of collateral on default by the debtor. (Paragraph 5.63.)

6.141 We provisionally recommend that the scheme should incorporate a provision to the effect that:

(1)   The sale may be by public sale (including auction or competitive tender) or private sale.
(2)   The secured party may buy the collateral, but only at a public sale, and only for a price that bears a reasonable relationship to its market value.
(3)   Collateral may be sold in its existing condition or after 'repair, processing or preparation for distribution'.
(4)   Collateral may be sold as a whole or in commercial units.
(5)   The secured party may delay disposition of all or some of the collateral.
(6)   If the agreement so provides, payment for the collateral may be deferred or the collateral may be disposed of by lease. (Paragraph 5.67.)

6.142 We provisionally recommend that a secured party need not apply or pay over non-cash proceeds of disposition unless the failure to do so would be commercially unreasonable, but where a secured party does apply or pay over such non-cash proceeds, it must do so in a commercially reasonable manner. (Paragraph 5.70.)

6.143 We provisionally recommend that the secured party should be permitted to buy the collateral:

(1)   at a public sale, or
(2)   at a private sale if the collateral is of a kind that is customarily sold on a recognised market or the subject of widely distributed standard price quotations, subject to special rules about calculating the surplus or deficiency after such sales. (Paragraph 5.72.)

6.144 We ask consultees whether, where there is no organised market (or where the collateral is neither perishable nor likely to decline rapidly in value if not disposed of immediately), the secured party should have to give notice a reasonable time before the sale or disposition. If so, do they agree that 10 business days' notice should be sufficient? (Paragraph 5.83.)

6.145 If there is to be a notice requirement, we provisionally recommend that the notice should have to be 'sufficient', and that it will be sufficient if it indicates:

(1)   the debtor (or party who owns the collateral);
(2)   the secured party, and gives an address at which it may be contacted in sufficient time;
(3)   the collateral to be sold or disposed of;
(4)   the intended method of disposition;

(5)　the time and date of any sale or after which any other disposition will be made.

We would welcome views on whether it would be useful to provide a standard form of notice in the draft regulations. (Paragraph 5.84.)

6.146　We provisionally recommend that, when a notice is required before collateral is disposed of, it should be sent to:

(1)　the debtor or any other person who is known by the secured party to be an owner of the collateral;

(2)　a person with an SI in the collateral if, before the day on which the notice of disposition is given to the debtor, that person has filed a financing statement;

(3)　any person who has given an indemnity or guarantee for the debt, if the secured party knows that one exists and knows the name and address of the person, and

(4)　any other person with an interest in the collateral who has given a written notice to the secured party of that person's interest in the collateral prior to the day on which the notice of disposition is given to the debtor. (Paragraph 5.86.)

6.147　We provisionally recommend including a provision on the effect of disposition. (Paragraph 5.87.)

Retention of collateral by secured party ('foreclosure')

6.148　We provisionally recommend that the statement of remedies should include provisions for the secured party, on the initiative of either party, to take the collateral in full or partial satisfaction of the obligation secured, provided that the debtor has agreed in writing and other interested parties have been notified and have not objected within 20 business days. (Paragraph 5.93.)

Redemption

6.149　We provisionally recommend that a person entitled to notice of disposition under DR 63 may, unless otherwise agreed in writing after default, redeem the collateral by tendering fulfilment of the obligations secured by the collateral and paying a sum equal to the reasonable expenses incurred by the secured party in preparing etc the collateral for disposition and enforcing the security agreement. (Paragraph 5.95.)

Cumulative remedies

6.150　We provisionally recommend that it be provided that the rights and remedies of each party against the other are cumulative, and may be exercised simultaneously so long as they are not mutually incompatible and simultaneous exercise is not commercially unreasonable. (Paragraph 5.97.)

6.151　We also provisionally recommend that it be provided that the secured party may enforce its personal rights under the obligation secured by the SI, and may seek to execute any judgment against the debtor's property, including the collateral, without extinguishing the SI. (Paragraph 5.98.)

Appointment of receiver and secured party acting through receiver

6.152 We provisionally recommend that it be stated specifically that a security agreement may provide for the appointment of a receiver and for the rights and duties of a receiver (save as provided for by the draft regulations or another enactment). We also provisionally recommend that the rights, powers and duties of a secured party under Part 5 and DR 17 of the draft regulations should apply equally when the secured party acts through a receiver. (Paragraph 5.101.)

Provisions not recommended

6.153 We provisionally recommend that the scheme should not contain a provision relating to the interpretation of an acceleration clause. (Paragraph 5.104.)

6.154 We provisionally recommend that the scheme should not contain a provision dealing with the measure of damages relating to leases or consigned goods seized when the lessor's or consignor's interest is ineffective because it is unperfected. (Paragraph 5.109.)

6.155 We provisionally recommend that the secured party should not be under an obligation to give other secured parties a written account of the nature of the disposition, the amount raised and how it was distributed. (Paragraph 5.110.)

6.156 We provisionally recommend that the scheme should not contain a provision dealing with reinstatement of the security agreement. (Paragraph 5.113.)

6.157 We provisionally recommend that the statement of rights and remedies should not contain provisions relating to the powers of receivers. (Paragraph 5.118.)

Applications to court

6.158 We provisionally recommend that there be a provision relating to court orders to ensure compliance, enforcement, stay etc. (Paragraph 5.119.)

Financial collateral

Security financial collateral arrangements

6.159 We provisionally recommend that the statement of rights and remedies set out in the draft regulations should be without prejudice to any agreement in a financial collateral arrangement within the meaning of the FCAR. (Paragraph 5.125.)

Title transfer financial collateral arrangements

6.160 We ask whether in respect of a title transfer financial collateral arrangement:

(1)   the statement of remedies should be without prejudice to any contractual right to retain, appropriate or dispose of financial collateral under a title transfer financial collateral arrangement, within the meaning of the FCAR; or

(2)   whether title transfer financial collateral arrangements should be exempted from the statement of remedies in Part 5 of the draft regulations; or

(3)   whether title transfer financial collateral arrangements should be exempted from the scheme as a whole. (Paragraph 5.133.)

Good faith and commercial reasonableness

6.161   We provisionally recommend that there be no general requirement of good faith included in the draft regulations, but that a specific requirement of commercial reasonableness be included in relation to DRs 59(1)–(2), 60(5)–(6), 62(6) and 65(5). (Paragraph 5.135.)

6.162   We provisionally recommend that the parties to a security agreement should be able to determine the standards which fulfil the rights of a debtor or obligations of a secured party under any provision mentioned in DR 59(3), provided that the standards are not manifestly unreasonable. (Paragraph 5.137.)

6.163   We provisionally recommend that the scheme should include guidance on steps that are sufficient to ensure that particular methods of collection, enforcement, disposition or acceptance are 'commercially reasonable' within the meaning of the draft regulations. (Paragraph 5.141.)

Mandatory or default rules?

6.164   We provisionally recommend that the requirements to act in a commercially reasonable manner should be mandatory. (Paragraph 5.156.)

6.165   We provisionally recommend that the parties should be free to set standards as to the notice to be given before disposal of collateral, provided that the standards set are not wholly unreasonable; but, subject to that, even as between debtor and secured party any notice requirements should be mandatory. (Paragraph 5.159.)

6.166   We provisionally recommend that the provisions on surplus should be mandatory. (Paragraph 5.163.)

6.167   We provisionally recommend that the provisions on acceptance of collateral in full or partial satisfaction of the obligation secured should be mandatory. (Paragraph 5.164.)

6.168   We provisionally recommend that the provisions on redemption should be mandatory. (Paragraph 5.165.)

6.169   We seek consultees' views as to whether the draft regulations should deny effect to any provision in a security agreement or other agreement purporting to exclude or limit the secured party's liability for failure to comply with any provision of the scheme of rights and remedies. Should any other provision in the draft regulations that gives rise to a duty be capable of being excluded or limited? (Paragraph 5.169.)

6.170 We ask whether it is necessary or desirable for the draft regulations to contain provisions setting out when a debtor may waive its mandatory rights or agree to an exclusion or restriction of liability as part of a settlement agreement. (Paragraph 5.171.)

APPENDIX B – CHANGES NEEDED TO THE DRAFT REGULATIONS TO OMIT TITLE-RETENTION DEVICES

6.171 If the draft regulations were amended to apply only to traditional securities and sales of accounts, and not to title-retention devices, we ask whether consultees think that the draft regulations should continue to contain:

(1) provisions relating to PMSIs,
(2) the statement of the rights and remedies set out in Part 5 of the draft regulations. (Appendix B.9.)

INDEX